RETHINKING LATINO(A) RELIGION AND IDENTITY

RETHINKING LATINO(A) RELIGION AND IDENTITY

**EDITED BY
MIGUEL A. DE LA TORRE
AND GASTÓN ESPINOSA**

THE
PILGRIM
PRESS
Cleveland

*To those Hispanic scholars who came before us
and carved a niche in the academy:
their scholarship made this book possible.*

*And to those Latino/a scholars who we hope will follow us
and build upon the work in this book.*

The Pilgrim Press
700 Prospect Avenue
Cleveland, Ohio 44115-1100
thepilgrimpress.com

10 09 08 07 06 5 4 3 2 1

Library of Congress Cataloging-in-Publication Data
    Rethinking Latino(a) religion and identity / Miguel A. De La Torre and
Gastón Espinosa, editors.
        p. cm.
    ISBN 0-8298-1658-5 (alk. paper)
    1. Hispanic Americans – Religion – Congresses. I. De La Torre, Miguel A.
II. Espinosa, Gastón.
    BL2525.R4735 2006
    200.89′68 – dc22

                                                            2006001189

ISBN-13: 978-0-8298-1658-7
ISBN-10: 0-8298-1658-5

Contents

Part Three
RETHINKING THEORY, POWER, AND IDENTITY
IN LATINA/O RELIGIONS

Introduction

Rethinking Latino/a religions and identity is risky. The mere fact that it is so, makes the need all the more great. The Hispanic scholarly community is no more immune to intellectual disagreements, infighting, and turf-building than any other community. For so many, so much is at stake — their careers, their writings, their legacies. One of the goals of this book is to rethink Latina/o religions and identity in a way that openly addresses some of these concerns. Our goal is to build, not destroy, a bridge of understanding and mutuality through critical analyses of the field. This bridge is deeply rooted in the rich soil of the U.S. Latino/a and Latin American community on the one hand and the U.S. academy on the other. As the metaphor implies, the bridge is a two-way thoroughfare that involves constant movement of ideas, people, and visions back and forth. The bridge, however, is also a place, space, and location in its own right — loaded with human emotion, activity, and, occasionally, conflict. To borrow a phrase coined by the Aztec Indians in the wake of the Spanish conquest of Mexico, it is a *nepantla* location — of being in the middle. Persons in the middle seek neither to deny their ancient customs and ancestors nor the new religions, ideas, and methodologies brought on by the winds of change. This is a fascinating New World insight that, like *mestizaje* itself, was birthed in the painful crucible of conflict. Being in the middle does not imply a running away — from or to another place — but rather it describes an attitude, an outlook, a worldview, a state of being in its own right. So too the scholarship here.

While to be sure some of the essays in this volume are pointed and push the envelope of accepted opinion and interpretations of Latina/o theology and religion, most of the authors also warmly affirm the rich soil out of which their own intellectual ideas and journeys have grown and been nurtured. In many respects, this volume represents the coming-of-age of a new generation of Latino/a scholars who are

1

fully aware of where they have come from and are in the process of charting new courses for the future. We are creating maps on the middle of the bridge all the while painting *la(s) tierra(s)* as the center(s) of the universe. For some, this will be shaky and potentially dangerous ground. For others, including many of the senior scholars referenced in these works, it will be liberating and refreshing. Their work, example, and guidance have contributed to the birthing and unleashing of a new generation of scholars who are now beginning to come into their own. However, still others may be threatened by what is written. Retribution may follow. However, we want to state from the very outset that our goal is not to debunk our theological and intellectual role models and friends. Their scholarship, like Hispanic identity itself, is built on the foundations laid by our forebears and co-laborers. Their ideas and points of view, like the very stones the Aztecs and Incas used to build the beautiful cathedrals of Latin America, reflect the imprint, carving, painting, and handiwork of their original makers — reshaped, repainted, transformed. These stones have, in one sense, become the substance of the cathedral itself. In many ways, they are the cathedral. Perhaps more importantly, these stone and plaster temples pointing to the sacred embody the blended multiple *mestizo* and mulatto identities that constitute the physiology, psychology, and spirituality of many people of Latin American ancestry. This book, like a cathedral, is a limited human attempt to create bridges and visions that connect and blend past, present, and future all in one place, one space, and one location — one that continues to be contested and reimagined with each successive generation. While we do not endorse everything written in the book, we do endorse the desire and the need to reflect and rethink what Latino/a religions and identity mean to each and every one of us both now and in the years to come.

The very idea of "rethinking" implies a revision of previous thought. However, almost all these essays in one way or another draw upon and affirm the work of our colleagues' rich insights and successful attempts to speak on behalf of our communities and carve out a niche in the academy. We seek to reflect on and rethink the various ways scholars of Latina/o religions have gone about their calling to write about the Hispanic religious community. We have no grand schemes or single overarching vision of what Latino/a religions should look like for everyone, nor should we — especially given the growing methodological, disciplinary, theological, and national diversity within the field. Different recommendations and theories are made by scholars working from different disciplinary perspectives, themes, and points of view. What unites all of the essays is the fundamental conviction that each successive generation needs to critically reflect on what has gone before it and consider what still needs to be done in the future. This process honors our intellectual forerunners while at the same time using their work as a foundation and springboard from which to explore new methodological and theoretical vistas on the horizon.

It is our hope that this volume will in some small way do precisely this. We also hope that it will move the dialogue and discourse — which has for so long taken place largely within our community — into a new public space between the secular academy on the one hand and the powerful faith-based Hispanic community of scholars on the other. In fact, most Latino scholars (and scholars in general) are somewhere in the sticky middle. This *nepantla* space and bridge has in many ways already been created. What we are doing is merely highlighting and platforming what has already been written and explored by scholars active in the field, albeit with our own unique twists and interpretations.

Any attempt to rethink Latino/a religions and identity should be in conversation with and build on the important findings of the previous generations of scholars who have labored in the academic vineyard (some might say desert). The best place to begin any attempt to rethink Hispanic religions and identity is with the various historiographic essays on the field and state of Hispanic theology (Aquino, 1993; Medina, 1993; Eduardo Fernéndez, 2000; Espín, 2000; De La Torre and Aponte, 2001; Espín and Díaz, 1999), religious history (Barton and Maldonado, 1998; Daisy Machado, 1998), and social science research (Maduro, 1991, 1995; Stevens-Arroyo and Pantoja, 1995; Anthony M. Stevens-Arroyo and Ana María Diaz-Stevens, 1997; Gilberto Cadena, 1995; Peña and Frehill, 1998, 2002; Edwin Hernández, 1995, 1998, 1999; and McGuire, 1994). All of these authors are cited and/or explored to varying degrees in the essays in this volume.

The need to rethink Latina/o religions and identity is not new. In fact, U.S. Hispanic and Latin American scholars of religion have been earnestly engaged in a process of rethinking since at least the 1960s, although the roots of this reflection go back much earlier. César Chávez, Gustavo Gutiérrez, Enrique Dussel, Virgilio Elizondo, Orlando Costas, Ada María Isasi-Díaz, Yolanda Tarango, Justo González, and many others served as major catalysts in the subsequent development of the field. The field itself has expanded to include not only theological analyses but also historical, sociological, anthropological, political, cultural, feminist, Chicano/a studies, Latin American, literary, gay/lesbian, and pop culture analyses. The field is moving outward like the ever-expanding universe — into the dark unknown, with occasional sparkles of light that pull our eyes and hearts into their spheres of influence.

This ever-expanding universe was initially birthed in conflict. So too our book. Despite this fact, we still have a strong sense for a common *Latinidad* that, regardless of all of our different ethnic, theological, generational, sexual, and disciplinary identities, still anchors our scholarship and our psyches in our respective Latino/a communities, countries of origin, religious traditions, and subcultures. It is from these places, spaces, and support networks that we speak and seek to examine hitherto new and sometimes unexplored religions, theories, experiences, worldviews, and ways of life.

The book is the direct outgrowth of a panel proposed for the Hispanic Religion, Culture and Society Group at the American Academy of Religion (AAR) in the fall of 2001 in Denver, Colorado. Miguel A. De La Torre and Gastón Espinosa organized the panel as a means to explore the various ways Latino/a scholars were rethinking Hispanic religions and identity. They invited a number of scholars, including Laura Pérez, Manuel Vásquez, and Luis León to present their research. Espinosa chaired the session.

In order for us to remain in active conversation with the very scholars upon whom so much of our own work was built, one of our panel's primary concerns was to find a recognized Hispanic scholar who could offer a critical but fair-minded analysis of our papers. We decided to ask a senior Latino scholar to serve as respondent. We made it absolutely clear that our goal was not to debunk Hispanic theology or religion or the founders of the field. The response was surprising. The respondent sent us a lengthy e-mail outlining the various reasons why he would not and could not serve as a respondent. We were all caught off guard by his tone and rationale. He made a number of assumptions that we felt were as unfair as they were inaccurate. Furthermore, we were surprised to see that he publicized his response to us by copying over half a dozen of the highest-ranking Latina/o scholars in the field. The message was clear: not only did he not support our desire to examine and rethink Hispanic religions on our own intellectual reconnaissance at the AAR, but he also apparently did not want anyone else to do so either. Although we contemplated publishing his response to our invitation along with our own response in this book, we decided against this as a matter of professional courtesy.

No doubt the respondent, in turning down our invitation, raised valid concerns — many of which we acknowledge. Still, the response seems to us to typify the rift that exists between a few highly visible Latino/a theologians and junior Latina/o scholars of religion. Although the respondent felt that the discourse we engaged in should have been done apart from a public setting at the AAR, we thought otherwise. Some junior Latino/a scholars find limited space within the Latino/a scholarly community for disagreement. In fact, some younger scholars who made the "error" of critiquing the works of senior scholars have been "punished" by not having their works published in Hispanic-centered journals or by being denied funding to complete their dissertations by organizations and institutes where senior scholars preside.

Despite all the concerns and fanfare about jeopardizing the field of Latino/a theology, our session took place in the morning without protest. Approximately forty to fifty people attended the morning session, including about eight non-Hispanics. While the papers were stimulating and the discussion thought-provoking, there was no major outcry or protest, just a warm reception and affirmation of our desire to critically reflect on the field of Latina/o religions from our own unique points of view. However, we left the event with the

knowledge and memory of the events that had transpired that fall —
memories that still live with us.

The larger result of the episode was just the opposite of what was
desired. We decided to expand the project into a full-length book
manuscript and found a publisher who put the project under contract
almost immediately. This is the book you now have in your hands.

One of the goals of the book is to rethink Latino/a religions from
multidisciplinary perspectives by first looking at various methodological approaches to the subject, followed by an analysis of key terms
that have shaped and continue to help shape and define the field. This
is followed by theoretical reflections and case studies of what this rethinking might look like. The first part of the book, "Rethinking
Methodological Approaches to Latino/a Religions," examines some
of the historiographical, social scientific, and theological methodological approaches and innovations in the field of U.S. Latino/a religions.
In chapter 1, Gastón Espinosa examines the work of Hispanic social scientists over the past hundred years and then uses the Hispanic
Churches in American Public Life (HCAPL) national research project
as a case study to explore some of the methodological limitations and
breakthroughs in social science research among Latina/os. The keys
to creating an excellent social science national survey are a first-rate
design team, a large urban and rural sample, a bilingual Hispanic-
framed survey, and a religious classification system that cuts across
country of origin, gender, and generation and reflects the religious
profile of the Latino/a community. He found that major shifts in U.S.
Latino religious affiliation took place in the 1920s and 1930s and not
just in the 1960s as is often assumed.

While Espinosa's chapter focuses primarily on quantitative research, Edwin Aponte (chapter 2) explores qualitative research by
examining what a Changó botánica in Dallas reveals about the texture, fluidity, and diversity of Hispanic religiosity. He suggests that
botánicas become a legitimate strategy for survival, health, guidance, and wholeness, which are religious/metaphysical decisions and
actions in the everyday experience of Latinas and Latinos.

This is followed in chapter 3 by Espinosa's examination of the
historical development of Mexican American religious studies in the
United States. He proposes that one possible route for Latino scholars

at state and private secular universities is an ethno-phenomenological methodological approach to the study of Latina/o religions. This approach blends race, class, gender, and phenomenological analyses that are grounded in their historical, social, theological, and political contexts. It further seeks to bridge the growing chasm that separates secular religious studies from theology.

In chapter 4, Jorge Aquino explores the theme of rethinking Hispanic religions in his examination of the role that the prophetic horizon plays in Roberto Goizueta's vision of a "U.S. Hispanic" subaltern community. He suggests that Goizueta's theology may inadvertently sublimate deeply rooted fault lines of race, sexuality, and class. Because he does not fully contextualize the material conditions of the aesthetic imaginary world of Latinos in his social-scientific analysis, he runs the risk of potentially neutering its latent prophetic voice.

Building on the historical and contemporary methodological approaches to Latina/o religions, part 2, "Rethinking Critical Concepts in Latino/a Religions," analyzes some of the most important and original concepts in the study of Hispanic religions. In chapter 5 Manuel Vásquez examines the historical development and usages of *mestizaje* in the writings of Mexican American theologian Virgilio Elizondo and others. He argues that his task is not to jettison *mestizaje*, but to historicize and contextualize it and point out that it has very different, often contradictory, meanings (elite ideology, subaltern identity, historical process, and theoretically licensed banner of resistance) in different parts of Latin America and among U.S. Latino/as who trace their ancestry back to these regions. Despite this fact, he argues that it would be unwise to abandon *mestizaje* because it offers a powerful critique of the still hegemonic bipolar racial formation in the United States.

In contrast, in chapter 6 Miguel A. De La Torre interrogates the various interpretations of the term *mulatez* as popularized by Cuban theologian and ethicist Ada María Isasi-Díaz. He argues that the term has been widely incorporated by the Latino/a theological community to describe the ethos of those who define their identity through their association with Brazil and the Caribbean. Despite this fact, he argues that it is loaded with a racial history that tends to indirectly mask intra-Hispanic structures of oppression and racism.

Michelle González points out in chapter 7 that some feminist scholars like María Pilar Aquino question Ada María Isasi-Díaz's notion of *mujerista* theology because it engages in a kind of fictionalization and essentialization of Latina women. She notes that Latina feminist theologians need to be careful to avoid cultural and theological essentialism (assuming all Latinas are feminist or hold the same beliefs on a given topic), which has permeated feminism, ethnic studies, and theology. She also critically analyzes how Latino scholars indirectly marginalize women's voices by relegating their scholarship to women's spheres and sections in their historical overviews of the field. González ends by calling on scholars to reflect on how identity functions politically in the academy, what strategic value minority studies have, how feminists can work together to bring a gender critique to bear on Latino scholarship, and what role "the people" play in the future construction of Hispanic theology and scholarship.

In chapter 8 Manuel Mejido calls on scholars to avoid an essentialist understanding of U.S. Latino/as by rethinking liberation for the postmodern condition from the point of view of the U.S. Hispanic reality. He argues that U.S. Hispanic liberals and leftists are both falling captive to the postmodern condition, specifically to the eclipse of assimilation as the dialectic of anxiety and alienation. One possible solution is a psychoanalytic approach to U.S. Hispanic religion that analyzes the way U.S. Hispanic popular religious beliefs and practices function both *ideologically* to assimilate U.S. Hispanics into the Anglo-American mainstream, and *liberatively* as resistance and forward-looking hope in the face of fragmentation.

Parts 1 and 2 lay the groundwork for part 3, "Rethinking Theory, Power, and Identity in Latina/o Religions." In chapter 9, Luis León examines the roles of religion, erotics, and machismo in U.S. Latino/a religions and identity. He argues that machismo is a staged reality and cultural invention invested with authority by sacred symbols and the virginity of Guadalupe. While the mythology of Guadalupe and the myths she models have been subject to powerful scrutiny, for the most part theology and religious studies have failed to critique the baleful image of the macho and the homophobic drama it enacts. As a corrective, León explores the way Latina and Latino artists like El Vez have deployed irony, parody, and religious discourses to deconstruct the narrative and image of the macho.

In chapter 10 Lara Medina draws on the work of Gloria Anzaldúa to examine how a *nepantla* spirituality is a multifaceted psychic and spiritual space composed of complementary opposites, obscurity and clarity. She argues that *nepantla,* or the middle space, can become a psychological, spiritual, and political space that Latino/as can transform into sites of meaning-making and healing. To be *en nepantla* is to simultaneously exist on the border and in the center of things.

Also exploring the theme of sexuality and gender roles, Laura Pérez in chapter 11 analyzes the critical role of religion in Chicana visual arts and literature, for example, the works of Gloria Anzaldúa and Cherríe Moraga. These feminist artists and poet-writers challenge the traditional heterosexual patriarchy and Christianity of the Hispanic community by symbolically drawing upon their ancestral Mexican traditions in Mesoamerican Aztec art, religious worldviews, and society. She argues that these Chicana artists and poets engage in a political spirituality that seeks to use religious symbols, visions of the divine, and understandings to empower Latinas and Latinos.

Echoing the cautions about intra-Hispanic oppression, in chapter 12 De La Torre argues that as long as Latino/a scholars insist that their religious thoughts and paradigms originated among the oppressed and believe that their task is simply to articulate what the people are reportedly saying and doing, they can inadvertently mask their own power relationships with their subjects and colleagues in the academy. Although it is true that most Hispanic scholars ground their work within their marginalized faith community, a fine line exists between what comes from the faith community, and what is produced by scholars who then claim to speak on the community's behalf. De La Torre argues that the Hispanic religion scholars may find themselves creating absolutes wherein the good is defined as whatever a particular Latino/a professes to be the good. But the gravest danger is the refusal to seriously recognize and reflect on how power works *within* marginalized communities and how it can be used to silence and oppress dissenting voices. As Paulo Freire warned, the oppressed almost always, during the initial stage of their struggle, tend themselves to become oppressors (what he called "sub-oppressors"), rather than strive for liberation (1994:27).

While all the authors in this volume share a commitment to the Hispanic community and to rethinking, strengthening, and developing the field of Latino/a religions, they have proposed various ways to go about this process from their own unique (inter)disciplinary and intellectual vantage points. We hope that these essays will contribute to greater openness, dialogue, and critical reflection and discussion on the past, the present, and the future ways we go about understanding and interpreting Latina/o religions. These essays only scratch the surface of the growing scholarship on Hispanic religions. We nevertheless hope that this book will help broaden the field and create a creative and exciting academic space where alternative points of view are welcomed and encouraged. By so doing, we can create a vitally important bridge that is deeply rooted in *la tierra* and the academy.

Miguel A. De La Torre
Gastón Espinosa

Part One

Rethinking Methodological Approaches to Latino/a Religions

Chapter 1

Methodological Reflections on Social Science Research on Latino Religions

Gastón Espinosa

A major debate has erupted over Latino religious affiliation in the United States. Depending upon whom you believe, Latino Catholic religious affiliation runs from as high as 77 percent to as low as 50 percent (Hunt, 1998, 1999; Greeley, 1988, 1997; Gallup Jr. and Lindsay, 1999; Kosmin, Mayer, and Keysar, 2001; Gastón Espinosa, 2003a, 2004a; Espinosa, Elizondo, and Miranda 2003). These contradictory findings are due not only to the inherent methodological limitations of national data sets like the General Social Survey (GSS), the National Alcohol Survey (NAS), the National Survey of Religious Identification (NSRI), the American Religious Identification Survey (ARIS), and the Gallup Poll, but also to unique problems that social scientists face when conducting quantitative research in the U.S. Latino religious community.[1] Clearly there is a need to constantly rethink how scholars should go about conducting social science research among Latinos. This essay explores and rethinks some of

The author wishes to thank So Young Kim of Florida Atlantic University for her assistance in analyzing the data for this publication. Unless otherwise indicated, all statistics will be rounded to the nearest one hundred thousand for imputed numbers over one million and to the nearest ten thousand for imputed numbers over one hundred thousand. I would like to thank Miguel De La Torre, Edwin Hernández, and Ulrike Guthrie for their feedback on early drafts of this essay.

1. The GSS has clearly improved its methodology by recently fielding bilingual surveys and by including more questions that focus on popular religious practices. Roberto Suro's Pew Hispanic Center is also generating first-rate social science research like the 2004 National Survey of Latinos (NSL) and has created perhaps the most sophisticated national survey methodology to date (Suro, 2004). The HCAPL national survey still remains one of the best surveys for data analyses by religious affiliation because of its large Protestant oversample.

the current limitations in quantitative survey research among U.S. Latinos and then examines how the Hispanic Churches in American Public Life (HCAPL) research project attempted to address some of these limitations.

The keys to creating a first-rate social science national survey are an excellent design team, a large urban and rural sample, a bilingual Latino-framed survey, and a religious classification system that cuts across country of origin, gender, and generation to reflect the religious profile of the Latino community. The HCAPL research project attempted to address a number of these limitations and shortcomings. My research found that major demographic shifts in religious affiliation took place in the 1920s and 1930s and not just the post-1960 period as is often assumed. The Pentecostalization of Latino Protestantism along with the growth of denominational and religious pluralism via the Jehovah's Witnesses, Mormons, and metaphysical traditions goes back to the 1920s, if not earlier. One of the reasons why this had not been tracked very well before is that much of this growth took place predominately within Spanish-speaking indigenous Pentecostal denominations that English-language surveys could not capture adequately and because some tended to use a Mainline Protestant religious affiliation schematic and lump Jehovah's Witnesses, Mormons, and others into the category of fundamentalist or conservative Protestant.

My methodological reflections are based on more than a decade of social science research among Latinos in the United States, Mexico, and Puerto Rico. This research includes: (1) helping to theorize, frame, and construct the methodology and questions for four major survey instruments, (2) fielding four major surveys that polled more than twenty-eight hundred Latinos across the United States and Puerto Rico, (3) conducting numerous oral history interviews, and (4) coordinating, constructing, and overseeing ethnographic and community profile interviews and work with over three hundred Latino men and women from twenty-six different religious traditions in seven urban and two rural areas in Santa Barbara, Los Angeles, San Antonio, Chicago, Miami, New York City, San Juan, Puerto Rico, rural Iowa, and rural Colorado. Most of my comments will draw directly from my recent experience as project manager of the Pew Charitable Trusts–funded $1.3 million Hispanic Churches in American Public Life (HCAPL) research project (1999–2003).[2]

I ran the day-to-day operations for the project and directed the research in consultation with Jongho Lee, Harry Pachon, and Rodolfo O. de la Garza on behalf of principal investigators Virgilio Elizondo and Jesse Miranda. I oversaw all five phases of the HCAPL project: (1) a telephone survey of 2,310 Hispanics, (2) two national mail-out surveys of 434 Hispanic civic, public, and religious leaders, (3) community profiles of 45 congregations and 266 clergy and laity in eight urban and rural locations, (4) sixteen commissioned scholarly papers, and (5) four years of primary and secondary research.

Despite the comprehensive nature of the HCAPL national survey, from the outset it still faced a number of limitations. First, it did not survey Latinos without a telephone, which would include a small but important number of poor and underrepresented (largely undocumented) Latinos. Undocumented Latinos who had telephones, however, were included because the survey did not screen out respondents who were not citizens. Second, it only surveyed Latinos who were at least eighteen years of age. Thus it did not capture the attitudes of Latino youth. Third, it surveyed Latinos in seven urban and two rural areas. Although almost 80 percent of all Latinos live in urban metropolitan statistical areas, these cities do *not* account for all Latinos. Fourth, it did not survey Anglos or blacks for comparability purposes, although it did include select questions from other survey instruments for comparability. Finally, the small cell count on many of these religious affiliation survey responses means that some

---

2. The total of 3,153 people surveyed, interviewed, or profiled breaks down as follows:

1. HCAPL National Survey (2,310),

2. HCAPL Civic and Community Leaders Survey (229),

3. HCAPL Religious Leaders Survey (205),

4. HCAPL Community Profile Interviews with clergy, lay leaders, and laity (266),

5. Ethnographic Church Profiles (2 — Catholic and Pentecostal) for Wade Clark Roof and Ethnographic Church Profiles (5 — Catholic, Lutheran, American Baptist, Pentecostal, Independent Immigrant) for Cathy Albanese in Santa Barbara (46),

6. Latina Pentecostal Assemblies of God Women in Ministry Survey (n = 60),

7. Latina United Methodist Women in Ministry Survey (n = 25), and

8. Latino Protestant Oral Histories (n = 12).

of the estimates for smaller religious traditions are suggestive rather than conclusive.

Social Science Research and Demographic Shifts in U.S. Latino Religions, 1920s–1980s

The findings from the Hispanic Churches in American Public Life research project build on almost eighty years of modern social science research among Latinos. The first data collecting on Latino religions took place during the colonial Spanish and Mexican periods in the Southwest as Spanish and Mexican Franciscan and Jesuit priests and secular political leaders took inventories of the religious state of Indians, Mexican mestizos, and Spanish residents in California, Arizona, New Mexico, Florida, and Texas. Although in no way scientific or representative of the Latino population in that day, these records are nonetheless a valuable source for statistical figures. After the U.S.–Mexico War of 1846–48, Anglo-American Catholics and Protestants began to keep track of the size of their Spanish-speaking congregations. Throughout the late nineteenth and early twentieth centuries Catholics, Presbyterians, Methodists, Baptists, Congregationalists, and others produced books and reports that included statistical information on Latino religious affiliation, beliefs, and attitudes (e.g., Harwood, 1908–10; Stowell, 1920; McCombs, 1925; Bresette, 1929; Robert C. Jones, 1929; McLean, 1930; Jones and Wilson, 1931; Abel, 1933).

We do not begin to see any significant secular-oriented anthropological and sociological research on Mexican American religiosity until the early twentieth century, when Anglo-American and Mexican American faculty and graduate students from the University of Southern California, the University of California, the University of Texas, the University of New Mexico, and other institutions, institutes, and government agencies like the WPA Federal Writers Project began to produce quantitative social science research on Latino immigrants that included data on religion. Five of the most important social scientific and anthropological studies from this period are G. Bromley Oxnam, "Mexican Americans from the Standpoint of Religious Forces of the City" (1921), Evangeline Hymer, "A Study of the Social

Attitudes of Adult Mexican Immigrants in Los Angeles and Vicinity" (U.S.C. M.A. thesis, 1923), Robert C. Jones's *The Religious Life of the Mexican in Chicago* (1929), Manuel Gamio's classic study, *Mexican Immigration to the United States* (1930), and Samuel C. Ortegón's U.S.C. M.A. thesis, "Mexican Religious Population of Los Angeles" (1932). In chapter 3, I analyze these works more fully.

Contrary to popular stereotypes today that the growth of denominational and religious pluralism is a recent, post-1960 phenomenon, all of these authors document a vibrant and pluralistic religious marketplace. Jones, Gamio, and Ortegón's analyses include references to Catholics, Evangelicals, Pentecostals, Baptists, Presbyterians, Methodists, Mormons, Jehovah's Witnesses, Seventh-Day Adventists, Spiritualists, Theosophists, and others. Furthermore, they also document significant defections of Catholics to Protestantism. By the early 1920s both Oxnam and McLean argued that the Catholic population was around 60 percent in the Southwest, and Bromley suggested that Protestants might make up as much as 30 percent of the Latino community. These figures are too high and probably reflect a Protestant bias (both were Methodists).

A better read on Latino religious affiliation is Evangeline Hymer's ethnographic-based survey, which puts the percentage of Catholics at approximately 69 percent (1923:40). Several studies by both Catholics and Protestants seem to offer indirect support for their claims that Protestants made up approximately 10–15 percent of the Latino community in places like Los Angeles and Dallas (Bresette, 1929:30, 40–41; McLean, 1930:128). The number of Latino Protestant churches and members in the United States (primarily in the Southwest) had grown from 300 churches and 12,000 communicant members in 1921 to 367 churches and missions and 26,599 communicant members by 1931 (Roundy, 1921:366; McLean, 1930:43). In 1932, Ortegón reported 28 Mexican American Protestant churches in Los Angeles (1932:28–57). The number of Protestants increased to 500 churches and 50,000 people by the mid-1940s (Griffith, 1947:190).

Social scientists note that large numbers of Mexican Catholics were joining Pentecostal, Jehovah's Witness, Mormon, Spiritist, and

Spiritualist traditions. Gamio wrote that a "large number" of Mexicans had "abandoned" Catholicism in the United States. This was confirmed in his interviews with informants telling him that the "Aleluyas," or Pentecostals, were the most popular Protestant tradition in the Spanish-speaking community (Gamio, 1930:117–18; 1931:223). Both Jones and Ortegón make reference to Francisco Olazábal's Bethel Temple mother churches in East Los Angeles and in Chicago just across the street from Hull House (Robert C. Jones, 1931:7, 25; Ortegón, 1932:40, 50). Similarly, in 1933 Theodore Abel wrote that Pentecostals were the greatest competition to both Catholics and Mainline Protestants and in the late 1940s Ortegón stated that the Pentecostals were drawing "a large number of Mexicans into their fold" (Abel, 1933:54–55; Ortegón, 1950:152). These findings are consistent with the historical research on the large-scale evangelistic and healing campaigns conducted by Francisco Olazábal. He held mass evangelistic meetings (with as many as ten thousand attending) throughout the United States, Mexico, and Puerto Rico during the 1920s and 1930s. The meetings attracted some 250,000 Latinos and resulted in the planting of over 120 missions and churches. Olazábal organized large mother churches in the wake of his revivals (from which other missions and churches were planted) in East Los Angeles, Nogales, El Paso, San Antonio, Houston, Chicago, Spanish Harlem, and the Bronx. His evangelistic work was joined by other Mexican American and Puerto Rican evangelists, including Antonio Castañeda Nava, Roberto Fiero, A. C. Valdez, Juan Lugo, Carlos Sepúlveda, Natividad Nevarez, Francisca Blaisdell, Chonita Morgan Howard, Julia and Matilde Vargas, Aurora Chávez, and many others during the 1920s through the 1950s. All told, these attracted tens of thousands of Latinos to the Pentecostal movement throughout the United States, Mexico, and Puerto Rico (Espinosa, 1999, 2002, 2004b). These social scientific studies also note the growth of other important religious groups such as the Seventh-Day Adventists, the Jehovah's Witnesses, Mormons, Spiritualists, and Spiritists in the Latino community (Robert C. Jones, 1929:2; Gamio, 1931:197; Ortegón, 1932:15, 40–44).

This movement toward denominational pluralism is also borne out in qualitative anthropological and religious studies research interviews (Dolan and Hinojosa, 1994:54–55, 95–96). Many of the above cited surveys and reports leave out Seventh-Day Adventists, Jehovah's Witnesses, Mormons, and some indigenous Pentecostal groups, and many counted only communicant membership. Church growth studies generally argue that the total number of religious adherents is membership times three (Gastón Espinosa, 1999; 2004a; 2004b).

In addition to this important work in the Southwest, in New York City C. Wright Mills, Clarence Senior, and Rose Kohn Goldsen conducted survey research among Puerto Ricans for their book *The Puerto Rican Journey* (1950) and Meryl Muoss included statistical work on the Latino religious profile in New York City in her report *Midcentury Pioneers and Protestants* (1954). The Latino Pentecostal movement in New York City grew from 25 churches in 1937 to 143 by 1953 to 250 by 1960. By 1954, they made up approximately 70 percent (143 out of 204) of all Latino Protestant churches in New York City. In 1960 Wakefield wrote that the "flourishing" Pentecostal movement in Spanish Harlem was the greatest "challenge" to Catholics and Mainline Protestants and that these churches were "so strong that they also present a threat — which no other group seriously does — to the practice of spiritualism" (Muoss, 1954:17, 20; Traverzo Galarza, 1979:9; Wakefield, 1960:76, 78).

The quality of social science research among Latinos witnessed significant improvement in the 1970s. Perhaps the first major modern social scientific studies that included significant attention to Latino religions were Patrick H. McNamara's and Joan Moore's essays in Leo Grebler, Joan Moore, and Ralph Guzman, *The Mexican American People* (1970). The book drew on the findings from the 1960 U.S. Census and their own Mexican American Studies Project (MASP) survey conducted in Los Angeles and San Antonio in 1965–66 (Grebler, Moore, and Guzman, 1970:631–65). They drew on historical research and the MASP survey to analyze the role that churches played in both assimilation and social and political empowerment.

The findings from the MASP survey, however, are significantly flawed because MASP (a) conducted the survey in English only, (b) restricted its survey to primarily second- and third-generation Mexican

Americans in San Antonio and Los Angeles, and (c) only surveyed people living in urban centers. In addition, Moore's analyses and classification of Mexican American traditions were problematic for three reasons. First, she stated that "Protestantism is not important in the Mexican American population" and that only 5 percent of those professing religion were Protestant and thus "not worth much special attention." However, the survey is based only on English-speaking respondents, and she assumes that anyone who does not respond as "Protestant" is therefore not Protestant. In fact, as we shall see later, a majority of the HCAPL national survey respondents who self-identified as "other Christian," "no religious preference," "something else," and even "other religion" later self-identified as born-again or with a smaller Protestant denomination when asked to specify their tradition. Second, she classified Mormons as Protestants (even though she admitted that Mormons do not consider themselves Protestant) and the Church of the Nazarene as Pentecostal (even though that church explicitly rejects the Pentecostal movement and speaking in tongues). And third, she claimed that the Apostolic Assembly was the largest Mexican American Pentecostal tradition even though the Latin Districts of the Assemblies of God were much larger. She tended to treat Apostolic Pentecostals as if they were typical of Latino Pentecostals, despite the fact that they reject the doctrine of the Trinity, make up less than 20 percent of all Latino Pentecostals, and do not ordain women to the ministry — something that most Pentecostal groups have done since the early twentieth century (Espinosa, 2004a). Despite these limitations, her study is important because it is non-sectarian and pluralistic in orientation, includes groups often overlooked, such as Oneness Pentecostals and Mormons, and surveys English-speaking Mexican Americans in Los Angeles and San Antonio (Joan Moore, 1970:482–512).

McNamara's work draws less upon the statistical findings from the MASP survey, but he does nonetheless include important statistical information on Mass attendance, discrimination in the church, fear of Protestant defections, knowledge of Catholic social teachings, clergy civic activities, birth control, level of CCD (Confraternity of Christian Doctrine) instruction, Catholic marriage rates, and other findings. While McNamara later stated that his assimilationist framework soon fell by the wayside, his work has since influenced Latino social science researchers such as Anthony M. Stevens-Arroyo and Ana María Díaz-Stevens (1997), Milagros Peña (2002), and Anneris Goris (1995). The work of McNamara and Moore was augmented by surveys on Latino Catholicism by Gallup/*Our Sunday Visitor* (1978) and Roberto O. González and Michael Le Velle for their book, *Hispanic Catholics in the U.S.: A Socio-Cultural and Religious Profile* (1985).

Another study to examine Latino religious affiliation was the work of Catholic sociologist Andrew Greeley. After overlooking Latino Catholics in his previous analyses, he began to conduct work on Latinos in the 1980s. Drawing upon the findings from the GSS at the University of Chicago, he wrote three short but important essays that identified what he described as "seismic" "mass defections" of Latino Catholics to Evangelical Protestantism (1988, 1994, 1997). His work, however, was limited by the fact that the GSS only surveyed people in English. Although his work implied these major demographic shifts were new, we have seen that mass defections have been taking place since at least the 1920s with Francisco Olazábal, A. C. Valdez, Juan Lugo, Antonio Castañeda Nava, and many others. One of the main reasons why their work went largely undetected by social scientists and the 1936 U.S. Census is that newly arrived immigrants kept the percentage of Latino Catholics relatively stable at around 70 percent. Moreover most researchers fielded only English-language surveys, which were only able to capture the religious affiliation of English-speaking second-generation children when they (GSS, LNPS, NSRI, ARIS) began to target and analyze Latinos in the 1980s and 1990s. Greeley's larger findings about the growth of Latino Protestantism were echoed in Rodolfo O. de la Garza's *Latino National Political Survey* (LNPS) (De la Garza, DeSipio, Chris García, John García, and Falcón, 1992). Despite the small number of questions and response options regarding religious affiliation in the LNPS, it has served as a national standard by which social scientists have subsequently measured Latino religious affiliation.

Recent Methodological Reflections of Social Science on U.S. Latino Religions

The social scientific study of Latino religions received a major boost with the work of Otto Maduro (1991, 1995), Meredith McGuire (1994), Anthony M. Stevens-Arroyo and Gilbert Cadena (1995), Stevens-Arroyo and Diaz-Stevens (1998), Cadena (1995), Edwin Hernández (1995, 1998, 1999), Milagros Peña (1998, 2002), and others since 1990. Otto Maduro's important essay "Some Theoretical Implications of Latin American Liberation Theology for the Sociology of Religion" called on scholars to begin their social science research by asking themselves a series of critical questions about the method, goals, and objectives of their study such as: Why are we conducting the research? What are the implications? Who are our research partners? Whose opinions and concerns count? Does our research methodology actually include the "voice of the voiceless"? Do we make any effort to include the "other" in our research projects? Do we include them in an evaluation and critique of our work, rather than just as subjects of it? In an equally illuminating essay entitled, "Directions for a Reassessment of Latina/o Religion," Maduro calls on social science researchers to think of theories as maps that guide but do not determine our end results. A theoretical study of Latino religions should be conducted as an open exploration and humble quest to understand the lived experience of ordinary people that does not seek to impose a theoretical grid on the community. He suggests that scholars entering into the Latino community should avoid the tendency to inadvertently silence, objectify, and manipulate the people they are interviewing and surveying. He warns researchers to be wary of the temptation to naively believe that all research can be "value-free" and that all Latinos are monolithic. To this end, he calls on scholars to avoid an elitist approach to religious agency, ecclesiocentric analyses of popular religion, and static views of religious identity. Instead, he encourages social scientists to view religious agency as creative transformation. By so doing, social scientists can produce first-rate scholarship that also advances the cause, the community, and contributes to its creative transformation (Maduro, 1991, 1995).

Meredith McGuire echoes many of Maduro's recommendations. She notes that past interpretations of U.S. religion were founded on research that either overlooked or ignored Latino religiosity. The emerging social science quantitative research on U.S. Latino religions will push scholars to "rethink" past interpretations of American religions by forcing them to look at popular religion as a cultural resource rather than focus on fixed institutions. The exploration of religious pluralism, popular religion, religious syncretism, civil religion, "quasi-religion," and other non-official "patterns of religion" will offer rich insights not only into Latino religiosity but also into American religions. She tempers her optimism by cautioning scholars to "avoid romanticizing popular religion" lest their work be "biased" and their data "slanted or even useless." Just because it is a "religion of the people" does not mean that it is "any more benign or beneficial than official religion." In fact, she says, in some cases "popular religions are intolerant, oppressive, or even violent...and anti-democratic." Despite the fact that pure objectivity is impossible, she implies that scholars should nonetheless at least try to remain objective and even-handed in their methodologies and analyses (McGuire, 1994:198–99).

In an effort to address the lack of social science research on U.S. Latinos noted by McGuire, Díaz-Stevens and Stevens-Arroyo's book *Recognizing the Latino Resurgence in U.S. Religion* offers a historical, quantitative, and qualitative analysis of how Latinos use religion as a major cultural resource and symbolic capital to fortify their identity in American society (1998). They use their findings to argue that from 1967 through the 1980s there was a major resurgence in the study of U.S. Latino religions. They also challenge social scientists to include Latinos in their future analyses. This resurgence is further documented in chapter 3 of this book. Similarly, Gilbert Cadena's research examines how religious values, symbols, and meaning shaped Latino cultural awareness and self-determination. He then explores Latino religious and ethnic identity, commitment to social justice, demographics, institutional satisfaction and dissatisfaction, and Catholic religiosity. He ends by calling for more comparative and interdisciplinary qualitative and quantitative research on U.S. Latinos (1995).

Like Cadena, Edwin Hernández examines the scope and limitations of conducting social science research among Latinos. He argues that a sociological analysis of Latinos has to be theoretically driven and based on a Latino religiocentric cultural identity, empirical data, and objectivity. He argues that the "belief in supernatural forces or realities has to be 'bracketed' from any sociological investigation." He draws upon the work of Neuman (1991) and H. W. Smith (1975) to argue that scholars need to triangulate their research approach by "using different types of data-collection techniques [archival, quantitative, qualitative] to examine the same research problem from multiple approaches in order to establish a greater degree of validity." Hernández argues that triangulation will help reassure that biases, which are inherent to every methodology, are recognized and kept in check. It will also help ensure a more balanced and accurate "representation of reality without allowing any particular bias to dominate" (H. W. Smith, 1975:273; Hernández, 1995:69). Before this triangulation begins, however, there needs to be a process of deconstruction and question asking. He hopes that taking a holistic approach to the study of Latino religions will help avoid the various ideological and epistemological battles between those for and against social science survey research because the battles threaten the well-being of the community of scholars (Hernández, 1995:73).

Similarly, Milagros Peña's important articles "Latina Religious Practice" (1998) and "Devising a Study on Religion and the Latina Experience" (2002) open up new vistas of understanding in how social scientists go about conducting research among Latina women in the United States. She draws on race, ethnicity, and gender to challenge the way sociologists of religion have hitherto looked at religious practice and expression by exploring new methodological approaches and questions. She argues that social science research cannot simply be based on the kinds of religious measures found in Mainline Protestantism and traditional sociological surveys about churches. Instead, social scientists need to conceptualize new woman-centered theoretical frameworks that take into account what Ana María Díaz-Stevens calls the "matriarchial core" of Latino religion (1994). Scholars also need to examine the various ways that women use religion to subvert the religious and social order. For this reason, she proposes a methodological approach that focuses on popular non-institutional women's spirituality. The best way to access this knowledge is through qualitative face-to-face research with women on the ground through a process of *confianza,* or gaining trust in the interview process. In this respect, she challenges the insider vs. outsider methodological approach, which calls on scholars to keep a critical outside distance from their subjects. One of the critical ways that this *confianza* can be gained is by giving something back to the community. The best way to do this is to balance survey questionnaires with focus group interviews. She also argues that selecting the right wording for ethnographic interviews and surveys is important because it can help avoid contradictory findings. She cites as an example the fact that while Rodolfo O. de la Garza's *Latino National Political Survey* (LNPS 1990) found that 25 percent of all Latinos considered themselves born-again Christians, the survey by Ada María Isasi-Díaz, Milagros Peña, and Yolanda Tarango (1996) found that 38 percent of Latinos self-identified as born-again Christians in their study (Peña, 1998, 2002). This led her to the conclusion that their wording may have been unclear when in fact, as we shall see shortly, their figures were correct.

Quantitative National Survey Limitations — Advisory Board and Design Team

The contradictory findings on U.S. Latino religious affiliation are due, in part, to a number of methodological limitations of the General Social Survey (GSS), the Latino National Political Survey (LNPS), the National Survey of Religious Identification (NSRI), the American Religious Identification Survey (ARIS), the Gallup Poll, the National Alcohol Survey (NAS), and similar data sets. These limitations can be avoided by taking the following steps. The first step that any scholar must take who wishes to conduct a national survey in the Latino community is to ask a series of questions: What problem, theories, or hypotheses are to be explored? Why a national survey? What kind of national survey — a random sample telephone survey or an in-person interview survey? What is the purpose of the survey? What are the goals? Why should a foundation or institution want to fund such a survey? How will the potential findings differ from previous studies? What previous theories or hypotheses will it challenge or revise? These questions, theories, and/or hypotheses are critical because they will not only shape the survey itself, but also who is selected to serve on the advisory board.

The second step is to create an advisory board and design team that can represent, understand, and capture the diversity of the community.[3] This is especially true in the case of surveys on religiosity where denominational and religious classification can be confusing to a non-specialist. Given the increasingly political nature of scholarship today and the religious, national, and ethnic diversity of the community, selecting an advisory board is difficult. Any scholar conducting national research among Latinos should try to create an advisory board that captures (as much as possible) the social profile of the larger Latino community. One of the best ways to do this is to make sure that there is gender, religious affiliation, country of origin, and regional representation on the board. While it will be impossible to have 100 percent proportional representation, it is nonetheless a wise strategy to come as close as possible as people *will* inquire about the composition and representation of the board to make sure that their perspectives and values are accurately represented in the construction of the survey methodology, framework, and questions. Furthermore, it is important to keep the advisory boards small (five to eight people). This will make it easier to coordinate board meetings and reach consensus on important decisions.

The principal investigators and project manager of the HCAPL tackled this limitation by assembling an advisory board that attempted to reflect the diversity of the Latino community.[4] Unlike

---

3. The HCAPL survey design team included the project directors, manager, select HCAPL advisory board members, and the Tomás Rivera Policy Institute staff. They based the religious leaders survey, the civic leaders survey, and the community profile questionnaire on the national survey. Gastón Espinosa and Jongho Lee took the lead in the construction of these latter survey and profile instruments in direct conversation with Virgilio Elizondo, Jesse Miranda, Harry Pachon, Rodolfo O. de la Garza, and other members of the advisory board.

4. The seventeen scholars who helped shape the HCPAL national survey methodology, framework, questions, and language were Virgilio Elizondo (theologian), Jesse Miranda (theologian), Gastón Espinosa (historian/social scientist), Edwin Hernández (sociologist), Milagros Peña (sociologist), Daisy Machado (historian), Harry Pachon (political scientist), Rodolfo O. de

many national surveys, typically directed by Anglo-Americans, the HCAPL survey was led, managed, and coordinated by U.S.-born Latinos. The principal investigators were Virgilio Elizondo and Jesse Miranda, and the project manager and director of research was Gastón Espinosa. They not only selected a team of outstanding advisors, a majority of whom were also Latino, but they also sub-contracted Harry Pachon, Rodolfo O. de la Garza, Louis DeSipio, and Jongho Lee of the Tomás Rivera Policy Institute (TRPI) to help coordinate and oversee the three HCAPL national surveys and eight community profiles — an important addition because TRPI is the finest Latino social science policy institute in the nation and their strong reputation adds a level of secular credibility to the project re-sults. The advisory board included people of Mexican, Puerto Rican, Cuban, Dominican, Colombian, and other Latin American ancestry, women and men, people who lived (either currently or in the past) in the Southwest, Midwest, South, East Coast, and Puerto Rico, people from Roman Catholic, Protestant (Mainline, Evangelical, and Pente-costal), and Alternative Christian backgrounds, and also those with no religious affiliation at all. We also intentionally sought advisors who could bring to the project their unique methodological and dis-ciplinary insights from religious studies, theology, political science, sociology, history, and education.

The Question of Language

One of the most important decisions any director or advisory board will have to wrestle with in fielding a national survey is whether the

---

la Garza (political scientist), Jongho Lee (political scientist), Louis DeSipio (political scientist), David Leege (political scientist), Allen Hertzke (political scientist), Donald Miller (sociologist), Dean Hoge (sociologist), Wade Clark Roof (sociologist), Samuel Pagán (theologian), Elizabeth Conde-Frazier (theologian/Christian educator), and María Elena González, R.S.M. (theolo-gian). Of the ten Latinos/as who served on the board, five (50 percent) were of Mexican ancestry, three (30 percent) were of Puerto Rican ancestry, one (10 percent) of Cuban an-cestry, and one (10 percent) of Colombian ancestry. Four (40 percent) of the Latinos/as either grew up and/or were currently living in New York City, Miami, and/or Puerto Rico and four (40 percent) were women. Although we found it impossible to secure exact proportional rep-resentation among the Latino advisors given the limitations of scholarly availability, expertise, budget restrictions, and time, we tried nonetheless.

survey will be bilingual. Until just recently, most major national surveys like the GSS, NSRI, and ARIS were conducted almost exclusively in English. This skewed the sample in favor of second- and third-generation U.S. Latinos who are more likely to be English-dominant and Protestant. This is a major methodological limitation because it leaves out of the sample a large percentage of first-generation Latin American immigrants who speak exclusively Spanish. Kosmin and Mayer's ARIS survey, for example, only surveyed English-speaking Latinos. This helps to explain why their survey results found that only 57 percent of Latinos were Roman Catholic, while the HCAPL survey, which was conducted in both English (62 percent) and Spanish (38 percent), found that 70 percent of Latinos across all generations were Roman Catholic. The Kosmin and Mayer findings are more consistent with the HCAPL survey finding that 62 percent of third-generation Latinos (all of whom would be English-dominant) are Roman Catholic. Both studies reported Protestant and Other Christian affiliation at 22 and 23 percent respectively. Furthermore, because the HCAPL survey found that Latino Catholics are significantly more likely to be immigrants (54 percent) and thus more likely to speak only Spanish than their Protestant counterparts (33 percent), ARIS not only inadvertently undercounted Catholics within the U.S. Latino population, but also undercounted the total percentage of Latinos who make up the American Catholic Church (29 percent) and as a corollary the total percentage of Christians (77 percent) in the U.S. population (Kosmin, Mayer, and Keysar, 2001:8–9, 36; Espinosa, Elizondo, and Miranda, 2005:284; Espinosa, 2004b:289–91).

The language issue is further complicated by the fact that the English word choice of the survey also has to translate accurately into Spanish — and into a form of Spanish that can be clearly understood not just by Mexicans, but also by Puerto Ricans, El Salvadorians, Guatemalans, Dominicans, Colombians, and other Latin Americans. Because of the HCAPL design team's diversity, they were able to address this potential limitation by fielding a bilingual national survey that could be understood by U.S.-born Latinos and immigrants from different Latin American countries. Furthermore, it did not ask the interviewees to provide their name or contact information and thus protected the anonymity of the respondents. This effort resulted in 38 percent of all respondents answering the survey in Spanish.

Sample Scope and Size

The next major limitation scholars face in conducting survey research among Latinos is the scope and size of the survey. The survey research design team has to decide if they are going to conduct the survey via telephone, U.S. mail, in person, or some combination thereof. If they choose the telephone survey route, they have to further decide if they will use a random digit dialing method in high-density *barrios* and *colonias* and/or Hispanic-surnames in low-density areas. They also have to decide the number of states in which they will field the survey, how many questions will be on the survey, and the size of their national sample. The larger the number of questions on the survey and the larger the sample size, the greater the cost and difficulty in securing the sample. Many national surveys like the GSS include 1,100 to 1,500 respondents (National Opinion Research Center, 2001:147, 1289, 1295; Larry Hunt, 1999:1605), although 2,100–2,300 appears to be one of the most common sample sizes for recent Latino national surveys (Espinosa, Elizondo, and Miranda, 2003; Suro, 2004). This is probably because the large sample size allows for greater cross analysis and can help reduce the margin of error, thus making the results more representative and "accurate."

In addition to size, researchers have to decide in what seasons and on what days they plan to field the survey. This can be complicated for religious surveys because Sunday (the ideal time to conduct surveys) is usually the time when religious people are least likely to be at home. The same is true for Wednesday night for many Protestants and Catholics who attend mid-week Bible studies or Mass. This is where a Latino framework that takes into account cultural variables and religious attendance patterns is important. Furthermore, given the fact that the Latino population is disproportionately Catholic, it is critical to include a Protestant oversample in order to ensure enough English- *and Spanish-language* Protestant respondents to analyze the other survey questions by Catholic and Protestant religious affiliation and within the Protestant community itself. This is a limitation of virtually every other Latino survey to date, including the Pew Hispanic Center/Kaiser Family Foundation 2004 National Survey of Latinos.

The HCAPL design team attempted to address these limitations by deciding to field a national twenty-minute telephone survey with 2,310 Latino respondents across the United States (2,060) and Puerto Rico (250) over an eight-week period from August 29 through October 31, 2000. They chose to conduct the survey on days least likely to compete with Catholic and Protestant religious activities. The first draft of the survey questionnaire was based on sample questions from ten previous Latino- and non-Latino-framed national and regional surveys provided by social scientists and the directors of the other Pew studies on religion and public life, including Harry Pachon, Jongho Lee, Edwin Hernández, R. Drew Smith, John C. Green, and Robert Wuthnow, and from questions created from scratch by the design team. The initial draft of ninety-five questions was reviewed by the advisory board and, after ten major revisions over a four-month period, whittled down to sixty-three questions, four of which were screening questions.[5] Survey samples were drawn from Los Angeles, San Antonio, Houston, Chicago, Miami, New York City, rural Iowa, rural Colorado, and San Juan, Puerto Rico. According to a 2000 census estimate, 80 percent of Latinos live in urban metropolitan areas. Latinos living in just these seven metropolitan areas above (not including the rural area samples) comprise almost half (46 percent) of the entire U.S. Latino population. Given that Latinos are essentially an urban population, a sample from these seven metropolitan and two rural areas is an adequate and cost-effective way to secure a national random sample of Latinos.

Latino households were randomly selected drawing on a two-tier approach — using samples both from the random digit dialing method in high-density Latino areas and from directory listed households with Spanish surnames in low-density rural Latino areas. The

5. The best resources to review in preparing for a national survey are the methodological section of the National Opinion Research Center's (NORC) General Social Survey (GSS) and Pamela L. Alreck and Robert B. Settle, *The Survey Research Handbook: Guidelines and Strategies for Conducting a Survey* (Chicago: Irwin Professional Publishing, 1994).

sampling frame from which primary sample units were selected was a list of all telephone exchanges (i.e., area codes) that serve the aforementioned Consolidated Metropolitan Statistical Areas (CMSAs). Only exchanges whose proportion of listed households was within 50 percent of the sampled county were selected. In total, the national survey sample included a primary national sample of 1,709 respondents made up of a metropolitan base sample of 1,404 respondents and a rural sample of 305 respondents, an oversample of 351 Protestants, and an oversample of 250 Puerto Rican islanders (Espinosa, Elizondo, and Miranda, 2003).

Another related limitation in Latino national survey research is low response rates. According to Tortora, the Latino response rate to surveys is much lower than the national average (2004). Furthermore, he found that Latinos have one of the highest percentages (44 percent) of any major national subgroup that was *unwilling* to respond to a telephone survey (2004). This means that social scientists have to work significantly harder to secure a viable national sample among Latinos than among the general population. Although the reasons for a low response rate are complex, language, literacy, concerns about legal status in the United States, lack of leisure time, and apprehension concerning scams may all contribute.

Despite the various limitations in securing responses, the fact that all three of the HCAPL surveys drew on other survey questions enabled them to offer a limited level of comparability for certain questions. This proved especially insightful when we compared and contrasted, for example, how Latino clergy differed from African American clergy in their attitudes on political mobilization and social action. We were able to make these comparisons because we included questions from R. Drew Smith's Public Influences of African American Churches national clergy survey funded by The Pew Charitable Trusts (Smith, 2003:9–10, 58–83; Espinosa, Elizondo, and Miranda, 2005:288–89, 304, n. 17).

Survey Locations and Country of Origin

The next methodological limitation social scientists face in conducting national surveys among U.S. Latinos is deciding whether or not to include a rural sample. Rural samples are expensive and can be difficult to obtain because people tend to be scattered over a large geographical region, can normally only be identified by their surname, and often end up constituting a very small segment of the total sample. For this reason, many surveys do not include a true rural sample. However, a survey that does not include a rural sample is not, technically speaking, a national survey. Some social scientists argue that because the Latino population is so highly urban, a rural sample is unnecessary and will affect the results only in minor ways. However, this is just a methodological ruse used to justify a decision to make national claims about the Latino community with an exclusively urban survey sample. Although expensive and time-consuming, a rural sample is important because a large number of Latinos still live in largely historically rural communities, especially in states like New Mexico and Colorado. Furthermore, a growing number of Latinos are migrating to rural regions of the country in the Midwest and the South. In fact, the Latino population has grown by almost 400 percent in North Carolina, Georgia, and in other southern states.[6]

The HCAPL research team addressed this limitation by including a rural oversample in the national survey. However, they also wanted to include a historic rural population and a relatively "new" rural population. The decision was thus made to secure a Latino rural sample in southern Colorado (which along with northern New Mexico is a historic Hispanic community that goes back to 1598) and a rural sample in America's heartland— Iowa.

A related limitation is that there is often no way to ascertain an accurate picture of the country of origin of Latino respondents. Most surveys simply list as possible response options Mexico, Puerto Rico, Cuba, and other Latin America (LNPS). The result is that the "other Latin America" category often ends up being very large and analytically ambiguous. In order to address the country of origin limitation, the HCAPL design team sought a large sample size (2,060) and increased the number of country of origin self-identification

---

6. The eleven states with the most rapid Latino growth in the United States are Iowa, Minnesota, Nebraska, Arkansas, Georgia, Alabama, North Carolina, South Carolina, Tennessee, Kentucky, and Nevada. Gouveia and Saenz, 2000:305–28; Saenz and Torres, 2003.

possibilities to include not only Mexico, Puerto Rico, Cuba, and other Latin America, but also the Dominican Republic, El Salvador, Guatemala, Colombia, other parts of the world, and people of more than one ancestry. The relatively large sample size allowed for limited comparative analyses of Latinos by important variables like sex, country of origin, generation, language, religious affiliation (by family grouping or select denominations), citizenship, education, marriage, occupation, income, and political party affiliation.

Latino-Framed Survey and Classification Systems

Many of these concerns about language and rural representation can be addressed if the advisory board and survey design team create a truly Latino-framed survey. A Latino-framed survey should include questions and terminology that reflect the language, culture, society, and values of the Latino population. Yet it is likewise important for Latino-framed surveys also to include questions from other national surveys. This will help ensure a certain level of compatibility with other Latino- and non-Latino-framed national surveys and enable scholars to compare and contrast their findings across surveys, sexes, races/ethnicities, and time.

The importance of developing a Latino-framed survey is also critical in the creation of a religious affiliation classification system. As we have already seen, this limitation is very critical if one wants to make comparisons across religious traditions. Many national surveys, typologies, and meta-classification systems are largely based on an Anglo-American religious marketplace classification, a Mainline Protestant theological schematic (Peña, 2002), a lack of understanding of the historic and theological distinctions between Pentecostal, Evangelical, fundamentalist, and Alternative Christian (e.g., Jehovah's Witness and Mormon) traditions, and the inability of interviewees to specify with which religious tradition they self-identify after checking "independent/non-denominational," "other Christian," "something else," "other religious tradition or denomination," or "other religion." Furthermore, most national surveys (e.g., LNPS, NSRI, ARIS, NLS) use a Euroamerican rather than a Latino/Latin American religious classification system and inadvertently list large white Anglo-American denominations like the Presbyterians, Episcopalians, Lutherans, Methodists, and Baptists but not large indigenous Latino denominations and traditions. Some surveys list only one broad category of "Pentecostal" (LNPS); still others do not list Pentecostal at all (NSL).

The importance of a Latino-framed survey that included indigenous Protestant Pentecostal traditions was driven home when we included (for the first time in any national Latino survey) several indigenous Spanish-language Latino Protestant Pentecostal denominations in our national survey like the Assembly of Christian Churches, the Pentecostal Church of God, and the Apostolic Assembly of the Faith in Christ Jesus, Inc. The result was that the HCAPL national survey found that these Latino Pentecostal denominations were ranked the third, fourth, and tenth largest non-Catholic Christian traditions in the United States (Espinosa, 2004a). We also found that other Alternative Christian traditions also ranked in the top ten non-Catholic U.S. Latino Christian traditions. The Jehovah's Witnesses and the Mormons were the first and eighth largest non-Catholic Christian traditions in the U.S. Latino community. When we examined only the Protestant traditions and left out Alternative Christian traditions like the Jehovah's Witnesses and Mormons, Latino Pentecostal denominations or traditions were the first, second, third, and tenth largest Protestant traditions in the United States among Latinos (Espinosa, 2004a). Unlike denominational surveys, which normally can provide only data about Spanish-language congregations and districts, the HCAPL bilingual survey cut across the Spanish- and English-language congregation divide by securing responses from both.

The HCAPL national survey also addressed the problem of religious affiliation classification by providing a longer than normal list of twenty possible response options. We asked respondents who self-identified as "independent/non-denominational," "other Christian," "something else," "other religious tradition or denomination," and "other religion," to "specify" their tradition. These responses were written down and thus enabled us to secure a very precise read on the religious affiliation of an otherwise large and unknown group of survey respondents.[7] The findings from this methodological ap-proach challenge the general perception that movement away from denominational affiliation signals a movement away from Christian-ity and results in secularization (Hout and Fischer, 2002:165–75; Sherkat, 2001:1462). Although the HCAPL survey confirmed the growth of non-denominational religious affiliation (Steensland et al., 2000:295–98), we also found that the vast majority of those who did not self-identify with a particular denomination did self-identify as born-again Christian. This was true for national survey respondents who self-identified as "independent/non-denominational" (75 per-cent), "other Christian" (77 percent), "something else" (52 percent), "other religious tradition or denomination" (52 percent), and even "other religion" (50 percent), "don't know/unspecified" (48 per-cent). This finding was further confirmed by high levels of church attendance (almost every week or more) for those respondents who self-identified as "independent/non-denominational" (67 percent), "other Christian" (71 percent), "something else" (52 percent), "other religious tradition or denomination" (60 percent), "other religion" (40 percent), and "don't know/unspecified" (48 percent). Given that being born-again is one of the defining marks of both Evangeli-cal and Pentecostal Christianity and that high church attendance is more often associated with Evangelical Christianity as well (Roof, 1999:129, 303, 319), these data suggest that many Latino Evangel-icals and Pentecostals may have been misclassified in other national surveys. This kind of misclassification may also be a problem for analyses of other national surveys as well. Furthermore, as we have already seen and will continue to see shortly, other groups like Jehovah's Witnesses and Mormons have also been underreported be-cause they have often been inaccurately lumped under the label of fundamentalist or conservative Protestant.

---

7. HCAPL National Survey Question #23 included the following response options: "Amer-ican Baptist, Southern Baptist, Assembly of Christian Churches, Assemblies of God, Disciples of Christ, Episcopalian, Evangelical and Jehovah's Witness, Lutheran, Methodist, Mormon, Pentecostal Church of God, Apostolic Assembly or Oneness Pentecostal, Presbyterian, Seventh-Day Adventist, Independent/Non-denominational Protestant, Other Christian . . . Specify, Other Religion . . . Specify, Something Else . . . Specify and Don't know/Refused."

Latino unwillingness to self-identify with any one denomination may be due more to high rates of mobility, employment transfers, the search for affordable housing, and the search for higher paying jobs than to secularization, movement away from Christianity, or lack of religious commitment. The HCAPL national survey found that 93 percent of U.S. Latinos self-identify with Christianity, 6 percent self-identify as having no particular religious preference/other, 1 percent as practicing another world religion, and 0.37 percent as atheist or agnostic (Espinosa, 2004a). However, the most obvious reason why some people self-identified as "independent/non-denominational," "other Christian," "something else," "other religious tradition or denomination," or "other religion," and then later specified being born-again and/or attending a Protestant church on Sunday is probably because they were unaware of the historical and taxonomical distinctions between a religion and a denomination. Still others may in fact practice two or more religious traditions, although this is unlikely given the tendency of born-again Evangelicals and Pentecostals to criticize non-Christian religions and Alternative Christian traditions. These findings and others do reveal a high level of religious mobility and switching within the Protestant subculture (Espinosa, 2004a, 2004b). The implications of these findings are that many survey analysts may be misclassifying Evangelicals, Pentecostals, and Alternative Christians.

In light of the importance of creating a classification system that reflects the reality of the larger Latino community and yet is still useful for data analyses, the HCAPL design team created a more refined religious classification system based on the HCAPL national survey results. It broke down the U.S. Latino religious community into six groups of respondents:

1. Christian
   A. Catholic
   B. Protestant
   C. Alternative Christian
2. World Religions
3. Atheist and Agnostic
4. Other Unspecified
5. No Particular Religious Preference

6. No Response, Don't Know, Refused to Answer

It further broke down the Christian, world religion, and atheist/ agnostic categories by specific religious traditions/subgroups. For further refinement see the appendix on page 43. Clearly, each survey design team will need to create a religious affiliation classification system that works best for the purpose of their project and in light of the restrictions placed on it due to sample size, scope, and budget.

Although there is good reason to classify all Latino Protestants together into one family grouping (especially given the high rate of those self-identifying as "born-again" — 37 percent of all U.S. Latinos), we decided against this for two reasons. First, while it is true that most Latino Protestants regardless of family grouping see themselves as *Evangélicos* in the Spanish-speaking community (where Protestant religiosity is, in general, more Evangelical and theologically and morally conservative), this is not true for many second- and third-generation Latinos who attend English-language Mainline Protestant and Pentecostal congregations that emphasize their own unique liberal, conservative, or creedal views on religion and society. Second, the large percentage of Pentecostals in the Protestant community (64 percent) skews this family grouping and does not enable us to further analyze other large non-Charismatic groups such as the Southern Baptists and Seventh-Day Adventists. For these reasons and others, we decided to subdivide Protestants into three categories for the purpose of our data analyses. However, in other analyses we simply collapsed the three categories into one.

Another important methodological finding of the HCAPL national survey design team is that many classification systems may have a tendency to over-report Mainline Protestants and under-report Latino Evangelical and Pentecostal Protestants because there are a large number of completely indigenous and autonomous Pentecostal denominations in the United States with no administrative, ecclesiastical, or financial ties to white denominations within their same religious family grouping (Espinosa, 1999, 2004b). Those surveys (GSS, LNPS, NSRI, ARIS) that list the various Mainline Protestant traditions (e.g., Episcopalian, Presbyterian, Methodist, Lutheran, etc.) but only a few Pentecostal and non-Charismatic

Evangelical denominations (which are more numerous) and no indigenous Spanish-speaking Pentecostal denominations (e.g., Assembly of Christian Churches, Apostolic Assembly of the Faith in Christ Jesus, Latin American Council of Christian Churches, Pentecostal Church of God, Light of the World Church, Universal Church of the Kingdom of God, etc.) bias the findings in favor of Mainline Protestantism, other religious traditions, and no religious preference — the latter of which could very easily be read by respondents as no *particular* religious preference or no *one* religion rather than no religion at all — the way some scholars tend to interpret it (Hout and Fischer, 2002:165–89). Furthermore, Mainline Protestant representation is also often over-represented because no distinctions are made between the Mainline Protestant and the Evangelical wings of historic Protestant traditions such as the Methodists (Free Methodists vs. United Methodists), Presbyterians (PCUSA vs. PCA/OPC/EPC), Baptists (American vs. Southern, Conservative, etc.), and the Lutherans (ELCA vs. Missouri Synod). In most cases, all of the Evangelical wings of these denominations are lumped under the category of Mainline Protestant even though the Evangelical wings of these traditions also have a growing number of Latino adherents and congregations.[8]

Some survey teams are aware of the presence of Pentecostals in the Latino community and have tried to address this by providing one or two religious affiliation response categories — almost always "Pentecostal" or "Assemblies of God." The problem with this is that there are approximately 150 distinct indigenous and autonomous Latino Pentecostal denominations, councils, and independent movements in the United States, Mexico, and Puerto Rico. Furthermore, according to David Barrett and the World Christian Encyclopedia Research Center, there are an additional 1,991 Pentecostal denominations, traditions, and councils in Latin America of which 1,767 are completely indigenous and independent of American influence (Espinosa, 2004b:275–80). Many of these, such as the Universal Church of the Kingdom of God, the Light of the World Church, and Congregation

---

8. For example, when I contacted various denominations I found that there was a growing number of Evangelical Methodist (68 Free Methodists churches vs. 550 UMC churches) and Lutheran (159 Missouri Synod churches vs. 133 ELCA churches) congregations in the United States. Espinosa, Elizondo, and Miranda, 2003:27.

Mita, have had organized churches in the United States since at least the 1970s, and in many cases since the 1950s (Espinosa, 2004b).

Not all Pentecostals are alike. They differ in *theology* (Trinitarian vs. Oneness), *indigeneity* (Anglo-American affiliated vs. indigenous Latino), *language* (English and Spanish vs. Spanish only), *denominational identity* (denominational vs. independent non-denominational), *regionality* (the New York City–based Assembly of Christian Churches vs. the Texas-based Latin American Council of Christian Churches vs. the California-based Apostolic Assembly of the Faith in Christ Jesus), *social attitudes* (pacifist oriented Apostolic Assembly of the Faith in Christ Jesus vs. just-war oriented Assemblies of God), and *gender attitudes* (non-ordination for women like the Apostolic Assembly of the Faith in Christ Jesus vs. full ordination for women in the Assemblies of God vs. ordination restricted to pastoring, teaching, and preaching but no weddings, funerals, and baptisms in the Latin American Council of Christian Churches) (Espinosa, 2002, 2004b). Furthermore, in my twelve years of ethnographic and oral history research on Latino Pentecostals, I found that most Pentecostals simply self-identified as "Christian," "Charismatic," or "non-denominational." Many are part of independent Pentecostal/Charismatic storefront churches that avoid the label of "Pentecostal" because they de-emphasize the public practice of speaking in tongues. Perhaps the most important reason why they tend not to self-identify with a traditional Pentecostal or charismatic denomination is that most Latino Pentecostals tend to be less familiar with the history and theological distinctiveness of their own denominations and traditions than their Mainline and non-charismatic Evangelical (e.g., Southern Baptist, Seventh-Day Adventist) counterparts.

Another limitation of many past national survey religious classification systems is that they tended to overlook transdenominational movements, beliefs, and practices. This is evident in transdenominational movements and experiences like liberation theology, the Cursillo movement, the "born-again" movement, and the Pentecostal/Charismatic movement. As is true among African Americans but is less true among Anglo-Americans, the HCAPL national survey found that the Pentecostal/Charismatic movement had made significant inroads into Latino Mainline Protestantism and Roman Catholicism. It found that 28 percent of all U.S. Latinos self-identify as born-again and Pentecostal, Charismatic, *and* spirit-filled and that 21 percent of all Latino Mainline Protestants did the same. Perhaps more surprising to some, the HCAPL survey also found that 22 percent of all U.S. Latino Catholics said they were Catholic, born-again, and Pentecostal, Charismatic, or spirit-filled (Espinosa, 2004a; 2004b). These findings seem to be confirmed by the recent finding that 27 percent of all Christians in Latin America are Protestant Pentecostal and Catholic Charismatic (Espinosa, 2004b). Furthermore, when Protestants and Catholics are combined, approximately 37 percent of all U.S. Latinos self-identify as born-again or with an Evangelical denomination. The findings from the HCAPL national survey confirmed the findings of Isasi-Díaz, Peña, and Tarango. The percentage of Latina women who self-identify as born-again in the HCAPL national survey (39 percent) was virtually identical to what Peña and her colleagues found (38.7 percent) in their survey of Latina women four years earlier (1998, 2002:288). In fact, the LNPS biased its question by adding to it, "There are deeply religious people who have not had an experience of this sort." If this kind of negative qualification and framing were applied to questions about abortion, gay rights, affirmative action, and feminism this would rightly be flagged as biasing the question and leading the respondent. Regardless, the significance of the born-again experience among Latinas is evident among women of Mexican (35.8 percent), Puerto Rican (41.3 percent), and other Latin American ancestry (43 percent). This topic clearly needs further investigation (Espinosa, 2002; Sánchez-Walsh, 2003).

The HCAPL classification system also avoided the common problem that the GSS FUND variable faced when it lumped Pentecostals and Evangelicals together with Jehovah's Witnesses in a broader category of conservative or fundamentalist Protestant (Hunt, 1999:1606; Hunt, 2000:350). This is problematic as few Jehovah's Witnesses would self-identify as "fundamentalist" or even "conservative Protestant." The reverse is also true. The reason that the HCAPL national survey did not classify Jehovah's Witnesses and Mormons as Protestant is because they do not self-identify with the Protestant

Reformation nor with the larger Protestant movement or theology. They view their movements as uniquely Christian. This has inadvertently led scholars to imply that most of the Latinos leaving Catholicism are joining Evangelical, Pentecostal, fundamentalist, or conservative Protestant movements (Greeley, 1988, 1994, 1997). The problem with this reporting is that those using the GSS may be lumping together Pentecostals, Evangelicals, Jehovah's Witnesses, and fundamentalists into the metacategory of "fundamentalist" or "conservative Protestant" without offering any further classification nuance or distinctions (Greeley, 1988; Hunt, 1999, 2000). However, there are clear historical, theological, and social reasons for separating these traditions and groups into separate categories not only among Anglo-Americans, but also and especially among English-speaking second- and third-generation Latinos who have acculturated to the larger Anglo-American set of religious traditions and values. In fact, the term "fundamentalist" as applied to Latinos is not only historically inaccurate, but also pejorative and sociologically problematic. Latino Protestant Evangelicals and Pentecostals generally do not fit the sociological profile of Anglo-American fundamentalists. While Latinos are morally conservative on abortion and same-sex marriage (as are many moderate Catholics and Mainline Protestants), a majority cast their votes (69 percent) for Bill Clinton in 1996, support giving aid to illegal immigrants even when giving such aid is illegal, generally support affirmative action and civil rights struggles, believe illegal immigrants should be eligible for government assistance such as Medicaid or welfare, oppose the death penalty, want their churches to talk about the pressing social issues of the day, and support the ordination of women (Espinosa, Elizondo, and Miranda, 2003; Espinosa, Elizondo, and Miranda, 2005:296–98). In fact, Latino Protestant Evangelicals and Pentecostals have more in common with their African American counterparts on many social issues and attitudes than with their Anglo-American brethren.

The result of refining the religious classification in the HCAPL survey was that we found that many of the Latinos who are supposedly leaving Catholicism for Evangelicalism and Pentecostalism are in fact switching to the Jehovah's Witness and Mormon traditions. The HCAPL survey also found that although seven hundred thousand

Latinos indicated that they "recently converted" or returned to Catholicism from a non-Catholic denomination or tradition, it also found
that over 3 million Latinos recently converted away from Catholicism.
Thus for every one Latino who returns to Catholicism, four leave it.
Furthermore, a clear majority of Latinos (57 percent) who recently
converted from Catholicism to Protestantism were second- or third-
generation U.S. citizens. That Jehovah's Witnesses and Mormons are
a major recipient of these seismic shifts was evident in the HCAPL
survey, which found that the single largest non-Catholic Christian
tradition among Latinos was the Jehovah's Witnesses, with more than
800,000 adherents and more than 2,200 Spanish-language congregations, followed by three Pentecostal traditions, the first of which was
the Assemblies of God (770,000). The Seventh-Day Adventists ranked
seventh and the Mormons ranked as the eighth largest traditions. All
combined, there are more Latino Jehovah's Witnesses and Mormons
(1.1 million) than all Latino Baptists (1 million) combined. Further
supporting this, the HCAPL national survey found that the Jehovah's
Witnesses had a higher conversion rate among Latino immigrants
than any other Latino-serving non-Catholic Christian tradition in the
United States. Despite the significant growth of Alternative Christian
traditions, the HCAPL survey also found that Latino Protestant Pentecostals and Charismatics make up 64 percent (4.5 million) of the
Latino Protestant community (Espinosa, 2004a; 2004b).

Conclusion

Despite the limitations researchers face, the future of Latino social science research on religion looks bright. There is a great need not only for
more scholars specializing in Latino social science research, but also for
a rethinking of our quantitative methodological strategies. As we have
seen, very little social science research was conducted among Latinos
until the 1970s and 1980s, and most of it focused on particular cities or
regions of the country. The vast majority of national bilingual surveys
of Latinos (in addition to the work of the GSS) were not fielded in large
numbers until the 1990s. While bilingual studies date back to the work
of Manuel Gamio and others in the 1920s and 1930s, most of this work
since then has been fraught with various limitations and difficulties.

The HCAPL research project attempted to address a number of these shortcomings despite facing a number of key limitations of its own. In so doing, it found that the Pentecostalization of Latino Protestantism along with the growth of denominational and religious pluralism via the Jehovah's Witnesses, Mormons, and metaphysical traditions goes back to the 1920s, and not the 1960s as it is often assumed. One of the reasons why this had not been tracked very well is that much of this growth took place within Spanish-speaking indigenous Pentecostal denominations that English-language surveys could not capture and because some tended to use a Mainline Protestant religious affiliation schematic and lump Jehovah's Witnesses, Mormons, and others into the category of fundamentalist or conservative Protestant. It is my hope that these methodological reflections will in some small way help scholars to continue to conduct groundbreaking social science research on Latino religions and society well into the twenty-first century.

Appendix
Hispanic Churches in American Public Life
Religious Affiliation Classification System
Based on Survey Responses
(Created by Gastón Espinosa)

This classification system was based not only on the original twenty response options listed in the HCAPL national survey, but also on all of the responses given when people who self-reported "other Christian," "other religion," "something else," and "other religious tradition or denomination" were asked to specify their religious tradition.

I classified the Mennonite, Christian Reform Church, and the Reform Church in America respondents as Evangelical not only because their Spanish-language congregations tend to be Evangelical in orientation but also because it is the Evangelical wings of these denominations that have historically conducted outreach to Latinos. CRC, RCA, and Mennonite colleges and seminaries also have ties to the Evangelical community and are part of the Evangelical-based Christian College Coalition (CCC) and other Evangelical associations.

I. Christian
   A. Roman Catholic
      A1. Traditional Catholic
      A2. Charismatic Catholic
   B. Protestant
      B1. Mainline Protestant
         a. Methodist
         b. Presbyterian
         c. American Baptist
         d. Episcopalian
         e. Disciples of Christ
         f. Lutheran
         g. United Church of Christ
         h. Unitarian
         i. Other Mainline Protestants
         j. Non-"Born-Again" Non-Catholic Christians, Denomination Unspecified
      B2. Evangelical Protestant
         a. Southern Baptist Convention
         b. Baptist General Conference
         c. Conservative Baptist
         d. Missionary Baptist
         e. Independent Baptist
         f. Other Baptist
         g. Church of Christ
         h. Seventh-Day Adventists
         i. Mennonite
         j. Christian Reformed Church
         k. Reformed Church in America
         l. Salvation Army
         m. Other Evangelical
         n. "Born-Again," Non-Catholic, Denomination Unspecified
      B3. Pentecostal/Charismatic
         a. Assemblies of God
         b. Assembly of Christian Churches
         c. Pentecostal Church of God
         d. Apostolic or Oneness Pentecostal

            e. Calvary Chapel
            f. Vineyard Christian Fellowship
            g. Victory Outreach International
            h. Light of the World Church (Iglesia la luz del Mundo) (Oneness)
            i. Pentecostal Name of Jesus Christ (Oneness)
            j. United Pentecostal (Oneness)
            k. United Pentecostal International (Oneness)
            l. Church of Christ (Pentecostal)
           m. International Church of the Foursquare Gospel
           n. Other Pentecostal or Charismatic
      C. Alternative Christian (Non-Protestants)
         C1. Jehovah's Witness
         C2. Mormon
         C3. Christian Science
  II. World Religions
      A. World Religion
         A1. Judaism
         A2. Islam
         A3. Buddhism
         A4. Hinduism
         A5. Taoism
         A6. Confucianism
      B. Metaphysical/Alternative World Religion
         B1. Deism
         B2. Metaphysical/Spiritual
         B3. Native American Spirituality
         B4. Paganism
         B5. Satanism
         B6. Unspecified other religion
 III. Other, Unspecified
 IV. No Religious Preference
  V. Atheist or Agnostic
      A. Atheist
      B. Agnostic
 VI. No Response/Refused/Don't Know

Chapter 2

Metaphysical Blending in Latino/a Botánicas in Dallas

Edwin David Aponte

Changó in Oak Cliff

Like many U.S. cities, Dallas, Texas, is divided by race, class, language, and geography in both real and imaginary ways. Many of the city's segments are bordered by the Trinity River. This river of multiple meanings symbolizes the fragmentation of Dallas. Flowing from the west the Trinity River runs through central Dallas, skirts downtown, and forms the northern boundary of the section known as Oak Cliff. For many of the inhabitants of the north side of the river divide, the separation is more than geographic. For them, Oak Cliff is where "those people live" — people too poor, too different, and too much trouble as neighbors. In the minds of many people living north of the Trinity River, Oak Cliff fosters violence and crime, a place to be avoided at all costs by "good folk."

While some people live south of the Trinity River because the housing is more affordable, other residents choose to live in Oak Cliff because of its geographic and cultural beauty and variety. Many of the inhabitants of Oak Cliff, some of whom still resent its annexation by a grasping Dallas, perceive those living north of the Trinity as too focused on ostentatious presentation, too white, too oppressive, and just too bigoted. For them, North Dallas is a place of exclusive wealthy communities and racial profiling by police and shopkeepers. Noticeable cultural diversity is viewed suspiciously and North Dallas residents demonize the southern section of Dallas. Given their mutual suspicion, it is not unexpected that some residents on each side never cross the river. But the fact is that there are diverse communities on both sides of the Trinity River as well as communities that continue to strive for exclusivity. And so the separation of the Trinity River is a porous boundary that defies any urge to be finite and final.

It may or may not be coincidence that Oak Cliff is where multicultural populations of broad economic diversity reside, including large African American and Latino/a communities. It is that type of otherness that makes some Dallas residents uncomfortable. Moreover, there are places in Oak Cliff where the otherness becomes even more extreme. Traveling west on Davis Street (Texas Highway 180) through a seemingly exotic Oak Cliff, one is met with an interesting manifestation of the area's cultural diversity. After passing a popular Salvadoran/Tex-Mex fusion restaurant, the *Librería Cristiana* (Christian bookstore), a fast food restaurant advertising tacos and tortas, and a number of auto repair shops with Spanish signs, the traveler will come to the intersection of Davis Street and Edgefield Avenue. This is a literal crossroad of Latino/a and ethnically diverse neighborhoods where lower income multiple dwellings and middle-and-upper-middle-income neighborhoods of single family bungalows adjoin.

Across the street from a discount dollar store and a Salvadoran specialty market, Changó Botánica has in its display windows lifelike figures in unfamiliar garb. People passing on the sidewalk often look twice at this unusual exhibit. This particular type of striking cultural diversity even has some residents of Oak Cliff scratching their heads trying to figure out the name of the shop and what it sells. The word "Changó" is usually associated with the religious or metaphysical traditions of the Afro-Caribbean — certainly geographically distant from Oak Cliff. But it is not solely the name emblazoned in large red letters on the side of the building that draws the attention of the passerby. There is something both compelling and eerie about the life-size specially clothed mannequins, one female dressed all in white, another in blue sitting in the display windows surrounded by candles and crucifixes with a full-sized stoic-looking Indian chief standing with full-feathered head bonnet, statues and images of the Virgin Mary, and a fat Buddha. It is clear that Changó Botánica stands apart from the other shops along Davis Street, or indeed from many shops on both sides of the Trinity River. The physical location of this store in Dallas, Texas, south of the Trinity River, coupled with the perceived cultural location of the population of Oak Cliff reasonably prompts the question, "What is Changó doing in Oak Cliff?"

While there is a substantial and growing Latino/a population in Dallas and especially in Oak Cliff, it is not primarily of Caribbean origin. The 2000 U.S. Census counted 422,587 Hispanics making up 35.6 percent of Dallas's official total population, as compared with a figure of 12.5 percent nationally. In March 2002, the Latino/a population of the United States was numbered at 37.4 million, up from 32.8 million in 2000 and representing 13.3 percent of the national population. In June 2005, the Census Bureau announced that one out of every seven persons in the United States is Hispanic, thus estimating that there were 41.3 million Hispanics, an increase of 3.9 million in less than five years.[1] Across the United States persons of Mexican descent make up about 66 percent of those called Hispanic or Latino/a.

Likewise, although the Latino/a population of Dallas is diverse, those of Mexican and Mexican American descent dominate. Even the view from a car window will show any observer that Dallas's Hispanic neighborhoods are not monolithically Mexican. There are a significant number of Central American residents, officially totaling 14,972 in 2000, with the largest groups being Salvadoran and Honduran.[2] In the same period of time the percentage of persons of Mexican descent grew to 66.9 percent.[3] The 2000 Census showed that in some parts of the city, including many areas of Oak Cliff the Hispanic population was between 66.7–94.6 percent of the population. Oak Cliff's Latino/a population is mostly, but not exclusively, Mexican, followed by growing numbers of Central Americans. This gives some information about Latino/a diversity and population concentration in Dallas, but the Census demographics do not address the question, "What is Changó doing in Oak Cliff?"

---

1. Pauline Jelinek, "Hispanics Make Up a 7th of U.S. population," *Philadelphia Inquirer*, June 9, 2005, A17.

2. U.S. Census Bureau, *Current Population Survey*, March 2000, P-4; U.S. Census Bureau, Census 2000 Summary File 1, Matrix PCT11.

3. Ibid., P-5.

This chapter explores the nature, influence, and creative presence of African-Caribbean metaphysical (religious) traditions within this predominant Mexican American Latino/a population of Dallas, Texas, in the section of the city known as Oak Cliff.[4] This should show, in part, that the metaphysical practices of people are not limited by any definitions of religious devotion. People have the ability to adapt their metaphysical practice and use any resource that appears to be helpful to them. The diversity of metaphysical practice within the Oak Cliff Hispanic population serves as a corrective to those who would like to name boundaries between one tradition and another without paying attention to the specific context of the community.

African Presence and Influence in Latin American Religions

One way to begin to discover what Changó is doing in Oak Cliff is to review the profound and lasting influence of African traditions in the Americas. This influence is often overlooked in historical, religious, and theological discussions of religious convictions and practices among Latinos/as in the United States and in Latin America.

When discussed at all, the African influence on Latin American Christianity is usually seen as confined to Caribbean cultures in Cuba, Puerto Rico, and the Dominican Republic.[5] Yet the African presence

---

4. This essay enters the discussions that differentiate between "religion" and "spirituality." Often religion connotes an institutional form of "metaphysical" practices. In deference to people who are sensitive about the meaning of religion, I have incorporated the use of "metaphysical." According to *Webster's Universal College Dictionary*, one definition of "metaphysical" is that it is "beyond the physical; incorporeal or supernatural." Yet when understood as encompassing more than institutional hegemonic expressions, "religion" might be a better term than "metaphysical" in the case of beliefs and practices that have African roots (like some within Latino/a communities) because it includes both communal physical (or liturgical) aspects of metaphysical practice alongside the invisible (but still perceived real) metaphysical practice (or theology). In fact, to be precise, the term "physical/metaphysical" could probably be employed. For the sake of the discussion in this volume I will merely use "metaphysical practice" to indicate what in other contexts would be called "religious practice," "spirituality," or other similar terms.

5. For this discussion "Latin America" is understood to refer to those nations and entities where Spanish or Portuguese is spoken as part of the Iberian cultural heritage transplanted through conquest and colonization. Nevertheless, it should be remembered that the African heritage in the Americas is more widespread than this, notably in the non-Spanish-speaking

is more pervasive than the Caribbean. Certainly, during the long period of slavery the African settlement was heavy in the Caribbean, especially in Cuba; Havana was the leading slave city in the world in the nineteenth century. An even larger number of Africans were brought to Brazil, eventuating in the development of Luso-Brazilian culture. Other African slaves were brought to other areas of Spanish America, including Mexico, Colombia, and Venezuela.[6] African slaves were introduced into Peru in 1669 to do the hardest work required by Spanish *conquistadores* (Bakewell, 1995:114). Shortly afterward slave traders brought thousands of black Africans to Peru, Chile, and the Río Plata region (today the nations of Argentina and Uruguay) between 1701 and 1713 (Rout, 1976:30). In these and other contexts the evidence of African heritage has persisted to the present day. The scope of this African influence throughout Latin America and the Caribbean calls for a greater understanding of the origins and different manifestations and evolutions of African religions and cultures as they developed there.

The development of the European system of transatlantic African slavery adds another set of cultural confrontations. As Europeans, especially Iberians (the various Christian kingdoms that later emerged as the modern nation states of Spain and Portugal) and Italians in their service, explored alternative ways to eastern Asia by traveling along the coast of Africa, they came upon the Canary Islands, Cape Verde, Madeira, and the African coast, where they eventually established a permanent presence. During these journeys, they made contact with different African cultures where a system of slavery existed. Accustomed to the practice of slavery from the medieval period, the Iberian Europeans developed sugar plantations on their Atlantic island possessions and found that black African slaves could be used effectively there. As the need for slaves increased with new plantations, the Africans who were forcibly brought to the Americas became a more highly diverse group in ethnicity and metaphysical (religious)

Caribbean, e.g., Haiti and Jamaica, and of course in the United States. See Coniff and Davis, 1994; Dayan, 1995; Holloway, 1990; Murphy, 1994.

6. African slaves in Mexico were present both on the Gulf and Pacific coasts. On African presence in Mexico see Hernández Cuevas, 2004; Laurence Iliff, "Black Mexicans See Pride in Lost History," *Dallas Morning News*, April 3, 2002, 1A, 12A.

practice. They came from a wide geographic span of west and central Africa from contemporary Cape Verde to Angola and from ethnic groups like the Yoruba from Nigeria, the Fon from contemporary Benin, and the Bakongo peoples from the Congo region.

From such complex roots, this confluence of African cultural and religious traditions and practices became enmeshed through slavery in the Americas. The resulting physical and metaphysical cross-cultural fertilization of language, cultures, practices, and beliefs impacted the direct descendants of these slaves as well as the broader multi-cultural societies in which they lived and toiled. The enslaved Africans brought their religious-cultural cosmos to the Americas in their holistic understanding of the world with a rich and active spiritual dimension of everyday life that repeatedly was contextualized.[7] The Muslim slaves from West Africa added a different understanding of monotheism, which was transplanted across the Atlantic and added to the mix. Others from West Africa shared some features of what may be called a multiethnic West African cosmology. Thus many in the African Diaspora possessed a common religious-cultural heritage that Joseph Murphy refers to as a "family of traditions, cousins shar-ing common ancestors and set apart by the 'intermarriages' made in the line" (1994:4). Despite the calamity of a common social history of subjugation, racism, and achievement, traditions from Africa were remembered, re-membered, and re-created by the enslaved Africans.

African ways of knowing and being confronted transplanted Iberian understandings of Christianity at both the institutional and popular (or folk) levels. It was at the popular level of religious/spiritual beliefs and practices that generations of blending took place in ways that could not be predicted and often were not sanctioned officially. Indeed, despite efforts to define them the boundaries between institutional and popular religion frequently are not as clear as the Trinity River going through Dallas. But it is at the popular level of lived religion, or spirituality, or the metaphysical/physical that we begin to answer the question of why Changó is in Dallas, Texas. Anthropologist Harold Recinos states that "popular refers to a defining characteristic of a

---

7. Anita de Luna writes, "Spirituality is mediated through lived experience, and experience is contextualized in culture" (2002:38).

social class which has a common identity, based among other things, upon a situation of inequality" (2001:116). For centuries the vast majority of the populations of Latin America has lived with inequality and suffering. It is often "popular" culture and "popular" religion that nurture a community, particularly a community on the underside of a society. In this way the inequalities of class dynamics came into play in areas of society and culture, including religious or spiritual beliefs, attitudes, and practices for both slave owners and those who were enslaved.

This innovative metaphysical cultural blending that took place in a milieu of oppression exerted a powerful influence on the development of Latin American religion and culture and is sometimes referred to as *mestizaje*.[8] Originally an exclusively pejorative term that referred specifically to the mixing of European and Amerindian/indigenous peoples, it gained wider usage to refer to the cultural mixing of all peoples in the Americas (see chapter 5 by Manuel Vásquez). Today theologians like Ada María Isasi-Díaz strongly advocate a renewed understanding of the concept of *mestizaje* that embraces the African heritage of people in the Americas. Some have suggested that this can be done through the reappropriation of the term "mulatto" and its cognates that refer to the cultural mix of African and European peoples. Isasi-Díaz states, "I have found it absolutely necessary to add *mulatez* to *mestizaje* using it as a binominal: *mestizaje-mulatez*. I have added *mulatez* to make it absolutely clear that there is no Hispanic culture in the U.S.A. (and no culture in our countries of origin) that is without elements of African culture and race" (2004:44).[9] While the concept of *mulatez* is criticized by some (see chapter 6 by Miguel De La Torre) the debate surrounding its link to *mestizaje* highlights the growing awareness of Latino/a scholars of religion to give fuller account of the African dimensions of Latino/a religious life, even beyond Afro-Latino/a communities. In a very provocative and yet helpful way, theologian Loida Martell-Otero examines the cultural identities and locations of Latino/a through the alternative

---

8. For a helpful discussion on *mestizaje* and a theological and pastoral appropriation of the concept see Elizondo, 1988.

9. See also Segovia, 1992; and Valentín, 2002:69–72.

metaphor of *sato/sata* ("mixed breed" or "mongrel") arguing for a re-capturing of the original "stereotyped, rejected, insulted" experiential connotations of the terms *mestizaje* and *mulatez* (2001:8–9).

Whether under the rubric of *metizaje* or *mulatez,* or some other designation to describe the mixture, fusion, and re-creation of race and cultural perspectives, distinctive African ways of healing and folk wisdom blended over time with aspects of Iberian Christianity and indigenous Native American beliefs and practices. Often this religious fusion is referred to as "syncretism," a term perceived by some as carrying negative and pejorative connotations. In any case, whether understood as syncretism or a physical/metaphysical blending, the religious options available at a popular level — which in some locales included an African stream — were more varied, complex, and localized than often perceived by those who see the religious history of Latin America as defined by four centuries of Roman Catholic religious monopoly. African influence in Latin American religions is significant and widespread with regional variations throughout Latin America, which in turn influence Latino/a religious perspectives and practices in the United States. Unique metaphysical (religious) practices blossomed in each specific locale from indigenous seeds and multiple transplanted traditions. And then there were significant waves of religious-cultural-spiritual-metaphysical blending that occurred with the shift of international borders and the periodic movements of peoples starting in 1848. These particularized practices amalgamated with other localized practices as people found themselves in the United States. In this way religious options for Latin Americans and Latinas/os in the United States developed in the context of local communities and parallel to officially sanctioned beliefs, resulting in a tapestry of everyday metaphysical beliefs and practices.[10]

One such stream of religious options is the way that African-based diasporic beliefs and practices are reworked in the Americas.

---

10. For example, Chestnut, 2003:3–4, states that "after four centuries of religious monopoly in which the main choices for the popular classes were either to consume the Catholic product or not to consume any religion at all, impoverished believers, and indeed all Latin Americans, can now select from among a dizzying array of religious options that range from the African-Brazilian religion of Umbanda to the New Age group known as the Vegetable Union ('União do Vegetal' in Portuguese)."

The surviving African traditions that persisted through slavery and colonial life empowered the African–Latin American communities by providing beliefs, rituals, and practices that were perceived to address spiritual, psychological, and social needs. Variations of this theme occurred throughout Latin America, including the islands of the Caribbean and portions of Mexico, Central America, and South America.

Candomblé and Umbanda are prominent examples of metaphysical practices with African roots that survived in Brazil. Candomblé is a religious system that has blended elements from Yoruba traditions, Roman Catholicism, and indigenous religions. Espiritismo, especially as influenced by the nineteenth-century spiritualism movement associated with Allan Kardec, whose actual name was Hippolyte Rivail, involves the belief that people can converse with the dead. Umbanda is related to espiritismo and emerged from an urban context, drawing on European, African, Asian, and Indigenous elements to form its distinctive metaphysical practice. Dianna DeG. Brown describes the majority of Umbanda practitioners as displaying "an eclectic blend of Catholic belief and practice, Kardecism, and Afro-Brazilian practices with aspects of Hinduism, Buddhism, and other currents of mysticism" (1994:1). And so while it is not a direct descendent of the African diaspora tradition, espiritismo becomes a cousin through its absorption of some of the practices that survived (Brandon, 1993:86). Another expression of physical/metaphysical blending is Santería, which evolved in Cuba as a distinct slave religion characterized by a fusion of Afro-Cuban beliefs and practices with Spanish Catholic folk culture. During the period of slavery Africans exerted a major influence in shaping the developing Cuban culture in its entirety through attitudes, music, dance, and religion.

We can see from this discussion that the metaphysical practices brought to the United States from Latin America and the Caribbean cannot be viewed as primarily Catholic tradition with some indigenous religion scattered across the landscape. In exploring Latino/a religiosity in the United States we do well not to accept the premise of a religious monopoly composed of a strict Catholic/Protestant two-party paradigm without giving additional attention to the rich diversity of expression under the umbrellas of those two rubrics, as well as what is happening at the popular/folk level. There are complex religious options that include officially sanctioned institutional beliefs and practices in addition to the rich metaphysical mélange transported from Latin America. New combinations of religious practice constantly develop and evolve within the heterogeneous context of Latino/a communities in the United States. We return to our question of what Changó is doing in Oak Cliff.

Changó and Metaphysical Blending

As noted, the everyday presence and accessibility of the spiritual realm was a common African sensibility that crossed the Atlantic through the slave trade. African religious-cultural or metaphysical traditions emphasized maintaining good and balanced relationships with all of life, especially between human beings and "spirits," or *orishas* (Spanish: *orichas;* Portuguese: *orixas*). Another characteristic of Africa-based metaphysical practice is the conviction that the spirits of ancestors are honored and are believed to exert a continuing influence in everyday life. The belief in a Supreme Being who exists over and above all of life is part of these faith systems. While this Supreme Being is usually perceived as being remote from the everyday, the multiple intermediary spirits, or *orishas,* are seen as the active invisible beings with which humans have the most daily contact. The African–Latin American synthesis results in a worldview that considers all of existence as infused with the spiritual and connected to the supernatural, rather than dividing life into the sacred or the secular, a common European-American modernist viewpoint. Maintaining balance and keeping good relationships between the different realms of existence becomes the vehicle that ensures that the resources needed to negotiate life are available on a daily basis. This balance is accomplished through ceremonies combining beliefs with symbolic objects and actions.

Different forms of divination establish balance, seek guidance, address spiritual problems, obtain knowledge, and commune with the ancestors and orishas and are central to Afro-Latino/a traditions. The alignment of human action with the spiritual realm and the proper treatment of various spiritual, physical, and psychological illnesses calls for the insight of a trained specialist. In Santería the *babal-awo* serves as the expert who recognizes the nature and spiritual dimension of specific life-problems. Addressing these troubles may involve a type of sacrifice as a means for deeper relationship with the spirits/orisha. Drums and dances figure prominently into ceremonies where divination and sacrifice combine into a single event/experience of orisha consciousness. This description is typical of many practices of African-based religious traditions in Latin America.

As it developed, Santería not only spread beyond its original slave adherents, but also proved to be extremely adaptive. African orishas/orichas were paired with particular European Roman Catholic *santos* (saints) who were perceived to share particular characteristics.[11] Illustrations of connections made between the saints and the orishas include Changó with St. Barbara, Yemaya with Our Lady of Regla, and Oshun with the Virgin of Cobre. While Santería is distinct from its African antecedents there is a simultaneous continuity with Africa even as it embraces or blends elements of folk Christianity and indigenous beliefs into a distinct religious/metaphysical approach used in special ceremonies and everyday life.

Santería and other religious-cultural systems like it emerged as a means for continuity with an African past in the colonial present while accessing elements of Spanish Christianity (especially folk or popular religion) and of the indigenous cosmovisions (worldviews). As the transplanted African religiosities were taking root and developing in their new contexts within Latin America, there were instances of reciprocal influence from one region or location to another. Examples of this influence include that of Cuban Santería on Puerto Rican expressions of spiritualism and Haitian Vodou on Dominican culture on the island of Hispaniola. Partly through the influence and impact of Cuban exiles Santería is increasingly known in the United States, gaining adherents from other Latino/a groups and among non-Hispanics, especially African Americans. In the growing and diverse U.S. Latino/a communities new types of spiritual/religious/metaphysical/physical blendings take place as people come

---

11. In different parts of Latin America and Hispanic/Latino/a communities in the United States the term *santo* has another meaning as a common referent to hand-carved statues (usually wood), painted and used devotionally. This is the case in Puerto Rico and New Mexico.

together in everyday life. African diaspora influence is growing in certain expressions of broad-based religiosity. Popular religious practices, the music and rhythms of worship, and approaches to health and healing reflect many religious/metaphysical influences. And a key metaphysical meeting place for initiated followers of Santería, non-initiated Latinos/Latinas, African Americans, other searchers, seekers, and the spiritually curious are the botánicas in Latino/a barrios, such as the Changó Botánica in Oak Cliff.

Botánicas as Spiritual Meeting Places

Botánicas, which are a combination of spiritual resource center, folk pharmacy, metaphysical purveyor, and bookstore, have become a center for another type of religious fusion within Hispanic/Latino/a communities in the United States (DeStefano, 2001:5). Servicing physical, psychological, religious, and spiritual needs, botánicas provide information, tools, supplies, and sometimes additional services. They sell special bath water, sprays, votive herbs, teas, incense, oils, and perfumes. Tall, glass-jar votive prayer candles with pictures of Roman Catholic saints sit on the shelves of the botánicas, supermarkets, discount stores, and other shops in Dallas. The reverse side of most of these votive candles has a prayer in Spanish and/or English to be recited with a particular request or purpose. Specialized books and pamphlets in Spanish and English are available on a variety of topics, and the botánica provides ritual supplies, statues and other images, as well as tarot cards. And because the botánica is more than a retail outlet, often there is space reserved for spiritual consultations.

While rooted in Santería, the Changó Botánica in Oak Cliff has a self-proclaimed eclectic mission to be "a provider of spiritual supplies for all beliefs including but not limited to: Santería, Buddhism, Confucianism, Christianity, Hinduism, Islam, Jainism, Judaism, Shinto, Sikhism, Taoism and Zoroastrianism."[12] A walk through the aisles of this Oak Cliff botánica reveals that the merchandise is offered by someone who sees needs beyond those of the small Afro-Latino/a community in Dallas.

---

12. *www.changobotanica.com/about.cfm.*

The Changó Botánica in Dallas was launched in 1977 by Francisco Díaz, an exile from Cuba. His story is a common one of the Cuban diaspora in that Díaz was born and spent his early life in Havana, arriving in the United States in 1968. Once he moved to Texas, Díaz opened the botánica in Oak Cliff. Oak Cliff is not the only place to find a botánica around Dallas because Latinos/as of all types of national and racial heritage frequent botánicas. There are other botánicas on Davis Street in both directions from the Changó Botánica. A few blocks away on Jefferson Street, the de facto downtown of Oak Cliff, near a large supermarket that caters to the Latino population, there are several more botánicas, both large and small. Indeed, on both sides of the Trinity River, defying the major geographic boundary of the city in neighborhoods where Latinos/as reside there are still more botánicas. And botánicas are found not just in Dallas or in the Cuban communities of South Florida. It appears that across the United States wherever there are Latino/a communities of whatever origin there is a good chance that there will be some type of botánica. "In communities with sizable Hispanic populations, such as El Barrio (East Harlem) in Manhattan and the South Bronx, the presence of neighborhood botánicas — stores that sell ritual materials used in Santería and other ritual practices such as espiritismo — increases the visibility of the religion vis-à-vis the general public" (Gregory, 1999:66).

But to be sure, not everyone who goes to a botánica is a practitioner of Santería. Some people go just to get particular objects for their home *altarcito* (altar), and this indicates that something else is going on. Increasingly non-Latinos have become frequent visitors of places like the Changó Botánica in Oak Cliff. Whether they are non-Latino/a followers of African-based traditions, practitioners of an expression of New Age spirituality or a form of Buddhism, looking for solutions to troubles, healing for ills, help in love, guidance in life, or other types of seeking, the botánica has become a place of wider spiritual significance and increasingly eclectic metaphysical blending. But metaphysical blending does not necessarily mean that the distinctions between religious traditions are forgotten or obliterated. It is quite possible for "good" Latina or Latino Catholics or Protestants to stop by the botánica as needed and not see any contradiction with their religion, although they may risk chastisement from a disapproving priest or pastor. This suggests a far more complex understanding of metaphysical and religious realities than typically imagined. Many Latinos/Latinas blend popular religious or metaphysical attitudes and actions of multiple traditions in everyday practice.

While it is the case that in many botánicas and spiritualist specialty shops there readily are found aspects of orisha devotion like Changó, Eleggua, and Obatala, there also are found evidences of cultural cross-fertilization among diverse Latin American traditions in the United States where previously there was no direct link. In the botánicas of Oak Cliff, as well as in other Latino/a communities across the United States, African-based religious expressions from the Caribbean have merged with other forms of Latino/a popular religiosity with roots in Mexico and Central America among urban Latinos/as. For example, Mexican American *curanderismo* is one form of a healing tradition that finds a welcome in the botánicas.

Curanderismo can be understood as a type of folk healing that addresses physical, psychological, and metaphysical dimensions of healing and illness (James S. Griffith, 2003:122). Perrone, Stockel, and Krueger offer this definition of *curanderismo*:

> *Curanderismo* consists of a set of folk medical beliefs, rituals, and practices that seem to address the psychological, spiritual, and social needs of traditional...people. It is a complex system of folk medicine with its own theoretical, diagnostic, and therapeutic aspects. *Curanderismo* is conceptually holistic in nature; no separation is made between mind and body, as in western medicine and psychology. (1989:86)

Although in the U.S. Southwest the most common expression of *curanderismo* has its roots in Mexico, localized expressions drawing on indigenous and European traditions are found throughout Latin America, for example, in Argentina, Honduras, Guatemala, and Nicaragua. All of these forms of *curanderismo* share an understanding of the interconnectedness of the physical and spiritual dimensions of life, as well as the assumption that both play a role in illness and healing. The agent of healing is called *curandero* (male healer) or *curandera* (female healer).[13] Some famous *curanderos/as* in the Southwest and the Mexico-U.S. Borderlands continue to be objects of intercession and devotion even after their deaths, most notably Don Pedrito Jaramillo (d. 1907) and Niño Fidencio (1898–1938).

The Mexican and Mexican American communal tradition of *curanderismo* has three levels of healing: physical, mental, and spiritual. Healing on all three levels may include prayers, candles, rituals, and herbs. While *curanderismo* often is criticized formally by Roman Catholic and Protestant church leaders as inappropriate, as evil, and sometimes as demonic, at the popular level within many Latino/a communities it is accepted and widely practiced, particularly when there is no readily available alternative avenue for health care (West, 1989:138–40). In the foreword to the reissue of Trotter and Chavira's study of Mexican American *curanderismo*, Luis León asserts that

> *curanderismo* is a border phenomenon that exists throughout the Chicano Southwest, Chicago, and in all parts of the country. For wherever Mexican communities are found within the United States borders, one encounters the transformation of Mexican traditions; geopolitical boundaries are, in effect, meaningless — the borderlands are everywhere. (1997:xiii)

Among some Latinos and Latinas *curanderismo* is seen to be compatible with the healing practices of Santería without one becoming an adherent of Santería. Prayer candles with images of the *Virgen de Guadalupe, los Siete Potencias Africanas* (the Seven African powers), and *La Mano Más Poderosa* (the most powerful hand) are sold side by side with plain white votive candles in botánicas, supermarkets, and discount stores. While innocuous in their supermarket locations they function as a shared spiritual/metaphysical focus point for a wide variety of beliefs, desires, hopes, and commitments. These objects have multiple parallel functions depending on the orientation the user brings to them. The appropriation of African-based religious expressions demonstrates their ongoing influence and presence among

---

13. For a fictionalized but very helpful entry into the world of the *curandera* see the novel by Anaya, *Bless Me, Ultima* (1994).

U.S. Latino/a groups with very little or no direct African connection. Commenting on this phenomenon, Miguel De La Torre states that "as Santería attracts more individuals of different ethnicities and socioeconomic classes, it will become less Cuban-centric. Spanish is already being used less, and specifically Cuban procedures are being discarded.... The Americanization of Santería is redefining how the faith is practiced and understood" (2004b:206).

Not only is Santería undergoing an internal "Americanization," its presence in the United States has an external influence on the popular religiosity of some Latinos/as in the United States who are not devotees of Santería. Its interaction with other Latino/a metaphysical or religious traditions is indicative of larger cultural transformations in our midst and points to a growing U.S. Latino/a pan-ethnic reality.

One of the manifestations of this pan-ethnic reality is verbalized through "Spanglish," a phenomenon with some history, although the term itself seems to have appeared in the mid-1960s, well after the appearance of its actual practice. Spanglish combines elements of the English and Spanish languages, with the latter's verbal patterns dominant. The language uses many English words as substitutes for existing Spanish words, resulting in a type of linguistic fusion that is reflective of larger contextual cultural creativity and synthesis. Scholar and essayist Ilan Stavans, musing on Spanglish, writes,

> I've learned to admire Spanglish over time. Yes, it is the tongue of the uneducated. Yes, it's a hodgepodge.... But its creativity astonished me. In many ways, I see in it the beauties and achievements of jazz, a musical style that sprang up among African-Americans as a result of improvisation and lack of education. Eventually, though, it became a major force in America, a state of mind breaching out of the ghetto into the middle class and beyond. Will Spanglish follow a similar route? (2003:3)

In describing Spanglish both as a language and as a cultural phenomenon, Ed Morales asserts that it "is the active state of cultural mixing, the endless pursuit of resolving contradictions in politics and art, the upside-down overhaul of class structure, the carnival of multinational culture," and "Spanglish is the state of belonging to at least two identities at the same time, and not being confused or hurt by it"

(2002:6, 8). If spoken Spanglish (despite protests from both Spanish and English linguistic purists) expresses a milieu of emergent Latino/a pan-ethnic reality, botánicas as spiritual meeting places indicate a stream of pan-ethnic eclectic spirituality and reciprocal religiosity.

Another example of reciprocal religious influence is seen in the presence of El Santo Niño de Atocha on the shelves of botánicas, pharmacies, discount stores, and supermarkets. The contemporary devotion in the United States to the Holy Child of Atocha has its roots in Mexico, especially in the state of Zacatecas. But far from Zacatecas, El Santo Niño is adored at the El Santuario de Chimayó shrine in New Mexico. The Sanctuary is known as a place of healing, and the Black Christ crucifix of Esquipulas is featured behind the altar of the church. El Santuario de Chimayó remains a major destination of pilgrimage, as well as the home of El Santo Niño de Atocha. Representing the Christ Child dressed in blue pilgrim clothing, Atocha is known for healing, especially of children. Devotion to El Santo Niño de Atocha is far from limited to Mexico and New Mexico. In Latino/a communities throughout the United States, Latin America, and in Spain *curanderos* and *curanderas* ask the Santo Niño de Atocha to intervene on behalf of those in need.

Interestingly in Santería the Santo Niño de Atocha also has become recognized as a representation of the Santería orisha Eleggua, known in other traditions as Legba and Eshu-Elegba. Because Eleggua/Legba/Eshu-Elegba is associated with a crossroads in these traditions, he is known as the gatekeeper to the realm of the orishas, a trickster, and sometimes as a messenger of the High God Olodumare.[14] Of course, this does not mean that everyone who purchases a prayer candle with the image of El Santo Niño de Atocha affirms or even recognizes the possible double meaning, practices Santería, and is devoted to Eleggua. Some people purchase El Santo Niño because he is perceived as assisting healing, but others see in Atocha a manifestation of Eleggua, who needs to be consulted as the gatekeeper before the devotee can progress. At the Changó Botánica, the customer leaving with a candle with the image of El Santo Niño de

---

14. See Cros Sandoval, 1995:86; and Murphy, 1993:46.

Atocha could be a practitioner of Santería, a Roman Catholic seeking healing, or a person who simply likes the picture of Atocha.

The only thing that is certain about the customers of Changó Botánica is that something about the store is alluring, that it had something they needed or wanted. The meanings of the religious/metaphysical aids inside Changó Botánica in Oak Cliff represent a variety of practices either exclusively or simultaneously. There can be no single snapshot that captures the religious practice in a botánica because people bring their own beliefs and expectations with them, automatically weaving them into the tapestry of countless combinations of tradition represented by the examples of material religion found in each place affected by the changing needs, challenges, struggles, uncertainties, and desires of everyday life.

The Beliefs of the People

In places like Oak Cliff we can see the diverse and creative beliefs of the people at work, namely, the popular religious or metaphysical practices. Theologian Orlando Espín, one of the primary voices describing the importance of Latino/a popular religion, asserts that the practitioners of popular religion are the marginalized in a society (1994:66). Espín states that "the people's faith [should] be taken seriously as a true *locus theologicus* and not solely or mainly as a pastoral, catechetical problem" (1997:2). While he focuses primarily on Latino/a popular Catholicism, Espín specifically mentions Cuban Santería and Palo as examples of popular religion. Even though it is discounted by some within institutional religion, popular religion is a dynamic rather than a static phenomenon of extensive variety and appeal. Popular religion finds its roots in the past while it continues to be meaningful for its adherents in the present and as such is said to be the standard bearer of tradition but nevertheless adapts to new contexts, and therefore affects the future. C. Gilbert Romero defines popular religion in the Hispanic Catholic context as "a form of popular devotion among Hispanics based more on indigenous cultural elements than on official Roman Catholic worship patterns" (1991:2). Isasi-Díaz has identified popular religiosity as a creative communal way of being and a means of cultural self-identification for survival (2004:45–48).

As an expression of popular religion the botánica in Latino/a communites across the United States may be seen not only as a theological site but also more broadly as a *locus religious* that likewise wrestles with the needs, challenges, struggles, uncertainties, and desires of everyday life. Moreover, the different metaphysical beliefs and practices that converge in the spiritual meeting places of botánicas reconfigure the religious traditions into new practices, in turn impacting the development of new religious understandings, some of which overlap Christian theological understandings. The recognition of this religious/metaphysical blending in the daily life of Latinas, Latinos, and others is an attempt to describe and name the "facts on the ground." The intellectual, theological, or pastoral responses to the practices that find a home in U.S. botánicas invites a set of questions, concerns, responses, and commitments that allow for a greater multiplicity of grassroots options.

An illustration of naming and responding to the diverse practices of popular religion is found in a tale related by Carlos Cardoza-Orlandi. When he was the pastor of a small Dominican congregation in New York City, a child in the congregation became ill. The congregation prayed and after a period of uncertainty, the child returned to good health. Everyone rejoiced in the child's recovery. A problem occurred when Cardoza-Orlandi discovered that the family had visited a botánica and consulted a *santero*, behavior that many considered outside the parameters of Latino/a *evangélico* belief and practice.[15] When Cardoza-Orlandi made his pastoral visit to speak with the family about this inconsistency:

> the father, uncomfortably, shared what the *babalawo* had prescribed. They still had some of the potions and natural treatments that they administered to their son. As the conversation continued I asked more questions and the father was less reluctant to speak about the experience. The *santero* had encouraged them to continue visiting the doctor. He also told them to continue praying in the church, while celebrating some rituals for

---

15. For a helpful discussion on *evangélicos/as*, see Traverzo Galarza, 2006.

a particular *orisha*. . . . In a moment of confusion and surprise, I asked the father, "Whose miracle is it? Is it your *orisha*? Is it Jesus Christ?" The father, puzzled by the question, looked at me and said: "It was God, pastor, it was God. It is your problem to decide whose miracle is it, not my problem." (1995:56)

Cardoza-Orlandi lays out both the metaphysical synthesis that took place in this family and the separate but equally important theological and pastoral issues that are generated. The important lesson in this story is that despite confusion in people around them, the family was clear that God had acted. There was no metaphysical question or confusion for them in their everyday experience of the divine or in the healing of their child.

This type of religious/metaphysical synthesis in a Dominican congregation in New York City is not an isolated event. Reflecting on the broadening appeal of Santería, Griffith suggests why people may opt for a religious/spiritual synthesis:

Most important, perhaps, is the fact that these animas or folk saints, or whatever they should be called, produce results. Many people pray to them or go to séances in which they are channeled because they have "come through" for friends and relatives. Most of these people do not have access to many sources of power — be they medical, legal, or economic — available to their more fortunate contemporaries. All lives are filled with uncertainty, and none more so than those of folk who for one reason or another must exist on the fringes of mainstream society. (2003:152)

This perspective of religious synthesis raises more questions about the metaphysical practices nurtured in places like Changó Botánica. What do the people who go there for help believe about prayer? What produces spiritual and physical results and how can you tell you are successful? Who decides? Do relatives and friends have greater influence in recommending spiritual and metaphysical resources than do institutional clergy and pastoral workers? To what extent do Latino/a communities allow or endure divergent metaphysical systems without a sense of contradiction? Is frequenting a botánica an indication of social marginalization, economic class, spiritual orientation, education, length of residence, generational location, all these factors, or something altogether different? To what extent are the needs, challenges, struggles, uncertainties, and desires of everyday life the deciding factors in what spiritual, religious, or metaphysical paths people will choose?

Conclusion

I started this chapter with the geographic and cultural boundaries and perceptions that divide Oak Cliff from North Dallas and contribute to reciprocal demonization. This may be illustrative of a divide among some scholars in the formal study of Latino/a religious and metaphysical traditions — often the specific practices of popular religious traditions are disparaged by those who follow more formal and authorized forms of practice. It is difficult to see how the study of alternative Latino/a metaphysical traditions and practices differs from the study of Latino/a religion and theology. In the study of Latino/a religion, the challenge includes recognizing the fluidity with which people adapt their beliefs and practices. A wholesale discounting of certain beliefs and practices because they seem strange or exotic or fall beyond the boundaries of a particular orthodoxy will leave us with a truncated picture of what is going on. This is not to say that theological issues of orthodoxy are unimportant, but rather that those discussions may be more fruitful when there is greater awareness and acknowledgement of the varied beliefs and practices of the people.

The Latino/a people are of many faiths and within families and for individuals there are de facto different faith traditions (or at least selected individual elements) that are appropriated concurrently, many times without any sense of conflict or inconsistency. The case of Latinos/as who are not practitioners of Santería and yet frequent botánicas challenges certain religious studies research models that do not allow for such boundary crossings. In Latino/Latina communities where several metaphysical options are operating simultaneously there is a need for broader interpretive categories.

Changó Botánica is geographically, culturally, and even academically separated from other parts of U.S. American society, a site of exotic and dangerous otherness. But such places are right where many Latinos and Latinas live. Latinos/as and non-Latinos cross multiple boundaries to go to the botánicas. The Changó Botánica is a reminder that there are various ways and approaches to tell the stories of Latino/a faith, religion, and religiosity. What we see in Oak Cliff and other places is a type of "inculturated spirituality" (Groody, 2002:116) that it is important to explore further in order to contribute to a fuller understanding of Latino/Latina spiritualities. Some of the spiritualities are Christian, some draw on an African heritage, and others draw on indigenous roots; some are a shifting contextual mixture. All lie within the matrix of the European colonial conquest, and all defy the simplistic binary categories of Christian/non-Christian, European/non-European, African/non-African, Indigenous/non-Indigenous. And that in turn points to the richness of Latino/a religious/spiritual/metaphysical experience that calls out for comprehensive examination. In the eclectic mix of multiple day-to-day spiritualities running in parallel and sometimes interacting with one another, it can be argued that a new version of U.S. Latino/a spirituality is emerging. This spirituality has clear connections to its antecedents and has a distinct context within the United States, practiced alongside other communal spiritualities with multicultural, multiethnic, and transnational (i.e., communities with ongoing connections between the United States and points of origin) dimensions (Aponte, 2006).

The divisions in Dallas are not just geographic, not just cultural, but also spiritual and metaphysical. Part of the metaphysical division means privileging some religious expressions and practices while demonizing others. Cardoza-Orlandi states:

> Given historical and theological ambiguity regarding syncretism, the theologian either protects the elements of the Christian faith in the popular religion by connecting their presence with traditional theological discourse, keeping silent when the Christian elements have been reinterpreted in the context of the popular faith (in a way that threatens the Christian discourse), or he/she demonizes the entire religious experience. (1995:60)

This observation begins to help answer the question of what Changó is doing in Dallas as Cardoza-Orlandi names the ongoing historical and theological ambiguity regarding religious beliefs and practices that are both distinct from the norm and also clearly a mixture of multiple traditions. It is not the relatively small number of Cubans (2,283 in the 2000 Census) who are keeping the Dallas botánicas in business, but the wider Latino/a community. In Oak Cliff and other places with a multinational, transnational, and multiethnic Latino/a population (e.g., Mexican, Salvadoran, Honduran, Puerto Rican, Cuban, Guatemalan, and Peruvian) there are multiple beliefs, practices, and traditions operating and beginning to influence each other. As Latinos/as and others of different backgrounds come into residential contact, there is a metaphysical exchange and blending of traditions at various levels. New methodological approaches to the study of Latino/a metaphysical traditions are needed that will help researchers avoid judgments that fall between the polarities of demonization and romanticization.

Issues of communal and individual self-identities and ways of negotiating daily life must be examined. People who need help, counsel, relief, direction, health, and safety will try whatever works and usually believe that "whatever works" must be good and that in the end all good finds its ultimate source in *Dios,* that is, God. In the context of such beliefs, visits to botánicas therefore become a legitimate strategy for survival, health, guidance, and wholeness — religious/metaphysical decisions and actions in the everyday experience of Latinas and Latinos. If this is how metaphysical practice works, then it is really no surprise to find Changó in Oak Cliff or indeed wherever Latinos/Latinas live in the United States.

Chapter 3

History and Theory in the Study of Mexican American Religions

Gastón Espinosa

The academic study of Mexican American religions traces its origins to 1968, although important historical, sociological, and anthropological writing on the topic stretches back more than a century. That year the writings and intellectual foment stimulated by César Chávez, Virgilio Elizondo, Gustavo Gutiérrez, Enrique Dussel, and others served as major catalysts in the future methodological and theoretical development of the field. Between 1970 and 1975, some of the first academic books, articles, and centers were written and created by scholars like Virgilio Elizondo, Enrique Dussel, Moises Sandoval, Juan Romero, Juan Hurtado, Patrick McNamara, Joan Moore, and others. The Mexican American Cultural Center (MACC) was co-founded by Virgilio Elizondo in 1972. It played a decisive role by publishing many of the first academically oriented biographies, histories, and studies in the field. The study of Mexican American religions received a boost in 1987–88 with the publication of the work of feminist-informed Chicana/o literature and theologies by Gloria Anzaldúa, Andrés Guerrero, Ada María Isasi-Díaz, and Yolanda Tarango. The next major turning point came in 1994–96, when Anthony Stevens-Arroyo and PARAL (Program for the Analysis of Religion among Latinos) published a four-volume series on U.S. Latino religions; when Jay P. Dolan and the University of Notre Dame Press published a three-volume series on Latino Catholicism; and when Gastón Espinosa and Mario T. García attempted to help define

I wish to thank Davíd Carrasco, Virgilio Elizondo, Miguel A. De La Torre, Rudiger V. Busto, and Ulrike Guthrie for their thoughtful feedback on this chapter.

the field at their "New Directions in Chicano Religions" conference at the University of California, Santa Barbara.

Over the past thirty-five years, scholars have often taken one of five approaches to the study of Mexican American religions: (1) traditional church history (e.g., Brackenridge and García-Treto, Dolan and Hinojosa), (2) interdisciplinary liberation theology church history (e.g., Sandoval, Romero), (3) interdisciplinary popular theology and religion (e.g., Elizondo, Guerrero, Rodríguez, Espín), (4) anthropology, psychology, and sociology (e.g., Madsen, Kiev, McNamara, Moore), and (5) interdisciplinary phenomenological religious studies (e.g., Carrasco, León, Espinosa). Still other scholars have blended approaches or taken a Chicano studies/ethnic studies approach (e.g., Busto, Medina). Many scholars have drawn on Chicano literature and poetry (Castañeda, Valdez, González, Anaya, and Anzaldúa), the writings of Reies López Tijerina, the Chicano student movement, Chicana feminism, black studies, and secular religious studies, as well as the emerging scholarship on postcolonialism, transnational issues, critical theory, ethnicity, race, class, gender, and sexuality.

After sketching the historical development of the field of Mexican American religions, I will propose a *nepantla*-based ethnophenomenological method as one of many possible alternatives to rethink how one goes about studying and interpreting Mexican American religions at secular colleges and universities where one is required not to promote or endorse a theological worldview.[1] This approach blends race, class, gender, and phenomenological analyses that are grounded in their historical, social, theological, and political contexts in order to identify, recognize, and interrogate religious leaders, structures, traditions, movements, and experiences on their own plane of reference. Such an approach is taken in order to understand how

---

1. Denominational and religiously affiliated institutions are often not bound by the Supreme Court decision on the separation of church and state and are thus free to follow any methodology they desire. I do not use "secular" and "atheistic" interchangeably. A person can take a secular social scientific approach to the study of Mexican American and U.S. Latino religions and at the same time be a devout practitioner of a particular religion in his or her private or non-academic public life. By "*nepantla*-based" I mean a methodological position that seeks to be in the middle and that serves as a bridge between different methodologies and ideological perspectives.

such leaders and structures provide hope and meaning to practitioners and contribute to their larger culture. It also seeks to bridge the growing chasm that separates secular religious studies from theology as described in Donald Wiebe's controversial book *The Politics of Religious Studies: The Continuing Conflict with Theology in the Academy* (1999) by listening to, dialoging with, and drawing upon the important insights from theology and the above-noted influences. While Mexican American and U.S. Latino religions are organically connected, due to time, space, and regional limitations, I will focus on the historical development of Mexican American religions in the Southwest. The best place to review the literature on Mexican American religious historiography are the bibliographies and essays edited or written by Anthony M. Stevens-Arroyo and Segundo Pantoja (1995), Paul Barton and David Maldonado (1999), Justo L. González (1998), and Daisy Machado (1998). Although beyond the scope of this study, there are also overviews on U.S. Latino theology and history by Saragoza (1999), Aquino (1993), Medina (1993), Eduardo Fernández (2000), Espín (2000), De La Torre and Aponte (2001), and Díaz (2001).

Why Mexican American Religious Studies?

Despite the growing scholarship on Mexican American religions, no one has mapped out its historical development over the last hundred years. This is largely because the study of Mexican American religions has been subsumed under the rubric of U.S. Latino religions. However, there are a number of reasons why it should be an academic field of intellectual inquiry in itself. People of Mexican ancestry have lived in the Southwest for over four hundred years — since 1598. Their history in the American Southwest predates that of the Pilgrims and Puritans at Jamestown in 1608 and Plymouth Rock in 1619. People of Spanish and Mexican ancestry have a number of rich and unique religious traditions (e.g., New Mexican popular Catholicism, the Santero tradition, the Chimayó pilgrimage site, Día de los Muertos), saints and spiritual healers (e.g., Our Lady of Guadalupe, El Niño Fidencio, María Teresa Urrea, Don Pedrito Jaramillo, Juan Soldado, Francisco Olazábal), brotherhoods and social-spiritual movements (e.g., the Penitente Brotherhood, the Cursillo, PADRES, Las Hermanas, La Raza Churchmen), political leaders (e.g., Padre Antonio José Martínez, César Chávez, Reies López Tijerina, Dolores Huerta), and religious leaders (e.g., Junípero Serra, Eusebio Kino, Francisco Olazábal, Antonio Castañeda Nava, Archbishop Patricio Flores), which have influenced U.S. Latino and American religious history (Espinosa, Elizondo, and Miranda, 2005). People of Mexican ancestry have shaped the history, architecture, politics, culture, and cuisine of the Southwest for over four hundred years. They continue to do so. The 2005 U.S. Census Bureau notes that people of Mexican ancestry currently make up 65 percent (27 million) of the nation's 41.3 million Latinos. They are now more numerous than all Asian Americans (13.5 million), Jewish Americans (6 million), and Native Americans (4.4 million) combined, all of which have their own discrete intellectual fields of study. And finally people of Mexican ancestry are the fastest-growing Latino subgroup in the United States and account for 52 percent (8.2 million) of all Latin American immigrants to the United States (16 million).[2]

Genealogy of Mexican American Religious Studies

The origin of the academic study of Mexican American religions is difficult to determine. The first systematic records of Mexican religious experiences in the Southwest were written from the sixteenth to the nineteenth centuries by Catholic Franciscan and Jesuit missionaries, diocesan priests, lay leaders, and American and European clergy, missionaries, and traders such as Father Alonso de Benavides, Father Eusebio Kino, Father Junípero Serra, Richard Henry Dana, and others (Moises Sandoval, 1983; Ramón Gutiérrez, 1991). In the late nineteenth and early twentieth centuries, we see the rise of slightly more formal institutional church histories such as Jean Baptiste Salpointe's, *Soldiers of the Cross: Notes on the Ecclesiastical History*

---

2. ArriveNet Politics Press Release, "Census Bureau: Hispanic Population Passes 40 Million; Number of Elementary School-Age Children in Nation Totaled 36.4 Million," June 9, 2005; 2004 U.S. Census Bureau url: *http://press.arrivenet.com/pol/article.php/650602.html* and *www.census.gov/popest/*.

of New Mexico, Arizona, and Colorado (1898), and Thomas Harwood's, *History of Spanish and English Missions of the New Mexico Methodist Episcopal Church from 1850–1910,* 2 vols. (1908, 1910). However, these were written almost exclusively by clergy about their own institutional churches and for a Christian audience.

In the wake of the first massive wave of Mexican immigration to the United States from 1880 to 1920, we begin to witness in the 1920s and 1930s a number of church-sponsored or church-affiliated Catholic and Protestant books, reports, and articles on Mexican Americans in the Southwest. The most important books include Jay S. Stowell's, *A Study of Mexicans and Spanish Americans in the United States* (1920); Vernon M. McCombs's, *From over the Border: A Study of the Mexican in the United States* (1925); Linna Bresette's, *Mexicans in the United States* (1929); Robert N. McLean's, *The Northern Mexican* (1930); Robert C. Jones and Louis R. Wilson's, *The Mexican in Chicago* (1931); and Theodore Abel's, *Protestant Home Missions to Catholic Immigrants* (1933). Many other articles, reports, and books were also published (Sandoval, 1983).

In the early twentieth century we also note a growing number of university-affiliated humanistic and social scientific theses, books, reports, articles, and studies on Mexican Americans that include attention to religion (Kienle, 1912; McEuen, 1914; Culp, 1921; Hymer, 1923). One of the first social scientific studies on Mexican American religions was Methodist bishop G. Bromley Oxnam's article "The Mexican in Los Angeles from the Standpoint of Religious Forces of the City" (1921). This research was more social scientific than the previous church-sponsored literature. It was augmented by a number of articles, folklore, museum, and WPA Federal Writers Project studies, and histories on religion and culture in New Mexico (A. M. Espinosa, 1926, 1937; Scholes, 1929, 1935, 1936, 1942; Hodges, 1931a, 1931b; Lucero-White, 1932, 1941; Lawrence, 1935; M. J. Espinosa, 1936; Park, 1936; Hackett, 1942; Tatum, 1939; Campa, 1943; A. Chávez, 1948).

Among the first significant humanistic interpretations of Mexican American religiosity were Manuel Gamio's classic anthropological studies, *Mexican Immigration to the United States* (1930) and *The Mexican Immigrant: His Life Story* (1931). Gamio, who was a highly respected anthropologist from Mexico, conducted his field research in the United States over a two-year period in 1926–27. His books were among the first to examine the role that religious beliefs played in helping Mexican immigrants transition into American society. Unlike previous church-sponsored work, the methodological orientation of his work was almost entirely secular, humanistic, and anthropological. His work touches on anti-clericalism, church attendance, popular Catholic practices, and why many Catholics were switching to Protestantism (1930:13–29, 117–18). Perhaps more important for the future methodological development of Mexican American religions, his pluralistic and non-sectarian work noted the importance of Evangelical Protestantism and non-Christian traditions like spiritualism, spiritism, and *brujería*.

Oxnam's and Gamio's work influenced Robert C. Jones's report "The Religious Life of the Mexican in Chicago" (1929) and his subsequent book, *The Mexican in Chicago* (1931). Similarly, American Baptist Samuel M. Ortegón drew upon Oxnam's and Gamio's work for his M.A. thesis at U.S.C. entitled, "Mexican Religious Population of Los Angeles" (1932). Like the work of Gamio and Jones, Ortegón's work was pluralistic in scope and included brief mention of Mainline Protestants, Evangelicals, Pentecostals, Seventh-Day Adventists, Spiritualists, Theosophists, Jehovah's Witnesses, and Roman Catholics. His study was perhaps the first significant qualitative and quantitative ethnographic study of Mexican American religions in Los Angeles. Gamio's work was later picked up with vigor by Chicano movement scholars hungry for Mexican authors (Acuña, 1972:150; García, 1981:306; Romo, 1983:215; Sandoval, 1983:237, 253, 266; García, 1989:356; Sánchez, 1993:356; Dolan and Hinojosa, 1994:368; David G. Gutiérrez, 1995:313).

The flurry of scholarship on Mexican American religions in the late 1920s and early 1930s continued as a steady stream throughout the 1940s (Weatherby, 1942; National Catholic Welfare Conference, 1943; A. Fernández, 1943; A. Chávez, 1946, 1948; Kibbe, 1946; Griffith, 1947) and especially the 1950s in the wake of the Bracero guest worker program agreement between the U.S. and Mexican governments (Grijalva, 1950; Harrison, 1952; Stratton, 1953; Garza, 1954; Burma, 1954; Stapleton, 1954; R. E. Smith,

1958; Gibson, 1959). The two most notable book-length manu-
scripts were Samuel M. Ortegón's massive U.S.C. Ph.D. dissertation,
"The Religious Thought and Practice among Mexican Baptists of the
United States, 1900–1947" (1950), and Carlos Eduardo Castañeda's
monumental seven-volume history, *Our Catholic Heritage in Texas,
1519–1950* (1936–58). Although both works were clearly rooted in
their respective theological and ecclesiastical traditions, they mark a
major leap forward in the academic study of Mexican American religions because they also included social scientific interpretations and
explanations that were not strictly shaped by a theological method.
Perhaps more important, they represent two of the first major histories of Mexican American Protestantism and Catholicism written
by, about, and for the Mexican American and Anglo-American communities. A number of scholars picked up their work in the wake
of the Chicano movement (McNamara, 1970; Moore, 1970; Sandoval, 1983:168, 194, 237; García, 1989:356; Dolan and Hinojosa,
1994:363).

Ortegón and Castañeda were part of what Mario T. García has
called the Mexican American G.I. Generation (1930s–1950s), which
sought to uncover and reclaim a Mexican American historical consciousness and fight for civil rights by working within the existing
political and social system (1989:13–22). Although they were professionally trained intellectuals and church historians with doctorates
living in the American Southwest and were engaged in a historical
retrieval, their work does not mark the birth of the field because
they (like Gamio before them) did not see themselves as scholars of
Mexican American religions per se and because they did not seek to
self-consciously define or construct a field as such.

César Chávez and the Birth of the Study of
Mexican American Religions

The key turning point in the development of Mexican American religious studies took place in 1968. That year the writings and foment
stimulated by César Chávez, Reies López Tijerina, Virgilio Elizondo,
Gustavo Gutiérrez, Enrique Dussel, Carlos Castañeda, and others

served as major catalysts in the future methodological and theoretical development of the field. The spark that helped ignite the field came from an unlikely source — a former Community Service Organizer (CSO) named César Chávez (Espinosa et al., 2005:8–9, 35–64; Dalton, 2003). Inspired by Father Kilian McDonald to fight for social justice and to unionize Mexican American migrant farmworkers in 1965, Chávez and Delores Huerta organized the United Farmworkers Union in Our Lady of Guadalupe Church in Delano, California, to fight for better wages, housing, and civil rights. In March 1968, during his first major fast for social justice, Chávez penned one of the first significant historical, social, political, and theological critiques of the Catholic Church by a Mexican American; his essay was titled "The Mexican American and the Church." Echoing other Latinos throughout the Americas struggling for justice, he criticized the institutional Catholic Church's lack of support for the Mexican American people and called it to sacrifice with the people for social change and political and economic justice. His critique differed from that of Gamio and Castañeda because it called on the Catholic Church to takes sides, affirmed indigenous popular Catholicism, and blended faith, writing, and activism. Chávez and Chicano movement activists differed from the Mexican American G.I. Generation activists because they were willing to work outside of the system and because they openly drew on their faith in their activism.

Chávez's critique and faith-based activism had a profound influence on the future development of Mexican American religious studies. His essay and activism were widely cited and followed in Chicano periodicals like *El Grito del Sol* (1968) and by a number of Chicano and Latino scholars including Rodolfo Acuña, Octavio I. Romano, Francisco García-Treto, Virgilio Elizondo, Juan Hurtado, Antonio Soto, Moises Sandoval, Anthony M. Stevens-Arroyo, and later by Andrés Guerrero, Gilberto Hinojosa, and others to this present day. Chávez's critique and faith-based activism along with that of the African American, Chicano, American Indian, feminist, and liberation theology movements inspired an emerging generation of Mexican Americans and U.S. Latino scholars to use their scholarship to fight for social, political, and economic justice on behalf of their communities. It also inspired many religious clergy and laity to participate in the Chicano cultural renaissance, which sought to celebrate their Mexican and indigenous cultural and religious identity (Espinosa, Elizondo, and Miranda, 2005).

Chávez's United Farmworker's Union struggle in California was important because it helped spotlight the struggle of other Mexican American activists, like former Assemblies of God Pentecostal evangelist-turned-activist Reies López Tijerina. His *Aliancista* land grant struggle in New Mexico along with his Poor People's march in 1968 inspired many Mexican Americans to fight for civil rights and social justice (Busto, 2005). However, his activism and writings were largely overlooked by scholars writing on Mexican American religions because most were Catholic and tended to resonate more with Chávez's openly ecumenical Catholic pacifism than Tijerina's magical-literalist militant activism (Busto, 2005; Espinosa, Elizondo, and Miranda, 2005).

The critical role that popular Catholicism and indigenous religious symbols played in the Mexican American civil rights movement was influenced by Chávez's fasts, pilgrimages, and decision to march behind the colorful banner of Our Lady of Guadalupe. It was also influenced by Reies López Tijerina's land grant struggle, by the religious themes in Luis Valdez's *Plan of Delano* and *Teatro Campesino La Pastorela* play, by Rodolfo "Corky" González's epic poem, *I am Joaquín,* and his call for a national Chicano homeland (Aztlán), and by hundreds of *barrio* wall murals, poems, songs, theater troops, and student movements popping up across the Southwest in the 1960s and 1970s (Espinosa, Elizondo, and Miranda, 2005; Rosales, 1997). This first generation of Mexican American activists provided *el movimiento* with a spiritual impulse, a sacred set of symbols (Our Lady of Guadalupe, Aztec Eagle), a sacred genealogy (*la raza cósmica* — a cosmic racial heritage going back to the "brilliant" civilizations of the Aztecs and Mayas), a set of sacred traditions and history (pilgrimages, fasts, penance, ecclesiastical history), and a sacred homeland (Aztlán — the American southwest) that gave ordinary Mexican Americans a collective "Chicano" identity and mission that they could understand, appreciate, and rally behind.

Their grassroots activism contributed to the birth of a Mexican American/Chicano cultural renaissance that promoted cultural nationalism and a sense of pride that manifested itself in Chicano art, music, poetry, theater, politics, and historical recovery. Chicano cultural nationalists argued for an oppositional "us vs. them" attitude toward Anglo-American society. "Corky" González called for the creation of a national Chicano homeland in the Southwest called Aztlán, named after the mythical homeland of the Aztecs and Mexican people. Drawing upon the work of Paulo Freire, Acuña argued that Chicanos were an internal colony suffering oppression like other "Third World peoples" (1972: iii, 1–5; Freire, 1972). This led many Chicano scholars like Juan Gómez-Quiñones to argue that in their struggle for liberation there could be no neutrality because "to acculturate is not merely to exercise a cultural preference but to go to the other side" (1977:29, 33, 35, 39; Sánchez, 1993:6). Acuña's vision of internal colonialism was further refined in Mario Barrera's 1972 essay, "The Barrio as an Internal Colony" and in his 1979 landmark study on internal colonialism, *Race and Class in the Southwest: A Theory of Racial Inequality,* which were later picked up by U.S. Latino scholars of religion (Stevens-Arroyo and Díaz-Stevens, 1997).

Despite their important contributions, Chicano historian Alex M. Saragoza argues that the work of Acuña and others led to a kind of nationalist romanticization and mythologization of Mexican American history that painted an "us vs. them" struggle. This minimized internal conflict and dissension, focused on local community studies rather than comparative analyses, and exaggerated the continuities and downplayed discontinuities in Chicano and *mexicano* cultures (Saragoza, 1999:9–10). Seeking to create a collective history and identity, Saragoza argues that authors like Acuña tended to project normative value judgments in a world where there were largely good people (Mexican Americans/Latinos/Ethnic Minorities/Poor/Women/ etc.) and bad people (largely white males or ethnic minorities that sought to accommodate or to transform society within the existing social and political system). Furthermore, there was a certain moral urgency and rightness to their scholarship; they assumed that because they were either describing or promoting tolerance, pluralism, diversity, or social justice that they were therefore justified in offering an otherwise explicitly and unapologetically negative ideological interpretation of their opponents, all the while purporting to be engaging in critical, fair-minded academic scholarship (Saragoza, 1999:5, 8–11).

Latin American Influences on Mexican American Religious Studies

At the same time Chávez, Tijerina, and others were fighting for social justice, civil rights, land rights, and human liberation in the United States, Catholics and Protestants in Latin America were engaged in a similar struggle. The same year that Chávez penned "The Mexican American and the Church," hundreds of Catholics met at the Second General Conference of Latin American Bishops (CELAM) in Medellín, Colombia, where they began to articulate a theology of liberation (Dussel, 1981:244–47; 1992:391–96). The critical development of liberation theology took place when Peruvian priest and theologian Gustavo Gutiérrez asked his colleagues if their theology of socio-economic empowerment would "be a theology of development [i.e., capitalism] or a theology of liberation" (Dussel, 1981:327). Blending conviction with academic precision, Gutiérrez penned Latin America's most important contribution to global Christian theology, *Teología de la liberación* (1971), which was subsequently translated into English as *A Theology of Liberation* (1973). In this book he argues that Jesus was a scorned suffering servant and revolutionary who preached a gospel of liberation to the poor and oppressed. He fought for spiritual, political, social, and economic justice against the religious and political establishments, and as a result was martyred on behalf of his people in order to help usher in the kingdom of God (Dussel, 1992:1–2).

Liberation theologians like Gutiérrez, Hugo Assmann, Leonardo Boff, Clodovis Boff, Juan Luis Segundo, José Míguez Bonino, Enrique Dussel, and many others argue that their movement is a theological and practical movement that emphasizes present deliverance of the oppressed from their sinful oppressors. The authentic starting point for any Christian theology is commitment to the poor, the nonperson. The Christian message, they argue, has to be interpreted out of the context of the suffering and struggle of the poor. Drawing on the story of Moses leading his people out of slavery in Egypt, they preach a revolutionary and prophetic praxis-based message that maps the trajectory of human history from "captivity" to "exile" to "liberation." Conscientization, contextualization, and praxis are the keys to realizing this liberation, they teach. They believe God is on their side — and the side of the poor against the symbolic pharaohs of this life. They tend to focus on the importance of economic factors in the oppression, pay close attention to class struggle, argue for the mystifying power of ideologies, including religious ones, emphasize the role that society plays in oppression of individuals and communities, and argue that suffering is the result of social and political structures. Liberation theologians have been criticized as being Marxists. However, this is unfair and inaccurate because they tend to use Marxism in a purely instrumental way (Gutiérrez, 1973; Boff and Boff, 1987:28; Belli and Nash, 1992).

Latin American liberation scholars like Enrique Dussel also influenced the rise and methodology of Mexican American religious history. He formulated a praxis-based historical methodology that reframed history as a struggle for liberation from neocolonial dependency on Anglo-Saxon English and American industrial capitalism. Echoing Marxist, leftist, and social historians, Dussel argued that no description of a historical fact is obvious or neutral. Every historical account presupposes an "interpretation" based on one's ideological and theological worldview that either upholds the capitalist structure of society or promotes a revolutionary movement toward human liberation and freedom. For this reason, he argued that scholars must create a Christian faith-based interpretation of history and society that blends the rigors of a critical scientific methodology with an equally rigorous contextual and praxis-oriented commitment to the suffering, aspirations, and perspectives of the poor and the oppressed (Dussel, 1981:293–333).

Dussel's methological influence is clearly evident in Moises Sandoval's groundbreaking history, *Fronteras: A History of the Latin American Church in the U.S.A. since 1513* (1983). In the preface of the book, Bishop Ricardo Ramírez states that the idea for the book came from Dussel, who was then president of the Commission for the

Study of the History of the Church in America (CEHILA) (Sandoval, 1983: vii). This influence is also confirmed in Virgilio Elizondo's introduction to the book, where, echoing the language of Paulo Freire's conscientization (Freire, 1974), he states that one of the reasons that so many Latinos are confused and divided over their ethnic identity is that they have been deprived of a "real consciousness of our historical becoming." The best way to address this problem, Elizondo argues, is to follow the example of Dussel, and especially of Acuña, whose work "beautifully brings out the Chicano struggle for liberation." Far from being a dead and fossilized past, Elizondo writes, Mexican American history and religion are very much alive in the dynamic and creative imagination of *corridos, leyendas, cuentos, murales, pinturas,* and religious celebrations of the saints and cultural heroes like Our Lady of Guadalupe. After thanking Enrique Dussel and CEHILA for inviting Sandoval to write the book, he ends his introduction by stating that it fills him with great joy that MACC was able to publish this first general history of Latino Christianity in the United States (Elizondo, in his introduction to Sandoval, 1983).

Virgilio Elizondo played a pivotal role in the birth of Mexican American theology and religious studies. A native of San Antonio, Elizondo stated to me in an interview that his praxis-oriented scholarship wove together a Mexican American/Chicano theology that reflected the influences of his seminary training's emphasis on social justice, Archbishop Robert Lucy's grassroots work in the war on poverty and farmworkers' movement, and especially Vatican II's insistence on incarnational theology, the need for inculturation, and the dynamic notion of divine revelation. Furthermore, the Constitution on Divine Revelation (*Dei Verbum*), the Decree on Missionary Activity (*Ad Gentes*), and the Constitution on the Church in the Modern World (*Gaudium et Spes*) also significantly influenced his theological reflection. In addition, his thought and method were directly shaped by Chávez, Gutiérrez, Dussel, Acuña, and others in the Chicano cultural renaissance. Perhaps his most important influences were Johannes Hoffinger and Alfonso Nebreda of the East Asian Pastoral Institute, because they introduced him to the need for cultural anthropology in any kind of Christian theological reflection. These influences were further clarified and deepened by Jacques Audinet of the Institute Catholique de Paris. He insisted on using the social sciences in creating local theologies. Elizondo not only knew Chávez first hand and learned about the promulgations of Vatican II from Cardinal Archbishop Robert Lucy, who had attended the event, but he also accompanied Lucy to the preparatory meetings of the now historic CELAM Conference in Medellín, Colombia, in 1968, where he met and conversed with Gustavo Gutiérrez, Enrique Dussel, and other pioneer Latin American liberation theologians. These influences are evident in Elizondo's groundbreaking 1968 essay, "Educación religiosa para el méxico-norteamericano," published in the Mexican journal *Catequesis Latinoamericana* (Medina, 1994). He was also influenced later by Chicano historian Jesús Chavarria at the University of California, Santa Barbara, who said that "as long as you do not write your own story and elaborate your own knowledge, you will always be a slave to another's thoughts." Those influences were later refined in his *Anthropological and Psychological Characteristics of the Mexican American* (1974) and in his classic study *Christianity and Culture* (1975). Elizondo's theological reflection came into intellectual maturity in his germinal works *Mestizaje: The Dialectic of Birth and Gospel* (1978), *La Morenita: Evangelizer of the Americas* (1980), and especially *Galilean Journey* (1983) and *The Future Is Mestizo* (1988).

Not only do Elizondo's academic writings signal the birth of Mexican American theology (Medina, 1993:13; M. T. García, 2005:88), but his vision to publish revisionist theologies and histories led to the publication of the first history of Latino Christianity in the United States. Drawing upon the methodology of Gutiérrez, Dussel, Acuña, and others, he argued that Mexican American scholars should create and publish collective revisionist scholarship on Mexican American theology and religious history from the perspective of the poor and marginalized. He also insisted that this scholarship should be "objective" and academically rigorous (Sandoval, 1983: xiii). He brought this vision to fruition by publishing some of the foundational biographical, sociological, and theological books on Mexican American religions through the Mexican American Cultural Center (MACC), which he co-founded in San Antonio in 1972. In addition to three of his own books, under his influence MACC also published

Juan Romero and Moises Sandoval, *Reluctant Dawn: Historia del Padre A. J. Martínez, Cura de Taos* (1975); Juan Hurtado, *An Attitudinal Study of Social Distance between the Mexican American and the Church* (1975); Moises Sandoval, ed., *Fronteras: A History of the Latin American Church in the U.S.A. since 1513* (1983); and other books, reports, and articles.

Although Elizondo was proactive in publishing the work of other scholars and writers, it was his own aforementioned books that heavily influenced the theological agenda of Latino theology of the day. His *mestizo* paradigm argued that Mexican Americans are like Jesus because they are religious outsiders who are rejected by the racial and religious establishment for being from a racially and theologically impure bloodline (a popular tradition taught that Jesus' father was a Roman soldier). Elizondo called on all Mexican Americans to be proud of their mixed racial and popular Catholic heritage. The work of and other U.S. Latinos contributed what Anthony M. Stevens-Arroyo and Ana María Díaz-Stevens have called a resurgence in the study of U.S. Latino religions (1997).

The work of Elizondo, Chávez, Gutiérrez, Tijerina, and others in the 1960s and 1970s influenced, to varying degrees, the work of later Mexican American and U.S. Latino/a scholars in the 1980s and 1990s, like Andrés G. Guerrero, *A Chicano Theology* (1987), Ada María Isasi-Díaz and Yolanda Tarango, *Hispanic Women: Prophetic Voice in the Church* (1988), and Jeanette Rodríguez, *Our Lady of Guadalupe: Faith and Empowerment among Mexican American Women* (1994). Elizondo, Isasi-Díaz, and Tarango exerted tremendous influence on the study of Mexican American and U.S. Latino religions. Guerrero's book was, by comparison, largely overlooked despite the fact that he cites Chávez, Gutiérrez, and Elizondo (1987: 166–81). Guerrero's theology (based on a set of nine interviews with Chicano Catholic and Protestant leaders) stated that the Christian Church was the last hope of Chicanos. However, he also accused it of working against Chicano liberation, practicing sexism, preaching the inferiority of women, and using Our Lady of Guadalupe to both liberate and oppress Chicanos. Some interviewees in his *Chicano Theology* promoted fighting for communal lands taken by Anglos in the wake of the U.S.-Mexican War of 1848 by whatever means necessary (including violence), a position that the pacifist Guerrero did not personally support. Despite his rejection of violence in the struggle for liberation, his book has been overlooked by scholars because it is seen as romanticizing the Chicano struggle, being too academic and too militant, falling into a simplistic "us vs. them" binary, and being too quick to condemn the institutional Catholic Church which, love it or leave it, was and still is the religious home of most Mexican Americans (Guerrero, 1987:156–65).

Mexican American and U.S. Latino scholars have promoted a largely liberationist methodological outlook and praxis-based orientation through a number of pan-Latino interdisciplinary associations, organizations, and journals, including the Association of Catholic Hispanic Theologians of the U.S. (ACHTUS, 1988), the Program for the Analysis of Religion among Latinos (PARAL, 1988), *La Comunidad* of Hispanic Scholars of Religion (1992), the Hispanic Fund for Theological Education, the Hispanic Theological Initiative (HTI), and interdenominational journals like the United Methodist affiliated *Apuntes: Reflexiones teológicas desde el margen hispano* (1981), and the Roman Catholic affiliated *Journal of Hispanic/Latino Theology* (1994). Through these endeavors, Mexican American and U.S. Latino theologians and scholars have been able to keep alive, institutionalize, and mainstream their largely Christian liberationist theological praxis-based methodology.

Chicana Feminism and Women in Religion

The influence of Gustavo Gutiérrez and Virgilio Elizondo on Chicana feminist and *mujerista* theology is evident in Yolanda Tarango and Cuban-born Ada María Isasi-Díaz's pioneering work, *Hispanic Women: Prophetic Voice in the Church* (1988). Their Latina feminist liberation theology was based on a series of interviews with Hispanic women and the writings of Rosemary Radford Ruether, Margaret Farley, Elizabeth Schüssler Fiorenza, Mary Elisabeth Hunt, Clifford Geertz, Antonio Gramsci, Paul Tillich, José Míguez Bonino, Paulo Freire, and others. They sought to create a Hispanic cultural, feminist, and liberation theology that captured the sentiment and struggles of ordinary women. They saw themselves first and foremost as activists struggling for justice and peace and saw no conflict in combining theology and activism. They sought to fight "militantly" against both Anglo-American and Latino multilayered sexism, patriarchy, classism, and economic oppression. Their work was methodologically important because it (a) provided a sharp critique of Latino sexism, classism, elitism, and patriarchy, (b) called on Latino men to share leadership and the theological enterprise with women, (c) called for more inclusive theologies, and (d) gave voice to Latina women and sought to shift the focus away from *orthodoxy* (right belief) to *orthopraxis* (right practice) (Isasi-Díaz and Tarango, 1988:116–23).

Despite the pivotal role that Tarango and Isasi-Díaz's book played in the development of Latina feminist liberation theology, María Pilar Aquino has warned scholars to be careful not to assume that their work represents all Chicana and U.S. Latina feminist theologians. In fact, Chicana and Latina feminism is much broader, pluralistic, and effusive than the work of Isasi-Díaz/Tarango, Gutiérrez, or Elizondo. Furthermore, Aquino argues that Isasi-Díaz's *mujerista* theological perspective is a "creative fiction" because "there are no *mujerista* sociopolitical and ecclesial subjects in the United States or Latin America." The problem with Isasi-Díaz's work, Aquino argues, is that she created a theology that "glorifies difference" and produces " 'discursive . . . locations . . . and false oppositions' that weaken the political force of feminism." For these reasons and others, she suggests that Chicana/Latina "theology must be clearly characterized by a *non-mujerista* orientation" (Aquino, Machado, and Rodríguez, 2002: 138–39). Furthermore, she calls on Chicana and U.S. Latina feminist theologians to draw on the work of Chicana and other feminist writers like Norma Alarcón, Ana Castillo, Gloria Anzaldúa, Cherríe Moraga, Vicki Ruíz, Chela Sandoval, Dena González, Olga Villa-Parra, Alma García, Cynthia Orozco, Elisabeth Schüssler Fiorenza, and others.

Aquino equally distances Chicana feminist scholarship on religion from Loida Martell-Otero's 1994 work on Latina *evangélicas* because of her subject's lack of commitment to social transformation (Martell-Otero, 1994; Aquino, 2002:139). Espinosa's work on Latina Pentecostal women in ministry, along with that of Elizabeth Ríos and Arlene Sánchez-Walsh, argues that there is a long tradition of Latina

Pentecostal women engaging in social ministry (Espinosa, 2002; Sánchez-Walsh, 2003; Ríos, 2005). Mexican American Pentecostal women have been engaging in social ministry (albeit with an evangelistic goal) since 1906, and most have historically voted Democrat, despite their very conservative position on abortion and same-sex marriage — which they reject as unbiblical. In fact, 69 percent of Latino Pentecostals voted for Bill Clinton in the 1996 presidential election and in 2000 they looked to split their votes between Gore (35 percent) and Bush (35 percent). However, although Latina Pentecostal women are morally conservative, women like Aimee García Cortese engaged in a kind of feminist discourse and protest (although she was uncomfortable with the word) as early as the late 1950s in their struggles against blatant sexism within the Latino Assemblies of God. Despite this fact, Cortese and others rejected feminism because of its association with a pro-abortion position and "the gay movement" (Espinosa, 2002:25–48; Sánchez-Walsh, 2003:125).

Taken as a whole, Chicana feminist interpretations of religion are critically important to understanding and interpreting the Mexican American religious experience. Every effort should be made to support feminist scholarship and scholars. There is also a great need to uncover, discover, and analyze the stories of millions of non-feminist women from new and hybrid theoretical and methodological interpretive frameworks based on quantitative and qualitative oral history, community profile, and ethnographic interviews with women from Catholic, Mainline Protestant, non-Pentecostal Evangelical, Pentecostal, Islamic, Jewish, Jehovah's Witness, Mormon, Spiritualist/Spiritist, *brujería*, Buddhist, Hindu, atheist, agnostic, Native American, mixed religion, New Age, and other religious backgrounds. This pluralistic framework is important in light of the growing religious diversity within the Mexican American and U.S. Latino communities.

The *Hispanic Churches in American Public Life National Survey* (n = 2,060)[3] found in 2003 that: (1) 70 percent of all Latinos are

---

3. Milagros Peña (sociologist), Daisy Machado (historian), Elizabeth Conde-Frazier (theologian/Christian educator), and María Elena González, R.S.M. (theologian) served on the advisory board and helped shape the framework, language, and questions on the Hispanic Churches in American Public Life National Survey instrument.

Catholic and 22 percent of these are Charismatic; (2) almost 30 percent (10.6 million out of 35 million) of all Latinos self-identify with a non-Catholic tradition; (3) 7.2 million of the 8 million U.S. Latino Protestants self-identify as with an Evangelical denomination and/or as a "born-again" Christian; (4) 64 percent of all Protestants are Pentecostal, Charismatic, or spirit-filled; (5) Latino Mainline Protestants make up 14.8 percent of all Latino Protestants; (6) there are more Jehovah's Witnesses (810,000) and Mormons (260,000) than all Southern (430,000) and American Baptists (530,000) combined (1 million); (7) 28 percent (9.2 million) of all Latinos are Protestant Pentecostal or Catholic Charismatic Christians, and 37 percent (12.2 million) claim to be born-again Christians; (8) 17 percent of all Latinos believe in the practices of spiritism, *curanderismo, brujería,* or all of the above; (9) 6 percent of all Latinos (2 million) have no one particular religious preference; (10) over 350,000 Latinos practice Buddhism, Islam, Judaism, Hinduism, Native American spirituality, or some blend thereof; and (11) 0.37 percent of the Latino community reports being atheist or agnostic (Espinosa, 2004a, 2004b, 2005:6). There is a great need for research on non-Christian and hybrid Mexican American and U.S. Latino religions and spiritualities.

Secular Interpretations of Mexican American Religions

Like Gamio, Jones, and Ortegón forty years earlier, Anglo-American scholars like Patrick McNamara and Joan Moore published important sociological and historical essays (Grebler, Moore, and Guzman, 1970), which included brief attention to Presbyterians, Methodists, Baptists, Evangelicals, Pentecostals, and Mormons. Their essays sketched the role that churches played in assimilation, socialization of values, and furthering social change, which together contributed to socioeconomic advancement and social justice. McNamara argued that Latino "folk" Catholicism combined "normal" Catholic practices with "pagan (Indian) rites" (1970:450), and he claimed that unlike the "ideologically-tinged ethnic spokespersons and activists who as insiders had their own agendas," his survey research findings could "influence the objectivity of outsiders" (1995:25). He further claimed that his essay provided data for a new generation of

Chicano scholars like Acuña who were "bent upon rewriting the history of the Southwest in a conflict/internal colonialism framework" (McNamara, 1995:27). Although McNamara's study was cited by Mexican American scholars for hard facts, it does not mark the birth of the field because McNamara stated that his sociological focus was *not* on Mexican American religiosity and because he did not attempt to define or construct a field as such (McNamara, 1995:25). However, McNamara and Moore's research is methodologically important because of its social scientific approach and because it clearly built on the previous writings of Salpointe, McCombs, Abel, Ortegón, Castañeda, Gibson, Soto, Chávez, and others.

In addition to the rise of secular-oriented social science research, we also see humanistic anthropological research on Mexican American religions. From the 1930s through the 1960s, we see the rise of secular anthropological, historical, psychological, and folklore research and literature both on Mexican American Christian healing traditions like Pentecostalism and Catholic *curanderismo* and on metaphysical traditions like spiritualism, spiritism, and *brujería* (Jones, 1929; Gamio, 1931:78–81, 197; Dodson, 1932, 1951; McNeil, 1959; Madsen and Madsen, 1965, 1972; Kiev, 1968). This literature has continued to grow from the 1970s through the present thanks to the work of Juan Castañon García (1979), June Macklin (1979), Marc Simmons (1980), Robert T. Trotter II and Juan Antonio Chavira (1981), Beatrice A. Roeder (1988), Davíd Carrasco (1982a, 1990), Luis León (2002, 2004), Gastón Espinosa (1999, 2004a), Lara Medina (2005), Inés Hernández-Avila (2005), and many others. Little, by contrast, was written on Latino Mormonism, Jehovah's Witnesses, Seventh-Day Adventists, and world religions, with the notable exceptions of Ortegón (1932:15, 40–44, 50), J. Moore (1970:505–7), and Espinosa (2004a:312–17; 2005:282–302).

During this period from 1965 through the publication of *Fronteras* in 1983 we also see the rise of a number of histories, biographies, and other works about Mexican American and U.S. Latino Mainline and Evangelical Protestants (Morales, 1964; Lara-Braud, 1968; J. M. Fernández, 1973; Reyes, 1974; Holland, 1974; Nieto, 1975; A. Nañez, 1980; Atkinson, 1981; Grijalva, 1982, 1983; Sylvest, 1983; Atkins-Vásquez, 1988) and Pentecostals (Cantú and Ortega,

1966; Galvan, 1969; De León, 1979; Valdez, 1980; Guillén, 1982; Bazán, 1987) that were not explicitly liberationist in orientation. This church-based scholarship was supplemented by a number of books by Chicano historians like Ramón Gutiérrez (1991), Davíd Carrasco (1990), Mario T. García (1981, 1989), Vicki Ruíz (1987, 1998), George Sánchez (1993), Tomás Almaguer (1994), and others. They provided alternative theoretical and methodological frameworks for interpreting Mexican American history and religions that clearly went beyond the purview of traditional church history and liberation theology.

The work of these Chicano historians is important because they moved away from the static "us vs. them" cultural nationalistic oppositional mentality of the 1970s and instead argued for more complicated, contradictory, and nuanced histories of the Mexican American experience (Saragoza, 1999). Mario García, for example, wrote that the "Mexican border culture [was] neither completely Mexican nor American, but one revealing contrasting attractions and pressures between cultures" (1981:231). George Sánchez echoed this when he wrote in *Becoming Mexican American: Ethnicity, Culture and Identity in Chicano Los Angeles, 1900–1945* that "any notion that individuals have occupied one undifferentiated cultural position — such as 'Mexican,' 'American,' or 'Chicano' — has been abandoned in favor of the possibility of multiple identities and contradictory positions" (1993:8). Their work has in turn shaped an emerging generation of Mexican American religious studies historians and scholars like Luis León, Gastón Espinosa, Alberto Pulido, Lara Medina, Roberto Ramon Lint Sagarena, Daniel Ramírez, and others.

Chicano Literature, History, and Mexican American Religious Studies

The field of Mexican American religions has been shaped not only by the faith-based activism of Chávez and Tijerina, the Chicano movement and cultural renaissance, liberation theology, denominationally sponsored church histories and theologies, and social scientific and humanistic scholarship, but also by Chicano literature. Although writing outside the academy, literary authors like Carlos Castañeda (*The Teachings of Don Juan: A Yaqui Way of Knowledge,* 1968), Rudolfo Anaya (*Bless Me, Ultima,* 1972), and Gloria Anzaldúa (*Borderlands/La Frontera,* 1987) have also indirectly contributed to the interdisciplinary and canon-busting movement away from institutional theology by focusing on non-institutional forms of religiosity and by treating the U.S.-Mexico borderlands as a hybrid shamanic space that challenges Catholic and Protestant hegemony, traditions, and ways of knowing.

Castañeda's anthropological foray into the world of Don Juan, a *diablero,* or satanic sorcerer, from northern Mexico then living in Los Angeles, explores shamanistic cognition and ways of knowledge and power that challenge modern Western categories, medicine, religion, and epistemology. Like Castañeda's emphasis on Mexican American healing traditions, Anaya's novel analyzes the influence of Native American indigenous history, spirituality, and mythology on the magico-realist outlook on life and the world in popular Catholicism through the life and work of a *curandera,* or folk healer, named Ultima. She teaches her coming-of-age grandson and apprentice Antonio that life cannot be reduced to a simple binary of good vs. evil. Knowledge, like the world, is fragmented, and yet one can find liberation and hope through moving beyond one's individual identity (Köhler, 2000). This magical-realist outlook has been shaped by a number of other writers and has influenced the writing of Mexican American scholars like Rudiger Busto (2005).

Castañeda's and Anaya's work inspired and influenced Gloria Anzaldúa's new *mestiza* paradigm, which calls for the celebration of a shamanic state and consciousness that challenges traditional Western conceptualizations of religion, gender, sexuality, and identity. Her work explores in prose and poetry the ambivalence of Chicanos in Anglo culture, women in Latino culture, and lesbians in a straight world. She criticizes anyone who oppresses people who are culturally or sexually different. Although her work has been overlooked by some Mexican American scholars of religion who have strong ties to the institutional church or were trained in seminaries and divinity schools, she has found vibrant sponsorship by many Chicano/a scholars of religion trained in secular public Chicano, ethnic, or religious studies programs and by Latina feminist theologians who have strong interests in borderlands studies, gender, race, ethnicity, or sexuality (Aquino, Machado, and Rodríguez, 2002; León, 2004; Busto, 2005; Laura Pérez, 2007; Isasi-Díaz, 1993, 2004; Carrasco, 2006).

Davíd Carrasco, Chicano Literature, and the Decentering of Mexican American Religious Studies

The intellectual and methodological development of the emerging field of Mexican American religious studies comes to its maturity in the work of Davíd Carrasco. His work marks the methodological crystallization of a Mexican American religious studies paradigm that expanded the methodological and theoretical boundaries beyond the field and scope of liberation theology. His work in the early 1980s along with that of Chicano/a writers like Gloria Anzaldúa and others contributed to the decentering of the scholarship on Mexican American religions away from the orbit of liberation theology and institutional church histories to increasingly pluralistic religious studies and Chicano studies analyses that no longer privileged a liberationist or institutional methodological approach. Perhaps the best example of this shift are Carrasco's analysis of Rudolfo Anaya's novel *Bless Me, Ultima* published in *Aztlán: A Journal of Chicano Studies* (1982a), his groundbreaking books *Quetzalcoatl and the Irony of Empire: Myths and Prophecies in Aztec Tradition* (1982b) and *Religions of Mesoamerica* (1990), and his work on Gloria Anzaldúa (2007).

Unlike most contemporary scholars writing on liberation theology, Carrasco takes many of his main theoretical and methodological cues from Mircea Eliade, Charles Long, Paul Wheatley, the Chicago School of the History of Religions, cultural anthropology, and Virgilio Elizondo's theological anthropology of *mestizaje*. He also uses Chicano literature as primary source texts to illustrate the native indigenous elements in Mexican and Mexican American religions. Drawing upon the work of phenomenologist Mircea Eliade and the urban ecologist Paul Wheatley in particular, Carrasco applies and reimagines a series of potent interpretive categories within the context of Mesoamerican and Mexican American history. These interpretive categories include sacred time, sacred centers, sacred spaces, world-making, world-centering, world-renewing, and what Carrasco calls center/periphery dynamics.

Unlike Gamio's negative view of Mexican Indian influences on religion, Carrasco celebrates the cultural and religious hybridity of the Mexican American religious experience. He explores the benefits of using the categories of both syncretism and transculturation in attempting to capture the rich texture of Mexican American religious hybridity in the most important cultural and political symbol of Mexican American community — Our Lady of Guadalupe. Carrasco writes: "In Guadalupe we see a curious and even furious syncretistic mixture. She is Indian and Spaniard. She is an Earth Mother and Holy Mother. She is a comforter and a revolutionary. She is the magnet for pilgrimages and she is a pilgrim herself, traveling in front of the rebel soldiers and entering every heart who needs protection and comfort" (Carrasco, 1990:124–57). Carrasco inadvertently challenged and transformed McNamara's relatively negative theological depiction of Mexican popular Catholicism as rooted in "pagan Indian rites" by shifting the locus of Mexican American religions away from institutional Catholicism and concerns about the theological orthodoxy of religious practices (McNamara, 1970:450; Stevens-Arroyo and Díaz-Stevens, 1994:9–36).

However, Carrasco's work does not necessarily represent an ideological or a theoretical break with the goals and aims of the Chicano movement or even liberation theology's commitment to the poor and marginalized. Instead it represents a methodological break with the largely theological orientation and methodology of his colleagues. His interest in a phenomenological approach to Mexican American religions is largely the result of his training in the history of religions at the University of Chicago and of his interest and experiences in non-Christian Mexican, metaphysical, Mesoamerican, and U.S. Native American religious traditions. At Chicago, Carrasco studied closely with both Charles H. Long and Paul Wheatley, who taught him the value of the comparative study of religions and the importance of putting phenomenology into constant dialogue with the study of social stratification and literary expressions. Carrasco's current work argues that we are entering a "Brown Millennium" that will forever change history and the study of religion both in the United States and around the world. Chicano/Latino growth in our megacities represents a new dynamic mestizo Latino aesthetic that will reorient and rejuvenate our understanding of how the current *"cultural and religious change"* will transform "the *religious, economic, civic and social ordering* of our socially stratified societies" (Carrasco, 2007).

History and Theory of Religious Studies

Carrasco's phenomenological approach to religious studies has a very distinct genealogy and method that traces its origins back through Mircea Eliade, Rudolf Otto, and Geradus van der Leeuw to Enlightenment philosophers like David Hume, Immanuel Kant, John Locke, and late nineteenth-century anthropologists like as Max Müller and E. B. Tylor (Wiebe, 1999:31–50). It purports to be entirely naturalistic in orientation and does not assume an a priori belief in the existence of God. This naturalistic approach developed slowly into the field of religious studies until the 1963 *Schempp* decision along with the work of Mircea Eliade and the Chicago School of the History of Religions led to four decades of unprecedented expansion from the 1960s to the present (Sharpe, 1987; Capps, 1995; Wiebe, 1999).[4] Although some variation of this religious studies approach has been embraced by almost all of the major secular Ph.D.-granting institutions in the United States, most Catholic, Mainline Protestant, and Evangelical Ph.D.-granting institutions and seminaries have not strictly embraced this secular approach as it is seen as running contrary to their Christian roots, their theologically and professionally oriented seminaries or divinity schools, and many of their faculty's a priori beliefs in God.

---

4. Kathryn Alexander argues that the *Schempp* decision "altered the total picture of the study of religion in America by introducing the language which has governed its subsequent development in secular public colleges and universities." Donald Wiebe further argues that "The distinction it [*Schempp*] introduced into the field was that between the teaching *of* religion and the teaching *about* religion, with the former being excluded from public institutions by the Constitution, and it opened a window for the inclusion of the academic study of religions in the curriculum of the modern public university" (emphasis in the original). Alexander and Wiebe as cited in Wiebe, 1999:86, 107, 110, 297.

Some religious studies scholars (also known as historians of religion and scholars of comparative religions) trained in the classical and contemporary history of comparative religions described in Sharpe, Capps, and Wiebe distinguish themselves from their theological counterparts in their attempt to: (1) take a scientific, non-apologetic, non-value-laden (good vs. bad theology or morals), and non-sectarian pluralistic approach to the study of religion; (2) suspend or bracket belief in God and the divine origin of religion in their writings; (3) compare two or more religious traditions, regions, or religious phenomena; (4) identify religious rituals, myths, and social patterns and phenomena that transcend many religious traditions; (5) offer non-theological interpretations and explanations of religious rituals, traditions, beliefs, and events; (6) take an interdisciplinary and often humanistic or a social scientific approach to interpreting religion; and (7) interpret the meaning, purpose, and function of religion in culture and society. In the words of William Paden, religious studies attempts to "create a language that explains what is otherwise expressed only by the language of religious insiders" (1996:37–49). What generally differentiates history of religions scholars from theologians or ethicists is their comparative emphasis and their attempt to avoid making normative theological, ethical, and political faith statements about what society should look like or believe. This job they leave primarily to their colleagues in ethics and theology.

Mircea Eliade, perhaps the most famous exponent of religious studies, argued that the phenomenological approach to the study of religion assumes that the sacred is "an element in the structure of [human] consciousness, not a stage in the history of consciousness." He suggested that religion is important because it helps people make meaning out of life by imitating paradigmatic experiences with the sacred. The aim of the phenomenologist is to identify, recognize, decipher, and understand the religious structures in society in order to better interpret and understand the meaning behind these private worlds and imaginary universes. Eliade believed that the historian of religions must make an effort to understand religious experiences and movements on their own plane of reference in order to understand their deeper meaning. Finding this deeper meaning is not an end in and of itself, but rather a means to understand its contribution to the *"entire culture"* (1984: preface, 4, 7–9).

As important as Eliade's theories are to the study of comparative religions, they tended to be, in the words of Richard Hecht, ahistorical, apolitical, and consensual, and assume what Donald Wiebe has identified as a theological a priori (1999:59–61, 100–101). Furthermore, one could also argue that some religious studies scholars like Wiebe engage in a modernist intellectual and ideological program whose findings are passed off as objective truth but in fact are nothing more than the projections of a neo-colonial and neo-orientalist enterprise. Recognizing these limitations, recent historians of religion such as Jonathan Z. Smith have emphasized the need to ground one's study of religions in their historical, social, and political contexts. Furthermore, Smith argues that "there is no data for religion" [*sic*], only the scholar's creative imagination. For this reason, it is incumbent upon scholars to be "relentlessly self-conscious" of their subjects and subjectivities. Scholars must gain mastery of the primary sources and secondary interpretations, select an appropriate methodology for interpreting the data, and then argue for a new paradigm, theory, or some fundamental question. This approach along with what Eliade calls the perspective of the sympathetic but critical outsider may yield one useful interpretive framework for analyzing religion (Eliade, 1984; Smith, 1988:xi, xii).

Toward a Mexican American Religious Studies Framework

The years 1994–96 proved the next critical turning point in the field of Mexican American religions with the publication of a number of important historical, social scientific, and theological works, including Anthony M. Stevens-Arroyo's four-volume *PARAL* series on Latino popular religiosity, identity, syncretism, and bibliography, and Jay P. Dolan's three-volume series *Notre Dame History of Hispanic Catholics in the U.S.*, both of which offered sustained attention to Mexican American religiosity. These multivolume works were soon joined by a number of other important books that focused exclusively or in part on Mexican American religions (Sandoval,

1990; J. González, 1991; Elizondo, 1992, 1997; Elizondo and Matovina, 1998; Dolan and Figueroa Deck, 1994; Rodríguez, 1994, 1996; Jeanette Rodríguez-Díaz and Cortés-Fuentes, 1994; Goizueta, 1995; Matovina, 1995; Matovina and Poyo, 2000; Bañuelas, 1995; Rodríguez and Martell-Otero, 1994; Espín and Díaz, 1997, 1999, 2000; Maldonado, 1999; Pulido, 2000; and F. Fernández, 2000).

The next critical turning point in the development of the field of Mexican American religions took place in February 1996 with the "New Directions in Chicano Religions" conference held at the University of California, Santa Barbara. The conference was initiated by Gastón Espinosa and co-directed with Mario T. García. Sixteen scholars were invited to come together to reflect on and help define the emerging field of Mexican American/Chicano religions.[5] This was the first academic conference to explore and map out the field of Mexican American/Chicano religious studies from a multidisciplinary scholarly perspective that was largely shaped by a religious studies methodology and discourse. It was decidedly pluralistic, humanistic, non-sectarian, and non-theological in its basic framework and orientation. Although several authors drew upon liberation theology to frame their work, most engaged in theoretical and methodological approaches from anthropology, sociology, religious studies, history, literature, ethnic studies, and political science. The conference included essays that examined the role of religion in Chicano literature and gay liberation theology, perhaps the first

---

5. In 1994, Gastón Espinosa initiated a discussion with Mario T. García about creating an academic, non-sectarian, non-institutional yet theologically informed approach to the study of Mexican American/Chicano religions at the University of California at Santa Barbara (UCSB). Over the next two years other critical conversation partners included Luis Léon, Alberto Pulido, Richard Hecht, Rudy Busto, and others. This dialogue led to the UCSB "New Directions in Chicano Religions" conference. The sixteen scholars invited to present original papers were Gastón Espinosa, Mario T. García, David Carrasco, Anthony M. Stevens-Arroyo, Luis Léon, Deborah Baldwin, Ellen McCracken, Lara Medina, Rudiger V. Busto, Daniel Ramírez, Alberto Pulido, Daryl Caterine, Allan Figueroa Deck, Gilbert Cadena, Ines Talamántez, and Alma García. Catherine Albanese, Charles Long, Wade Clark Roof, Phillip Hammond, and Richard Hecht served as the five panel respondents. The UCSB Department of Religious Studies was perhaps the first doctoral-granting university in the nation to create a *permanent* course in a religious studies department on "Mexican American/Chicano" religions. Luis León, Alberto Pulido, Mary Rojas, Inés Talamántez, Gastón Espinosa, and Rudiger V. Busto have all taught courses on Chicano/Latino religions for the UCSB Department of Religious Studies. Busto is presently professor of Chicano/Latino and Asian American Religions at UCSB.

conference on Mexican American and U.S. Latino religions to do so. The conference helped stimulate the creation of a two-year long UCSB Chicano religions evening colloquium that met in García's home, the short-lived National Association for the Study of Chicano Religions (NASCR) (1996), the UCSB Religions of Aztlán course designed by Luis Léon, the book *Mexican American Religions* (2007) and many other articles and books that were developed or refined as a result.

Toward a Working Definition of Chicano Religions

At the conference, religious studies scholar Charles Long challenged the participants to define what they meant by Mexican American/ Chicano religions and to then show how it was different from any other kind of religious phenomena. While no immediate or systematic response was given at the time, I argue that it is precisely the Mexican American blending and combinative reconstruction of Mexican and "American" traditions, customs, practices, symbols, and beliefs in the United States that we call Mexican American/Chicano religious expressions or Mexican American Chicano/a religions. To be sure, religious rituals found in Mexican American religions can also be found in non–Mexican American religions. However, I argue that the Mexican American cultural reimagination, blending, rearticulation, and reconstruction of "Mexican" and "American" religious rituals, customs, traditions, practices, beliefs, and symbols in the United States give them a Mexican American or "Chicano" inflection that sometimes differentiates them in application and form, though not necessarily in function, from non-Mexican American religious practices. Because of this blending, Mexican American religions share common ritual functions with African American, Asian American, Native American, and Euroamerican religious expressions. At the same time their application, inflection, and expression are also noticeably and often qualitatively different in their execution. Chicano religious practices and traditions resonate with their Mexican counterparts while at the same time exhibiting a blending, a combining, a fusing, and a mixing with non-Mexican U.S. practices and traditions to create a new hybrid reality that is neither entirely Mexican nor entirely American but is in fact Mexican American or "Chicano." Some of these practices have combined and blended Mexican and American religious and cultural traditions and have in turn transformed themselves into a new hybrid reality (e.g., U.S. Latino liberation theology). This combinative hybrid spirituality has given birth to what Rudiger Busto calls the predicament of *nepantla,* or of being in the middle in their views and practices of other religions (Busto, 1998; Espinosa, Elizondo, Miranda, 2003).

Ethno-Phenomenological Approach to the Study of Religion

One approach to interpreting Mexican American religions is an ethno-phenomenological methodology that seeks to bridge the open hostility between religious studies and theology through an interdisciplinary, transnational, and a phenomenological religious studies method. Such a method listens to, dialogues with, and draws upon the important discoveries and insights from theology and the above-noted disciplines and influences. This approach should also seek to enter into and analyze the world of its historical and contemporary subjects on their own plane of reference through a methodology that respects and holds in balance both the perspective of the devout and committed religious insider and that of the skeptical, irreligious, and non-committed secular outsider. An ethno-phenomenological approach to the study of Mexican American religions should offer a scholarly framework that engages in what Ninian Smart has called "bracketed realism," whereby the scholars' own religious beliefs (or lack thereof) and ideological political positions are bracketed or suspended and not superimposed on their subjects in order to try to understand, analyze, and interpret a religious leader, tradition, movement, practice, belief, or phenomenon on its own plane of reference (Smart, 1973:31–34, 60; Wiebe, 1999:53–67). While personal subjectivities and values are unavoidable, a scholar should nonetheless try to fairly present the community in a way that is both critical and yet recognizable to the insider.

Although scholars taking this approach should (in their scholarship and classroom teaching) seek political and theological neutrality regarding the value, truth, or falsity of their subjects' theological beliefs and moral behavior out of consideration for the religion itself and their diverse student body at secular institutions where they teach, this does not mean that they cannot engage in advocacy on behalf of their own community or religious and political beliefs outside of these forums. Scholars should be free to advocate their own educational, social, racial, political, and religious views provided that they do not intentionally seek to use their classroom lecterns and scholarship as bully pulpits to force, coerce, or manipulate their students or colleagues into adopting their position as the one and only legitimate approach to their subject for all truly "open-minded" and "tolerant" people. Given that all knowledge and truth are provisional, relative, and perspectival, any attempt to force, coerce, or manipulate someone to embrace one's own position represents a kind of intellectual violence and neocolonialism that can silence, oppress, or marginalize dissenting voices and points of view even among one's own people, all the while demanding freedom, tolerance, liberation, and empowerment for oneself in the Euroamerican dominated academy. This kind of ideological proselytizing can have a chilling effect in the classroom and in the field because it can stifle the introduction of new and creative ideas, theories, methodologies, and points of view out of fear of reprisal and retribution for not towing the party line.

An ethnophenomenological approach to the study of Mexican American religions should strive to be politically and methodologically pluralistic, multidisciplinary, humanistic, social scientific, comparative, and transnational in its orientation, assumptions, and use and evaluation of evidence. Ideally, scholars should be trained not only in Mexican American religions, but also in U.S. Latino, Mexican, Mesoamerican, Latin American, and Native American religions and theology, both historical and contemporary. They should also be at home working in archives and, when possible, in conducting quantitative and qualitative ethnographic and oral history/*testimonio* research.

Conclusion

The academic study of Mexican American religions stretches back more than a century. The contemporary field of Mexican American religions traces its origins back to 1968 and the writings of César Chávez, Gustavo Gutiérrez, Enrique Dussel, and Virgilio Elizondo. Their work was joined by writers in history, sociology, anthropology, Chicano studies, literature, and others. All of these forces along with the contributions of the Chicago School of the History of Religions helped shape and give rise to the work of David Carrasco and others in the 1980s. The field went through a period of tremendous growth and refinement throughout the 1990s to the present. I have proposed that an ethno-phenomenological method is one of many possible ways to go about studying and interpreting Mexican American religions at secular colleges and universities where one is required by the state not to promote or endorse a theological worldview. This methodology seeks to bridge the chasm that often separates religious studies from theology by remaining in dialogue with theologians and religious studies scholars. Perhaps more importantly it seeks to generate new scholarship that examines the way ordinary people find hope and interpret their very real and imaginary universes.

Chapter 4

The Prophetic Horizon of Latino Theology

Jorge A. Aquino

In *Caminemos con Jesus* (1995), Roberto S. Goizueta bases his aesthetic theology[1] on an interpretation of the history of the term "praxis" as a means of situating not only the cultural milieu of Latino life, but also the intrinsic, culturally inflected humanity of Latinos. Goizueta's work embraces key emancipatory themes of liberation theology, including the notions of theology as a "critical reflection on praxis"[2] and the "preferential option for the poor."[3] However, while affirming these values, Goizueta's work tends to marginalize from the center of the U.S. Latino theological project both the theme of socio-economic liberation and the recourse of theology to the social sciences as indispensable auxiliary tools. Without an intellectual apparatus for analyzing the condition of marginality that confronts the majority of Latinos in this country, there is no secure foundation

---

1. Alejandro García-Rivera proposes a definition of aesthetics as "the science which asks...what moves the human heart," and theological aesthetics as that domain of aesthetics that "recognizes in the experience of the truly beautiful a religious dimension." The experience of the beautiful is a transcendental mystery, "an experience that transcends geological space and prehistoric time." For García-Rivera, "beauty's trace reveals a divine starting point" (1999:9–10).

2. The "critical reflection on Christian praxis in the light of the Word" is the formula Gustavo Gutiérrez uses to mark liberation theology as a new way of doing theology. See *A Theology of Liberation*, 1973, 1988, especially chapter 1 ("Theology: A Critical Reflection").

3. Born in the Latin American church in the 1960s and 1970s, the "preferential option for the poor" was as much a theological sensibility as an ecclesial policy. In that time of revolutionary activism and the liberalizations of Vatican II, the church offered a stronger prophetic voice against the condition of poverty. The poor should be listened to — the church vocally insisted — as moral agents deserving of greater control over their material socio-economic destinies.

for affirming the sorts of emancipatory options Goizueta otherwise supports.

While Goizueta's writing does speak to the reality of Latino poverty, racism, and marginality, he does not adequately trace those conditions to causes such as the coloniality of power exercised through global capital, the international division of labor that gives rise to the Latino diaspora, and global racial and gender formations that remain central axes of neocoloniality. Instead Goizueta shifts his emphasis from liberation theology's foundational concern with "social transformation" to an aesthetics of empathic fusion, first traced out by the Mexican philosopher José Vasconcelos.

This has important theological consequences. By not contextualizing the material conditions of the aesthetic imaginary through social-scientific analysis, Latino theology risks diluting its latent prophetic voice (see Mejido, 2001). I will consider these points by examining several dimensions of Goizueta's text.

Ambivalent Identity. Goizueta's ambivalence about his own ethnoracial identity is brought into dialogue with his claim that Latinos self-identify more on the basis of language and culture than race. I will hypothesize this connection as part of the widespread denegation of racialization in Latino culture. Such a denegation is characteristic of a bid to induct Latino thought into the religious academy's "liberal paradigm" (Mejido, 2002). Such a denegation operates according to long-established U.S. minority identity practices: those seeking entrée into the affluent classes deliberately array themselves with the vestments and affectations of the affluent class's culture — in this case, the cultures of whiteness (see Lipsitz, 1998, and Jacobson, 1998).

Praxis, Beauty, and Social Change. I critique Goizueta's analysis of praxis for the way it overdetermines Marxian elements, while sidelining core prophetic Christian elements that are indispensable to comprehending liberation theology's interest in praxis. Goizueta's interpretation of the term "praxis" demotes "social transformation" and dispenses altogether with the social sciences (especially history and sociology) as auxiliary tools — in favor of an aesthetics of "empathic fusion" as the true hermeneutical paradigm for U.S. Latino theology.

Option for the Poor. Goizueta's reinscription of liberation theology's "preferential option for the poor" understands solidarity with the poor in terms of a gesture of middle-class transgression: solidarity with poor persons *in their environs*. But while Goizueta supports his option for the poor with biblical citations, his argument overlooks the prophetically charged nature of the biblical situations he cites. Moreover, while emphasizing that his option for the poor must be established on the basis of relationships with living, flesh-and-blood people, *no poor person speaks for herself in his text.* Where Goizueta invokes supposedly living persons, they are neither named nor quoted directly. This has the effect of authorizing the author's positions on U.S. Hispanic popular Catholicism without letting his sources speak for themselves.[4] It is striking that his emphasis on the relationship between poverty as a *locus theologicus* and popular sacramentality as a distinctive U.S. Hispanic theologeme should not rely on ethnographic research.

In all these examples, Goizueta's discourse unwittingly supports the assimilation of Latino theology by the liberal North American theological academy, even as his work claims to represent the subaltern interests and religious imaginary of U.S. Hispanics. I will begin by examining the ways in which Goizueta represents his biography and identity in *Caminemos con Jesús.*

Positionality: Race and Identity in Goizueta's Text

If all theology is contextual then the social location of the writer of theology also influences the content of that theology. How does Roberto Goizueta's location influence his theology? In particular, by claiming that cultural and linguistic categories are more reflective of

---

4. This is especially true of "an elderly Mexican woman" who appears several times in *Caminemos.* She becomes the privileged example of how Latino religious devotion activates a divine-human encounter through the mediation of religious symbols and material artifacts — a crucifix, the veil of the Virgin Mary of the triduum procession, etc. — hewed from ordinary materials. Goizueta never names this woman, nor presents any statement *from her* as to her perception of the divine-human encounter. On the scholarly ventriloquism of "the poor" — writing about poverty without citing poor people in their own voices — see Gayatri Spivak's essay "Can the Subaltern Speak?" (Spivak, 1988).

Latino identity than racial ones, has he sublimated too deeply the per-
nicious influence of racism? On the one hand, Goizueta affirms his
experience as a Latino subject who has suffered — and resisted — per-
nicious racist practices in the United States. On the other hand, there
are abundant signs in his autobiographical narrative (given largely
in chapter 1: "Learning to Walk in an Alien Land") that Goizueta is
ambivalent about his own racial identity, an ambivalence suggesting
that he — and perhaps his theology — have not adequately comprehended the forces of racialization, or the assimilation those forces
push on those who resist racial subordination.

The theme of exile figures large in his narration. Goizueta identifies
himself as a first-generation Cuban American, who left Cuba with his
family as a small boy. On the first page of his book he describes his
"first memory" in life: of his mother coming into his room one day
after he returned home from kindergarten to tell him that they would
soon be moving to Miami.

> The only other memory of Cuba is that of sitting in a Miami-
> bound airplane on the airport tarmac, straining to see my father
> and paternal grandfather standing on the viewing deck atop the
> terminal building, and waving goodbye to them through the
> plane's scratched-up window — not knowing when or if I would
> see either of them again.... My earliest memories, then, are not
> of life in my homeland, Cuba; they are, on the contrary, mem-
> ories of leaving that life behind. My earliest memories are not
> of family and community, but of their destruction. They are not
> memories of home, but of homelessness, not of personal growth
> but of loss, not of life but of death. (1995:1–2)

He speaks of his subsequent exilic life as an attempt to recover what
was lost: "my connection to a community which, spanning many
generations, had given me birth. I bear that community, those men
and women, in the deepest recesses of my soul; what I thus seek is not
only a connection to others, both dead and living, but a connection
to my very self" (Ibid.:2).

The recovery project was challenged by the condition of double deracination Goizueta experienced as a Cuban exile raised in
"Bible-belt" Atlanta, a culture removed from both Cuba and such

established, post-revolutionary Cuban exile communities as Dade County, Florida; Union City, New Jersey; and New York City. Being removed from such communities, Goizueta struggled to determine his sense of place — a person no longer of Cuba or even its exilic communities, but not quite of America either.

> The Cubans in South Florida could continue to identify with their life "before" in Cuba; indeed, they virtually recreated that life in Miami. Thus, they were sometimes tempted to deny the reality of the passage itself, the reality that, for better or worse, we live *between the Cuban past and the North American present.* (Ibid.:2, emphasis added)

This desire to resolve his place *in between* cultures posed a risk for him that he might become too easily estranged from the culture of his parents, and too assimilated to white American culture.

> Since, at the time, U.S. Hispanics were a minute minority in Georgia, the danger I faced was the opposite [of what Cubans in Miami faced], that of identifying exclusively with life "after" Cuba, becoming thereby a fully assimilated *"americano."* This was easy for me, since I spoke English without an accent, am economically privileged, and I am white. (Ibid.:2)

Goizueta says he became conscious of the challenge of assimilation in college, where he was exposed to Chicano students "who were self-consciously affirming their own identity as distinct from the larger U.S. culture" (Ibid.:3). He described feeling that his "schizophrenic" life in-between Latino and Anglo cultures could not continue. "Having spent my youth, like so many Latinos and Latinas, trying to be accepted as a full-fledged *americano,* I would now self-consciously affirm my Latin American roots" (Ibid.:4).

But the struggle for cultural self-affirmation was not a simple matter. For one thing, Goizueta was often taken to be something other than Latino — presumably the white, assimilated person that, before his college years, he had attempted to become:

> I have often been told, for example, that I don't look or talk like a "Hispanic." Likewise, I have often been insulted by persons

who have made ethnic slurs to my face without realizing that I
was one of "those people." (Ibid.:2–3, n. 2)

He pivots from these claims to a remarkable conclusion:

> Consequently, such categories as "people of color" can, when
> used to categorize Latinos and Latinas, simply perpetuate stereo-
> types by imposing the dominant culture's own racial self-
> definition on a people whose self-definition is primarily cultural
> and linguistic. For Latinos and Latinas generally, *self-identity is
> more closely linked to culture and language than to race.* (Ibid.,
> emphasis added)

What are the identity positions implied in this narration of exilic
identity? I begin with its conclusion, that "for Latinos and Latinas
generally, self-identity is more closely linked to culture and language
than to race." Throughout the narrative his identity performance
navigates, first, toward Anglo-assimilation and away from Latino-
identification; and subsequently, toward Latino-identification and
away from... *what?* Goizueta has disputed the racialized "stereotypes" of those who would regard Latinos as "people of color."
In narrating his Latino identity, Goizueta seems to disclaim *color*
as a basis of that identity. Does this also unwittingly disclaim *race*
as a foundational identity marker for Latinos? We might criticize
as stereotype the idea that Latinos are "people of color" from the
standpoint of refusing an ascribed (and potentially oppressive) racialization. But that claim can bear a different reading if the thesis
of linguistic-cultural identity Goizueta pitches belies the fact that
racism predominates in Latin America as much as in North America.
Goizueta says as much when he writes:

> To suggest that U.S. Hispanics do not identify *primarily* with
> race is not, in any way, to suggest that our communities are not
> seriously divided along racial lines or that racism is not a major
> form of oppression *within* our communities. (Ibid.:2–3, n. 2)

This is all his text has to say about intra-Hispanic racism, but it is not
insignificant: Goizueta does not say that racism is merely significant

or pervasive; it is a *major* form of oppression within Latino communities. This comes as the second movement in a passage denying that the self-identity of Latinos is based primarily on race.

Goizueta does not link the two claims. He is not mistaken in thinking that "U.S. Hispanics do not identify *primarily* with race"; it is likely that many white Hispanics do not self-identify primarily on the basis of race. Yet this non-self-identification could also be read as a refusal, one that would operate as a *denegation:* one that obscures the complex, often contradictory strategy of identity claims that arise around cultural identities of whiteness in the United States and elsewhere. The positive content of this denegation gathers in implicit claims that: (a) we Latinos operate in a racialized cultural economy that we did not create, i.e., the cultural economy of the United States; (b) this cultural economy imposes racial identities upon us; (c) we refuse such imputations; (d) (ergo) we do not benefit from the racial economy; (e) we are "Americans" — or as Goizueta puts it, *americano* — apart from race.

Can matters be so straightforward? Is race so fictive a social construct that Latinos can make racism go away by *refusing* to be color-coded? Even if we refuse the color-codings given in Euroamerican history, we apparently do not refrain from color-coding one another. The difference between racial self-identification and imputed racialization is of critical importance to this discussion. What is race? In their classic work on racial formation in the United States, Michael Omi and Howard Winant argue that "there is a continuous temptation to think of race as an *essence,* as something fixed, concrete, and objective. And there is also an opposite temptation: to imagine race as a mere *illusion,* a purely ideological construct which some ideal non-racist social order would eliminate" (1994:54).

Instead, race is "an unstable and 'decentered' complex of social meanings constantly being transformed by political struggle." Omi and Winant define race as "a concept which signifies and symbolizes social conflicts by referring to different types of human bodies." Despite civil rights laws and anti-discrimination consciousness, such categorization of bodies and cultural identities still "plays a fundamental role in structuring and representing the social world"

(Ibid.:55). Omi and Winant conceive race in terms of *racial formations* — "a process of historically situated projects in which human bodies and social structures are represented and organized" (Ibid.:55–56). Racial formations are historically oriented as hegemonic projects, within which power is contested through complex negotiations of identity formation. Omi and Winant conceive of the structural dimension as an institutional and legal "racial dictatorship" that historically has "defined 'American' identity as white, *as the negation of racial otherness* — at first largely African and indigenous, later Latin American and Asian as well. This negation took shape in both law and custom, in public institutions and in forms of cultural representation. It became the archetype of hegemonic rule in the U.S." (Ibid.:66, emphasis added).

In terms of negotiating identity, racial formation became a project of designating, through law and custom, racial types and subjects who would be marked for inclusion in certain enterprises and social projects, and exclusion from others. The reservation of citizenship rights to "free white persons" in the nation's first nationalization act (1790); the enslavement of African Americans; the "reservation" of marginal lands for indigenous peoples; the exclusion of Asians from immigration rights between 1924 and 1965; and the establishment of the Mexican *bracero* worker program during and after World War II, are all paradigmatic social projects in which political, social, and labor privileges were disbursed on the basis of racialized identities. Such policies have historically produced, by negative determination, the freedom of white subjects (as theoretically *un-raced* persons) to pursue the most privileged positions and vocations available in U.S. society. They have also produced the identity-trope of "white" as that which was not determinable according to any racial category, except perhaps "European." Choosing to identify as white in America is tantamount to refusing affiliation with other racial identities.

Latinos in the United States live in the most marginal spaces of any racialized group in the United States. Goizueta regularly alludes to this, yet his manner of denegating the racialized construction of that world suggests that he has not adequately deconstructed America's contradictory, liberal racial logic. Such a logic would lead us to overlook the contradiction between the belief that Latinos don't self-identify on the basis of race, and the fact that Latinos still practice racism as a "major form of oppression within our communities" (1995:2).[5]

How do these logics inflect Goizueta's theological project? In the next section I describe his project in two phases. First I consider how he establishes an aesthetic theory on the basis of a critique of liberation theology. Then I consider how that theory rewrites a fundamental option of liberation theology — that of the preferential option for the poor.

Beauty, Praxis, and Oppression

Goizueta's aesthetic theology begins with a review of the history of the term "praxis," a term which he suspects instrumentalizes human action and is inherently alienating for a theory of religious identity such as might be expressed in Latino theology. The term reaches Latino theology through liberation theology, which in turn develops a theory of praxis through its engagement with Marxist social theory. According to Goizueta, Marx believed that human beings were distinguished from animals through the human capacity for "conscious life activity," or praxis. For human beings, "life-activity is thus defined as productive labor.... For Marx, then, the human person is *homo faber*" (Goizueta, 1995:82). Marxist theories of alienation stem from the idea that the productive relations of capitalism appropriate human labor in the interests of the capitalist classes. But Goizueta takes issue with an alienating tendency in Marxist thought that occurs even before the social relations imposed in capitalist political economies have alienated the fruits of human work from the *homo faber.* For Goizueta, the very idea of *homo* as *faber* itself entails

---

5. A characteristic contemporary liberal complicity in post–civil rights expressions of white supremacy is critiqued in Robyn Wiegman's essay on whiteness studies (Wiegman, 1999), a recent academic field seeking simultaneously to study and destroy the phenomenon of modern white supremacy. She argues that the post-1965 white subject is split "between disaffiliation from white supremacist practices, and disavowal of the ongoing reformation of white power and one's benefit from it." That split "is constitutive of contemporary white racial formation," underlying what Winant calls "white racial dualism." See Winant, 1997. The denegation by white Latinos of their ambivalent place in the American racial condition follows the ideological lines taken by the split white subject that Wiegman and Winant identify in their work.

an alienation, one rooted in an ambiguity deriving from Marx's use of the term "praxis."

Goizueta turns to Aristotle to pin down the ambiguity, discerning two sorts of "practice" signified in ancient Greek philosophy. First, there is praxis, which is "all human activity whose end is internal rather than external to itself, i.e., all human activity which is an end in itself" (Ibid.:82). Then there is poiesis, the sort of practice that tends to have other objects, products, or practices as its aim. Poiesis is instrumentalized practice, or productive activity, while praxis is human activity in, of, and for itself and its own ends. For Goizueta, praxis is what makes human beings human. "What makes human life human is precisely that it is an absolute value in itself — regardless of its productivity, usefulness, or practicality" (Ibid.:84).

On the other hand, he argues that Marx and others defined praxis in a manner more resembling what Aristotle conceived as poiesis, thus fudging a classical distinction between two types of practice. Though "it would be an oversimplification to suggest that Marx at no time views human life as intrinsically valuable" (Ibid.:85), the alienation Goizueta identifies in the Marxian history of praxis is fundamentally dehumanizing because the fruit of human labor is valued not by how a human being enjoys the undertaking of that work, but by a measure of utility that is removed from human experience through a violence of abstraction.[6]

Goizueta capitalizes on this claim to extend the supposedly alienating logic in Marx's notion of praxis to liberation theology's notion of praxis as oriented to social transformation. For Goizueta, liberation theology presents three senses of the term "praxis" (Ibid.:87ff.): First, there is *historical praxis,* which is simply human action in history, or the "active [human] presence in history."[7] According to Goizueta, this form of praxis most closely resonates with Aristotle's idea of "praxis": human actions as ends in themselves. Second, there is *Christian praxis:* "the specifically Christian form of active presence

---

6. Goizueta writes: "For Marx ... what defines human action as human is precisely its productive capacity, the human ability to transform the environment. Whether one is transforming raw wood in order to make a house, or social structures in order to make 'a just society,' or one's very self in order to make a 'better person,' what defines human life and action is its usefulness in achieving the desired result" (1995:84).

7. Goizueta's internal quotation is from Gutiérrez, 1988:6.

in history, namely, prayer and commitment to justice" (Ibid.:87). He notes that Gustavo Gutiérrez defines liberation theology as "a critical reflection on Christian praxis in the light of the Word," as well as "a critical reflection on historical praxis." Finally, what Gutiérrez called "liberating praxis" is:

> a historical praxis of solidarity with the interests of liberation and is inspired by the gospel. This liberating praxis endeavors to transform history in the light of the reign of God. (Ibid.:87)[8]

Goizueta regards the idea of "liberating praxis" as:

> perhaps the most significant contribution of liberation theology to the church, reminding Christians that the lived commitment to social justice is not superfluous to but a precondition for authentic Christian faith. The struggle for justice is not an option for Christians, over and above their Christian belief and worship; the lived commitment to social justice is itself an essential, intrinsic dimension of any authentic Christian faith. (Ibid.:88)

Having said this, however, Goizueta takes a step backward, a step that I will quote in full before undertaking an analysis of what is transacted by this passage:

> Yet this identification of human action with social transformation also leaves liberation theology susceptible to the modern tendency to define human action as production or technique, that is, as a means to some external end — in this case, the end of liberation. What, in other words, is the relationship between historical praxis, or praxis-as-an-end-in-itself, and liberating praxis? Is liberating praxis *foundational* insofar as it is "the praxis on which liberation theology reflects"? If so, the starting point, or *locus theologicus,* of theology will be the "endeavor to transform history." Yet such an understanding of praxis, as transformation, remains ambiguous. Is liberation theology fundamentally a reflection on human action as an end in itself (historical praxis), or on human action as an *instrument* of liberation (liberating praxis)? Is liberation but a *by*-product of

---

8. Goizueta quotes Gutiérrez, 1988:xxx.

the struggle *within which* we become full human subjects? Or is liberation the end *product* of this struggle?

As indicated in the first chapter, their insistence on the intrinsic connection between social transformation and the Christian faith has been, for me, one of the most inspiring insights of Latin American liberation theologians. My own experience in Latino communities, such as San Fernando, has also led me to question, however, any emphasis on the social transformative dimension of human action which would make this dimension itself foundational. In these communities, I have witnessed a type of empowerment and liberation taking place which, at least initially and explicitly, seems to have relatively little connection to any social or political struggles. Indeed in many cases, empowerment and liberation are not explicit goals at all. Seemingly, the only explicit goals are day-to-day survival and, especially, the affirmation of relationships that are essential to that survival. Central to the struggle for survival and relationships, moreover, is the community's life of faith, which also, at least on the surface, seems little related to social transformation. (Ibid.:88)

In sum: since Marx's notion of praxis values production/productivity as the hallmark of human life, then the goal of social transformation — as liberation theology's "foundation" — is infected by this structure of (human de)valuation. This is because Goizueta sees the project of "social transformation" as one that "reduces human action to mere technique, or instrumentality" (Ibid.:84). To reduce human action to social transformation is to reduce it to productive activity, which is to reduce it to technique; and to reduce human action to technique is to reduce the human person to but a passive object, a mere instrument of production (Ibid.:84).

What is puzzling here is the question, From whence does this *reduction* enter? How has Goizueta proceeded from a critique of praxis to the conclusion that a theology of "social transformation" should *of necessity* be involved in producing something *alien, external,* and dehumanizing to those who would practice it? How is it that the "identification of human action with social transformation also leaves liberation theology susceptible to the modern tendency to define human action as production or technique"? What sort of an "identification" has Goizueta conceived? Where would it take place? If Goizueta accepts that Latinos live in a society that marginalizes too many of their number, in what sense can the "identification" of human action and social transformation be reductive? Here we are not far from being told that liberation theology's concern with biblically inspired notions of justice and prophetic activism are dehumanizing, as if liberation theology's reflection on Christian traditions of resistance to poverty and oppression has been co-opted by the logic of instrumentalization that Goizueta cites in Marx.

The crucial question on which his whole analysis turns — from a demotion of a liberation analytics to the privileging of aesthetics — is whether

> liberation theology [is] fundamentally a reflection on human action as an end in itself (historical praxis), or on human action as an *instrument* of liberation. (Ibid.:88)

The drift of this question makes us wonder under what conditions it would be possible to live a life in which one's actions could spin toward a destiny of their own, and not a destiny conditioned by natural necessity or socio-economic compulsion. Toward the end of his text, Goizueta speaks of the way that ethico-political poiesis mediates affective-aesthetic praxis. Poiesis is the domain of the productive, the external. To emphasize this prong of practice is to instrumentalize human life, he argues. However, to overemphasize praxis, as though material needs were not relevant to the question of one's humanity, would be to fall into idealism and sentimentality. In fact, Goizueta concedes, "human praxis is mediated by poiesis" (Ibid.:190), therefore,

> human relationships are mediated by material relationships. Consequently, all the abovementioned forms of marginalization [race, gender, age, class, etc.] are mediated by economic marginalization. (Ibid.)

If Goizueta critiques the propensity of liberation theology to instrumentalize praxis through its foundational attention to "social transformation," but praxis is mediated by poiesis, how are these two forms of practice distinguishable *in practice?* This question shows how his discourse of affective-aesthetic praxis and ethico-political poiesis risks contradiction. For example, toward the end of his discussion on the preferential option for the poor, Goizueta parses "the everyday struggle for survival" of Latinos as falling on the prong of praxis; indeed, it does so in a privileged way:

> The *everyday struggle for survival*, the simple, seemingly insignificant acts of familial affection and care through which we affirm our life-giving relationships with our brothers, sisters, and neighbors *become, in the gospel, the norm for all human praxis.* God is revealed first and preferentially not in the grand political projects of liberation and transformation, but in the "insignificant," everyday, common struggle for survival — though this latter is always intrinsically related to the larger political and economic struggle. (Ibid.:195–96, emphasis added)

I have yet to hear any liberation theologian express the reductive sentiment that God is preferentially revealed in "grand political projects of liberation." Moreover, it must be said that the whole question of *struggle* in Latino life has a context whose energies are largely centered outside the Latino communities Goizueta otherwise celebrates with such compassion. That outside has its places in corporate boardrooms and the institutions of government that hold the power to shape the political economy in ways that require subaltern people to struggle for their living and their dignity. An anti-instrumentalist critique of liberation theology cannot succeed by opposing a liberating praxis to an instrumentalizing poiesis — as though the first path invoked a divinely inscribed *don* of human agency, while the other robbed us of agency. Instead, any life that is *compelled* to struggle for survival because the political economy has unduly imposed necessities of productivity on racialized (or gendered) subjects is forced to act on terms decidedly beyond its control. An instrumentalization that has made productive pawns out of Latino people has already entered into their condition and options, before they have made any decisions concerning the investments of their energies. So the suggestion in Goizueta's critique of liberation theology — that Latinos can *opt for* a praxis that humanizes them, and *against* the poiesis of "grand political projects of liberation" — too much privileges the idea that Latinos who struggle to survive are free to choose their ways of practice. Poverty stubbornly inhibits the freedom to choose one's destiny and practice. But more practically, if capital has instrumentalized the lives of impoverished people, then the option to dwell in the sacrament of the *beautiful* can be illusory and self-defeating.

In fact, the privilege to choose between such options truly belongs to those who have privilege: the economic capital to earn a dignified wage and live in a dignified way; the social capital to enter and leave well-to-do domains at leisure; and the intellectual capital to discern between non-comestible abstractions such as praxis and poiesis. It is to the subalterns of the Global South that the preferential option for the poor was addressed by the Latin American church. For a theologian to propose a praxis that celebrates the "everyday struggle for survival" of Latinos *at the expense* of political action to ameliorate socio-economic marginality misplaces the history of prophetic engagement that has been the crucial center of Judeo-Christian traditions. Such a position is not consistent with the scriptural witness of a Jesus who was a social activist, who stridently preached against religiously sanctioned impositions of poverty, and who was executed because he refused to simply walk anonymously with his people in Galilee.

Acompañamiento: Preferential Migration to the Poor?

In this section I join the question of the aesthetic option for praxis with Goizueta's version of the "preferential option for the poor," which marginalizes scriptural prophetic narratives taken up by liberation theology. Goizueta begins by asking how the preferential option for the poor might be reinterpreted in the light of the anthropological and theological perspectives he has presented as underlying U.S. Hispanic popular Catholicism. After affirming the biblical foundation for the option, which envisages the gratuity and universality of God's love, he concludes that the preferential option for the poor is "the most important *epistemological precondition for Christian faith:* to know God we must opt for the poor" (Ibid.:177, emphasis in the original). He has previously established the fundamentally sacramental character of popular Hispanic Catholicism, whose liturgical artifacts such as the banal objects of "wood, plaster, flower petals, candle, wax, cloth, clay, bread...in their particularity mediate and reveal a universal spiritual reality" (Ibid.:179). This sacramental structure of revelation is part of the theological justification for the preferential option for the poor, Goizueta argues, showing that divine-human communion proceeds through the least of things.

But what about the pragmatics of observing the option? How does his claim that the option is "the most important epistemological precondition for Christian faith" suggest ways that the option becomes a praxis? Goizueta argues that the option for the poor is the Christian gateway to "the development of a truly pluralistic, multicultural society, academy, and church." As a predicate to unmasking inequalities of power in American society, the option for the poor:

> requires us to begin any discussion of pluralism, multiculturalism, or intercultural dialogue with the acknowledgment that, before there can be a genuine dialogue or conversation among different social groups (racial, cultural, gender, class, etc.), these must be recognized as equal partners in the dialogue. (Ibid.:180)

He qualifies this claim by adding:

> There can be no true pluralism of equal positions, or dialogue between conversation partners, in a situation where one of the positions or "partners" has power over the other. A master cannot have a dialogue with a slave.... The concrete, historical situation *de facto* precludes the possibility of genuine collaboration between teacher and students as co-equal partners — regardless of the teacher's intentions. Nor would I be having an authentic intercultural dialogue if I, as a white teacher, were engaged in a classroom discussion with an African American student. However noble my intentions, the structural inequality of the historical context makes it impossible for me to truly carry out those intentions. (Ibid.:181)

If Goizueta's option for poor is (a) the solidarity that levels unequal power relations; *and* (b) the precondition for authentic dialogue destined to construct a "truly pluralistic, multicultural society, academy, and church," then the option seems stuck in a vicious hermeneutical loop: a truly multicultural society is the end, not the beginning, of the dialogue; yet, as demanded by Goizueta's expression of the preferential option for the poor, that dialogue presupposes the leveling of power relations among its interlocutors. If power relations were level at the beginning of such a dialogue, there would be no need for either a dialogue or a preferential option for the poor. The parties would have agreed — before the dialogue — to practice what the dialogue would have *persuaded* them to practice: *justice*. In short, Goizueta's vision of multicultural society is one that will be negotiated by reasonable people dialoguing around a table as equal partners in a social project.

Is this realistic? Goizueta seems to know that the powers of this world are not subject to persuasion from subalterns:

> In a historical context of asymmetrical, or unequal relationships, what the master thinks or says will always *ipso facto* be more true, more ethical, and more rational than what the slave thinks or says. (Ibid.)

In fact, Goizueta has sidelined reflection on the phenomenology of social conflict and struggle[9] as a necessary background to any subaltern theology. The relevant question is not how the option for the poor can bring about an altruistic society through dialogue. The more crucial and radical question is rather: How should Christians respond in the face of the fact that power does not surrender? This happens to be the literal *crux* of the Christian tradition: the crux of the cross. Theologies of the cross have often appeared as the backgrounds to political strategies: altruistic self-sacrifice in the name of justice work. For example, the performance of unmerited suffering, in nonviolent direct-action campaigns, was the core theologically informed strategy of the southern, black-church-centered, civil rights movement of the 1950s and 1960s.

Goizueta addresses the question of Christian responses to oppressive power as he traces a pragmatics of "human solidarity" through

---

9. Mejido centers his vision for the reconstruction of Latino theology as a project in an analysis of "the phenomenology of struggle as the primordial element of U.S. Hispanic reality." See Mejido, 2002:62.

acompañamiento — accompaniment. How do we accompany the poor? What does this idea mean? Goizueta speaks of "identification with the poor," "preferential identification with one concrete, historical, flesh-and-blood, *particular* person: the poor person." This sort of identification is how "we will come to recognize ourselves as implicated in their struggles and intrinsically related to them in their suffering" (Ibid.:182). It will also reveal "our common complicity in the injustice" of poverty (Ibid.:181–83). Goizueta also speaks of sharing in the suffering of the poor, and of participating in "the concrete reality of the cross" by participating in the abandoned condition of poor people. He notes that identifying with "the half-breed, the racially and culturally marginalized" (Ibid.:188) is tantamount to following Jesus, who himself was so identified in his time.[10] Such a commitment requires confronting the threefold nature of poverty as liberation theology has conceived it: (a) *material* poverty, characterized by the "lack of the goods of this world and even by misery and indigence";[11] (b) *spiritual* poverty, which is a "spiritual childhood [being] totally at the disposition of the Lord";[12] and (c) *solidarity*.

This expression of solidarity is the only place where the notion of protest appears as a legitimate exercise of the option for the poor. But it is an apolitical protest: Goizueta does not state that protest should go beyond walking in the everyday life of U.S. Latinos toward, say, a politics of protest against discrimination, or political and social enfranchisement. Neither specific political strategies nor the very idea of political action as a theological option are mentioned as part of the praxis of *acompañamiento*.

Goizueta does speak of identifying with certain socially marginalized groups, such as women, the elderly, and youth as part of the preferential option for the poor. But the option should also include, at its core, friendship and family-making with poor persons:

to love concrete, particular, poor persons *as members of our family.* The foundation of the preferential option for the poor is

---

10. Here Goizueta is citing the work of Virgilio Elizondo on *mestizaje*. See, for example, *Galilean Journey,* 1983; and *The Future Is Mestizo,* 1988.

11. Goizueta cites Gutiérrez, 1988:170.

12. Goizueta cites Gutiérrez, 1988:169.

the aesthetic, affective praxis of friendship with poor persons. (Ibid.:195)

But perhaps the most important way in which the preferential option for the poor is expressed in a North American context is in situations of *transgression,* Goizueta writes, especially when persons of good conscience (and middle-class-or-better means) take it upon themselves to refuse the safe solace of suburban boundaries to walk with poor people in *their places and spaces.* This is the basis for Goizueta's naming of "physical location, or space, as a theological category."

> In its fundamental sense, the *locus* of theology is the *physical, spatial, geographical place* of theological reflection. To walk with Jesus and with the poor is to walk *where* Jesus walks and *where* the poor walk. (191–92)

This includes naming the home, the city, and the church — where the first two domains meet in the life of poor Latinos, as Goizueta sees it — as the privileged places of the preferential option for the poor. Here Goizueta's version of the preferential option for the poor finds its truest register:

> To "opt for the poor" is thus to place ourselves *there,* to *accompany* the poor person in his or her life, death, and struggle for survival. A U.S. Hispanic theology will thus be preferentially... a *domestic, urban theology of accompaniment.* (Ibid.:192)

There is a striking effect written in this narrative, with its seemingly transgressive breaching of social boundaries in the name of solidarity with the poor, that is not evident without a close reading: Goizueta consistently envisages Christians moving into the *barrios* to stand with poor people (and against their plight). His version of the preferential option for the poor goes to *where the poor are.* On the other hand, the well-to-do are never urged to invite "the poor" to the suburbs, much less is there any mention of leveling class distinctions. In fact, the migration is from the "burbs" to the city:

An essential element of God's own identification with the poor is, thus, the transgression of the spatial, geographical boundaries which separate rich and poor in order to walk with the poor *where they walk* and live with the poor *where they live*. (Ibid.:201, emphasis added)

Not only does the migration go in only one direction, but the biblical authority for this *preferential migration to the poor* draws frequently on biblical narratives that are set in highly charged prophetic situations. That prophetic charge, however, is not cited in Goizueta's text to underscore his theological option. For example, Goizueta supports his reading by citing Mark 3, a story in which Jesus is shown shamelessly casting out demons, making contact with troubled people so far beyond the sanctions of his outcast-phobic society that he would be pursued by worried family members who wanted to restrain him.[13] What Goizueta does not read is that this narrative places Jesus *in his own home*. On the next page (Ibid.:202), Goizueta cites the passage in Matthew (22:2–14) of the rich man who gives an ill-fated banquet for guests, none of whom come. According to Goizueta, "the man instructs his servant to go *outside* to the streets and bring back [*inside*] those whom you happen to meet." Goizueta concludes by reading this passage, again, as an admonition to *go out* to the poor — but he does not draw on the next step of the narrative: that they should be brought back *into* the house of wealth or well-being.

Invitations to the Reign of God are extended randomly to whomever happens to be walking by, or standing around, or passing through.... We must be willing to walk out through the gate, out into the streets, for that is where we will find Lazarus. (Ibid.:202)

In our society it is not a scandal for a wealthy person to walk among the poor; according to the social code it is a privilege that is not shared in reciprocity by poor persons regarding the geographical

---

13. New Testament scholar L. William Countryman has traced what he calls the "purity" and "property" ethics that formed the foundation of the Hebrew *socius* of Jesus' times — ethics against which Jesus often preached. See Countryman, 1988.

spaces that the well-to-do are entitled by custom (and law enforcement) to inhabit. Goizueta states that because such boundaries are established to keep the poor in ghetto zones, away from the zones of comfort inhabited by the well-off, transgression must become part of any conscientious exercise of the preferential option for the poor. But Goizueta's strategy of transgression could be more radical with respect to the boundary that he claims must be breached: to truly breach the geographical boundary would be to bring poor people into the territories of the well-to-do, in effect, destroying (or surrendering) differentials of wealth and poverty.

> Jesus' life represented a threat to all those who would limit and impose an order, including a spatial and geographical order, on God's Reign. He was not crucified so much for what he did as for where he was; he "walked with" the wrong people and in the wrong places. That was enough to get him beaten up, enough to get him crucified. . . . To accompany the poor and the outcasts was to transgress the established and accepted boundaries which separate "us" from "them." Consequently, by walking with the poor, by accompanying the outcasts, Jesus put himself in the "wrong" place and was crucified as a result. He should have stayed in his proper place. To walk with Jesus is to walk with the wrong persons in the wrong places. To note that Jesus was not a political revolutionary is both to state the obvious and to miss the point; the fundamental political act is the act of transgressing boundaries, the act of walking and living with the outcast where he or she walks and lives. (Ibid.:203)

Because Goizueta has failed to attend to the prophetic situations marked by Jesus' divine outrage, he has overlooked a riskier, more transgressive "preferential option" for poor North American Latinos. First of all, the Scriptures present an image of Jesus as a humble man, not a wealthy, well-to-do person. A reading of the fiery sermons he gave in Jerusalem in the days before his crucifixion indicates that he was persecuted because he tried to bring his poor-people's Good News to the Jerusalem establishment (during the holiest season of the Jewish year, no less: the Passover). His real transgression was to bring before the powers of his time an attitude of protest against the prevailing structures of oppression and hypocrisy in his society. The "wrong place" that Jesus walked with his impoverished and outcast followers was not so much the geographical ghetto of poverty and marginality — in his case, Galilee and its environs — but Jerusalem: the capital of a Jewish world under Roman occupation. He brought his rabble before the powers and got into a lot of hot water.[14] Jesus was a prophet, and a daring and angry one at that, judging from the situations of his discourses and his high-and-mighty audiences.

Goizueta does not write of a different transgression: in which well-off persons would invite the poor into *their own homes* — and then undertake a prophetic march on the powers *right in the hallways of power*.[15] It is not a polite "dialog" with those we presume we can convert, though there may be strategically appropriate moments for such dialog, but a loud and unruly and confrontational protest *in the face* of those who benefit from oppression and social division. That is how Jesus' ministry might be an example of upholding a preferential option for the poor. But nowhere is this reverse transgression entertained in his text. On the contrary,

> If one takes seriously the concreteness and particularity of human praxis, and if one wants to walk with the poor, he or she must be willing to walk *where* poor persons walk. (Ibid.:203; emphasis in the original)

Theological Aesthetics and Latino Prophetics

In key aspects, then, Goizueta's preferential option for the poor overlooks much of the prophetic power that might be harnessed in the Latino experience: in its preference for dialog without sufficient attention to the tangled roots of social conflict; its failure to fathom the

---

14. The Gospel of Matthew, for example, is filled with examples of transgressive actions Jesus committed *in the domains of power, in Jerusalem,* in the days before he is arrested and crucified.

15. Martin Luther King Jr. had been planning a huge "poor people's march" on Washington at the time he was assassinated in 1968. This campaign was designed to extend the civil rights agenda beyond the quest for entrist political rights to seek economic rights for poor Southern blacks.

depths of racism that inhibit solidarity and fraternal dialogue; its one-way transgression of ghetto frontiers; its anemic appetite for activism; its sidelining of social theory and prophetic theological resources. This option for the poor offers up *accompaniment* as a response for Latino subalternity instead of the more confrontational form of struggle invoked by liberation theology a generation earlier.

That invocation has deep roots in the traditions animated by the ministry and fellowship around Jesus of Nazareth. Founder of a ragged reform movement within Roman-occupied Palestinian Judaism, Jesus was a prophet who held in thrall a band of un-exalted disciples. They were the ordinary people of society, and Jesus preached a gospel that spoke to their lives and their situations. He was not the sort of man who would have had to travel far from his bed to inhabit the margins, so his "preferential option for the poor" is decidedly different from Goizueta's. He was not content simply to *walk* to or among his people: though he preached in their synagogues — as well as in the Jerusalem temple — he offered little solace to those whose control of the lion's share of society's goods licensed them all the hypocrisy and piety in the world. Jesus was strident in calling for a love-centered praxis of social justice for poor people, ethnic others (Samaritans), prostitutes and other unseemly women (including widows), children (and orphans), the insane, the demon-ically possessed, the otherwise sick, and the outcast. By courageous and frequent example, he spoke outrage against the barbarity of poverty and stigmatization that his society had, more than *tolerated,* actually *ordained,* practically by religious decree. And in his parables we see the fabric of social reality as it would have been understood by those in places both low and high.

Sometimes he put his life on the line with the simple act of telling stories; for even in the simplest of narratives, Jesus showed an aston-ishing capacity for touching the raw nerve of his society's situation. In the Gospel of Luke, early in his ministry, Jesus returns to his hometown, Nazareth, after forty days of fasting in the wilderness. He enters the synagogue and is handed a scroll. He proceeds to read one of the most beautiful passages ever written as a religious scrip-ture, from Isaiah 61: "The Spirit of the Lord is upon me, because he has anointed me to bring good news to the poor. He has sent me to proclaim release to the captives and recovery of sight to the blind, to let the oppressed go free, to proclaim the year of the Lord's favor." He concludes his reading with the claim that this prophecy has been fulfilled right there in their midst, in his simple act of reading that Scripture. For Jesus the enunciation of justice is itself a graced transmission, and his reading performed its own prophetic fulfillment. That impression was not lost on his audience. But when they fell over themselves to congratulate Jesus, he reminded them that "no prophet is accepted in the prophet's hometown" (Luke 4:24). This seeming ingratitude enraged his erstwhile adorers, who proceeded to run him out of his hometown. Already in his inaugural acts, Jesus was performing prophetics in both senses of that term: crying out against injustice, and auguring a future-yet-to-come.

Jesus' readings could dishearten those who sincerely believed themselves to be ready for the burdens of discipleship.

> A certain ruler asked him, "Good Teacher, what must I do to inherit eternal life?" Jesus said to him, "Why do you call me good? No one is good but God alone. You know the commandments: You shall not commit adultery; You shall not murder; You shall not steal; You shall not bear false witness; Honor your father and mother.'" He replied, "I have kept all these since my youth." When Jesus heard this, he said to him, "There is still one thing lacking. Sell all that you own and distribute the money to the poor, and you will have treasure in heaven; then come, follow me." But when he heard this, he became sad; for he was very rich. (Luke 18:18–23)

The truth was strong medicine when prescribed through Jesus' words. And those who had a materially good life would not emerge unscathed. The prophetic demand for change was personal and political — and it was unrelenting. Indeed, Jesus' prophetic genius can be summed up in his capacity to deconstruct reassuring, but artificial, distinctions between the personal and the political. In his theology there is no room for claims that we are not responsible *in*, or *to*, or *because of* history.

Throughout his critique of liberation theology's notions of praxis and the preferential option for the poor, Goizueta subordinates the prophetic Christian admonition for social transformation to an aesthetics of empathic fusion and solidarity, through an option for the poor that makes the *site* of poverty the privileged locus. He admirably invokes a form of social transgression in which those who are well-off take themselves to the realms of poverty. He does not, however, urge the sort of political and social transgression that would make poverty a visible blight upon the polite hypocrisies of our world. That would involve a prophetics for which theological aesthetics seems inadequate because it has sidelined tools that might make a contemporary prophetics viable: the social sciences, and particularly history, sociology, and theories of the political economy.

If theology matters, it does so where its discourse activates the faith-intelligence of believers who are historically embedded, even if they do not *seem* to be politically engaged. Goizueta's reinscription of the prophetic options enunciated by liberation theology — the notions of "critical reflection on praxis" and the "preferential option for the poor" — becomes the foundation of Latino theology's "aesthetic turn." Yet this aesthetic turn does not equally take up liberation theology's prophetic risks. What is diluted in this transaction is the possibility that Latino theology and its theologians may become part of the cry of protest that must attend to the situation of Latinos in the United States, a people whose material condition is limited in formidable ways by structures of the U.S. political economy, and its labor markets, that all but guarantee them second-class citizenship.

Part Two

Rethinking
Critical Concepts
in Latino/a Religions

Chapter 5

Rethinking Mestizaje

Manuel A. Vásquez

According to Arturo Bañuelas (1995), *mestizaje* is "a core paradigm" in Latino history. Not surprisingly, *mestizaje* also occupies a central place in Latino theology, since the latter is a sustained reflection on that rich and evolving history. In this chapter, I discuss the continued relevance of the notion of *mestizaje* in the light of significant transformations in Latino communities. More specifically, I explore whether this notion helps make sense of the increasing diversity of Latino lives. Does *mestizaje* explain the power asymmetries that still exclude and divide many Latinos? Can it help us organize and mobilize resistance against domination?

I undertake this task not simply as an abstract exercise in a hermeneutics of suspicion, but in response to my location as a member of one of the "newer" Latino groups, often classified under the catch-all category of "Central and South Americans," a highly heterogenous category that includes people hailing from about twenty countries in the Americas. Besides the question of where new Latino groups fit in the growing Latino population, I am concerned about appropriations of the notion of *mestizaje* that silence difference. I grew up in El Salvador, a country where *mestizaje* is a dominant national ideology. One of my earliest memories is being told by my parents and elementary school teachers, all of whom considered themselves "good liberals," that "here there are no *indios*. They mixed with white Spaniards and so we are all *mestizos*. We are all Salvadorans." This ideology glosses over the fact that the modern Salvadoran *mestizo* nation was built on the violence of the 1932 *matanza,* in which more

I thank Anna Peterson and Brandt Peterson for their helpful comments.

than ten thousand Salvadoran peasants, many of them of indigenous descent, were massacred by the military (T. Anderson, 1992). Moreover, the ideology of *mestizaje* obscures persistent socio-economic and racial divisions in Salvadoran history that led to a bloody civil war in the 1980s.

While deeply concerned about the homogenizing dangers of the notion of *mestizaje*, I would also like to avoid an unqualified celebration of difference, which may end up "Balkanizing" Latino populations in the United States further, making it difficult to build emancipatory alliances among us and with other minorities. Difference can also serve as an ideology that resonates with neoliberal pluralism and consumerist individualism at the heart of the current episode of globalization. Thus, my task is not to jettison *mestizaje*, but to historicize and contextualize it, showing the interplay of lights and shadows that accompanies this notion. Throughout the history of the Americas, *mestizaje* has meant very different, often contradictory things: an "elite ideology, subaltern identity, historical process, and theoretically-licensed banner of resistance (to name a few)" (Hale, 1996a:3). One way to relativize *mestizaje* is by confronting it with its *otredad*, with its surplus, that which resists falling within its compass, not with aim of replacing one term for the other, but seeking to enrich and sharpen our approaches to the changing realities Latinos face in the United States.

Latinos and Their Evolving Communities

Post-1965 changes in U.S. immigration law, together with economic, political, and cultural processes associated with the current episode of globalization, have contributed to significant changes in the composition and patterns of settlement of Latino populations (Vásquez and Marquardt, 2003). Whether fleeing political repression and civil unrest, or dislocated by economic crises due to the implementation of neoliberal structural reforms, or in search of jobs in the expanding service and informal sectors of the U.S. economy, growing numbers of people from Central and South America have migrated north during the last three decades. As a result, while Mexican Americans, Puerto Ricans, and Cuban Americans are still the largest "national" groups among U.S. Latinos, the population of immigrants of Latin American descent in the United States has diversified considerably. According to the recent census, just between 1990 and 2000, Mexicans went from 60.4 percent to 58.5 percent of all Latinos, while Puerto Ricans went from 12.2 percent to 9.6 percent and Cubans from 4.7 percent to 3.5 percent. In the meantime, the category of "other Hispanics" grew from 22.8 percent to 28.4 percent (Guzmán, 2001). The table below shows the heterogeneity of U.S. Latino populations, particularly those labeled "other Hispanic" by the 2000 census.

These numbers belie the socio-economic and racial diversity within national categories. "Other Hispanics" include Honduran Garifunas, Dominicans and Colombians of African descent, indigenous groups

National Origin/Descent	Number	Percentage
Total Hispanic/Latino Population	35,305,818	100.0
Mexican	20,640,711	58.5
Puerto Rican	3,406,178	9.6
Cuban	1,241,685	3.5
Other Hispanic/Latino	10,017,244	28.4
Dominican	764,945	2.2
Central American	1,686,937	4.8
Costa Rican	68,588	0.2
Guatemalan	372,487	1.1
Honduran	217,569	0.6
Nicaraguan	177,684	0.5
Panamanian	91,723	0.3
Salvadoran	655,165	1.9
Other Central American	103,721	0.3
South American	1,353,562	3.8
Argentinean	100,864	0.3
Bolivian	42,068	0.1
Chilean	68,849	0.2
Colombian	470,684	1.3
Ecuadorian	260,559	0.7
Paraguayan	8,769	0.0
Peruvian	233,926	0.7
Uruguayan	18,804	0.1
Venezuelan	91,507	0.3
Other South American	57,532	0.2

This table is adapted from Suárez-Orozco and Páez, 2002.

like Guatemalan Maya K'iches, Ecuadorian Quechuas, and Bolivian Aymaras, as well as upper-middle-class, white, urban, and professional Peruvians, Argentinians, and Brazilians, many of whom overstayed their tourist visas in the face of deteriorating economic situations in their countries.

In the meantime, Latino groups with a longer history of presence in the United States have also shown increasing differentiation. The case of Cubans is well known. Following the generally affluent, well-educated, and white Cubans who immigrated in the wake of the revolution in 1959, we have seen multiple migratory waves, including the "Marielitos" in the 1980s, with increasing numbers of working-class and Afro-Cuban persons. These later waves have not always been well received by and incorporated into established Cuban communities in Miami or Union City, New Jersey (Portes and Stepick, 1994). In a study that I have been co-directing, we have found also increasing heterogeneity among Mexican farm workers in Florida.[1] In addition to differentials of salaries and job opportunities based on time of arrival, with long established Chicanos serving as the crew leaders while recently arrived Mexicans work for low wages and no benefits, we have seen the increasing presence of Mexicans of indigenous descent, particularly from Oaxaca and Chiapas.

Demographic heterogeneity is matched by an increasingly pluralistic religious field among Latinos. In their preliminary report on Hispanic churches and public life, Espinosa, Elizondo, and Miranda found that 70 percent of Latinos are Catholic, a number that has held steady despite prognostications that in less than three decades only half of all Latinos would self-identify as Catholics (Greeley, 1988, 1997). According to Espinosa, Elizondo, and Miranda, the influx into the United States of large numbers of Latin American Catholics, particularly from Mexico, which is still overwhelmingly Catholic, has balanced Protestant growth. However, the authors of the report observed that "the percentage of Latino Catholics drops from 74 percent among the first generation to 72 and 62 percent among second and third generations. The percentage of Latino Protestants and other Christians simultaneously increases from less than one in

---

1. See *www.latam.ufl.edu/fordproject/*.

six (15 percent) among the first generation to one in five (20 percent) and almost one in three (29 percent) among second and third generations" (Espinosa, Elizondo, and Miranda, 2003:15). There are other trends that add complexity to religious practices and affiliations among Latinos: the significant presence of "other Christians" like Jehovah's Witnesses and Mormons, the revitalization of indigenous traditions, the simultaneous re-Africanization and mainstreaming of African-based religions, particularly of Santería, the renewed interest in spiritism and *curanderismo*, the large percentage of born-again Evangelicals among Protestants, and the rapid growth of Charismatic Catholicism.

Heterogeneity among Latino populations is enhanced by the emergence of transnational social fields (see Basch, Glick Schiller, and Szanton Blanc, 1994, and Levitt, DeWind, and Vertovec, 2003). Using some of the same advances in communication and transportation technologies that have propelled the current episode of globalization (e.g., cheap phone calls and travel and the Internet), many Latino immigrants maintain close ties with their societies of origin, often building dense networks of exchange and reciprocity, while, at the same time, establishing stable connections in the United States. This multiple embeddedness in fields of thought and practice that span national borders represents an attempt by Latino migrants to adapt and respond creatively to the dislocation generated by economic globalization and to the effort of nation-states to control and police populations, even as they open their borders to an expanding neoliberal capitalism. Multiple embeddedness contributes to fragmented and hybrid identities among Latinos. On the one hand, by allowing people to maintain ties with the societies of origin, transnational linkages lend support to the affirmation of national, regional, and even local (village level) identities. In the religious field, this is illustrated by the proliferation throughout Latino communities of *fiestas* honoring local patron saints, which are often organized by hometown associations working in close connection with *cofradías* and *hermandades* in Latin America (Ruiz Baia, 1999). On the other hand, multiple embeddedness may lead to transculturation, the mixing of various ideas and practices across the transnational networks (Nederveen Pieterse, 2004). Thus, we have transnational youth gangs, like the

Mara Salvatrucha, which undergo a process of *choloization,* adopting some of the language and practices of long-established Mexican American gangs in Los Angeles and blending them with elements of Salvadoran and Guatemalan culture (Vásquez and Marquardt, 2003).

Often affirmation of particularistic and hybrid identities occurs simultaneously, as when Latinos affirm their national identities and in the same breath declare themselves to be part of a pan-Latino culture standing at the margins of a world dominated by Euroamericans. This simultaneous affirmation is undoubtedly a source of great cultural creativity in our communities. A clear example is the way in which Latinos are challenging the Census Bureau's attempt to categorize them within the bipolar racial model still dominant in the United States. In the 1980s, 58 percent of Hispanics identified themselves as white. In contrast, in 2000 only 48 percent self-identified as white. During the same period the percentage of Hispanics who identified themselves as neither white nor black, but as being of some other race or of more than one race grew from 38 percent to 49 percent.[2] However, fluid identities are a double-edged sword. They also demonstrate the tensions of being Latino in the United States, of leading transnational lives in a nation-state which, especially after September 11, has become ever more invested in patrolling its borders and in ensuring the uncritical patriotism of residents and citizens.

In addition to the diversifying composition of U.S. Latino populations and their increasing embeddedness in transnational circuits, new patterns of settlement have emerged. The Latino population is still predominantly urban, concentrating in large "gateway" cities in six states, including California, Texas, New York, Florida, New

---

2. See Mireya Navarro, "Going Beyond Black and White, Hispanics in Census Pick 'Other,'" *New York Times,* November 9, 2003. According to Navarro, 97 percent of those who marked the category "some other race" in the census where Latino. Many of these respondents wrote in next to the category "such disparate identities as Mayan, Tejano, and mestizo." Other responses included "indio," "mulato," and "jabao." Clearly, Latinos are destabilizing the U.S. racial formation, which predicated on juridical and spatial segregation. However, we should be careful not to overstate the destabilizing force of Latino identities. Only 2 percent of Hispanic respondents chose the category black, indicating among other things the stigma still attached to negritude. Here Hispanics seem to have assimilated the prejudices of the larger culture.

Jersey, and Illinois. However, due to the decline of the manufactur-
ing sector, which was has been the traditional anchor of social and
cultural life for immigrant groups in cities like New York and Chicago, and to the expansion of the service sector, some of the fastest
growing Latino populations are now in nontraditional states in the
Midwest and the South, including Iowa, Nebraska, Georgia, North
Carolina, and Kentucky (Vásquez and Marquardt, 2003; Zúñiga and
Hernández-León, 2005). This shift is intensified by the growth of
transnational agricultural and food industries that require abundant
and cheap labor.

In terms of the cartography of Latino presence in the United States,
the rule of thumb used to be: Cubans in Florida and New Jersey, Mexicans in California, the Southwest, and Chicago and its surrounding
rust belt, and Puerto Ricans and other Caribbeans in the Northeast, especially in New York and Philadelphia. While this rule has
always been purely heuristic, there are increasing exceptions to it.
For example, Mexicans are the fastest growing Latino population in
New York City, numbering now anywhere from 250,000 to 400,000,
while Puerto Ricans continue to migrate to Florida or return to the
island. Cities like Houston and Los Angeles now have large numbers of Guatemalans and Salvadorans, while in Miami, Nicaraguans,
Peruvians, Ecuadorians, and Colombians have a visible presence.

Now more than ever, the picture of U.S. Latinos as a fairly homoge-
nous, Catholic, Spanish-speaking urban population is misleading.
What does this increasing diversity and complexity of Latino lives
mean for Latino/a theologies, theologies that, as Ada María Isasi-Díaz
tells us, are concerned with *lo cotidiano,* the daily experiences and
struggles of our communities? Can the concept of *mestizaje* reflect
and respond to the evolving nature of U.S. Latino life?

Mestizaje in Latino/a Theologies

Debates about *mestizaje* are not new. Arguably, they go back at least
to the conquest and the colonial period. This is illustrated by the
hold of *La Malinche (Malintzin)* on the Mexican national imagination. This Aztec woman of royal lineage, who was sold in bondage
to Cortés and acted as his translator, has been commonly thought of

as the mother of a new, mixed people, born out of a violent and illicit sexual encounter.[3] *La Malinche*, the mistress, is often counterposed to Our Lady of Guadalupe, who according to legend appeared to native Juan Diego at Tepeyac Hill (an ancient pilgrimage site to a goddess of fertility) dressed in indigenous grab and speaking Nahuatl. If *La Malinche* functions as the contested metaphor for the biological genesis of *mestizos,* the Virgin of Guadalupe, in blending the religions of the conquered and conqueror, represents their spiritual mother. While interpretations of *La Malinche* and *La Guadalupana* have varied through the centuries, the point is clear: *mestizaje,* with all its contradictions, has been from the outset a unifying thread in debates about identity and power in the Americas (De Castro, 2002:21).

It is impossible to provide a detailed account of the multiple appropriations of *mestizaje* here. Thus, I would like to focus on some of the key ways in which Latino/a theologians have used the notion of *mestizaje.* I will then bring these uses into conversation with the emerging anthropological and historical literature on *mestizaje.* In Latino/a theology, there is no better place to start than with Virgilio Elizondo's *Galilean Journey* (1983), a ground-breaking synthesis of post–Vatican II liberationist themes and a long "cultural-aesthetic" tradition of Latin American and Latino thought, powerfully exemplified by José Vasconcelos.

The influence of liberation theology on Elizondo is clear. Like Gustavo Gutiérrez, for example, he takes the experiences of those on the underside of history as the new productive locus for theological reflection and pastoral action. And like Gutiérrez, Elizondo seeks to transcend the abstract humanism of progressive European theologies, addressing specifically the historical plight of those at the margins of society. While Latin American liberation theology has always been interested in popular culture and religion, it has tended to concentrate on the dehumanizing socio-political situation experienced by poor people in the region. This has been a logical response to Latin

---

3. For the most influential contemporary reading of *La Malinche,* see Paz (1959). Cypress (1991) argues that the identification of *Malinche* as traitor to her people only emerged in the nineteenth century, as the Mexican nation was in the process of consolidation. Chicana writer Gloria Anzaldúa (1987) offers a more positive reading of *Malinche,* drawing from her own location of double marginality, as an immigrant of a subaltern race and as a woman. This double marginality allows *La Malinche* to serve as the empathetic translator between cultures.

America's long history of economic dependency vis-à-vis the United States and other colonial/imperial powers and to the ever present reality of deep class divisions and repressive totalitarian regimes in the hemisphere. In contrast, Elizondo's theology, while recognizing the destructive power of economic injustice and political exclusion, has focused more on the symbolic and racial violence faced by Latinos in the United States. This, again, is a natural response to the omnipresence of racial segregation and discrimination against people of color throughout American history, as well as the dominant role of the politics of recognition in the construction and mobilization of collective identities in the United States. This politics of recognition has consistently obscured its linkages with class struggles.

To be able to address symbolic and racial violence, Elizondo has placed *mestizaje* at the center of his theology. Here Elizondo's work strongly resonates with José Vasconcelos's *La Raza Cósmica*.[4] In this work, Vasconcelos argues that humanity is in the midst of an evolutionary process that is taking it from a materialistic era, primarily defined by sensory perception and the fulfillment of physical needs, through an intellectual/political epoch ruled by modern rationality and formal ethics, toward a spiritual/aesthetic era characterized by the exercise of expressive creativity and mystical enjoyment of beauty and passions like joy and love. This evolution is played out in four successive "racial trunks: the Black, the Indian, the Mongol, and the White." Each of these races has dominated different periods of human history, seeking to carry out its specific mission and, in the process, thinking of itself as the fulfillment of the progress of human consciousness. According to Vasconcelos,

> the white race, after organizing itself in Europe, has become the invader of the world, and has considered itself destined to rule, as did each of the previous races during their time of power. It is clear that domination by the whites will also be temporary, but

---

4. Elizondo does not refer directly to Vasconcelos in his discussion of *mestizaje*. Vasconcelos does not even appear in the bibliography in *Galilean Journey*. However, at several points in his work Elizondo writes about *la raza cósmica* to characterize a *mestizo* future. What we have here is a case of "family resemblances," as philosopher Ludwig Wittgenstein would put it, where conceptual clusters like *mestizaje*, cosmic race, and Aztlán are shared but expressed in different ways by those influenced by Chicano thinking and politics (Guerrero, 1987).

their mission is to serve as a bridge. The white race has brought the world to a state in which all human types and cultures will be able to fuse with each other. The civilization developed and organized in our times by the whites has set the moral and material basis for the union of all men into a fifth universal race, the fruit of all the previous ones and amelioration of everything past. (1997:9)

This new "cosmic race" is the *mestizo* race developing in Ibero-America out of the "fusion and mixing of all people." In the creation of this race the "Indian has no other door to the future but the door of modern culture, nor any road but the road already cleared by Latin civilization." For his part, the "white man," "having fulfilled [his] destiny of mechanizing the world...will have to depose his pride and look for progress and ulterior redemption in the souls of his brothers from other castes" (Ibid.:16). In other words, the mission of the cosmic race is to redeem humanity, drawing from its hybrid vigor and multiplicity to usher in the spiritual/aesthetic era. Addressing the Hispanic world, Vasconcelos writes: "a sensitive and ample heart will be taking shape within us; a heart that embraces and contains everything and is moved with sympathy, but, full of vigor, imposes new law upon the world" (Ibid.:22). The fifth *mestizo* era will thus be one of fullness, understanding, and reconciliation.

The extent of Vasconcelos's racism is a matter of intense debate. His thought has far more in common with Romantic notions of the *Volk* and Herder's and Hegel's philosophies of the evolution of human consciousness and civilization than with the pseudoscientific theories of eugenics dominant in the early 1900s. Vasconcelos was interested in elevating humanity through a narrative of racial inclusion, assimilation, and unity, not in creating hierarchies that exclude certain races by virtue of their phenotypes or mental capacities. Nevertheless, there is in Vasconcelos's work a precarious "slippage back and forth between culture and race," which is characteristic of the uses of *mestizaje* in the texts of his time (De Castro, 2002:20).

When approaching *mestizaje,* Elizondo stresses the cultural and religious angle even more strongly, thereby avoiding the most dangerous implications of Vasconcelos's racial essentialism. Nevertheless,

Elizondo shares with Vasconcelos the idea that the *mestizo* is a new creative universal subject. Elizondo defines *mestizaje* as the painful but hopeful process whereby "a new people, a new ethnos — *la raza mestiza* ('mixed clan, family,' or 'race')" was born out of the encounter of "two disparate parent peoples." This birth is marked most powerfully by the apparition at Tepeyac, for Our Lady of Guadalupe stands not just for the emergence of a new American Christianity, but is the "symbol of a new creation." "She is the new woman from whom the new humanity will be born, *la raza cósmica de las Americas*. She is herself the prototype of the new creation. She is *la Mestiza*. She combines opposing forces so that in a creative way new life, not destruction, will emerge. On December 12 is celebrated the beginning of the new human-divine adventure" (Elizondo, 1983:43–44). For Elizondo, *mestizaje* thus carries a powerful liberatory impulse, despite its tragic origin. *Mestizaje*, he tells us, "is feared by established groups because it is the deepest threat to all humanly made barriers of separation that consecrate oppression and exploitation. It is a threat to the security of ultimate belonging — that is, to the inherited national/cultural identity that clearly and ultimately defines who I am to myself and to the world" (Ibid.:18). Because *mestizos* cannot be reduced to the groups that begat them, and yet, because they carry elements of the parent cultures, they are "outsider-insiders," capable of both "objective distance" and "intimacy." This "in-out" existence, what Elizondo characterizes as an "unfinished identity," gives Latinos a great creative potential.

Moreover, Elizondo sees *mestizaje* not just as a widespread phenomenon in human history, challenging the obsession with purity and assimilation among dominant groups. For him, *mestizaje* is not just emancipatory but clearly eschatological, an essential constituent of Jesus Christ's salvific work. For Jesus, the Galilean, was himself *mestizo*, laboring at a crossroads of peoples and cultures at the margins of the empire to build a new, inclusive reign of God. In Jesus, "God becomes not just a human being, but the marginated, shamed, and rejected of the world. He comes to initiate a new human unity, but the all-important starting point is among the most segregated and impure of the world. Because the world expected nothing good to come out of Galilee, God chose it to be the starting point of God's human presence among us. The principle behind the cultural image of the Galilean identity is that God chooses what the world rejects. What is marginal to the world is central to God" (Elizondo, 1995:19). By crossing the most insurmountable borders "between the eternal and the temporal, between the divine and the human," Jesus affirms the Christian "conviction that a universal human family is truly possible and desirable, one that transcends the blood and ethnic bonds which usually identify and divide us" (Elizondo, 2000:180).

By reading *mestizaje* through the lenses of liberationist Christianity, Elizondo has gone beyond Vasconcelos's provincial, nationalist perspective. For Elizondo, *mestizaje* is not the inalienable property of Ibero-American civilizations or any other ethnic or national group, but the core of humanity itself. "When we look at the history of humanity, we quickly discover that throughout history there have been migrations, *mestizajes,* and new identities. As new groups forge their geographical-social identity, they tend to forget their ancient origins. Immigrations, *mestizajes,* and new identities are as old as the planet itself and as natural as life itself but they are feared worse than hell itself" (Ibid.:177). The present episode of globalization, with its drastic time-space compression, only makes us more aware of the ubiquity and power of *mestizaje.* "The term mestizo, originally used in Latin America to categorize the children of Native American and European parents, is now being applied to any person of racially or ethnically mixed origins" (Ibid.: ix). It is in this sense that the future is *mestizo,* for in the "*mestizo* peoples of the world, the new identity of the Third Millennium is beginning to emerge and proclaim its presence" (Ibid.:179).

This is an extremely sketchy account of Elizondo's compelling reading of *mestizaje.* A fuller discussion would have to explore in detail the connection *mestizaje* has with themes such as sin, popular devotions, ecclesiology, and the experience of God, as part of Elizondo's complex theology. Nevertheless, this account allows us to get a sense of Elizondo's innovative appropriation of *mestizaje* and the powerful effect this appropriation has had on subsequent generations of Latino/a theologians. In *Caminemos con Jesús,* for example, Roberto Goizueta highlights the aesthetic, ludic, and performative aspects of Latino Christianity, arguing very effectively that they provide a powerful critique of the excessive rationalism, instrumentalism, and individualism of Enlightenment-based rationality. *Mestizaje's* in-betweenness challenges the arbitrary but power-laden Cartesian dichotomies (between mind and body, between thought and praxis, between the self and the other) at the heart of Western modernity. Moreover, "popular Catholicism — and U.S. Hispanic culture in general — presupposes an integral, holistic, and organic anthropology" that bridges the dichotomy between modernity's obsession with reason and unchanging foundations and postmodernity's "idealization of irrationality," its celebration of ambiguity and undecidability (Goizueta, 1995:140–51).

Ada María Isasi-Díaz, for her part, introduces *mulatez* in full force, rightfully acknowledging the great contributions that Africans forcibly brought during the slave trade have made to racial, cultural, and religious mixing in the Americas. These contributions have been particularly prominent in what Paul Gilroy (1993) calls the "black Atlantic," an intercultural and transnational formation that included countries as diverse as Brazil, Cuba, the Dominican Republic, Colombia, Nicaragua, and the United States. In the next chapter, Miguel De La Torre explores in greater detail the concept of *mulatez*. Isasi-Díaz also grounds the notion of *mestizaje* more tightly in daily lived experience, *lo cotidiano,* particularly as it concerns the struggles of Latinas to survive, "to earn money to feed and clothe their children and to keep a roof over their heads" (1996:68). These struggles are made more difficult by the sexism, racism, and class oppression that penetrate every aspect of social life (Ibid.:92). This is why Isasi-Díaz builds her *mujerista* theology in conversation with ethnographic approaches to the shared day-to-day experiences of Latinas. "Using ethnographic principles, *mujerista* theology presents the understandings and opinions of Hispanic women, as much as possible, in their own words" (Ibid.:179).

By bringing in gender, Isasi-Díaz also enriches and broadens the notion of *mestizaje,* seeing it as a "new way of valuing and embracing diversity and difference." She writes in her *Mujerista Theology,* "for us differences are not something to be done away with but rather

something to be embraced. In our theology we do not aim at assimilation, at making all that is different fit into a preconceived norm
or center" (Ibid.:80). She continues, "Usually in mainline discourse,
in traditional theological discourse, difference is defined as absolute
otherness, mutual exclusion, categorical opposition. This is an essentialist meaning of difference in which one group serves as the
norm against which all others are measured" (Ibid.). "In *mujerista*
theology difference... means not otherness or exclusive opposition
but specificity and heterogeneity. Difference is understood as relational rather than as a matter of substantive categories or attributes"
(Ibid.:81). According to Isasi-Díaz, *mestizaje* operates with an "ontology that emphasizes non-opposition and non-exclusion," which
"de-centers" us, allowing us to see the "partiality of all human perspectives and... [admit] others' point of view as a possible corrective
lense to our own" (2001a:164). Thus, *mestizaje* does not homogenize or normalize (creating a deviant Other that is then rejected),
but makes possible an "empathic fusion" with others. It generates a
condition of "world-traveling" and intersubjectivity that allows us to
build mutuality and solidarity (Isasi-Díaz, 2001b:208–9, 216–17).

Placing *mestizaje* at the center of Latino history and theology and
defining it as essentially liberatory and eschatological, undeniably
carries positive effects for Latino communities. Privileging *mestizaje*
enables Latinos to challenge modern Western social epistemology,
particularly taken-for-granted Euro-dominant notions of racial purity
and segregation. It also helps Latinos recover and celebrate the richness of their religious and cultural resources. "We can drink from our
own wells," in Gustavo Gutiérrez's phrase. For what was considered
impure and primitive is now seen in a new light as transformative, a
signpost for the coming reign of God. Latinos can then "name their
reality," in Paulo Freire's words, reappropriating their long devalued
traditions, including those that come from the experiences of women,
Native Americans, and people of African descent, to build prophetic
voices that challenge the exclusionary status quo.

The alternative spaces of resistance and utopia opened up by *mestizaje* do not have to be restricted to Latinos. They can serve as
incubators and models for truly multicultural and multiracial national and transnational civil societies. As Elizondo writes, "From

the old and separate ethnic and racial ghettos of the United States is arising a new phoenix, the new human person in whose very body and soul are contained the blood and spirit of every human race upon the earth. A new humanity is emerging. This universal mestizaje is a natural product of the society started by the founders of this country who postulated as a foundation stone of this new government that all are created equal!" (Elizondo, 2002:ix). Universal *mestizaje* opens the possibility of the coming of a *"mestizo democracy"* that transcends the either/or of the American *unum vs. pluribus*. As Burke (2002) notes, democratic thinking in the United States has been caught in the dichotomous struggle between assimilationists fixated on *unum* and separatists obsessed with *pluribus*. Assimilationists insist on the timeless value of the melting pot, where immigrants shed their previous histories and cultures to blend in a shared American culture that holds them together as a moral and national community. However, acceptance of this shared American culture has meant the internalization of a hegemonic Protestant Anglo-Saxon worldview. To the extent that immigrant cultures persist, it is only as light flavoring to the dominant culture. On the other side of the coin, separatists affirm the distinctiveness of groups that have made up the American experiment, as well as their right to voice and political enfranchisement. However, this affirmation comes at the cost of an impoverished and ahistorical view of cultures as static and self-contained wholes, not open to transcultural creativity and exploration. Culture becomes a possession and enclave, opening the door to exclusionary politics. Thus neither assimilationism nor separatism is truly democratic. Drawing from Elizondo and other Latino thinkers, Burke argues for a *mestizo* democracy as an alternative model that recognizes and values the distinctiveness of each culture but allows for "multicultural interaction," for the construction of truly dialogical, intersubjective public spaces. *Mestizaje* points to a "unity-in-diversity" that transcends the dichotomies between universality and particularity and between communitarian conformity/uniformity and individual difference/identity.

The notion of *mestizaje* also complements a growing literature on postcolonialism, which focuses on hybridity as a way to highlight the contradictory legacy of Western colonialism and imperialism for both metropolitan and colonial subjects (García Canclini, 1995). In the process, the teleological narrative that places the West as the universal source and paragon of civilization is destabilized. According to Homi Bhabha,

> Strategies of hybridization reveal an estranging movement in the "authoritative," even authoritarian inscription of the cultural sign. At the point at which the precept attempts to objectify itself as a generalized knowledge or a normalizing, hegemonic practice, the hybrid strategy or discourse opens up a space of negotiation where power is unequal but its articulation may be equivocal. Such negotiation is neither assimilation nor collaboration. It makes possible the emergence of an "interstitial" agency that refuses the binary representation of social antagonism. Hybrid agencies find their voice in a dialectic that does not seek cultural supremacy or sovereignty. They deploy the partial culture from which they emerge to construct visions of community, and versions of history and memory, that give narrative form to the minority position they occupy; the outside of the inside: the part in the whole. (1996:58)

Bhabha's text shows that hybridity and *mestizaje* are powerful critical tools that Latino theologians and religious scholars do well to keep in their arsenal. But what are we to make of the late Peruvian literary scholar Antonio Cornejo Polar and his pointed indictment of *mestizaje*? According to him, despite the tradition and prestige of the concept of *mestizaje* in Latin America, "it falsifies in the most drastic manner the condition of our culture and literature. It offers harmonic images of what is obviously fragmented and agonistic [*desgajado y beligerante*], proposing figurations that in the end are only pertinent to those for whom it is useful to imagine our societies as smooth and conflict-free spaces of coexistence" (Cornejo Polar, 2002:867). Anthropologist Jorge Klor de Alva is even more explicit, calling *mestizaje* a "foil" and "fetish" articulated by the *criollo* elites "as the fissuring of Spanish America into separate countries led to growing micropatriotism." In this context, *mestizaje* homogenized "ethnically and politically distinct native peoples . . . into 'Indians' and mercilessly transformed [them] into Spanish subjects." *Mestizaje* functioned as the nation-building myth that has helped link dark to light-skinned hybrids and Euro-Americans, often in opposition to both foreigners and the indigenous "others" in their midst. And it has been effectively used to promote national amnesia about or to salve the national conscience in what concerns the dismal past and still colonized condition of most indigenous peoples of Latin America. (1995:256–57)

The Trouble with Mestizaje

Like any other theoretical concept or political category, *mestizaje* is not exempt from contradictions and limitations. The historical record offers ample evidence of the deployment of *mestizaje* as a functionalist ideology, a homogenizing and reductive discourse that elites in post-independence Latin America used to "imagine community," to construct territorialized nation-states out of the disparate populations that inhabited the colonial world. The case of Nicaragua is instructive on this point. In *To Die in This Way,* historian Jeffrey Gould (1998:10) analyzes the process of "ladinoization" involved in the creation of a modern Nicaraguan nation.[5] This process included, on the one hand, the use of symbolic violence through "an array of friendly and antagonistic interventions in the indigenous communities by the church, the state, political parties, local intellectuals, and landed elites" which "discredited indigenous identity, exacerbated cultural alienation, and enhanced the elites' claim to rule the nation." On the other hand, the process involved "real violence," including land expropriation and coerced labor. In Gould's estimation, "the birth of *mestizaje* [as a national discourse in Nicaragua] and the demise of the indigenous communities were closely interconnected."

On a local level, ladino elites phrased their struggles against the Comunidades indígenas in a language that would gain national support. They called upon democratic notions of citizenship and

5. According to Grandin (2000:238–39), during colonial times in the Spanish Americas, the term *ladino* referred to "baptized or Hispanized Indians." Eventually, the term acquired a class dimension. Now non-Indian urban elites use it to refer to poor peasant and migrant workers in the city, of both indigenous and non-indigenous decent. In Guatemala, *ladino* came to mean non-Indians, Mestizos, Creoles, and Spaniards included.

equal rights to question the legitimacy of the Comunidades and their claims to land. Their political success hinged to an important degree on their appropriation and creation of those key elements of the emerging national political discourse. Equally important was their questioning of the authenticity of the indigenous organizations that had become the "hard" border within which its members reproduced their identities. In every significant legal battle with the Comunidades, the denigration of indigenous authenticity was the most powerful weapon in the ladino discursive arsenal, one that facilitated their use of state repression against their adversaries. (Ibid.:285)

This could not be farther from the ideal of *mestizo* democracy presented by Elizondo and Burke. What we have here is the intertwining of the discourses of *mestizaje* and liberal democracy in order to legitimize the destruction of the indigenous Other, those at the margins of post-national Latin American societies. Like the Orientalism that Edward Said describes, the erasure of the Other, its emptying out, also involved a projection of the colonizer's desires and fantasies. In Nicaragua, Gould documents genderizing strategies that accompanied ladinoization. Intellectual elites constructed "virile images of pre-Hispanic Indian warriors, while simultaneously "feminizing" contemporary indigenous males, "presenting visions of cowed, effeminate indigenous males that could only be redeemed through mestizo progress" (Ibid.:161). We have already seen this "engendering" at work in Vasconcelos's affirmation of the virility of the Spaniard which elevates the primitive meekness of the noble savage to the next civilization level. Gould points out that the gender dimension of the discourse of *mestizaje* in Nicaragua extended all the way to César Augusto Sandino's *indohispanismo*, the forging of a mixed race that he felt could resist repeated U.S. interventions. The Sandinistas certainly used this anti-imperialist discourse effectively to mobilize the nation against the Reagan administration's destructive and illicit Contra War. This discourse of *mestizo* national liberation, however, exacted a high price for the Sandinistas, blinding them to Miskito and other local claims to recognition and autonomy. The point here is that in Nicaragua *mestizaje* led not to gender empowerment, as *mujerista* theologians might expect, but to the disciplining of local populations under essentialized gender categories where male = power = mestizo = progress = nation, and women = impotence = Indian = primitive = tribe.

Perhaps the misuse of *mestizaje* occurred only in the past. Perhaps now, in the wake of postmodern and postcolonial critiques of hegemonic narratives of nation, and facing growing transnational and global processes, it may be possible to advocate an emancipatory reading of *mestizaje*. Yet, recent events in Guatemala compel us to be cautious. According to anthropologist Charles Hale, just as a pan-Mayan movement began to gather steam in the mid-1980s, "decoupling the association of 'ladino' with 'Guatemalan,' reinscrib[ing] ladinos as one 'people' among many, and contrast[ing] self-assured Maya identity with the *ningunidad* of being ladino," ladino intellectuals began to draw on the discourse of *mestizaje* to ridicule and delegitimize what they referred to as "Maya fundamentalism" (1996a:43; see also Warren, 1998:41).[6] Responding to the imagined threat of "the insurrectionary Indian," Guatemalan ladino intellectuals have sought to discredit the Maya movement by showing its naive obsession with racial/ethnic essentialism and by affirming that the movement has no local referents. For example, Estuardo Zapeta wrote in 1994:

> Our [i.e., Mayan] discourse is a recycling of European neo-leftist ideas, patched together with gringo environmentalism, and seasoned with Latin American defeatism.... With false claims of purity we are creating closed communities at a time when throughout the world one only hears talk of openness. We have not yet come to understand that the pure does not exist. The purity of our culture is its continuous transformation. (Quoted in Hale, 1998:300)

Often ladino critiques of the Maya movement are presented in the language that mimics progressive theorists of postcolonialism and globalization, such as Homi Bhabha, Arjun Appadurai, and Néstor

---

6. *Ningunidad* literally means "nobodiness," which is the term that Gúzman-Bockler (1975) associated with *ladino* identity. Ladino identity is essentially empty and negative, defined against that which it is not.

García-Canclini. A case in point is journalist and literary scholar Mario Roberto Morales, who studied at the University of Pittsburgh, where he was associated with the Subaltern Studies group. "With a lively cynical postmodern tone, Morales employs images of globalized popular culture, hybridity, mimesis, culturally fabricated otherness and *mestizaje* to argue against the existence of 'the Maya' in Guatemala" (Warren, 1998:42). For example, Morales writes: "Evidence indicates that what is dominant now are hybrid identities — impure (Indians with Reeboks or Pierre Cardin, depending on whether they work washing cars or for international organizations), negotiable, plural, and mediated by the laws of the market" (Morales, 1996, quoted in Warren, 1998:42). Or more explicitly: "It is obvious, then, that the cultural policies of a multicultural country, and especially a cultural hybrid country, should have as their central theme, not cultural 'purism' but rather, mestizaje. At the same time, these policies should provide the impulse for a deepening of this mestizaje, such that in this country's future there will be no Indians or ladinos, but only Guatemalans" (Morales, 1993, quoted in Hale, 1998:301).

The net result of these critiques of the pan-Maya movement is to prevent any debate on the persistent racism and political and economic exclusion that indigenous people in Guatemala suffer at the hands of *ladinos*. In this case, the discourse of *mestizaje* does not open but rather closes spaces where collective identities and rights at the margins can be affirmed.

When the term mestizo is applied specifically to Maya identity and politics — even shorn of assimilationist intent — the consequences become deeply ambiguous. They entail both an important constructive critique of Maya essentialism, and a thinly veiled threat of delegitimation. The unintended consequences of Maya cultural activism add to this ambiguity. In comparison to a decade ago, Maya people, especially when they acquire money and education, move with much greater ease between the the Indian and ladino worlds. The discourse of mestizaje, by reinforcing [a] broadened space of ethnic indeterminacy, threatens to blur the message of Maya cultural activism, and to undermine the movement's ability to forge a unified front of support. (Hale, 1996b:48–49)

According to Hale, the ambiguous impact of the discourse of *mestizaje* on the Maya movement is in large part due to the fact that this discourse "may not travel well." "Analysis inspired by theories of 'hybridity' and its close affine 'mestizaje' have traveled widely, informing all sorts of quasi-universal theories of identity and subjectivity, setting ambitious theoretical agendas for conference and edited volumes, and lending support to a disturbingly wide range of political projects. My own 'travel warning,' then, is against any theory of 'hybrid' identity politics that is not grounded in militant particularism" (1998:303).

I do not quite agree with Hale that the solution to the contradictions in the narratives of *mestizaje* lies in simply grounding these narratives in "an active engagement with the politics of a particular place, time, and people." While I applaud his decision to position himself as a committed intellectual among indigenous peoples in Central America, grounding oneself in a particular place, time, and people does not guarantee that one's theoretical discourses and politics will be progressive. Moreover, privileging "theoretically informed particularity" runs the risk of reinscribing anthropology's often decontextualized localism. Nevertheless, Hale is correct in challenging unreflective attempts to universalize *mestizaje* as the next emancipatory narrative. And I believe that some Latino/a theologians come close to engaging in this type of universalizing in their efforts to blend Christian eschatology with *mestizaje*. As a result, they present *mestizaje* as the inescapable condition and future of a redeemed humanity. This excessively sanguine use of *mestizaje* leaves itself open to surreptitious drives toward totalization and homogenization, no matter how much "in-betweenness" and "border-crossing" are celebrated. *Mestizaje* can continue as a viable metaphor only if this cluster of discourses is historicized, contextualized, and relativized, that is, confronted at all times with the otherness that it contains and fails to contain. *Mestizaje,* like globalization, can only provide a contingent, fallible tool box with which to think about and act in the face of complexity.

Moreover, *mestizaje* is intertwined with globalization in trouble-some ways. As Appadurai (1996) and Nederveen Pieterse (2004) argue, globalization cannot be equated with American homogeniza-tion, with the creation of a single global culture made in the United States. Nor is it simply characterized by the return of tribal iden-tities and "strong religions," which are simultaneously deployed in response to the economic and cultural dislocation and transported by informal transnational networks. Rather what one sees is the mixing of the logic of the capitalist market with a powerful desire for dif-ference and the exoticism offered by cultures at the margins. The production of this desire among baby boomers and generations X and Y is the sine qua non of global culture industries and media conglomerates. The so-called traditional cultures are mined for new scripts and symbols that can be detached from their geographical bearings and recombined in a pastiche with Western pop culture and beamed globally through the mass media or the Internet. We are in a world in which hybridity has become a prime commodity, in which multinational corporations like Benetton appropriate the symbols of multiculturalism and the mixing of the races to promote a brand of cosmopolitan consumerism. In this world, there is the danger that the destabilizing power of *mestizaje* will be sapped by globalization. As Hardt and Negri (2000: xii) put it, we live in an age of "Empire," a new global form of governmentality that "manages hybrid iden-tities, flexible hierarchies, and plural exchanges through modulating networks of command. The distinct national colors of the imperialist map of the world have merged and blended in the imperial global rainbow." For Hardt and Negri, then, the idea that the discourse of *mestizaje* by itself can liberate us is not only naive but is part of the problem because it blinds us to new forms of global power that use aestheticized hybrid identities and narratives of transculturation as points of relay.

At the very minimum, the examples in this section, which are drawn from countries where "other Latinos" come from, problema-tize the discourse of *mestizaje*. We are faced with contradictory visions of *mestizaje*. On the one hand, we have a view of *mestizaje* in line with Elizondo and other Latino/a theologians, namely, as:

a liberating force that breaks open colonial and neocolonial categories of ethnicity and race. This is a resistant mestizaje, one that questions authenticity and rejects the need to belong as defined by those in power. As a discourse of militant hybridity, it is a counterhegemonic claiming of intermediate identities that, by its very indeterminacy and flexibility, escapes the use of ethnic and racial categorizations for the purposes of social control.

On the other hand, mestizaje also emerges as an official discourse of nation formation, a new claim of authenticity that denies colonial forms of racial/ethnic hierarchy and oppression by creating an intermediate subject and interpellating him or her as "the citizen." As a discourse of social control, official mestizaje is constructed implicitly against a peripheral, marginalized, dehumanized Indian "Other" who is often "disappeared" in the process. (Mallon, 1996:171–72)[7]

How are we to deal with this contradiction? Does it mean that we have to reject *mestizaje* because it is implicated in enduring forms of domination? Does it mean that we have to return to exclusionary otherness, with its quest for purity?

Recognizing *Otredad* in *Mestizaje*

It is unwise for Latino/a theologians, scholars, and activists to abandon *mestizaje*. Despite serious drawbacks, the concept offers a powerful critique of the still hegemonic bipolar racial formation in the United States, which places Latinos in an inferior position in race hierarchies. The discourse of purity and segregation is alive and well in the United States, even exacerbated by the perceived threats of globalization, particularly immigration and terrorism, to the nation-state, imagined as an Anglo-Saxon bastion of civilization (Vásquez

---

7. Proponents of *mestizaje* in Latino theology recognize this contradiction. For example, Isasi-Díaz observes that *"mestizaje/mulatez* is not always seen as a positive element in our societies back home" (2001b:215). She also notes how in countries such as Mexico and Peru politicians "refer to the Aztec and Incas in order to support claims of identity and greatness for their countries and to identify themselves with the people. This entails a certain ambivalent embracing of *mestizaje* even as laws and policies continue to oppress indigenous people" (Ibid.:215–16).

and Marquardt, 2003). *Mestizaje* also reflects the reality of daily life, *lo cotidiano*, for large sectors of Latino populations. However, I would use *mestizaje* with great care. Before we are tempted to universalize this concept, to render it as unequivocally emancipatory or salvific, we need to understand its genealogy and be attentive to its multiple historical and current uses. We must always ask: Who deploys *mestizaje*? For what purposes? How does the discourse of *mestizaje* play in the local, national, and global regimes of identity? What are the effects — including of resistance and domination — of this discourse in a particular social and cultural reality?

Nevertheless, it is not sufficient to contextualize and historicize *mestizaje,* as Hale advises us to do. Even if we begin with a strong "militant particularism," locating ourselves among those at the margins/borderlands, we can never assume that our narratives of *mestizaje* will be always liberatory. I believe that we need an epistemological critique of *mestizaje* which places it in the "regimes of truth" (Foucault, 1980) through which elites, particularly intellectual ones, interpellate the subaltern at the service of both conformity and liberation. It is vital that we acknowledge, along with the celebration of "unity in diversity," the silences, exclusions, and power asymmetries that criss-cross any *mestizo* discursive and institutional formation.

To begin with, no matter how "organic" we may be as Latino intellectuals, we must be aware of the "epistemological violence" we commit when we speak for, about, and to "our communities." Here we can draw from the work of postcolonial and subaltern scholars such as Gayatri Spivak and John Beverley. In her influential essay "Can the Subaltern Speak?" (1988), Spivak points to the role that the intellectual situated in the metropolitan academy has in constituting the postcolonial subject. According to Spivak, for the subaltern to speak with any authority and legitimacy, it must do it through the "thought of the elite." Under these conditions, even the progressive intellectual is complicit "in the persistent constitution of the Other as the Self's shadow," an Other that becomes reified as a unified emancipatory subject that allows the intellectual to claim prophetic authority. In our case, defining *mestizos* as a new emancipatory race, the artisans of a new humanity, while expressing a highly desirable ideal, may preclude us from self-critique, from recognizing the difficulties and contradictions in our own praxis: the power effects of essentializing Latinos as a fluid, all-embracing, and eschatological cosmic race. Latino communities, no matter how *mestizo* they are, always carry subalternity, those others, at the margins of the margins, which we theorists and theologians cannot present as part of our communities without to some extent reducing them. Whether we are referring to indigenous men from the Guatemalan highlands working in the tomato and strawberry fields in Plant City, Florida, who want nothing to do with "other Latinos" but want to build alliances with Native Americans in the United States, or to Afro-Colombians or Afro-Dominicans who find themselves doubly discriminated against by African Americans and brown and fair-skin Latinos, we need to acknowledge that in "giving voice to them" as *mestizos,* even as the God-chosen marginalized, we are re-presenting them, and thus doing symbolic violence to the multiplicity and uniqueness of their experiences. For our theologies and social theories, no matter how sensitive and progressive, emerged out of the knowledge-power nexus at the heart of the colonial enterprise, which included a combination of violent conquest, Christianization, and slavery. The same can be said of the ethnographic methods to which Isasi-Díaz appeals in her search for *lo cotidiano.* As Fabian (1983) and Clifford and Marcus (1986) among others have shown, ethnography partakes of modernity's disciplinary gaze and is deeply implicated in the colonial politics of representation. In other words, there is no innocent, transparent position where we can recover the authentic voice of the subaltern. As John Beverley (1999:2) writes, "the subaltern is subaltern in part because it cannot be represented adequately by academic knowledge (and 'theory'). It cannot be represented adequately by academic knowledge because academic knowledge is a practice that actively produces the subalternity (it produces subalternity in the act of representing it). How can one claim to represent the subaltern from the standpoint of academic knowledge, then, when that knowledge is itself involved in the 'othering' of the subaltern?"

While Spivak's attack on the metropolitan intellectual is on target, in her zeal to denounce the epistemological violence that constructs the subaltern, she runs the risk of presenting the latter as a mere "empty space," "an inaccessible blankness." Since the subaltern cannot be retrieved without imposing the language of the colonizer, Spivak ends up reducing the subaltern to a "theoretical fiction," a "subject-effect" (which she sometimes characterizes as an inchoate repressed will) that serves to unsettle the power of colonial discourse. Although I recognize the inescapably mediated and relational character of the subaltern, I would like to re-materialize the "Other." The Other is not simply an undecidable text, an absence endlessly caught in "a sign-system." The Other is an embodied, historical individual who is constituted not only by the subjectivizing discourses and practices of the nation-state, churches, and global capitalism, but also by his or her own creative work upon the fragments of the empire. More concretely, the Other is in our midst, at the heart of our Latino populations, in *lo cotidiano* of the recently arrived Chiapaneco, who is exploited not only by the white farmer but by other more established Latinos who subcontract or supervise his labor. No doubt, Spivak would accuse me of "refetishizing the concrete," of engaging in a kind of positivist denial of my own role in re-representing the suffering of the embodied Other as fully transparent (91). Yet, my plea here is not for recovering an authentic, uncontaminated, and unified Other that can be immediately accessed through his or her suffering body, independently of our own desires and ideological investments. I wish to avoid semiotic reductionism and recognize the uncomfortable material presence, the "viscerality," as Sanjinés (2004) puts it, of the Other, as a way to relativize the position that gives only metropolitan intellectuals the capacity to create the world through their discourses.[8]

Isasi-Díaz's effort to define *mestizaje* as non-exclusionary difference is valuable, and I concur with her on the need to understand identity as fluid, performative, and relational. This is a very strategic move in challenging Western essentialism and obsession with fixed boundaries, particularly with hierarchical binarianism: "either you

---

8. Spivak also commits epistemic violence. She silences the Other so that the Self (the intellectual) can write endlessly about its absence and the impossibility of ever encountering it. "Perhaps the greatest irony of 'Can the Subaltern Speak?'... is that if Spivak's account of subaltern silence were true, then there would be nothing but the non-subaltern (particularly the West and the native elite) left to speak to or write about" (Moore-Gilbert, 1997:104).

are with us or against us." I also appreciate her efforts to ground inter- and intra-ethnic solidarity and justice on *mestizaje*'s de-centering of self and on the empathetic world-traveling that hybridity encourages. However, I would argue that not all differences are created equal. Nor can all of them be embraced with the same ease. Some differences are more recalcitrant and traumatic, more resistant to pluralism, multiculturalism, and even empathic fusion. These differences stubbornly refuse to be part of *mestizaje*'s cosmopolitan and friendly diversity. They are not just another specificity to be playfully placed side-by-side with others, as if history and structural inequality did not matter. Some subaltern groups' long experiences of oppression have left deep traces of exclusion and non-being that mark a radical difference that no empathic love or aesthetic experience can completely and finally heal, in much the same way as Jesus Christ carries the wounds of his crucifixion in his resurrected body.

Fernando Segovia (1995:35) summarizes the predicament well: Latinos have not just "binding similarities" but also "unavoidable differences." "We are...not only a bicultural people but a multicultural people, the permanent others who are also in various respects others to one another." More specifically, given the increasingly heterogeneous composition and complex settlement patterns of Latino communities, we need to posit as the locus of Latino theology not just *mestizaje*, but the tensile relation between *mezcolanza* and *otredad*. It is in the dynamic tension between mixture and irreducible (but mediated) otherness that transgressive praxis lies; it is this tension that is, as Segovia puts it, "unsettling and liberating at the same time" (1995:31). This tension allows us not to fall into another destructive binarianism: either everything is a mixture, which is positive, or everything is the Other, defined by pure difference, defined negatively. This binarism is untenable if we understand the Other as relational without being dialectical (leading to a Hegelian synthesis or a peaceful coexistence). The Other is, in his or her particular history and embodied suffering, irreducible to the logic of sameness, homogeneity, or even *mestizaje*.[9] However, it is simultaneously mediated by and

---

9. Borrowing from Enrique Dussel and Walter Mignolo, Sanjinés (2004:10) calls for "constructing a discourse in which difference is not included within a totality conceived by power.... Today's indigenous movements counter the 'ethics of inclusion' that promotes the

in interaction with other historical discourses and practices, including those of the nation-state, globalization, and our own narratives of *mestizaje* and *otredad*. In other words, what I am suggesting here is another form of "in-betweenness" and "borderlands": *el ser entre mestizaje y otredad*.

I envision a praxis that is, on the one hand, cosmopolitan and unfinished, a challenge to established boundaries, and on the other hand, deeply aware of the irreducible otherness of the subaltern and their right to name their oppression, to mark alterity and unresolved opposition, even if this exercise may itself be problematic.[10] It is a praxis that at once celebrates and is energized by our shared ludic and aesthetic resources but also is soberly aware of power differentials, not just between Latino communities and dominant groups but also within Latino communities. I believe that a dual hermeneutic of recovery and suspicion would help us develop a clearer sense of the potentials and limits of narratives of *mestizaje* and a more realistic understanding of the difficulties involved in mobilizing our communities for transformative action. Rather than assuming that because we are all *mestizo* we carry in ourselves a necessarily emancipatory essence that just needs to be awakened, we need to acknowledge that *otredad* marks us not only vis-à-vis the dominant groups in mainstream society, but also within our own ranks. We must be wary of letting our rightful impatience for solidarity, reconciliation, and utopia overpower the humbling task of self-critique. In other words, we need to take seriously Isasi-Díaz's own call for "epistemological vigilance."[11] In the face of the rapidly evolving

---

fusion of races, in which mestizaje is portrayed as the synthesis of the nation, with an 'ethics of liberation'...that propounds a different path to understanding." The "indigenous Other" is not simply the "outside" of *mestizaje*. It is an altogether "exterior locus."

10. Hale (2002:524) raises the possibility of a "mestizaje from below" that "would extend a bridge to Maya people, to express solidarity while refusing to let 'mestizos' re-assume their previous claim to encompass, speak for, appropriate *lo indígena*." This *mestizaje* would recognize the exteriority and heterogeneity of the Maya movement, while encouraging "critique of neoliberal multiculturalism's investment in neatly bounded categories of cultural difference, each with pre-inscribed contributions to societal diversity."

11. Isasi-Díaz (1996:76) rightly calls us to assume "responsibility for our subjectivity." In addition to being "aware of how our own social situation colors our analysis of the religion of our communities and colors the way we say what we say in our theological writing,...we need to apply a hermeneutics of suspicion to our constructive proposals, to our narratives, to our whole theological enterprise."

character of Latino populations, awareness and critique of historic power asymmetries among ourselves, starting with the contradictory location of the Latino/a theologian and social theorist, is a necessary prerequisite for community building and collective transformative action.

Chapter 6

Rethinking Mulatez

Miguel A. De La Torre

When my parents arrived in this country immediately following the 1959 Cuban Revolution, they settled in New York City. Although a small Cuban community of recent refugees was living in the Big Apple during the early 1960s, a larger and more vibrant Puerto Rican community had become established since the Great Migration shortly following the Second World War. Soon my family began to develop relationships with non-Cuban Latino/a groups, learning their culture and traditions. It was not long before our Cuban family became friends with several of the Puerto Rican families living in our lower West Side *barrio*.

One evening, while my mother was visiting a new Puerto Rican acquaintance, the woman noticed a small reddish lump on my cheek. "*¿Qué le pasó a Miguelito?*" (What happened to Miguel?) she asked my mother. Wanting to say that some bug must have bitten me, my Cuban mother responded, "*Le picó un bicho.*" The Puerto Rican woman was both shocked and disgusted, for unbeknown to my mother, the Cuban word for pest or bug — *bicho* — is a Puerto Rican slang term for penis. After some awkwardness, both women discovered that each culture arbitrarily gave the linguistic sign *bicho* dissimilar definitions. Some months later, this same Puerto Rican woman offered to share with my mother a really juicy *papaya,* not knowing that the word *papaya,* a well-known tropical fruit, is vulgar Cuban slang for vagina.

Ferdinand De Saussure suggests that words as "linguistic signs unite, not a thing and a name, but a concept and a sound-image." This sound-image is a mental notion created by the name that is uttered. The sound-image is itself complex, with the power to either connote or mask relationships that the concept has with other sound-images. The mental entity of the concept is what is signified while the signifier is the mental entity of the sound-image to which the concept is linked through the linguistic sign. Although linguistic signs are arbitrarily chosen to engender what is being signified, still, a power relationship is created between those who name the object and those who accept the naming (1959:66–67).

Likewise, the linguistic signs *mulato* and *mulatez* provide coded access to the object they signify. But that which is coded can mask a relationship of power. Most Latina/o scholars of religion use the term *Mulato* or "*mestizo* Christianity" to describe the Hispanic Christian perspective. *Mestizo* usually refers to those whose roots lie in Central and South America where a mixture of Spanish and Amerindian stock is common. *Mulato* connotes a mixture of Spanish and African heritage and refers to a racial blend common in the Caribbean and Brazil. Because Manuel Vásquez provided an extensive exploration of the term *mestizaje* in the previous chapter, I will concentrate here on the term *mulatez* as used by Latina/o scholars of religion whose roots lie in the Spanish islands of the Caribbean.

The linguistic signs *mulato* and *mulatez* have been widely embraced and uncritically incorporated by the Latino/a theological community to describe the ethos of those of us who define our identity though our association with Brazil and the Caribbean. In an attempt to create a counterbalance to what Latino/as scholars of religion with indigenous roots have termed *mestizaje*,[1] predominately white scholars from the Caribbean have named their culture *mulatez*,[2] and in so doing, have masked their own complicity with internal Hispanic racism. Nevertheless, the miscegenation of Latino/as from the Caribbean as signifier is linked to what it signified, which is that Hispanics live in harmony through the linguistic sign of *mulatez*, defined as the positive identifier of Hispanics from the Caribbean. This chapter will critically analyze the existing intra-Hispanic structure of power and how the arbitrary choice of certain words, i.e., *mulato* and *mulatez*, contributes to the creation of power relationships centered on race.

---

1. For example see the classic texts: Bañuelas, 1995; Elizondo, 1988; Elizondo and Matovina, 1998a.

2. See for example, Isasi-Díaz, 2001b.

Ironically, while Hispanic groups find themselves resisting the dominant culture's societal structures originally designed to protect the power and privilege of Euroamericans, Latino/as must also struggle against their own forms of intra-Hispanic structures of oppression.

Latino/a community leaders and intellectuals (as is true of every ethnic group) can consciously or unconsciously take advantage of their position of authority within their marginalized group and use their power and prestige within that group for their own ends. Among the subjugated, the group's power holders can cause the submission and further intimidation of group members because their own position is assured by the overall system of white supremacy. Those whose skin-pigmentation is closer to the white ideal have greater access to privilege (although it is still greatly limited) than their darker compatriots. In short, these "whiter" Hispanics (including me) became important figures within the marginalized Latino/a group due to the sociopolitical vacuum created within the group by the dominant Euroamerican culture's ethnic discrimination against Latino/as in general. For example, by surveying the skin pigmentation of the Latino/a scholars of religion whose roots are from the Caribbean one discovers that very few of them represent the majority who possess more pronounced African features, and we must ask why.

To raise this question does not minimize the reality that all Latino/as, as people of color compared to the dominant Euroamerican culture, face institutional racism, individual bigotry, and collective discrimination. Yet while this fact is undeniable, seldom do Hispanic scholars of religion seriously explore the nuanced levels of racism faced by Latino/as. They assume that Hispanics are not and cannot be racist, because of their typically disenfranchised position within U.S. society. If traces of racism are to be found within the Hispanic community, so they say, it is a lingering influence of Euroamerican social ills. Regardless of these assertions, among Hispanics, and specifically among those who have learned to see themselves through the eyes of the dominant white Eurocentric culture, socioeconomic and political privilege is grudgingly bestowed on those who most appear to be "white." The mere fact that a Latina/o's skin coloration is lighter than that of other Hispanics generally assures that person greater success in this country than those who have darker skin and also display more pronounced African — or Amerindian or Asian — features.

This chapter suggests that the ethnic descriptor *mulatez*, fabricated by mostly white Hispanic scholars from the Caribbean, is not an entirely apt identifier or sign. For like the linguistic signs of *bicho* and *papaya* discussed earlier, the linguistic signs *mulato* and *mulatez* have different meanings depending on if one is a white, black, or biracial Hispanic. These linguistic signs signify racist concepts that perpetuate intra-Hispanic oppression while serving to mask and normalize light-skinned Hispanics' power within an overall disenfranchised group. The desire of Latino/a scholars of religion to evoke a pan-ethnic unity obscures the reality of how racism is rampant within the Hispanic constructed social space. Hispanic scholars of religion who cast themselves solely as victims of North American Anglos mask the dubious role Latino/as themselves play as victimizers of those among us who have darker skin pigmentations. Those of us who are white Hispanics are therefore both the oppressed and the oppressors, a fact that is often conveniently ignored when we define ourselves as the Hispanic Other to the U.S. hegemony.

To seriously consider how Latina/os define their identity requires an analysis of how internal Hispanic racism is masked by Latino/a religiosity. As a child of the Caribbean and a Latino scholar of religion, I find certain aspects of Hispanic theology problematic — specifically the term "*mulato* Christianity." To raise my concerns neither discredits nor rejects the work done thus far by many of those Latina/o scholars of religion who wrestled with these issues decades ago. Rather, a constant suspicion of how one's own social location masks oppressive structures is a foundational precept of any liberative ethics. Specifically, I am concerned when mostly white Latino/as describe their social location by using the term *mulatez*. Second, I am concerned that those of us constructed as being white within our Hispanic culture use language to mask our power and privilege by claiming to be *mulatos*. Third, I am concerned about how the linguistic sign *mulata* fuses racism and sexism. And finally, I am concerned that the whitening of Caribbean blacks through the term *mulatez* is but the latest problematic chapter of a racist historical process rooted in the mid-1800s.

Problematic Usage of the Linguistic Signs *Mulato/Mulatez*

Although simple linguistic signs are arbitrarily chosen, a complex sign like *mulato* is not arbitrary because it links the identity of a biracial Hispanic to that of a mule *(mulo)*. Because the meaning of the unfamiliar word *mulato* is unclear, the word it suggests, *mulo,* takes over the definition. The imposition by white Latina/os of the linguistic sign *mulato* masks an ideology of white supremacy prevalent within Caribbean culture by providing what appears to be a normative and legitimate word. Thus, I begin my critique by unequivocally stating that the word *mulato* is a racist term due to its association with the word "mule," the product of a horse and donkey that is unable to reproduce itself. Etymologically, *mulato* is a derivative of the Arabic *mulwállad* (pronounced *muélled*). *Muwállad* is defined as "one born of an Arab father and a foreign mother" — a possible passive participle of the second conjugation of *wálada,* "he begot." Dozy's monumental work on the Arabic language insists that the word *mulato* is actually a Portuguese word of contempt signifying mule. *Mulato,* literally "mule, young, or without domesticity," was influenced in form by a folk-etymological association with the Spanish word *mulo,* mule.[3] Fernando Ortiz, the famed Cuban ethnographical scholar, concurs with Covarrubias, the etymologist who clearly stated that *mulato* is a comparison to the nature of a mule (1975:40). The negative connotation of mule carries over to the word *mulato* regardless of the valiant efforts made by many white Hispanic scholars of religion to construct a positive definition.

Even if the whiter children of the Caribbean fail to make a connection between the word mule and *mulato,* U.S. African Americans make such a link and find the association offensive.[4] Since we construct our ethnic identity within the United States, sensitivity toward the U.S. contribution to our Latino/a identity should also be observed.

---

3. See *The Barnhart Dictionary of Etymology,* s.v. "Mulatto"; *Diccionario Crítico Etimológico de la Lengua Castellana,* s.v. "Mulo," by J. Corominas; *Supplément aux Dictionnaires Arabes,* 3d ed., s.v. "Begot" by Reinhart Dozy; *A Comprehensive Etymological Dictionary of the English Language,* s.v. "Mulatto," by Ernest Klein; *Diccionario de uso del Español,* s.v. "Mulato," by María Moliner; and *An Etymological Dictionary of the English Language,* s.v. "Mulatto," by Walter W. Skeat.

4. For a detailed discussion on the usage of the term "mulatto" within a North American culture, see Jordan, 1962; Mencke, 1979; Rueter, 1970; and Williamson, 1980.

True, it is the intention of Latino/a scholars of religion to use the word "mulatto" to indicate the positive mixture of races and cultures creating what José Vasconcelos termed *la nueva raza cósmica*. Vasconcelos, the Mexican philosopher and statesman, is credited with constructing the utopian concept of "the Cosmic Race." He did so as a way of combating the prevalent positivism of his time, which advocated the destruction of Mexican culture because of the belief in the evolutionary superiority of Euroamericans. But while we celebrate the defense of Latin American culture over against Eurocentrism, we need to recognize that philosophers like Vasconcelos still upheld positivism's hierarchical view on race. The maintenance of this hierarchical view is the primary reason I question the appropriateness of using the term *mulatez*, for the term's hidden meaning is to whiten the Africans (De La Torre, 2003:16–17).

Furthermore, *mulatez* creates a reductionist black-white dichotomy that fails to adequately encompass those of us who come from the Caribbean. Our roots contain more elements than just *mulato* (black and white) or *mestizo* (Amerindian and Spaniard). We are also Asian, and due to historical U.S. imperialism, Anglo. We are most truly a multicultural people, belonging to five cultural inheritances, yet fully accepted by none of them, making us simultaneously "outsiders" and "insiders" on all sides. It is from this existential space that we must construct the theological bases upon which we can reconcile our several selves to our "self." To insist on using only the racist term *mulato* detracts from our ability to represent the other elements of our ethnic identity.

This point is well made by Native American scholars like Ines Hernández-Avila and Andrea Smith, who remain suspicious of the claim that *mestizaje* is not destructive of indigenous cultures, leading them to call *mestizaje* a "colonizing" discourse directed against indigenous people. If *mestizaje* is truly concerned with preserving "the ancient religious traditions of the Americas," then why, asks Hernández-Avila, do so few mestizos know anything about indigenous cultures other than Aztec, Mayan, or Incan? Why is the language of *mestizaje* Spanish or Portuguese rather than an indigenous or African language? Where are the efforts of *mestizos* to recover these languages and cultures in more than a general way? (A. Smith, 2004:75–76).[5]

The critique these Native American scholars provide concerning the term *mestizo* is one that should also be raised concerning the term *mulatez*. What does *mulatez* have to say to the continuing social and economic genocide of those from African Caribbean descent? Why does a growing gap exist in the level of education, income, and status between white Caribbeans and black Caribbeans? Are these differences to be blamed solely upon the structural racism within the United States, or do similar structures exist on the islands — social structures that were imported along with the migration of the populations? If the future is *mulatez*, will black Caribbeans find acceptance only if they choose to "whiten" and Christianize themselves? Is the hope for the sacred traditions of Africans limited to the folkloric? The fact that *mulatez* fails to deal with questions like these reveals its masked hostility to those who choose *négritude* (black consciousness) as the ethnological starting point of Latino/a identity.

Language as of Form of Masking

Language, according to Michel Foucault, is an "opaque, mysterious thing," which both reveals and conceals (1994:34). As such, language is more than simply a collection of words; it is a conveyer of concepts. Within the generalized U.S. culture, the use of only English masks one of the many social structures that disenfranchise Hispanics, for identity among Latino/as is not restricted solely by a given race or ethnicity. As Deleuze and Guattari remind us: "There is no mother tongue, only a power takeover by a dominant language within a political multiplicity" (1987:7).

The stubborn resistance of uttering Spanish prevents the power takeover by the dominant English language as it attempts to link the diverse Hispanic cultural groups within the United States with their roots throughout Latin America. Within the United States, Latino/as

---

5. Also note the paper presented by Inés Hernández-Avila, "On Our Own Terms: Critical/ Creative Representations by Native American Women," during the 1995 American Academy of Religion conference.

attempt to establish a unity in identity, regardless of the glaring differences in history, culture, and traditions found, for example, in a Chilean, a Mexican, or a Dominican. It is this unifying symbol called Spanish that, unlike the tendency of other groups to consciously attempt to assimilate to the mainstream dominant Euroamerican culture, has led Hispanics to refuse to forsake their native tongue. To a great extent, Spanish (or Spanglish) represents the ethnic obstinance (stupidity as perceived by the dominant culture) that resists assimilation. With the act of speaking Spanish, Hispanics place themselves in direct conflict with the socio-political structures that would have us articulate self-oppressive expression with each linguistic utterance.[6]

Pierre Bourdieu suggests that language structures are established in such as a way as to endow the status of sole legitimacy upon the official language of the dominant group. Language, in the hands of this group, becomes an instrument of action and power. To purify thought by purifying language legitimates the dominant group's monopoly on political power (1991:1–37, 46–49). Hispanics (or any ethnic group for that matter) wishing to produce successful discourse so as to participate more fully in the structures of society must observe the cultural capital of that society — which is why this book is written in English rather than Spanish.[7]

---

6. This does not mean that Latino/as do not want to learn English — quite the contrary. Most Hispanics realize that to survive within the dominant culture, proficiency in English, the international language of commerce, is a must. But to learn English does not mean forsaking the language that symbolizes Latinidad. Ironically, at the same time that the dominant culture continues to insist on English only, it also continues to eliminate social service funding for ESL (English as a second language) programs.

7. In the case of the United States, fluent English becomes the prerequisite to cultural capital. Asserting one's ethnic language, or speaking the dominant language with an accent, disqualifies the speaker from social advancement. Regardless of the effort expended by the speaker, the attempt to speak English properly is viewed by others as a parody. The inability to master the dominant language signifies Latino/as in a symbolic system that they will never command, in fact, in a system that commands them. Defenders of an official language often insist on its predominance because of some alleged intrinsic virtue. In reality, they are defending their position of power. Power need not be overtly exercised. Rather, power can be transmuted into a symbolic form through the routine flow of day-to-day life that is conducted in the language of the dominant group. This process empowers the dominant group by bestowing a kind of legitimacy. Language, as a symbolic power, presupposes the values of the dominant culture in such a way that Hispanics attempting to speak English participate in their own subjection. The tacit acknowledgment of the dominant culture's legitimacy, and the power relation in which Hispanics are embedded, prevents Latina/os from recognizing that the present system is but an arbitrary social construction designed to serve the interest of the dominant group.

The use of language by the dominant culture as a means of creating normative structures that legitimize racism is not limited to the Euroamerican-Hispanic relationship. Among Latina/os, those privileged with whiteness can also use language to reinforce racism while masking it. The choice of *mulatez* as the linguistic sign by which to name the Latino/a identity betrays the power and privilege of those white Hispanics who impose this name upon the entire cultural group. Ironically, while Latina/o scholars of religion claim to do their theological work from the grassroots faith community, in those same communities which are predominately white, the usage of the word *mulato* to describe their spirituality would be considered insulting.

During my many years of research in Miami — a predominately white Cuban community — I studied several different churches, both Protestant and Catholic. During interviews with parishioners, I would bring up the term "*mulato* Christianity." The vast majority of the individuals I surveyed informed me that their faith was based in *nada negro* (nothing African); they were not *santero/as* (an Afro-Cuban religion), but rather, Christians. As I began to explain *mulatez* as an ethnic self-identification many became visibly upset that I would suggest that they were from a mixed cultural background, and instead insisted on their white "purity." Even the term "people of color" as an identifier for Miami Cubans was considered to be insulting. For a people who sees itself as white, terms like *mulatez* are objectionable. My research in Miami led me to wonder if the self-constructed identity of *mulatez* is in fact an academic fabrication created by scholars who then impose it upon Latino/as of Caribbean descent, or if it is truly a grassroots expression of self-description rising from the *comunidad*. Experience has led me to accept the former.

Yet, by claiming "color" within the overall Euroamerican culture, Hispanic racism is masked, a racism detected in the construction of *mulato* Christianity. While white Hispanic scholars of religion represent a narrative crucial to the overall discourse, informing and challenging dominant Eurocentric theological views, they too can fall into the fallacy of ignoring their own intra-Hispanic racism. This racism is generally evident in the overall Hispanic community's denial that racism exists among us. Latina/o racism is rooted in the belief that we, unlike the Euroamericans, are not racist, even though the primary criterion of social classification has always been color. The Latino/a community's first response to the accusation of racism is usually its denial. Unfortunately, the understanding of our Latina/o identity, based on "equality" between blacks and whites, benefited only white Hispanics. With Ada María Isasi-Díaz, we can quote the Venezuelan proverb, *Aquí todos somos café con leche; unos más café, otros más leche* (Here we are all coffee and milk; some more coffee, other more milk) (1993:15). However, *leche* has access to employment, state services, power, wealth and privilege, while *café* is disenfranchised. Although popular slogans like *mulatez* are constructed to describe the Americas' multiculturalism, white scholars like Isasi-Díaz romanticize the notion of *mestizaje* and *mulatez,* insisting that the terms, "do not carry the negative connotations associated with miscegenation, [but rather are] a *natural* result of the coming together of different races" (Ibid.; emphasis added). There was nothing natural about how Africans and Spaniards came together. Missing from her analysis is the existence of the transcript hidden among white Latino/as that a purer type of race mixing will be the organic result of miscegenation. The result of such a mixture is an acceptable "whiter" ethnic group that, by definition, excludes non-white Hispanics, especially those of pure African descent.

Mulatez as a linguistic sign masks white Hispanics' rejection of *négritude* (black consciousness) as a viable ideology. *Mulato* and *mulatez* seek assimilation, a conciliatory rather than divisive response to racism. With the proclamation of an elusive and romanticized notion of unity, the issue of race fails to be addressed. In effect, the so-called "black problem" within Hispanic culture is resolved by erasing the black race. White Latino/as can now identify and declare themselves "black," and also as suffering racism, because all Hispanics — not just blacks — are of color. For example, white dictator Fidel Castro was able to tell black South African leader Nelson Mandela during his 1991 visit to the island, "Look how far *we* slaves have come! Who wants to return to the days of the slave barracks? And how will *they* force *us* to return there?" (Castro and Mandela, 1991:44).

If there is no distinction between a black and a white Hispanic, then the abuse and suffering caused by slavery and racism in the

Caribbean ceases to be limited to blacks. Recounting a color-blind history makes all Latino/as descendants of slaves, not just the black ones. The linguistic sign *mulatez* masks the historical oppression of the Caribbean black by making whites both the victims of slavery and its perpetrators. Hence, if racism exists, it is not institutional; rather it is personal. Because all are Latino/as, racism cannot exist or occur as an inherent manifestation of social structures. Any exhibitions of racist actions must instead focus on the attitudes of the offending individual whose race-based actions indicate a personal rejection of the established color-blind society where all are simply part of a *mulatez* culture.

Yet, while white Hispanics "re-cognized" the presence of non-whites, people with pronounced African features had to shape their behavior according to white expectations and were unable to assert their own culture. As Frantz Fanon points out, within Caribbean culture, "Not only must the black man be black; he must be black in relation to the white man" (1967:110). When the term *mulato* is used, an assumption usually exists that a pure type will be the organic result of such a mixture. The result of such a mixture is an acceptable "whiter" ethnic group that, by definition, excludes Natives and Africans (Sathler and Nascimento, 1997:103). Among some Latino/as, the need to "whiten" Africans becomes the basis for developing racial reforms.

For some Hispanics the *only* legitimate claims Latino/a blacks can make or have made deal with labor discrimination, educational restriction, and segregationist offenses. Once those overt forms of discrimination are eliminated, racism will cease to exist. However, those of us who are whiter usually ignore the ethno-political and psycho-cultural ramifications of Hispanic white supremacy as manifested in our sociopolitical structures of power. White liberal paternalism, committed to integration, refuses to hear questions about racism asked outside of the official rubrics and thus establishes the boundaries of the discourse. Religious discourse and decisions concerning race among Latino/as from the Caribbean take place predominately among white Hispanic scholars of religion who enjoy the prestige and privilege of academia.

Fusing Racism and Sexism

Gender, race, and class domination do not exist in isolated compartments, nor are they neatly relegated to rigid uniform categories of repression. Rather, they interact and conflict with each other. Because all forms of oppression are identical in their attempt to domesticate the Other, it should not be surprising that the artificial boundaries separating sexism, racism, and classism are porous. The racism signified by the term *mulata* cannot be fully comprehended without seriously considering how the term also serves as a linguistic sign for sexual conquest.

A common saying from the Caribbean is "there is no sweet tamarind fruit, nor a virgin *mulato* girl." *La mulata* signifies an over-sexualized woman who is recognized for her prowess, thus fulfilling her nature as an object for consumption — specifically by young white Latino males hoping to learn the "art" of lovemaking. A white Hispanic male can engage in sex with her absolved of any culpability; for after all, it is she who is held responsible for compromising the virtues of the white men, either through her so-called seductive nature, or her "black magic." Fanon captures the white Caribbean sentiments about black sexuality when he writes:

> As for the Negroes, they have tremendous sexual powers. What do you expect, with all the freedom they have in their jungles! They copulate at all times and in all places. They are really genital. They have so many children that they cannot even count them. *Be careful, or they will flood us with little mulattoes.* (1967:157–59, emphasis added)

The *mulata* is constructed as a wild creature, who, because she contains black blood, is part savage, and because she contains white blood, is part civilized. White Hispanics project their own forbidden desires upon the black and *mulata* female body, even though it threatens white civilization. To engage in sex with her is for the white man to lose himself to primitive urges that heighten the sexual experience because of the added element of danger. Besides leading white men astray, the *mulata's* body is also viewed as a sexual cure. White Latino men have even gone so far as to create an illness that could be cured only by having sex with a black woman. Here it is described by Esteban Montejo, the former slave:

> There was one type of sickness the whites picked up, a sickness of the veins and male organs. It could only be got rid of with black women; if the man who had it slept with a Negress he was cured immediately. (1968:42)

This construction of *mulatas* as sex objects can also be profitable, as illustrated by their overrepresentation in numerous La Habana guidebooks for tourists published between 1930 and 1959. These directed uninhibited Euroamericans to nightly sex shows where mulatas were predominantly featured (Fox, 1973:278). The function of *la mulata,* specifically the exotic light-skinned *mulatas* known as *amarillas* (high yellows), was to provide sexual liaisons with white men. The usage of *la mulata,* specifically in tourist posters for Caribbean islands, signifies an exotic paradise free of racial conflict. Her body became a consumer good (De La Torre, 2003:109–10).

Mulato/Mulatez as the Latest Stage of Latino/a Racism

Among those Hispanics privileged with whiteness within the overall Latina/o culture there is a tendency to perpetuate the myth that the rules, traditions, institutions, and language of Hispanics are nature's way. Rejecting this naturalness, we turn to systems of encoding and decoding signs. Semiologist Roland Barthes's *Mythologies* consists of a series of short essays that examine aspects of popular French culture (i.e., the world of wrestling, soap commercials, wine and milk, steak and chips, and striptease) to reveal how every cultural phenomenon, regardless of how normative or natural it may appear, is contaminated with ideological assumptions. To the eyes of the myth-consumer, cultural norms appear as facts of nature. Norms are naturalized even though they can be construed as the unconscious propaganda of those who benefit from the myth. The myth succeeds, not because it is able to mask, but rather because it distorts the glaring contradictions existing within the social system so that they can appear both normal and natural. Myths do not deny, but rather purify — providing a natural justification to a historical intention so that it can appear innocent. Myth as a second-order semiological schema accomplishes this task (1972:111–15, 128–31, 142–43).

Specifically, the miscegenation of Latino/as from the Caribbean as signifier becomes an alibi for what is signified — that Hispanics live in racial harmony. *Mulatez* as sign ceases to be a symbol, but rather becomes the very ideology of the absence of racism among Hispanics. Still, the former linguistic sign of *mulatez* now becomes a new "depoliticized" signifier within a new system of meaning and, hence, creates a myth. Emptied from its original meaning, *mulatez* becomes a new signifier to a myth, a myth so entrenched within the Latina/o mind-set that its usage becomes second nature. *Mulatez* as the new signifier within this second-order semiological system now signifies that unlike in the United States, Hispanics have successfully integrated a multiracial and multicultural ethnic people, meaning that any oppressive structures that remain are imposed rather than internal. The real meaning of the original linguistic sign *mulatez* is perverted, giving the public a new sign, even as the history of the original linguistic sign is erased. This new sign as ideology maintains that Latino/as cannot be racist because racism is solely the product of the U.S. social and cultural milieu. Any racism that exists is just the expression of personal prejudices caused by the lingering effects of Euroamerican domination.

Myth distorts the full meaning of the original linguistic signs *mulato* and *mulatez,* emptying and depriving Hispanic blacks of their history. These linguistic signs have specific connections to the Caribbean milieu and as such cannot be separated from the social phenomenon that produces the system of language. The utterance of these two linguistic signs to denote Hispanic identity appears both natural and necessary, when in reality these signs of popular Caribbean culture mask a power relationship based on race even while attempting to construct a certain commonness to the words. Yet for the person versed in Afro-Caribbean history, *mulato* and *mulatez* stand as signifiers of a myth, providing the public with the image of a society were racism is minimal, if not non-existent. This myth has the power to connote a larger sign system that misconstrues society and its intrarelationships (Barthes, 1972:114–15). Using Roland

1. SIGNIFIER Miscegenation of Hispanics from the Caribbean	2. SIGNIFIED Latino/as live in harmony	
3. SIGN *Mulatez* as positive identifier for the identity of those Latino/as from the Caribbean I. SIGNIFIER *Mulatez* as positive identifier for the identity of those Latino/as from the Caribbean		II. SIGNIFIED Unlike the United States, Hispanics have success- fully integrated a multi- racial and multiethnic people so that those oppressive structures that remain are imposed rather than internal
III. SIGN Ideology that Latino/as cannot be racist because racism is solely a product of the U.S. social and cultural milieu, and any racism that does exist is reduced to personal prejudices caused by the lingering effects of Anglo domination		

Barthes's model, this relationship can be illustrated by the figure shown above.

I maintain that the whitening of Caribbean blacks through the term *mulatez* is but the latest chapter in a racist historical process — a historical process that focuses on the external oppressor while ignoring the internal oppressor. Throughout the history of the Spanish Caribbean islands, whenever the indigenous black population threatened to exceed the white population, a process known as *blanqueamiento* (whitening) occurred whereby land was freely given to poor white Spanish families who would leave Spain and come to live on the islands. For example, during the early nineteenth century on the island of Cuba, a corporation named the Junta de Población Blanca (Committee on White Population) was organized to carry out *blanqueamiento*. It received its proceeds from a six-*peso* tax imposed on all male slaves (Corbitt, 1971:2). During the first decade after the end of the Spanish-American War, approximately three hundred thousand Spaniards emigrated to Cuba, while laws denied blacks immigration. Other proposals to eliminate blacks from the Cuban social setting included the policy of dividing black from biracial Cubans by according some privileges to the latter and assimilating them (up to a point) as allies; hence the desire for some blacks to transform themselves into being whiter (McGarrity and Cárdenas, 1995:80).

Although Cuba and Puerto Rico attempted to create a type of color-blind society, blacks were usually blamed for being racist when they attempted to cultivate *négritude*. As José Martí, the intellectual giant of the Caribbean, writes, "The black man who proclaims his race, even if mistakenly as a way to proclaim spiritual identity with all races, justifies and provokes white racism" (quoted in L. A. Pérez, 1999:91). Although Martí poetically wrote articles to combat racism, his rhetoric fell short. He was still influenced by the prevalent racism of his time and place. Caribbean racism manifested itself in two distinct forms during the twentieth century. The most influential view at the start of the century was based on a Darwinian racial evolution that advocated the inferiority of Latino/as who were not "pure" descendants of the highly evolved white Spaniards. The second view, which gained greater prominence toward the end of the century, maintained that blacks had the potential to be equal to whites but were "stuck" in an earlier stage of cultural development. The solution required assimilation to the "superior" white culture through a process of de-Africanization. Hence *blanqueamiento,* the whitening of the Caribbean, became a prerequisite for black advancement. While scientists and intellectuals in the United States understood racial mixing as degeneration and mongrelization, those from the Caribbean saw *mulatez* as lifting the savage races toward civilization and progress (A. de la Fuente, 2001:178). This is evident in the work of José Elías Entralgo, a sociologist who was a proponent of a Caribbean version of eugenics. As chairperson of the 1959 Movimiento de Orientación e Integración National (Movement of National Orientation and Integration) of Cuba, he claimed a cause-and-effect relationship existed between "mulattoization" and national integration. He applauded the rape of African women by their white masters as the necessary evil of bettering Africans, allowing their integration into white society. Specifically, he said:

> The day . . . when a white slave master first had intercourse with a slave Negress in the bush or in the *barracoon* was the most luminous for mankind. . . . A vivifying transfusion took place that

engendered a fertile and plastic symbiosis. From such mixing was to emerge new physical attributes and ascending psychic and moral virtues. (C. Moore, 1988:47)

Mulatez is emptied from its original history and meaning and becomes the process of whitening blacks, where the rape of the black female body by white males is celebrated as a fraternal embrace across color lines. According to the dominant gaze the "savage" black female body willingly awaits domestication, as well as insemination from the white's male seed of civilization (De La Torre, 2002:49–50). White Hispanics who celebrate the birth of this new Caribbean child, born via miscegenation, ignore that such a birth occurs at all because millions of indigenous and African people, along with their cultures, languages, faith traditions, and civilizations, were subjugated.

In spite of miscegenation, "whiteness" remains synonymous with power and privilege. Blacks throughout the Antilles thus learn to self-impose the gaze of dominant white Caribbean eyes, a gaze that requires blacks to "whiten" themselves if they too wish to share in the privileges of society. Fanon describes this phenomenon well:

I still know people born in the Congo who pretend to be natives of the Antilles...[and] Antilles Negroes, who are annoyed when they are suspected of being [African]. This is because the Antilles' Negro is more "civilized" than the African, that is, he is closer to the white man; and this difference prevails not only in back streets and on the boulevards but also in public service and the army.... It [becomes] essential to avoid falling back into the pit of niggerhood, and every woman in the Antilles, whether in a casual flirtation or in a serious affair, is determined to select the least black of men. (1967:25–26, 47)

Yet Caribbean racism is somehow humanized by comparing it with the racism of the United States. Superficial comparisons to Hispanics' racial ethos conclude that racism exists among Euroamericans, not Latino/as. Growing up among Hispanics in the United States during its turbulent civil rights era, I recall white Latino/a adults debating the "U.S. African American question." They insisted that Hispanic blacks were more civilized and refined than U.S. blacks, due mostly to *blanqueamiento* and their integration into Latino/a culture facilitated by a lack of or minimal amount of racism among Hispanics. I still remember how one of the adults maintained that the sweetness of black Latina/os can be seen on their countenance, unlike the hatred visible in the eyes of U.S. blacks.

Racism is alive and well among Hispanics. Those closer to the Euroamerican white ideal are more privileged than their darker compatriots by the overall U.S. social structures that continue to support and sustain white supremacy. The concerns mentioned in this chapter give voice to some of the issues that the Latino/a community seldom discusses, specifically, the privileged space occupied by some Hispanics in this country due to their lighter skin pigmentation. We must be leery of how our choice of terms, *mulato* or *mulatez,* contributes to masking our own inner Hispanic structures of racism. The challenge Latina/os will be forced to face if we are to seriously rethink Hispanic religion and identity is how we have constructed and continue to use the words *mulato* and *mulatez.*

Chapter 7

Rethinking Latina Feminist Theologian

Michelle A. González

Essentialism, whether in relationship to gender, culture, or other identity categories, has been for some time a subject that has permeated the disciplines of cultural studies, feminist theory, philosophy, ethnic studies, and theology.[1] Whether one can authentically speak of categories such as "woman" or "Latino/as" without effacing the uniqueness that distinguishes the individuals that make up these categories is the subject of debate in feminist theory, cultural studies, sociology, and various other disciplines. In a similar vein, the growing interdisciplinary nature of the academy means that the lines that once sharply delineated various fields have become increasingly porous, forcing many to challenge and consequently reconstruct academic disciplines.

For Latino/a theology the challenge of essentialism is increasingly pressing. As a theology that claims to emerge from the perspective of Latino/a peoples in the United States, Latino/a theology is particularly susceptible to a constructivist attack on identity.[2] Who are the Latino/as this theology represents?[3] Is the construction of

---

1. Various texts have addressed the question of essentialism within numerous disciplines across the academy. See Benhabib, 1992; Butler, 1990; Chopp and Davaney, 1997; Fuss, 1989; Gracia, 2000; Gracia and de Greiff, 2000; S. Jones, 2000; Lugones, 1991:35–44; McClintock Fulkerson, 1994; Nicholson, 1990; Spelman, 1988; Young, 1997:12–37. On the history of the philosophical construction of gender see Allen, 1997 and 2002.

2. A constructivist approach emphasizes the socially constructed nature of identity. While emphasizing the importance of context and culture, Latino/a theologians claim to offer an accurate portrayal of Latino/a peoples. Even though we emphasize contextuality, however, do we at times gloss over concrete differences among our peoples?

3. Whether Latino/a theologians like it or not, within the dominant academy we represent the Latino/a population.

Latino/a identity found within this theology exclusive, representing only a fraction of the actual population in the United States? What is the understanding of Latinas found within Latino/a theological discourse? This chapter examines the construction of discourse within Latino/a theology, in particular the terms "Latina," "feminist," and "theologian." Beginning with the challenge to cultural essentialism, I then proceed to the category of gender and the role of feminism within Latino/a theologies. In the third section, I explore the implications of a constructivist critique on the nature of the Latino/a theologian. I conclude with some suggestions for advancing this necessary conversation.

Latino/a

My examination of the construction of Latino/a identity is shaped by three questions: Can we speak of a monolithic Latino/a identity? What are the political implications of claiming a Latino/a identity? And lastly, is Latino/a identity a racial, ethnic, and/or cultural construct and what are the implications if it is? Various Latino/a philosophers, critics, and sociologists inform my remarks. After presenting the questions and concerns laid out by these thinkers, I turn to the implications of their challenges for Latino/a theologians. These reflections will serve as a hermeneutical lens to examine Latino/a theology.[4]

Can we speak of Latino/a identity? According to philosopher Jorge Gracia we can, yet only in a limited sense. In his recent philosophical book, *Hispanic/Latino Identity: A Philosophical Perspective,* Gracia examines the nature of Latino/a/Hispanic identity, and discerns its pragmatic and philosophical viability. Discarding various theories of Latino/a identity, Gracia articulates his own philosophical construction of it, concluding that Latino/as must be understood historically, in terms of social relations. He writes, "What ties them together, and separates them from others, is history and the particular events of that history rather than the consciousness of that history; a unique web

---

4. "Hermeneutical lens" refers to one's interpretative approach.

of changing historical relations supplies their unity" (2000:50). Gracia's construction is heavily influenced by the philosophy of Ludwig Wittgenstein and his notion of family resemblances, a philosophical category based on the similarities that exist among members of a family. "Family resemblances" is a term that describes the network of commonalities that exist within a group. For Gracia, this is an especially useful analytic tool for Latino/as. Families cannot be reduced solely to those with genetic ties. Marriage, Gracia reminds us, is a contractual agreement, not a biological tie. The complexity, mixture, and diversity of families parallel the complexity of Latino/a communities. Differences and unique experiences do not render the term meaningless, for it is the history of Latino/a communities and not the particular consciousness of that history that grounds Latino/a identity.

Turning to the writings of Latino/a theologians, one finds that historical events and the interconnections that result from them play a significant role in the construction of the Latinos and Latinas who are the subjects and objects of this theology. This is seen, for example, through the widespread use of sociology and history as a methodological starting point for Latino/a theologians. A significant number of Latino/a theologians begin their books and articles with a chapter or section defining Latino/as through an overview of their historical and contemporary realities within the United States. Whether it is Roberto Goizueta's *Caminemos con Jesús,* Eduardo Fernández's *La Cosecha,* Alejandro García-Rivera's *Community of the Beautiful,* or Justo González's *Mañana,* to name a few, the reader is confronted in the first pages of each monograph with a chapter defining the Latino/a community, both historical and contemporary.

This first step, which I am not critiquing per se, is integral to Latino/a theology's method. By situating themselves as racial-ethnic theologians, Latino/a theologians must explain the very communities they belong to and represent. Often their introductory chapters highlight the complexity and diversity of Latino/a communities. Later chapters of these monographs often emphasize particular expressions or devotions within certain communities. All these methodological features are crucial in maintaining the particularity and diversity of

Latino/a communities. Starting by naming one's identity is fundamental to articulating a theology from a marginalized perspective.

Such acts of self-definition, are, however, subjected to an overarching homogenization found within these same works. One only has to look at their titles: *Caminemos con Jesus: A Latino/a Theology of Accompaniment; Mañana: Christian Theology from a Hispanic Perspective; Hispanic Women: Prophetic Voice in the Church; On Being Human: U.S. Hispanic and Rahnerian Perspectives.* Within the writings of many Latino/a theologians, the use of broad terms to describe Latino/a theology, Latino/a culture, Latino/a popular religion, and Latino/a experiences undermines the very particularity and distinctiveness of the various Latino/a communities.[5] There is a tension, therefore, between claiming the diversity of Latino/as while at times discursively negating it.

A concrete example is in order. The category of *mestizaje* has come to saturate Latino/a theology. The privileging of *mestizaje,* which refers to the biological and cultural mixture of Spanish and Indigenous, is intimately linked to Latino/a theology's emphasis on culture. *Mestizaje* has become the primary site of struggle for Latino/as and the *locus theologicus* of Latino/a theology. Anthropologically, *mestizaje* functions to name the ambiguity and in-between-ness of Latino/a identity. Contesting a monolithic understanding of Latino/as as a single race, Miguel De La Torre and Edwin Aponte note, "Hispanics are a *mestizaje* (racial mixture or combination of ethnicities), a *mestizaje* of races, a *mestizaje* of cultures, a *mestizaje* of kitchens, a dense stew of distinct flavors" (2001:13). In the concluding section of their text, Aponte and De La Torre describe the diversity of the current Latino/a community as an "evolving *mestizaje.*" The category, for them, no longer represents the mixture of indigenous and Spanish; it now refers to cultural mixture in any sense of the word, as long as it applies to Latino/a communities.

The 1995 anthology of Latino/a theology, *Mestizo Christianity,* cemented the primacy of this category for Latino/a theologians. As Arturo Bañuelas states in the opening paragraph of his introduction,

---

5. I myself am guilty of this in my own research and writing. Guerrero's *A Chicano Theology* (1987) stands out as a notable exception.

In this theology, *mestizaje,* the mixture of human groups, is a core paradigm because Latino history begins in the early sixteenth century with the Spanish conquest and the religious and cultural confluence of the Spaniards, Amerindians, and Africans in the Americas. This paradigm of the mixing of bloods and cultures also marks the birth of *mestizo* Christianity, the experience of God from within *mestizaje* reality. *Mestizo* Christianity is the Latino's heritage. Presently, Latino theology is attempting to elaborate the link between *mestizaje* and God's design for humanity. (Bañuelas, 1995:1)[6]

Like Aponte and De La Torre, Bañuelas sees *mestizaje* as encompassing mixture in general and not merely Spanish and Indian. However, there remains a strong ambiguity within Latino/a theology on the use of this term. In the more recent *From the Heart of Our People,* the editors note this ambiguity in their glossary (Espín and Díaz, 1999). *Mestizaje* is defined as the cultural and racial mixing of Spanish and Indigenous. However, they note that "the term is often used, in Latino/a theology, to refer to a much broader and deeper mixing of cultures, religious traditions, and so on." The following entry, *mulataje,* refers to the cultural and racial mixing of African and Spanish. "Although occasionally used in Latino/a theology, the term *mulataje* and *mulatto/a* are often and inaccurately subsumed into the categories of *mestizaje* and *mestizo/a*" (Ibid.:262).[7] *Mestizaje* has become equivalent to mixture and hybridity.

The subsuming of *mulatez* into the category of *mestizaje* is not present in the work of all Latino/a theologians. Ada María Isasi-Díaz and Fernando F. Segovia, both Cuban Americans, attempt to maintain the distinctiveness of each category while demonstrating their shared value. Within Isasi-Díaz's scholarship, these terms function at various levels: as descriptors of the Latino/a condition, as

---

6. In her contribution to *Mestizo Christianity* María Pilar Aquino defines Latino/a identity as *mestizo/a,* a combination of indigenous, African, and European (1995:192–208).

7. This position is a development on Espín's thought, for in earlier writings he uses the category of *mestizaje* to designate *mulato/a* realities. "Hispanic communities with their roots in the northeast, Florida or the Spanish-speaking Caribbean tend to be the result of *mestizaje* between Spaniards and Africans. Those communities with roots in the West and Southwest or in Mexico and central America tend to be the outcome of *mestizaje* between Spaniards and Native Amerindian population" (1995:151).

ethical standpoints, and as epistemological categories. *Mestizaje* and *mulatez* are a theological locus of her *mujerista* theology and function as a hermeneutical tool and paradigm that reveal the nature of Latino/a epistemology. For Isasi-Díaz, *mestizaje-mulatez* are both descriptors of the Latino/as' cultural condition and an explicit decision by Latino/as to embrace an identity within the dominant U.S. paradigm.[8] In embracing *mestizaje-mulatez,* Latino/as are expressing solidarity with other marginalized people of color and attempting to dismantle dualistic constructions of race that plague identity politics. For Isasi-Díaz, the choice to embrace the *mestizo-mulato* condition is a manner of contesting hegemonic constructions of identity within the academy and society.

Perhaps no other Latino/a theologian has attempted to explicitly maintain the categories of *mestizaje* and *mulataje* more than biblical scholar Fernando F. Segovia. Segovia describes Latino/as as a "hybrid people," both *mestizo* and *mulato.* "On the one hand, we are children of Spain and thus of Europe, Mediterranean and Catholic Europe.... On the other hand, we are also the children of pre-Columbian America and Africa — deeply rooted as well in other ancient cultures, histories, and languages" (1995:32). Segovia continues by noting that this *mestizaje* and *mulatez* permeates all aspects of Latino/a culture and identity, including religion, art, and epistemology. In his own work he resists the trend within Latino/a theology to collapse *mulatez* into *mestizaje.*[9] Segovia simultaneously maintains the shared value of the terms *mestizaje* and *mulatez* as markers of hybridity while preserving the distinctiveness of each term. In his

---

8. "*Mestizaje* and *mulatez* for Hispanas/Latinas are not a given but a conscious choice made obvious by how we move in and out of Latino and Anglo-American culture according to need and desire" (Isasi-Díaz, 2004:59).

9. The inclusion of the category of *mulatez,* while one avenue of rhetorically upholding the African elements of certain Latino/a cultures, is not without contention. Miguel De La Torre rejects the term *mulato* to describe the mixture of African and Spanish, and consequently Cuban culture. For him, the negative associations and racist connotations of the word's association with mule are too profound. De La Torre argues that *mulatez* is a fabrication by Latino/a religious scholars. Further, he argues, the term fails to encompass the totality of Cuban peoples, for example, and is not a "solution" to the problem of naming the racial complexity of Latino/a identity. "Cubans are heirs of a Taíno indigenous culture, of a medieval (Catholic, Jewish, and Muslim) Spain, of Africa (primarily of Yoruban culture), and of Asia (specifically Cantonese)" (2003:17); see also chapter 6 by Miguel De La Torre in this anthology.

efforts, he attempts to uphold the shared features of Latino/a communities while also maintaining their distinctiveness and not privileging certain aspects over others.

The privileging of certain Latino/a communities over others has concrete ramifications for the role of Latino/a theological discourse in the academy and the broader society. This leads to the second question, the political implications of claiming a broader Latino/a identity instead of a cultural identity defined by one's original nationality or national heritage. This practice, as many Latino/a authors indicate, is in fact more prevalent than self-identifying as a Latino/a. So, for example, I myself identify more readily as a Cuban American than as a Latina. Nevertheless, many Latino/a theologians continue to present their work as Latino/a theology (versus Cuban American or Puerto Rican theology), often for political reasons.

Of interest here are the implications of embracing the category of Latino/a within the socio-political arena of the United States and the academic discourse of theology. The political benefits of using the term "Latino/a" are manifold and known to many. Such naming increases visibility and allows for extensive coalition-building among Latino/as of various origins. Here, I only wish to ponder a potential pitfall in the use of this term. Cuban American philosopher Ofelia Schutte is helpful in discussing the question of identifying herself as a Latina versus a Cuban American. Schutte notes that "Latina" signifies one's status as a minority in the United States, while "Cuban American" refers to one's homeland and heritage (2000:69). "Latino/a" thus becomes a term that highlights one's context as a minority and makes that status the primary referent of one's political identity. This does not lead Schutte, however, to discard the term. Instead, Schutte embraces the category in spite of its negative political and commercial function. "What it leads me to do is to adopt the principle of *recognizing the internal differences* among women, Hispanics, Cuban Americans, or what have you. This principle allows one to identify as a member of a group without being coerced into compliance with the group's image of its normative type" (Ibid.:67). For Schutte, as for Gracia, the foundation of the ability to claim Hispanic identity without necessarily sharing all the attributes of other Latino/as lies in the shared cultural history of Latino/as. Again, we find a more fluid definition of Latino/a identity. However, when one takes the category "Hispanic" as descriptive of a socio-political minority, the boundaries become much more rigid. Without denying the political implications of the term "Latino/a," the question remains whether Latino/as constitute merely a political collective, or, as Gracia and Schutte indicate, a cultural or historical category. I argue for both, an emphasis on the ethnic *and* political dimensions of Latino/a consciousness. On one level, it is a political gesture to identify oneself as Latino/a, for it situates Latino/as within the national context of the United States as a large collective of peoples. However, given the increasing growth and cultural influence of Latino/a peoples, there appears to be a new ethno-cultural category of Latino/as, which is distinct from a "Hispanic" person's association with others from their nation of origin.

Theologians who write, teach, and publish under the banner of Latino/a theology must realize that this is not merely a category for the collectivity of Latino/a cultures, but a political gesture with multifaceted dimensions, both positive and negative. On the positive side, given the extremely small community of Latino/a theologians even today, our gathering under the common heading of "Hispanic" or "Latino/a" increases our visibility and prominence within the academy. This enables coalition-building and collaboration among ourselves to ensure that the voices of the masses that we represent to the elite academy are heard with greater frequency. However, in such coalitions we are often forced to negate the very particularities and complexity of our communities.

For the past few pages, I have used the terms "ethnicity" and "culture" interchangeably, for both terms are used by scholars to describe what is meant by the category of Latino/as. However, given the prominence of race in the broader identity politics of the United States, the actual nature of the socio-political category "Latino/a" and its function must be further explored. In other words, is Latino/a identity racial, cultural, and/or ethnic? Latino/as, as many authors have noted, do not fit into the rigid construction of race operating in the United States, for various races constitute Latino/a peoples. Latino/a "race" is not discernible. For philosopher Linda Martín Alcoff, echoing her colleagues, what unites Latino/as is culture. This

has led some Latino/a scholars and activists to identify Latino/as as
an ethnic group instead of a racial one. Yet Alcoff questions the ef-
fectiveness of this move. "African American," for example, a term
designated to emphasize the cultural identity of peoples of African
descent, in contrast to the racial category of "black," remains a
racial designator in dominant U.S. discourse. Thus a cultural category
can be transformed into an exclusive racial designator. In the United
States, a racialized group cannot embrace an ethnic identity that is
free of racial connotations. Alcoff notes, "The concept of ethnicity is
closely associated with the concept of race, emerging at the same moment in global history, as this meaning indicates. . . . For many people
in the United States, 'ethnic' connotes not only nonwhite but also the
typical negative associations of nonwhite racial identity" (2000:37).
In other words, "ethnic" comes to equal "nonwhite."

Two questions remain. The first concerns the political implications
of the category "Latino/as." For many, "Latino/a" is seen purely as
a political construct, an almost coalitional social construction. For
others "Latino/a" in fact represents a new ethnic reality, one that resonates with descriptions of mestizo/a peoples, who in their mixture
of Spanish, African, and indigenous heritages create a new reality, a
new people.[10] Latino/a theologians must decide where they stand on
this issue in an attempt to resolve the tension between pan-Latino/a
identity and particular Latino/a communities within Latino/a theological discourse. A second question, and one linked to the first,
concerns the role of Latino/a theology within minority discourse in
the United States and its connection to a pan-Latino/a identity. Also
important for consideration are the homogenization of Latino/a theological reflection and the manner in which Latino/as are received by
the theological academy.

In highlighting these questions, I am not arguing for the effacement
of the category of "Latino/a." A pan-Latino/a identity is after all part
of our intellectual and philosophical history. One only needs to remember, for example, the writings of the great nineteenth-century

---

10. See Elizondo, 1994; Goizueta, 1995, especially chapter 1. *Mestizaje* refers to the biological and cultural mixture of Indigenous and Spanish. A *mestizo/a* is the result of that
mixture.

Cuban writer José Martí, who argued for a pan–Latin American understanding of *América*. Also, when a marginalized people within the United States such as Latino/as name themselves, they both empower themselves and subvert a dominant society that seeks to erase the particularity of Latino/a culture and identity. I am, however, proposing that we Latino/as must critically examine the consequences of the discursive categories of "Latino/a" and "Hispanic," as well as the essentialist inclinations such categories contain. Let us now turn to the construction of Latina identity in particular, with special attention to the systematic marginalization of feminist discourse within Latino/a theology.

Feminist

Over fifty years ago Simone de Beauvoir wrote, "One is not born, but rather becomes, a woman" (1989:267). With this statement, de Beauvoir raised the question of gender essentialism in feminist theory, a matter hotly debated even today. The question of whether there are characteristics that essentially constitute the nature of a woman, or if we can even speak of a woman's essential nature, is not only discussed within women's studies, gender studies, and feminist theory, but also has permeated other disciplines within the academy. Primarily led by feminist scholars influenced by postmodern theory and cultural studies, many thinkers emphasize the construction of gender identity and the socio-political consequences of gender essentialism.[11]

A quick glance at recent publications in the field of feminist theology reveals that gender essentialism has been severely critiqued for over a decade. Unfortunately, this literature has been for the most part ignored by Latino/a theologians. As a result, we enter the conversation rather late. In his overview of Latino/a theology, Orlando Espín highlights the growing impact of Latina feminist contributions to Latino/a theology. "However," Espín notes,

> we would be daydreaming and lying to ourselves if we thought that this increased awareness and reception of feminist concerns

---

11. Gender essentialism is the belief that there are certain qualities that are essentially or a priori natural to men and women.

and issues has occurred without tension, that it's a "done deal," or that most of feminist critical theory has been understood, assimilated, or even read by most Latino/a theologians (who are males). Unfortunately, much Latino/a theology pays lip service to feminism, while ignoring it methodologically. We are certainly not where we were twenty years ago, but we are not even near where we should be. (2000:29)

Due to a lack of attention to the concerns and insights of feminist thinkers, Latinos have, for the most part, marginalized women's contributions to feminist critiques or matters pertaining solely to women's concerns. Thus nearly all theology written by women is uncritically deemed "feminist," and the term "feminist" itself remains inadequately defined within Latino/a theology.[12]

A few examples are in order. In their recent introduction to Latino/a theology, Edwin Aponte and Miguel A. De La Torre create four categories of thinkers representing Hispanic theology: Catholics, Protestants, Latina Women, and New Ecumenism (2001:103–15). The theological contributions of Latinas are only mentioned under the category of "Latina Women." While emphasizing the "invaluable contribution" of women, the authors end up marginalizing the voices of women as "women's theologies." Their contributions are limited to the domain of the feminine.[13] In addition to using the ambiguous category of "women's theologies," earlier in the text De La Torre and Aponte falsely categorize Ana María Pineda as an "important voice in feminist theology" (Ibid.:132). To my knowledge, Pineda does not see her theological method as feminist. The place of women within the other three categories is unclear. Indeed, one must ask what "women" means and why their voices are segregated from male theological contributions. An essentialized understanding of women's nature and writings is reflected in the tendency to segregate women's contributions.

---

12. By "feminist" I mean a thinker whose perspective is informed by feminist theory and analysis, looking at the power relationships that shape the historical and contemporary constructions of gender identity. While Ada María Isasi-Díaz describes her work as *mujerista*, she still remains heavily influenced by feminist analysis.

13. Whether intentionally or not, Aponte and De La Torre end up discursively marginalizing women's voices through this categorization.

Another challenge to an essentialized grouping of women is posed by the theology of Loida Martell-Ortero, who in her theology of *mujeres evangélicas* expresses reservations about both Latina feminist and *mujerista* theologies, because of their Roman Catholic emphasis and what she sees as their secular origins (1994:67–85). Martell-Otero articulates as an alternative her theology *evangélica*, whose sources are found in the faith and practices of Protestant Latina women. She thus rejects the blind categorization of all Latinas' voices as "feminist." In addition, the reduction of all women's theologies to feminist theology is a manner, whether intentional or not, of marginalizing their contributions to feminist studies, which have not been, historically, a central concern for Latino/a theologians.

Gender remains a secondary category of analysis within Latino/a theology. Similarly, in his recent monograph *La Cosecha: Harvesting Contemporary United States Hispanic Theology (1972–1998)*, Eduardo Fernández also discursively marginalizes the work of Latinas (2000). While Fernández is to be commended for his call to take seriously the lives and scholarship of Latinas, his decision to treat the female and male theologians separately in his analysis contributes to an understanding of feminist discourse as marginal. These monographs are not unique. In fact, they represent an all-too-common discursive practice within Latino theology.

A moment of clarification is in order. Aponte, De La Torre, and Fernández's work are of particular interest for this section for they are the first book-length introductions to Latino/a *theology*. This feature distinguishes them from other monographs and is why they are being scrutinized. Had I been examining the writings of Latino/a theologians regarding the exclusion of women in their construction of the Latino/a community, Latino/a identity, and/or Latino/a history, I would have included such groundbreaking works as those by Virgilio Elizondo, Roberto S. Goizueta, and Justo González. However, my interest here is examining in which arena Latino/a *theological discourse* is being presented. "Senior" Latino scholars would not fare much better in a broader critique of the absence of women's voices and experiences within Latino theology. However, unlike the authors cited above, these scholars have not written introductory monographs on Latino/a theology. In addition, I am not claiming that Aponte, De La Torre, and Fernández are intentionally marginalizing women's theological contribution in a malicious manner. However, they are, unfortunately, following the discursive practice of segregating Latinas' theological contributions.

Related to this issue is the failure to acknowledge and address the divisions that exist among Latina theologians. While we Latino/a theologians are quite comfortable speaking of "Latino/a theology," we seldom refer to the fact that within this category there are distinct and conflicting voices. I am speaking, of course, of the distinction between *mujerista* and Latina feminist theology, embodied particularly in the works of Ada María Isasi-Díaz and María Pilar Aquino. As demonstrated by a recent edited volume entitled *Religion, Feminism, and Justice: A Reader in Latina Feminist Theology,* there is a clear line between those who embrace the term *mujerista* and those who describe their theology as "Latina feminist." As the editors of the volume state in the introduction, "We acknowledge the important work and contributions of Ada María Isasi-Díaz in developing what she has defined as *mujerista* theology. However, we have opted to name ourselves Latina feminists" (Aquino, Machado, and Rodríguez, 2002: xiv). The exclusion of Ada María Isasi-Díaz's voice from this project obscures the distinctions among Latina theologians that claim a feminist hermeneutic.

In her groundbreaking text *En la Lucha/In the Struggle: Elaborating a Mujerista Theology,* Isasi-Díaz elaborates an early definition of *mujerista.* "A *mujerista* is a Latina who makes a preferential option for herself and her Hispanic sisters, understanding that our struggle for liberation has to take into consideration how racism/ethnic prejudice, economic oppression, and sexism work together and reinforce each other" (1993:4). Rejecting the term *feminist hispana,* she argues that for many Latinas, feminism is viewed as an Anglo creation which marginalizes Latino/a concerns. Isasi-Díaz also highlights the painful history and marginalization of Latinas within the white, Euroamerican feminist community (1989:410).[14] These factors contribute

---

14. White feminism is rejected due to the racism and ethnic prejudice that can accompany this movement.

to her rejection of "feminist" as an appropriate term to designate Latinas concerned about sexist oppression.

In response, Aquino argues that feminism is in fact indigenous to Latin Americans. Ignoring this reality erases the struggles of women against sexism and patriarchy. To those who call themselves *mujeristas,* Aquino writes, "With these views, not only do they show their ignorance regarding the feminist tradition within Latin American communities, but they also attempt to remove from us our authority to name ourselves according to our own historical roots" (1998:94). Aquino thus rejects the term *mujerista* because in her view it erases the history of feminism within Latin America. In addition, Aquino notes, "there are no *mujerista* sociopolitical and ecclesial subjects or movements in the United States or in Latin America" (Ibid.:139). At the same time, in my view it seems fair to ask if a Latina feminist theological movement exists outside of the academy.

I cannot speak for Isasi-Díaz or Aquino regarding their own views of their theological differences. I can, however, note that the tension between their theological contributions has largely been ignored by other Latino/a theologians. It seems to me that this refusal to seriously engage the theological tension between arguably the two most prominent Latina theologians in the United States turns their theological contributions into feminist "side-projects" that do not affect the core of Latino/a theology.[15] The division between Isasi-Díaz and Aquino is more than a quibble over names. Yet even names matter, as Elisabeth Schüssler Fiorenza reminds us: "Language is not just performative; it is political" (1999:93). In any case, beyond the use of the term *mujerista,* there has not been to date a dialogue that examines the methodological and theological differences between *mujerista* and Latina feminist theologians in order to uncover points of contention.

Linked to the debate over naming is the problem of the compression of Latina theological voices into two — and only two — camps. I am in no way contesting the pioneering contributions of Isasi-Díaz and Aquino to theology. I am, however, noting that their important

---

15. In addition, this tension is too often reduced to personal relationships, thus belittling the intellectual significance of the work of Isasi-Díaz and Aquino.

voices have eclipsed the complexity of Latina theology (an outcome not of their making). You are either a *mujerista* or you are not. So, for example, the soon-to-be published *Manual de Teología Hispana* has an entry for *Mujerista* Theology and an entry for Latina Feminist Theology. Discursively, therefore, you are either a *mujerista* or you are not, and in any case if you are a Latina, you are a feminist. While I commend and thank María Pilar Aquino, Daisy Machado, and Jeanette Rodríguez for editing the recent volume on Latina feminist theology and for inviting a group of younger scholars to contribute to this project, I am very concerned about the explicit framing of this book as non-*mujerista* theology. It is clear to me now, more than ever, that we need to open the doors of dialogue among all Latinas, for the manifold divisions among us can only enrich our theological projects.

The failure of Latino/a theologians to seriously engage the work of feminist theologians as a central concern is only one dimension of this gender trouble. An occasional footnote does not suffice. We Latino/as grow hoarse begging Euroamerican scholars to learn our intellectual history, yet among Latino/as there is a certain ignorance concerning the history and complexity of feminist thought. I am not denying the important role Latinas have played in the history and construction of Latino/a theology. As Allan Figueroa Deck highlights in his 1992 introduction to *Frontiers of Hispanic Theology in the United States,* a characteristic of Latino/a theology is "the unusually prominent role that women have had in this emergent theology" (1992:xvii).[16] The presence of these women is indisputable. I am, however, suggesting that Latino theologians have not taken feminist theology as a whole seriously and incorporated gender as a central category of analysis.[17] We must ask why.

---

16. Shawn Copeland also notes this when she writes, "From its beginning, Hispanic/Latino Theology has been informed by the insights of women" (1997:370).

17. At the 2002 meeting of the Academy of Catholic Hispanic Theologians in the United States, where I presented an abbreviated version of this paper, my claim was contested by Arturo Bañuelas. I do not find evidence of Latinos taking Latinas seriously in the writings of a majority of Latino theologians over the past twenty years. In my eyes, to take a discipline seriously is to study it and its interlocutors in order to understand the complexity and history of a given academic discourse.

In addition, Latino/a theologians must reflect on the manner in which Latinas are rhetorically constructed within Latino/a theology. They are most often portrayed as poor, associated with Marian devotions and popular religion. They are seen as mothers and grandmothers, not young women. They are the carriers of religion and culture. This is not to deny the centrality of poor, grassroots Latinas for theologians among us who identify profoundly with liberation theologies. This is also not to denounce popular religious practices as not genuine. However, in limiting our construction of Latinas to certain often-repeated categories and characteristics, as theologians we are restricting the nature and number of women that Latino/a theology is actually engaging and describing. Such a theology cannot claim to speak to the fullness and complexity of Latina experience, nor consider itself an authentic Latino/a voice. Similarly, to limit Latinas to the oppressed and the marginalized is to categorize them within a framework that strips them of any ability to transform their state of oppression (Lugones, 1990:504–5).

Within the realm of Latina theology exclusively, I would like to offer four future directions that build on the work of those groundbreaking scholars in the field. First, as this section has already implied, there needs to be a serious rethinking of the category "Latina theology" that includes the plurality of voices that make up this field. Latina theology cannot be reduced to a branch of feminist theology, for not all Latina theologians embrace a feminist voice. Nonetheless, the feminist concerns of a majority of Latina theologians cannot be dismissed and must be highlighted as an important dimension of Latina theologies.

Second, Latina theologians who embrace a feminist hermeneutic must offer a more explicit critique of the writings of Latino theologians. While these theologies do an excellent job of highlighting how sexism functions in Latino/a communities and in some traditional theological concepts, they have yet to apply that critique to the work of Latino theologians. This lack of critical engagement, in my eyes, allows Latino theologians to ignore Latina feminist voices since their feminist critiques clearly do not apply to them. Also, it reinforces the mistaken stereotype that feminism is an Anglo construction that does not apply to Latino/as.

A third area that would offer new points of departure for Latina theologies is further writings in more traditional theological categories. It is essential for voices deemed minority to write on traditional theological *loci* in order to enter into dialogue and challenge dominant theological constructions through this shared discourse. If not, our theological contributions are reduced to side projects that do not impact mainstream theological discourse. A point of departure is inspired by the work of Benjamín Valentín, who pushes Latino/a theologians not only to emphasize the category of culture but also to use Latino/a cultural production within their theologies. For Valentín, the use of Latino/a cultural artifacts is a fundamental starting point if one is to articulate an authentic Latino/a theology. I am thinking in particular of the work of Latina literature here as a vital area for Latina theologians to explore.[18] While a heavy emphasis on Latinas' experiences, most often via the lens of sociology and ethnography, has dominated Latina theologies, the time has come to explore other entry points into Latinas' theological contributions.

Theologian

We come now to the third and final area I would like to discuss: the construction of the theologian within Latino/a theology. There are two dimensions of this construction I wish to explore: the notion of the popular theologian and the danger of the "theoretical" in contemporary theology. Here, I will be brief. Regarding the popular theologian, my comments are influenced by the theology of Marcella Althaus-Reid, who has examined the construction of the Latin American liberation theologian. I find her insights, while in a different context, helpful for an analysis of Latino/a theology. Althaus-Reid notes that in liberation theology the popular theologian is constructed as a "mirror" of the poor, a reflection of the faith of the poor. "The popular theologian is not a person in diaspora but rather the conceptual product of Liberation Theology in the diaspora of the theological markets of Europe and the United States" (2000:37). The caricature of the popular theologian becomes a conceptual construct that

---

18. This area of literature and theology is beginning to be explored by some Latina theologians. See Delgado, 2002; M. A. González, 2003a and 2003b; Isasi-Díaz, 2004.

results in the co-optation and consequent powerlessness of liberation theologies in the face of dominant Western discourse. Liberation theologies become "theme parks" that Western theologians can visit while not having to alter the nature and structure of their theology. As theme park theologies, Althaus-Reid contends, liberation theologies become a commodity for Western capitalism (Ibid.:42). As theme parks, they can be visited at one's leisure; one is never forced to take them seriously.

This popular theologian is usually a priest or minister living with and working with the poor whose faith, suffering, and simplicity are acclaimed. "Western academia saw the popular theologian as a benevolent father dealing with ignorant, although sweet and well-disposed, native children.... Many Europeans would have liked to have submissive, faithful Christian natives in their parishes, instead of real people" (Ibid.:51–52). Two things are worth noting in Althaus-Reid's statement. First, and most obvious, is the gendered construction of the Latino theologian. True, women theologians are fewer than men, but if more male theologians would highlight the concerns and questions feminists raise, our awareness of the scholarship already done by women would increase. Second, Althaus-Reid sees a paternalistic attitude present in Latin American theologians. The educated elite are to translate the simple, beautiful faith of the people in order to transform the nature of the academy and the churches. This demonstrates a simplistic understanding of the faith of the people who are seen as uncritically pious and who do not have the ability to intellectually engage and challenge their own beliefs. "Luckily," they have theologians to do this. Do Latino/a theologians contribute to this? Are we aware of it? Does the non-Latino/a community embrace this? What better way to continue to view Latino/as as ignorant and backward peoples than accept a construction of them as people unable to intellectualize their faith!

A second matter concerns the role of critical theory in Latino/a theology. Critical theory is all the rage in theological circles. Demonstrating one's knowledge of critical theory, postcolonial studies, postmodernism, and globalization is the mark of a scholar who has seriously engaged and mastered some very complicated texts. This very essay, in fact, can be seen as an attempt to analyze Latino/a theology theoretically. However, Latino/a theologians must proceed with caution. There is a danger in the turn to theory, especially when too often Western European and Euroamerican sources are seen as the zenith of the discipline. Barbara Christian views the surge in theory within the writings of people of color as the victory, once again, of the West. "I have become convinced that there has been a takeover in the literary world by Western philosophers from the old literary élite, the neutral humanists.... They have changed literary critical language to suit their own purposes as philosophers, and they have reinvented the meaning of theory" (2000:11). What is considered good theory, Christian contends, is governed by white, Western, monolithic norms.

Christian is not denying the theoretical import of non-Western sources. "For people of color have always theorized — but in forms quite different from the Western form of abstract logic. And I am inclined to say that our theorizing (and I intentionally use the verb rather than the noun) is often in narrative forms, in the stories we create, in riddles and proverbs, in the play with language, since dynamic rather than fixed ideas seem to be more to our liking" (Ibid.:12). Instead, Christian is warning us against considering only certain types of writings to be genuine theory. Too often, in fact, scholars of color are shocked by the ignorance of the dominant academy regarding the contemporary and historical voices of marginalized groups.

This is seen in the curriculum at institutions where people of color are trained, leading to a vicious cycle of ignorance regarding the diversity of the history of thought.[19] This privileging of Western discourse also affects the very nature of theology. Liberation theologies that seek to emulate this methodology invariably see Western ways of thinking as normative.[20]

---

19. "Because of the academic world's general ignorance about the literature of black people and of women, whose work too often has been discredited, it is not surprising that so many of our critics think that the position arguing that literature is critical begins with these New Philosophers. Unfortunately, many of our young critics do not investigate the reasons *why* that statement — literature is political — is now acceptable when before it was not; nor do we look to our own antecedents for the sophisticated arguments upon which we can build in order to change the tendency of any established Western idea to become hegemonic" (Christian, 2000:15).

20. This concern was articulated over ten years ago in the writings of María Pilar Aquino. "Consequently, like all *liberation theology*, the theological task that Latina women develop

The popular theologian and the technical theoretician represent, in many ways, the tension that exists between the pastoral and the academic within Latino/a theology. Too often, theologians of a more pastoral persuasion have complained that their work is not taken seriously by other Latino/a academics. On the flip side, Latino/a theologians who rely heavily on theory and philosophy have been accused of abstraction and intellectual elitism. The challenge remains to find a balance between the two and to find strategies for incorporating the voices of Latino/a peoples while simultaneously transforming our view of what is theoretical or philosophical.

Concluding Comments

Underlying this entire essay is the question of essentialism. While well aware of the objections to a supposed essentialism in the writings of Latino/a theologians, I am not prepared to empty the term "Latino/a" of all meaning in Latino/a theology. I do not affirm an exclusively constructivist understanding of Latino/a culture, feminism, or theology. I am asking Latino/a theologians to focus our hermeneutics of suspicion upon ourselves and to examine carefully the way discourse has historically functioned within Latino/a theology. Form and content are organically united. Therefore, what we say and how we say it are intrinsically interconnected. In addition, the act of naming and the construction of any identity have political consequences.

---

cannot be understood apart from its own historical circumstances, nor can it avoid dialogue with contemporary theological movements. However, as with liberation theologies, this task consciously and critically distances itself from the postulates and aims of the current *liberal progressive* theological movement that developed in the Western world. This movement blatantly demonstrates its disinterest in the world of the poor and oppressed. Without minimizing the multiplicity of present-day theologies, the various axes of this theological movement are derived from what is generically called modern theology. The theological viewpoint that stems from the very situation and consciousness of women, although it recognizes its methodological accomplishments and its conceptual richness, tries to overcome the limited scope of this theology because of its contextualization in the First World. It is important to emphasize this point because I believe that among some Hispanic male theologians there is a preoccupation with clarifying the relationship between *modern* theology and the growing *Hispanic* theology. From their point of view, the questions to which modern theology aims to respond are the questions that concern the Latino communities; as such, this would be its primary partner in dialogue. As a Latina woman, I do not believe this is the case. Basically, the position that grants priority to *modern theology* — in its liberal strands — leads to disinterest in and postponement of the questions to which the liberation theologies want to respond" (1992:25–26).

I would like to offer four suggestions for further conversation. First, Latino/a theologians need to seriously examine the manner in which our identity functions politically in the academy, in churches, and within the broader society. Latino/a theology can perhaps glean some insights from feminist political philosophy. Iris Marion Young argues that searching for common characteristics of women's identity will only lead to essentialist constructions of women (1997:12). However, Young contends, there are valid political motives for conceiving of women as a group. The flaw in most feminist thinking, Young holds, is the desire to construct a systematic theory within feminist discourse. As an alternative Young offers a pragmatic view of theory. "By being 'pragmatic' I mean categorizing, explaining, developing accounts and arguments that are tied to specific practical and political problems, where the purpose of this theoretical activity is clearly related to those problems. Pragmatic theorizing is . . . driven by some problem that has ultimate practical importance and is not concerned to give an account of a whole" (Ibid.:17). For Young, the current practical problem is the simultaneous acknowledgement of the dangerous implications of essentialist notions of womanhood in feminist discourse and the need for a political subject for feminism.

Young contends that a reconceptualization of social collectivity offers us a way to view women as a collective without attributing a common or essential identity shared by all women. Young defines a series as, "a collective whose members are unified passively by the relation their actions have to material objects and practico-inert histories. . . . Their membership is defined not by something they are, but rather by the fact that in their diverse existences and actions they are oriented around the same objects or practico-inert structure" (Ibid.:27).[21] The series "women" is not based on attributes shared by all women. Instead, womanhood is situated in social realities that are exterior to one's personal identity and that condition women's lives. In one's relationship to these social realities gender is constructed. A key dimension in Young's understanding of identity

---

21. "*Woman* is a serial collective defined neither by any common identity nor by a common set of attributes that all the individuals in the series have, but rather names a set of structural constraints and relations to practical inert objects that condition action and its meaning" (Young, 1997:36).

is choice. One can decide which aspects of one's serial memberships are central to one's identity. "No individual woman's identity, then, will escape the markings of gender, but how gender marks her life is her own" (Ibid.:33). This statement removes the paradox of identity as choice and as imposed and as it resonates with the experiences of Latino/a communities. At the same time Young's notion of gender as seriality would seem to undercut Latino/a theology's emphasis on the cultural and historical unity of Latino/as. Gracia's notion of family resemblances, I find, offers a more persuasive philosophical framework for understanding the organic unity of Latino/a peoples.

In attempting to name and understand Latino/as in the United States, I propose a heuristic paradigm of two distinct realities functioning within Latino/a identity. The first is the cultural similarities of Latino/as, which if understood as family resemblances present the relationships between and diversity of Latino/a peoples. Also under this category I place Latino/a culture that is a mixture of various elements of all the Hispanic cultures found in the United States. Second, however, there is the purely constructed and political dimension of Latino/as. Here, Young's notion of seriality offers a suggestive paradigm for understanding one's ability to choose — that is construct — a Latino/a identity. The tension that exists between the two represents the unity and diversity, the organic and constructed nature of Latino/a identity. Latino/a theologians need to state explicitly which view, or both, they employ in their theological construction.

My second suggestion is linked to the first and focuses specifically on the academy. Latino/a theologians must begin to examine carefully the manner in which our theologies function within academic discourse. Are there ways in which we separate ourselves from the broader academy? How does our categorization as "minority voices" affect our theological contributions? Fernando F. Segovia emphasizes the problematic relationship between Western and non-Western theologies in his excellent overview of the relationship between Minority Studies and Christian Studies.

> From an academic point of view, the world of Christian studies — regardless of its specialization — is a world that revolves resolutely around the Western tradition and that approaches, if

at all, its non-Western expressions as extensions of the West.
In both regards, the operative vision of the center regarding
non-Western Christianity is one of undercivilization and underdevelopment — standing somewhere between the apex of
Western Christianity and the nadir of native religion. Given this
vision, the world of ethnic-racial minorities, as indeed the world
of non-Western Christians in general, is a world marked per-
force by marginalization and fragmentation — a world at the
periphery of the center, with a clear sense of its relationship to
the center but no sense at all of its relationship to others in the
periphery. (2001:30)

Collaborations between "minority" groups are thus sabotaged by
the very paradigm of Western dominance itself. In the concluding
comments of his essay, Segovia offers strategies for overcoming these
obstacles, opening up a dialogue among minorities, and undermin-
ing Western hegemony. For Latino/a theologians, the question of the
strategic value of the category of minority studies remains open.

A third suggestion concerns feminism. It is imperative that Latina
feminist theologians begin to explore the convergences and differences among their theological projects. This process must also include
the voices of those Latina theologians who do not employ a feminist
hermeneutic. The goal of such an exploration is not to find some
sort of resolution or to homogenize Latina theological expressions.
Instead, Latina theologians must find avenues for collaboration and
support in spite of their different theological standpoints. What hangs
in the balance is the role of feminism within Latino/a theology in
general. While Latina feminist theologians cannot force their male
colleagues to take feminism seriously, they can challenge their work
through the category of gender. Latinas can learn a lesson from wom-
anist theology's critique of black liberation theology. We must bring
the gender critique to bear on our own scholarship.

If one examines the writings of various Latino/a theologians, one
is struck by a fourth concern: the role of "the people" in their writings. The titles of our books tell the story: *From the Heart of Our
People, The Faith of the People,* and *"We Are a People!"* But who are
the people? While Latino/a theology has various sociological answers

to these questions, there remains ambiguity regarding the Latino/as of Latino/a theology. This has implications for the nature of the Latino/a theological task and the location of Latino/a theology within a broader theological discourse. Methodologically, this also has implications for the function of theory within Latino/a theology with pastoral and praxeological implications.

Concerning the diversity within feminist communities, Elizabeth Spelman writes, "If feminism is essentially about gender, and gender is taken to be neatly separable from race and class, then race and class don't need to be talked about except in some peripheral way. And if race and class are peripheral to women's identities as women, then racism and classism can't be of central concern to feminism" (1988:112–13). Spelman continues by arguing that if we assume that all women are the same, there is no point in learning about how women different from ourselves understand our womanhood. However, if what we have in common as women is viewed in concert with our differences, then examining race and class actually broadens and enriches our understanding of gender. For Latino/a theologians, we cannot assume that all Hispanics are alike, that all Latinas are alike, and that the theology written by men and women of Latin American descent living in the United States can be easily categorized under one rubric. Instead, we must look at the diversity of our communities, theologies, and identities and within that complexity articulate our theological contributions.

Chapter 8

Rethinking Liberation

Manuel Mejido C.

There is no Americano dream. There is only the American dream created by an Anglo-Protestant society. Mexican Americans will share in that dream and in that society only if they dream in English. (Huntington, 2004:11)

Notre syntaxe est en voie d'extinction minée, contaminée, déterminée par Shakespeare et ses sbires, Y'a pas d'quoi rire car j'ai malamalangue. (Loco Locass, 2000 Manifestif album)[1]

These reflections are an attempt to rethink liberation for the postmodern condition specifically from the point of view of U.S. Hispanic reality.[2] How does the postmodern condition appear to U.S. Hispanic reality? Global liberal-democratic capitalism presents itself

---

1. "Our syntax is nearly extinct, incinerated, contaminated, dominated by Shakespeare and his goons, This is no joke, 'cause I'm *malamalangue*." "*Malamalangue*" is literally "I'm-hurting-in-the-tongue" ("*mal-à-ma-langue*"), that is, *la langue française*, the French tongue: An allusion to the historical struggle for linguistic rights in Quebec. From the song, "Malamalangue" (2000 Manifestif album), written and performed by Loco Locass, the politically engaged francophone rap group from Montréal. All translations are my own.
2. Postmodernism is not simply a style of thought that is skeptical of "grand narratives." It does not simply refer to that way of seeing the world that gravitates around language, alterity, difference, fluidity, hybridity, playfulness, reflexivity. Postmodernism is first and foremost a cultural form that is related to the "rise of more flexible modes of capital accumulation, and a new round of 'time-space compression' in the organization of capitalism" (Harvey, 1989:vii). See also Jameson, 1991; and Eagleton, 1996. Today, after the fall of the Berlin Wall, the Treaty of Maastricht, and the emergence of, for example, the World Trade Organization (WTO), the World Social Forum, and, most recently, the global "war on terrorism," both the postindustrial societies of the center and the postcolonial societies of the periphery are merging in and through the international division of labor of global liberal-democratic capitalism. See Hardt and Negri, 2000. As the latest moment of the postmodern condition, liberal-democratic multiculturalism (i.e., "identity politics") and "deterritorialized" (i.e., global), advanced capitalism

to U.S. Hispanic reality as the Free Trade Area of the Americas, while the postmodern style of thought manifests itself as the decoupling of U.S. Hispanic reality from the history of the Americas. Indeed, the postmodern condition appears to U.S. Hispanic reality as assimilation into the Anglo-American mainstream, an assimilation that takes place in and through the anxiety generated by the loss of the Spanish language and in and through the alienation of U.S. Hispanic labor. U.S. Hispanic liberals and leftists are both falling captive to the postmodern condition, specifically to the eclipse of assimilation as the dialectic of anxiety and alienation.

U.S. Hispanic liberals, on the one hand, are comfortable with the idea that U.S. Hispanic reality is one among a plurality of ethnic groups in a multicultural society. Liberals believe that through public discourse, the U.S. Hispanic community will gradually open a space for itself in U.S. society. They believe that integration does not necessarily imply assimilation. Indeed, U.S. Hispanic liberals believe, for example, in the Congressional Hispanic Caucus, they believe in the U.S. Department of Education's Office of English Language Acquisition. But such a belief is possible only to the extent to which U.S. Hispanic liberals ignore the fact that U.S. Hispanic reality emerged in and through that dialectic of violence and domination that is the dialectic of Hispanic and Anglo America.

U.S. Hispanic leftists, on the other hand, are more skeptical about categories such as "community," "multiculturalism," and "identity politics." U.S. Hispanic leftists in addressing the problems of

---

present themselves as the "end of history." Today nobody thinks an alternative to liberal capitalism is feasible. It seems easier to imagine the "breakdown of nature" — "the end of the world" — than a change in the mode of production (Žižek, 1994:1–7). The postmodern way of seeing the world has contributed to the naturalization of global-liberal democratic capitalism. On the one hand, the postmodern critique of "meta-narratives" has augmented the efficacy of the liberal "blackmail" that any radical attempt to push beyond the basic coordinates of liberal capitalism will lead ineluctably to "totalitarianism." See *idem, Did Somebody Say Totalitarianism?* 2001. On the other hand, the leftist passage from the essentialism of the Historical Subject (i.e., the proletariat) to the postmodern plurality of liberationist struggles (e.g., feminist, gay, racial, ethnic) has pushed to the periphery the question regarding the totality of Capital (Žižek, 2000:90–135). Indeed, in the postmodern age both liberals and leftists are contributing to the liberalization of liberation: while the postmodern style of thought undercuts the idea of universal liberation in the name of "epistemological progress," the "triumph" of global liberal-democratic capitalism reveals the "futility" of any attempt to realize this liberation to the extent that such a project has historically implied the implementation of real socialism.

intra-Hispanic violence, sexism, and homophobia gesture toward the critique of political economy. They remember the Chicano movement and liberation theology. They want to believe in the Partido Independentista Puertorriqueño. They point to the problems in the *barrio* and the borderlands. Indeed, they situate themselves within postcolonial, diasporic, subaltern studies. But, in the final analysis, U.S. Hispanic leftists themselves fall captive to the postmodern eclipse of liberation to the extent to which their critique of liberalism, their critique of the "American way of life" is grounded in a radical turn to the particular that annihilates the totality, namely, the history of the Americas. This annihilation of the big picture results in the de facto naturalization of the basic coordinates of U.S.-style liberal democratic capitalism. It results in the de facto naturalization of the socio-historical conditions of possibility of assimilation.

To rethink liberation for the postmodern condition specifically from the U.S. Hispanic point of view is, on the one hand, to push beyond a naive multiculturalism and the radical turn to the particular: it is to reinsert U.S. Hispanic reality into the history of the Americas. And, on the other hand, it is to push beyond the naturalization of the latest manifestation of Anglo-American hegemony and the latest movement of the dialectic of the Americas: it is to struggle against the Free Trade Area of the Americas. Indeed, to rethink liberation for the postmodern condition from the U.S. Hispanic point of view is to struggle against the assimilation of U.S. Hispanics into the "American way of life." It is to struggle to construct (through labor) institutions for the production and reproduction of the Spanish language. It is to struggle against anxiety and alienation.

Together with the demographic transition that has transpired in the United States there has emerged a plurality of perspectives and base concepts that attempt to grapple with the coming of age of U.S. Hispanic reality. These include Chicano, borderland, Latina/o, postcolonial, and diasporic studies, U.S. Hispanic, *feminista,* and *mujerista* theology, *mestizaje, mulatez,* popular religion, etc. Yet these perspectives and concepts lack a common root or ground. This lack of a common ground is a reflection of the postmodern condition, and it is what is generating the postmodern eclipse of liberation. For the idea of a plurality of particular perspectives that reflect on this or that aspect of U.S. Hispanic reality from this or that point of view is the intellectual moment of the postmodern plurality of ethnic groups that gather around the public sphere in an attempt to negotiate the particularity of their ethnicity with the demands of abstract citizenship (see Balibar and Wallerstein, 1988).

While lurking behind "identity politics" and "multiculturalism" is a "disavowed, inverted, self-referential form of racism," i.e., the postmodern manifestation of Anglo-American hegemony (Žižek, 1999: 216), lurking behind the plurality of particular perspectives is the first and only autochthonous school of U.S. thought that emerged as a critique of the "ontologizing" philosophies of Continental Europe, namely, pragmatism.[3] Pragmatism is the ideological supplement of the "American way of life," the ideological supplement of U.S.-style, multicultural liberal democratic capitalism. Pragmatism's ahistoricism and integrationist bias, its reduction of the problem of social justice to the problem of "social engineering" makes it the intellectual moment of the "melting pot" (Habermas, 1973:210; Mannheim, 1936:254). Indeed, as the dominant school of thought in the U.S. theological academy, pragmatism serves as the implicit foundation for the plurality of U.S. Hispanic perspectives. Not searching for foundations, U.S. Hispanic intellectuals implicitly accept speaking the Master's discourse. The Master is the Anglo-American intellectual and his/her discourse is pragmatism. U.S. Hispanic intellectuals need to realize that, in this so-called postmodern age, to speak from a particular perspective is also to speak from the margins. For the particular is always mediated by the universal; and the margins are always marginalized by a center. Pragmatism is the universal of the North American academy; and the Anglo-American mainstream is the center of the "American way of life."

The idea of psychoanalysis as a critically oriented science can serve as the much needed foundation for the plurality of particular U.S. Hispanic perspectives.[4] It can serve as a metatheory for borderland,

---

3. See Peirce, 1934; James, 1975; Dewey, 1991; Rorty, 1982; and West, 1989.

4. The idea of psychoanalysis as a critically oriented science emerges in and through the attempt to use that science inaugurated by Sigmund Freud as a corrective to the reductionistic tendency of the Marxian tradition that does not fall captive to the hermeneutic or pragmatic reduction of the interest in emancipation. Psychoanalysis, unlike hermeneutics or pragmatism,

diasporic, and Latina/o studies, the sociology of Latina/o religion, and U.S. Hispanic theology, for example. It can serve as the frame of reference for base concepts such as *mestizaje* and popular religion. As U.S. Hispanic social theory, the idea of psychoanalysis as a critically oriented science takes as its point of departure the problem of assimilation as this assimilation takes form in and through the anxiety of losing the Spanish language and the alienation of U.S. Hispanic labor. Assimilation appears as an empirical, socio-historical problem for U.S. Hispanic reality only to the degree to which it appears as an existentio-ontological problem for U.S. Hispanic intellectuals. Indeed, what Martin Heidegger observed regarding the question of being is also true regarding the question of assimilation: its centrality can be gleaned from its circularity, from the vagueness of its "thereness." And this is precisely because assimilation is the socio-historical manifestation of the being of U.S. Hispanic reality. From here it is clear why assimilation also reveals the structure of U.S. Hispanic anxiety (Heidegger, 1962:1–64, 220–78).

---

is not satisfied with the understanding of intersubjective meaning structures. Instead it attempts to transform symbolic-cultural distortions through the therapeutic power of language. Rather than idealistically grasping symbolic-cultural conditions as intentionally communicated meaning structures that constitute an integrated lifeworld, psychoanalysis grasps these conditions in light of the problem of corrupted, distorted, and excommunicated desires, memories, and dreams that have been repressed. Psychoanalysis, like the critique of ideology, is driven by an emancipatory cognitive interest: both attempt, not only to interpret, but also to change the world. The revolutionary is driven by the interest in transforming the socio-historical conditions of misery. The analyst is driven by the interest in transforming the pathological state of the patient. With the guidance of psychoanalysis Marx's natural history of the self-formation of the human species is recast as the problem of the struggle to liberate the human being from both the external compulsion of nature and the internal compulsion of culture. The synthetic activity of social labor can now be properly understood as the dialectic of the poietic transformation of the material-economic through labor and the praxeological transformation of the symbolic-cultural through language. The problem of rectifying social labor becomes the problem of overcoming both alienation in and through labor and anxiety in and through language. This psychoanalytic corrective to the critique of political economy, moreover, becomes increasingly important as societies emancipate themselves from the compulsion of external nature. Indeed, in advanced capitalist societies the problem of internal compulsion is the primary problem. For a certain level of economic development does not automatically translate into symbolic-cultural integration. Here the idea of psychoanalysis as a critically oriented science becomes indispensable. As they struggle with the postmodern eclipse of liberation, U.S. Hispanic scholars of society and religion need to turn toward this trajectory that was inaugurated by Marcuse, 1966; and can be traced through the early Habermas, 1972; Deleuze and Guattari, 1972; and up to Lacan, 1966; and Žižek, 1999.

U.S. Hispanic Reality

U.S. Hispanic reality needs to be understood in light of the history of the Americas. The history of the Americas, however, is not a mythical synthesis; it is not a teleological unfolding of Manifest Destiny (see Rostow, 1962; Friedman, 1962). The history of the Americas is rather that asymmetrical life-and-death struggle that has relegated one region of the continent to the "periphery," to the "underside" (Cardoso and Faletto, 1969; Dussel, 1974). This history has taken form in and through four dialectics: (1) the dialectic of Cortés and *La Malinche*, of Spain and the Amerindian civilizations; (2) the dialectic of the *criollo* and the *peninsular,* of Hispanic America and Spain; (3) the dialectic of *civilización* and *barbarie,* of the urban elite and the rural peasant; and (4) the dialectic of Ariel and Calibán, of Hispanic and Anglo America.

Mestizaje came to be as the bastard of *La Malinche* — the absolute negation of the Amerindian civilizations by the Iberian Conquest-Colonialism, a negation that materialized through indigenous and African slave labor. This was the *Patronato regio,* the *Leyes de Indias,* the *Encomienda.* These were the viceroyalties of Nueva España and Perú founded upon the ruins of Tenochtitlán and El Tawantinsuyo. This was the desire for *El Dorado,* the education of the Inca Garcilaso de la Vega, and the scholasticism of Juan Ginés de Sepúlveda. But, from the outset, as resistance, this negation was itself negated: This was the blood of the first martyrs — Hatuey, Cuauhtémoc, Manco Capac, Túpac Amaru, Toussaint L'Ouverture. This was the prophetic voice of Bartolomé de las Casas (see de las Casas, 1957).

Mestizaje would then become the *criollo* — the positivity of the struggles of independence as the repudiation of the *peninsulares,* the repudiation of Iberian hegemony. This was Simón Bolivar, José de San Martín, Miguel Hidalgo, Carlos Manuel de Céspedes, the Manifiesto de Cartagena, the Grito del Dolores, the Grito de Yara. But as the *criollo,* as the first affirmation of Hispanic America, *mestizaje* would perpetuate its positivity only through the negation of part of itself. This was the tyranny of *civilización* over *barbarie*, the negation of the autochthonous and the bucolic, the longing for the enlightenment of France and the pragmatism of the United States. This

was Domingo Faustino Sarmiento — the project of a Europeanized
and Anglo-Americanized Hispanic America; this was Buenos Aires
over-and-against La Pampa, Caracas and Lima over-and-against Los
Andes (see Sarmiento, 1990). But already Martín Fierro would negate
the negation of the *bárbaro:* For the *gaucho* was not an impediment,
but the very possibility of Hispanic America (see J. Hernández, 1972).

Mestizaje would next become the *raza cósmica* — the abstract and
aestheticized synthesis of *civilización* and *barbarie* as the intellectualized recognition that a Hispanic America was possible only as
a unified totality (Vasconcelos, 1948). This is the coming-of-age of
Ariel, the repudiation of scientific rationalism, positivism, Yankee
ingenuity — the repudiation of Calibán (Rodó, 1930). Indeed, as
the *raza cósmica, mestizaje* was the coming-to-terms with Anglo-
American imperialism as the negation of *nuestra América* (Martí,
1977). But, like the overcoming of the diremption of *civilización* and
barbarie, the negation of Anglo-America by aestheticized *mestizaje*
was an intellectualized negation, a negation through interaction and
language alone. This was the Generación del 98, Ruben Darío's *A
Roosevelt* (Darío, 1955) and José Martí's critique of the annexation-
ists: *"Viví en el monstruo, y le conozco las entrañas — y mi honda es
la de David"* (1963–66:161).[5]

And *mestizaje* would then become the *raza de bronce*, the *revolucionario* — the coming-to-terms with the *raza cósmica* and *nuestra
América* as socio-historical projects, as tasks to be realized through
praxis and poiesis (Arguedas, 1919). This was the Mexican Revolution of 1910: the socio-historical concretization of the *raza cósmica*
as embodied in the Constitution of 1917. This was the Cuban Revolution of 1959: the socio-historical assertion of the autonomy of *nuestra
América* through expropriation as the concrete negation of Anglo-
American neocolonialism, and through the turn toward Moscow as
the concrete negation of the hegemonic logic of the Monroe Doctrine and its Roosevelt Corollary (Castro, 1973). The difficulties
and frustrations that have beset these socio-historical projects are
but an indication of the extent to which *mestizaje* as the *raza de*

---

5. "I have lived inside the monster, and I know its entrails — and mine is the sling of
David."

bronce, as the *revolucionario,* having concretely come to terms with its own fragmented reality and having attempted to overcome this fragmentation, has reached its limits. It has reached that point where forward-looking hope is negated by a fragmented history (i.e., conquest, colonialization, elitism, imperialism, underdevelopment) and becomes absurd. *Realismo mágico* is the literary expression of *mestizaje* as a Hispanic America that has come to terms with the limits of its own reality as absurd, as surreal: *"¿Qué es la historia de América Latina sino una crónica de lo maravilloso en lo real?"*[6]

Today the dialectic of Ariel and Calibán is being transformed in and through the globalization of U.S.-style liberal democratic capitalism. Indeed, today, under the conditions of postmodernity, *mestizaje* must grapple with a hyper- and ultra-Manifest Destiny. This new form of the dialectic between Anglo and Hispanic America came to the fore in the early 1990s as the conflict between the North American Free Trade Agreement (NAFTA) and the Ejército Zapatista de Liberación Nacional (EZLN)'s *Declaración de la Selva Lacandona* (Subcomandante Marcos, 2000); and today it has come to fruition as the tension between the Free Trade Area of the Americas and the World Social Forum (V. H. de la Fuente, 2004:3). Indeed, the *mestiza/o* must make a fundamental choice: S/he can either submit to the conditions of Anglo-American Empire and the tyranny of the dollar; or s/he can, in and through praxis and poiesis, language and labor, interaction and work, strive to construct a Hispanic American economic system and cultural community strategically linked to Europe and the euro (Fuentes, 2003:36). The fate of the *mestiza/o* disproportionately lies in the hands of the U.S. Hispanic population.

As I have already stated, U.S. Hispanics are not a particular ethnic group that form part of a multicultural society. If this is your point of departure then you have already fallen captive to the postmodern condition; you are already caught in the snares of Calibán. U.S. Hispanics are first and foremost part of Hispanic America. U.S. Hispanics are those Hispanic Americans who live within the contested borders of the United States of North America. And this holds

---

6. "For what is the history of Latin America if not a chronicle of the magical in the real?" See Carpentier, 1979.

a fortiori today given the time-space compression in the organization of capitalism we referred to at the outset. Who today under the conditions of globalization, who today, given the idea of a Free Trade area of the Americas, can continue to segregate U.S. Hispanic reality from the rest of Hispanic America? The dichotomy between "U.S. Hispanic" and "Hispanic American" is a manifestation of "scholastic epistemocentrism" (Bourdieu, 1997). The construction of "U.S. Hispanic" as a particular ethnic group decoupled from the history of the Americas is more a reflection of the position of U.S. Hispanic intellectuals in the U.S. academic field than it is a reflection of the position of U.S. Hispanics in the dialectic of the Americas. As it is currently used, the category "U.S. Hispanic" is more an object of analysis that can secure a job than it is an object of analysis that can contribute to the struggle for the liberation of the U.S. Hispanic people (Bourdieu, 1984b).

The ahistorically, free-floating category "U.S. Hispanic" is a clear example of the U.S. educational system functioning as an "ideological state apparatus" (Althusser, 1970). Indeed, the category "U.S. Hispanic" constructed within the frame of reference of "identity politics" or "multiculturalism" is rapidly becoming one of the most valuable ideological weapons in the United States. For the naturalization of the myth of the "melting pot" is a necessary cultural condition of possibility for the realization of the Free Trade Area of the Americas. Rethinking liberation from the U.S. Hispanic point of view must thus begin with a critique of the construction of the category "U.S. Hispanic." We argue that the best way to bring about this critique is to reinsert U.S. Hispanic reality back into the dialectic of the Americas.

U.S. Hispanic reality emerged in and through the fourth moment of the dialectic of the Americas: U.S. Hispanic reality is the mediation of Ariel and Calibán, the symptom of the back-and-forth between Anglo and Hispanic America. Indeed, U.S. Hispanic reality is that fragmented reality that has been generated by that perpetual tension, that logic of violence and domination that is the asymmetrical relationship between Anglo- and Hispanic America. The heterogeneity of U.S. Hispanic reality — i.e., its racial, gender, national, religious, socio-economic, political nuances — is subordinate to this movement of violence and domination in the mode of assimilation. The dialectic of Anglo and Hispanic America is the transcendental condition for U.S. Hispanic reality. Indeed, U.S. Hispanic reality is U.S. Hispanic reality in and through the dialectic of Ariel and Calibán. This dialectic has had two movements, through which U.S. Hispanic reality has taken form: First, Anglo-America moves south, initially as territorial expansion and later as neoimperialism and neocolonialism. And second, Hispanic America moves North, as escaping its own fragmented reality. In and through these two movements emerge, for example, a Mexican American, a Puerto Rican, a Cuban American. The fragmentation that is U.S. Hispanic *mestiza/o* reality manifests itself socio-historically as the problem of assimilation. In the final analysis assimilation is the conscious or unconscious losing sight of the tension between Ariel and Calibán as what radically constitutes U.S. Hispanic reality. Assimilation is the primary vehicle of intra-Hispanic violence understood as a U.S. Hispanic reality which, caught in the nihilism of the particular, has lost sight of its unity in and through the socio-historical fragmentation that is *mestizaje* and has turned against itself as East coast vs. West coast, *mujerista* vs. *feminista,* left vs. right, rich vs. poor, dark vs. light, Protestant vs. Catholic, Cuban vs. Mexican, etc. We may recall that the fundamental problem with U.S. Hispanic liberals and leftists is that they are explicitly or implicitly assimilationist: both, willy nilly, myopically ignore (or, more technically, perform the Husserlian *epoché* on) the dialectic between Ariel and Calibán and ahistorically grasp U.S. Hispanic reality as a particular (i.e., a minority group) in a community of particulars (i.e., a multicultural society) that will harmoniously integrate through pluralism and markets. That is, in other words, both U.S. Hispanic liberals and leftists are explicitly or implicitly grounded in that narrative we termed above the synthesis of the Americas. But the phenomenology of *mestizaje* invalidates such a narrative. Once again: U.S. Hispanic reality is not a concrete manifestation of the synthesis of the Americas. It is rather the concrete manifestation of the tension that is the dialectic of Ariel and Calibán, the dialectic of Anglo- and Hispanic America in the mode of the socio-historical problem of assimilation.

That fragmentation-as-assimilation that is U.S. Hispanic reality has taken form through both the material-economic and the symbolic-cultural, through both poiesis and praxis, through both alienation and anxiety. U.S. Hispanic reality is fragmented, on the one hand, to the extent that it is Anglo-Americans who have historically controlled the means of production. In this sense we say that U.S. Hispanic reality is an expression of alienated labor. On the other hand, U.S. Hispanic reality is fragmented to the extent that the Anglo culture is the dominant culture in the United States.

In this sense, submitting to the primacy of the linguistic turn and its motto: "the symbolic-cultural is mediated by language," we say that U.S. Hispanic reality is an expression of the anxiety generated by the loss of the Spanish language. Indeed, because they do not control capital U.S. Hispanics lack the means to perpetuate their language. And to the extent that Spanish is ghettoized a disproportionate amount of U.S. Hispanics have no choice but to sell their labor power to Anglo-Americans. Under the present socio-historical conditions the only hope for the *mestiza/o* is thus assimilation in and through the dialectic of alienation and anxiety. To survive in the United States the *mestiza/o* must overcome alienation in and through the life and death struggle for capital, and, now, overcome anxiety by replacing Spanish with English. Indeed, under present socio-historical conditions the *mestiza/o* is overdetermined to adopt the "American way of life." S/he must become a pragmatic, English-speaking capitalist.

The heterogeneity of U.S. Hispanic reality can be understood as different expressions of the relationship between *mestiza/o* labor and *mestiza/o* language. Thus, for example, the fragmented reality that is Puerto Rican reality manifests itself first and foremost as a problem of fragmented labor. Despite systematic attempts by the United States to impose Anglo-American cultural hegemony in the island, Puerto Ricans have, through the defense of the Spanish language, managed to secure the primacy of their Hispanic culture. No U.S. Hispanic American group enjoys greater cultural autonomy than the Puerto Ricans; and this to the extent that no U.S. Hispanic American group enjoys greater control over their educational system. The limit of this cultural autonomy, however, manifests itself through the fact that Puerto Ricans have until now lacked the material-economic leverage to break with the United States. Puerto Rico is, in the final analysis, a Spanish-speaking neocolony. Indeed, for Puerto Ricans, fragmentation manifests itself primarily as alienated labor, as the failure to objectify the Puerto Rican culture into nation-state.

The inverse holds for Cuban Americans: The fragmented reality that is Cuban American reality manifests itself first and foremost as a problem of fragmented language. Cuban Americans have, due to certain socio-historical reasons, managed to realize an impressive level of material-economic prosperity. This prosperity, however, has been achieved at the cost of cultural and linguistic autonomy. How many second- and third-generation Cuban Americans speak fluent Spanish? Indeed, one wonders why, given nearly three decades of economic prosperity, Cuban Americans have not been able to construct institutions for the perpetuation of their culture and language. Cuban Americans point to Miami — "the bridge to Latin America and the Caribbean" — as proof of the Cuban American ethic and the spirit of capitalism. What about the Cuban American educational system? In what language are classes taught? What literature is read? Whose history is studied? Miami, the "Cuban American dream," has been made possible by a materialism and consumerism that is driven by an attempt to compensate for the anxiety that is produced by the loss of the Spanish language and culture.

But no U.S. Hispanic group is more fragmented than Mexican Americans. Puerto Ricans have historically enjoyed relative cultural-symbolic autonomy. Puerto Rican fragmentation has been produced primarily in and through "Manifest Destiny." Cuban Americans have enjoyed relative material-economic autonomy. Cuban American fragmentation has been produced primarily in and through the "melting pot." Mexican Americans, however, have historically lacked both cultural-symbolic and material-economic autonomy. Mexican American fragmentation has been generated by Anglo-American imperialism par excellence: It has been generated in and through the dialectic of "Manifest Destiny" and the "melting pot," in and through the dialectic of territorial expansion and cultural extermination. Mexican Americans lack both capital and the Spanish language. They suffer anxiety and alienation. They are constituted by fragmented labor and language. Indeed, Mexican American fragmentation exemplifies the pathological state of the U.S. Hispanic *mestiza/o*.

And yet, as we suggested above, despite their differences, despite their heterogeneity, Puerto Ricans, Cuban Americans, and Mexican Americans are subordinate to the category "U.S. Hispanic." Indeed, Puerto Ricans, Cuban Americans, and Mexican Americans are all U.S. Hispanics. And this to the extent that these three groups sociohistorically emerged in and through the dialectic of Hispanic and Anglo America, the dialectic of Ariel and Calibán. Thus, for example, Cuban Americans and Puerto Ricans can be traced back to a common historical event: namely, the so-called "Spanish-American War," while Mexican Americans came to the fore as a result of the "Mexican-American War." Both of these "wars" were manifestations of the Monroe Doctrine and its Roosevelt Corollary.

Rather than idealistically grasping the fragmented U.S. Hispanic reality hermeneutically or pragmatically as intentionally or consciously communicated meaning structures that constitute a lifeworld or a conversation community, we should grasp this *mestiza/o* reality psychoanalytically as one that has been corrupted and distorted and as one that has excommunicated desires and repressed memories and dreams. The history of the human being, argued Sigmund Freud, is the history of his/her repression. This repression is what makes progress possible. In like fashion we argue that the history of the *mestiza/o* is the history of the repression of *mestiza/o* language and labor. The hermeneutic and pragmatic perspectives are grounded in an idealist conception of language (i.e., language as presence, disclosure, and understanding) that does no justice to the fragmented nature of U.S. Hispanic reality. This idealist conception of language today naturalizes the dialectic of Hispanic and Anglo America in and through the belief in communication, the public sphere, and multiculturalism.

To the extent that it deals with the problem of pathological states that need to be transformed in and through language and labor, praxis and poiesis, the idea of psychoanalysis as a critically oriented science is better suited to grapple with that fragmentation-as-assimilation that is U.S. Hispanic reality. On the one hand, a psychoanalytic perspective — and in particular the Lacanian post-structuralist conception of language as lack, dissimulation, and alienation — unravels the problem of fragmented *mestiza/o* symbolic-cultural conditions as a problem of anxiety generated by the loss of the Spanish language. On the other hand, when fused with the critique of political economy — when it understands itself to be a critically oriented science — this psychoanalytic perspective unravels the problem of anxiety generated by the loss of the Spanish language. It does so in light of the problem of fragmented *mestiza/o* material-economic conditions. And it does so in light of the problem of the alienation of U.S. Hispanic labor as this alienation takes form in and through U.S.-style liberal democratic capitalism, and specifically the Free Trade Area of the Americas.

Indeed, psychoanalysis as a critically oriented science is the post-modern turn to language that does not abandon the Marxian critique of political economy and totality. It is the linguistified corrective to the classical Latin American liberationist perspectives. The idea of psychoanalysis as a critically oriented science allows us to formulate the problem of liberation for the postmodern condition from the point of view of U.S. Hispanic reality as the problem of the relationship between the "inevitability" of the Free Trade Area of the Americas and the loss of the Spanish language: the repression of the Spanish language is what ideologically prepares the way for the Free Trade Area of the Americas, and the naturalization of the Free Trade Area of the Americas is what annihilates the Spanish language. One side generates anxiety in and through the "melting pot." The other side generates alienation in and through "Manifest Destiny." Both sides, however, are dialectically interlocked. This dialectic is precisely the structure of U.S. Hispanic assimilation into the "American way of life."

The *mestiza/o* is fragmented, marginalized. S/he is "thrown" into the dialectic of Hispanic and Anglo-America (Heidegger, 1962:232). This "thrownness," which socio-historically is no other than the phenomenon of assimilation, manifests itself as losing the Spanish language. *Mestiza/o* speech expresses this primordial loss. As the expression of the loss of the Spanish language, *mestiza/o* speech is at the same time the trace of the desire of the U.S. Hispanic, the trace of the lack of U.S. Hispanic being. U.S. Hispanics desire to "make a living," they desire to make a space for themselves in the United States. This desire is generated by the fact that they have "just arrived" or that they exist "at the margins." Indeed this desire stems from the socio-historical fact that the *mestiza/o* is still not integrated and still has not achieved the "American dream." This desire to make a world that the *mestiza/o* lacks is no other than the desire to be recognized by the Other; it is no other than the desire to be recognized by the Anglo and her/his "American way of life." But this desire for recognition is precisely what drives the movement of U.S. Hispanic fragmentation, marginalization, and thrownness: For to be recognized by the Anglo-American, the *mestiza/o* must speak in English and this speech is — so long as the *mestiza/o* identities him/herself as "Hispanic American" — stained with the loss, repression, and excommunication of the Spanish language.

We said that the desire to "make a living," the desire to make a space for him/herself is driven by the "American dream." But the "American dream" is not this or that empirical object that is lacked. It is not a socio-historical project that can be realized. It is not a world that can be constructed. Rather, the "American dream" is an existential-ontological property of the U.S. Hispanic. The "American dream" is what constitutes the structure of U.S. Hispanic anxiety. It is the movement of lack, the movement of U.S. Hispanic non-being. The "American dream" is the original lost object; the embodiment of U.S. Hispanic surplus-enjoyment. It is the pure void which functions as the object-cause of U.S. Hispanic desire: It is the object that, on the one hand, causes U.S. Hispanic desire, and, on the other, is posed retroactively by this desire (Žižek, 1989:65, 82, 95, 116, 145, 158, 163). Indeed, drawing on Lacan, the "American dream" is the U.S. Hispanic *objet petit a[utre]* (the little o[ther]) (1973:37–50, 63–75, 80–135): namely, that singularity "in the very heart of the [U.S. Hispanic] subject which cannot be symbolized, which is produced as a residue, a remnant, a leftover of every signifying operation, a hard core embodying horrifying *jouissance,* enjoyment, and as such an object which simultaneously attracts and repels us, which divides our desire and thus provokes shame" (Žižek, 1989:180).

That this is so, that the realization of the "American dream" is the U.S. Hispanic *objet petit a,* is clear from what we have just stated: namely, that the realization of the "American dream" is stained with the loss of the Spanish language; that the repression and excommunication of the Spanish language is the other side, the necessary condition of the "American dream." From here it is clear why the U.S. Hispanic is a broken and divided, barred Subject ($). This brokenness manifests itself in and through the difference between Spanish and English. Indeed, the bar (|) that covers the U.S. Hispanic Subject ($) is the failure of symbolization that is generated by the slippage between Spanish and English. U.S. Hispanic identity is the perpetual alienation of the Hispanic American "I" in the imaginary "me" of the discourse of the Anglo-American — an alienation that takes form through the symbolic order of the "American way of life" (Lacan, 1966:92–99). That something is not right, that things are out of joint, this is the result of the U.S. Hispanic Real that refuses assimilation and refuses to forget Spanish.

As the failure of symbolization, the slippage between Spanish and English appears primarily as an existentio-ontological property of the U.S. Hispanic; and as such it brings forth the structure of *mestiza/o* anxiety. But the difference between Spanish and English also manifests itself empirically as, for example, the tension between subject and object, consciousness and real-life process, private and public, lifeworld and system. As an empirical reality the difference between Spanish and English is no other than the socio-historical symptom or trace of assimilation. It should be clear from what we have said, however, that the existentio-ontological and the empirical are in fact dialectically related — and this to the extent that they mediate each other. Indeed, the value of psychoanalysis as a critically oriented science stems precisely from its ability to forth bring this dialectic. Once again: psychoanalysis as a critically oriented science grasps the problem of U.S. Hispanic liberation as a problem of the liberation from assimilation — an assimilation that takes form in and through fragmented symbolic-cultural and material-economic conditions, anxiety and alienation, the loss of the Spanish language, and the Free Trade Area of the Americas.

Whether s/he arrives in the States or whether the States arrive in his/her territory, every U.S. Hispanic engages in a life-and-death struggle that will undergird his/her life-trajectory: namely, the life-and-death struggle between Spanish — his/her maternal language, the language of his/her mother — and English — the foreign language, the language of "success." If, on the one hand, Spanish is the language of dreams and prayers, the language of meaning and intersubjectivity, English, on the other hand, is the language of work and rights, the language of power and the real-life process. The tension between Spanish and English thus brings forth and traces the fragmentation of the U.S. Hispanic as a fragmentation of private and public, subject and object.

The U.S. Hispanic structure of anxiety, the U.S. Hispanic failure of symbolization is rooted in this dichotomy: Spanish is excommunicated from the public life of political discourse and education. Spanish is repressed to the private sphere of the family and the community. Drawing on Habermas we could say that for the U.S. Hispanic Spanish is the language of the lifeworld, while English is the language of the system. Indeed, we could say that the fundamental problematic for the U.S. Hispanic is the problematic of the colonization of the language of the lifeworld — Spanish — by the language of the system — English (Habermas, 1984). It is in and through this tension, it is under these conditions that every U.S. Hispanic is "thrown" into the dialectic of the Americas. Or perhaps it is more accurate to say that it is this tension and these conditions that constitute the "thrownness" of U.S. Hispanics. While in the light of day U.S. Hispanics preach the "American dream," at night they must face the "American nightmare," that is, they must face the fact that their children will lose the Spanish language, they must face the fact that in the United States the means of cultural production and reproduction are controlled by the English language.

But U.S. Hispanics have struggled to "make a living," they have struggled to integrate themselves into the work force, they have struggled against the alienation of Anglo-American Capital, and thus lack the leisure time needed to struggle against the socio-historical conditions that ghettoize the Spanish language, the socio-historical conditions of assimilation. For the average, everyday U.S. Hispanic the solution to the "American nightmare" becomes clear: the future of the Spanish language is found in the family. And from here emerges the conservatism of the U.S. Hispanic population: U.S. Hispanics tend to naturalize the social system and tend to restrict the problem of the transmission of the U.S. Hispanic culture to the limits of the family.

Drawing on W. E. B. Du Bois, we could say that the U.S. Hispanic has a "double consciousness," that "sense of always looking at one's self through the eyes of others, of measuring one's soul by the tape of a world that looks on in amused contempt and pity" (Du Bois, 1995:45). But this "twoness" that constitutes the being of U.S. Hispanics, namely, the fact that they are, the fact that they are perceived to be, indeed, the fact that they are inasmuch as they are perceived to be, now, Hispanic (Americans), and, now (Anglo) Americans; this state of having "two souls, two thoughts, two unreconciled strivings" is the result of the failure of symbolization that is generated by the tension that exists between two languages, namely, Spanish and English. This linguistic dimension of the U.S. Hispanic double consciousness is what radically distinguishes the U.S. Hispanic and African American experiences.

The U.S. Hispanic double consciousness is, from the point of view of Freudian metapsychology, pathological: for the failure of symbolization disrupts ego-synthesis: Whether because they must struggle to learn English, whether they must struggle to communicate with their employer; or whether they must struggle to remember Spanish, whether they must struggle to communicate with their grandparents, every U.S. Hispanic has a pathological double consciousness, every U.S. Hispanic must — in one form or another — grapple with that failure of symbolization that emerges in and through the decoupling of the Spanish language from the Hispanic American culture (Freud, 1961; Marcuse, 1966). But precisely because the U.S. Hispanic pathological double consciousness is generated in and through language, the Lacanian linguistified understanding of mental illness and, in particular, of the psychotic disorder schizophrenia, can help us unravel its structure and dynamic.[7]

---

7. To the extent that in this essay we are drawing on the idea of psychoanalysis as a critically oriented science (see above p. 203, n. 4), it should be clear that we are using schizophrenia here

Lacan posits three dimensions of reality, three registers of thought, three psychoanalytic orders: the Imaginary,[8] the Symbolic,[9] and the Real[10] (Lacan, 1966:11–61). Human beings constitute themselves and their world in and through these three orders. For the most part, individuals are protected from the Real by the Symbolic and Imaginary. These function as a kind of filter, a kind of protective blanket. Psychotic persons have direct access to the Real due to the defectiveness of this filtering effect. This defectiveness skews reality testing, and it produces a tendency for abstraction, alienation, and detachment from their bodily experience. From here why for James Grotstein schizophrenic individuals have been born into the Real as ontological orphans for they have been denied the protective blanket of the Imaginary and Symbolic: these individuals seem to have subtle to profound difficulties in engaging or being engaged (attached) to and (bonded) by their mothers. They often seem to have engaged in double lives as true and false schizoid selves. What has recently attracted my attention is their propensity to be self-conscious, by which I mean that they seem almost literally beside themselves (1996:1–25). Following Grotstein we say that *U.S. Hispanics are born into the Real as ontological aliens.*

U.S. Hispanics also have a propensity for abstraction, alienation, and detachment from their bodily experience; they also have a feeling of being beside themselves. This is precisely another way at getting at the U.S. Hispanic pathological double consciousness. The Real for the U.S. Hispanic is "where I come from," "my mother tongue": Hispanic American. The "American way of life" is constituted in

---

not so much in the clinical nosological sense, but in the way it has been applied to social theory by, for example, Deleuze and Guattari, 1972.

8. The Imaginary is a synesthetic-visual dimension that generates the fundamental mis-recognition, namely, that "I am me," the false identity between the I and the "me"; The "me," for Lacan, is the "I" as fantasy, it is the Imaginary, the place of error.

9. The Symbolic is a linguistic-conceptual dimension, the world of language. This world of language is also the world of desire to the extent that the infant's passage to language coincides with the separation from the mother. Thus for Lacan the symbolic world always has the mark, the trace of loss.

10. The Real, on the one hand, precedes the Imaginary and the Symbolic. In this sense it is presence, the absence of desire, of loss. On the other hand, the real is constituted by the Imaginary and Symbolic as a fundamental failure, as a trauma. In this sense the real is unimaginable and unsymbolizable. Language for Lacan always expresses the absence of the Real as desire, as *objet petite a.*

and through the Imaginary and Symbolic. The U.S. Hispanic is born into the Real in and through the slippage that exists between Spanish and English. The "American way of life" exists, now, as the fundamental misrecognition. And it exists, now, as the object-cause of U.S. Hispanic desire, as that singularity that cannot be symbolized, namely, the "American dream." Indeed, recasting the discourse of one of Grotstein's patients, we can listen to the U.S. Hispanic speak: "When I was a child, I wasn't an '(Anglo) American.' I watched myself trying to be an '(Anglo) American' like the rest of the children. I learned to imitate them very well, but I always knew, and still know, that I'm not one of them; for I was, and I still am a Hispanic American."[11]

The pathological double consciousness is not a natural condition. It is rather the result of certain socio-historical conditions generated by the dialectic of Ariel and Calibán, and in particular of an educational system that systematically destroys rather than nurtures the maternal language of the U.S. Hispanic people. Indeed, the U.S. Hispanic double consciousness can be traced to the Marxian critique of political economy: Not controlling Capital, U.S. Hispanics lack the means to construct and shape institutions for the production and re-production of their language, and thus of their culture. U.S. Hispanics must traverse the primordial fantasy; they must bring forth their Real desire which has been eclipsed by the symbolic order of the Other, on the one hand, and the imagination of the "me" on the other. That is, in other words, U.S. Hispanics must come to terms with their desire, *objet petit a,* "the American dream," as the inverted and dissimulated form of their desire to realize the Real, Hispanic America, in and through the historical praxis of transforming language and labor.

Rethinking liberation from the U.S. Hispanic point of view has thus brought forth the problem of a *politics of language.* Once again: to rethink U.S. Hispanic liberation under the conditions of postmodernity is to grapple with the problem of the assimilation of U.S. Hispanics

---

11. The patient states the following, which Grotstein argues exemplifies the schizophrenic's feeling of "being beside him/herself": "When I was a child, I didn't play. I watched myself trying to play the way other children did. I learned to imitate them very well, but I always knew, and still know, that I'm not one of them" (1996:18).

into the "American way of life"; it is to grapple with the problem of losing the Spanish language in and through the ideological apparatuses of U.S.-style liberal democratic capitalism. Indeed, today a U.S. Hispanic liberationist project must be grounded in and guided by the idea of *linguistic rights*. This project, however, presupposes a critique of that socio-economic machine that hegemonizes the Anglo-American language and culture, namely, the Free Trade Area of the Americas.

To recast the problem of U.S. Hispanic liberation as a problem of U.S. Hispanic linguistic rights is to critique the meaning of the "American dream." From the point of view of a U.S. Hispanic politics of language the "American dream" no longer ultimately means the struggle to integrate oneself into the system of U.S.-style liberal-democratic capitalism. It no longer ultimately means the struggle for capital, the struggle for the U.S. dollar. The "American dream" rather now means the strategic use of U.S.-style liberal-democratic capitalism in order to construct the institutions that will ensure the perpetuation of the Spanish language and U.S. Hispanic culture. It now means the use of capital, the use of the U.S. dollar in order to construct a "U.S. Hispanic mainstream." The "American dream" in the traditional sense implied the annihilation of the Spanish language and the marginalization of the U.S. Hispanic culture in order to "make a living." It now means "making a living" so that my children and grandchildren can speak Spanish and learn the history and literature of their grandparents. The idea of U.S. Hispanic linguistic rights allows us to avoid both the technical reduction of labor and the interpretative reduction of language. It allows us to push beyond both an instrumentalist, empirical-analytical understanding of work and a romantic, historical-hermeneutic understanding of language. Indeed, the idea of U.S. Hispanic rights is the social theoretical insight that social labor is needed to perpetuate language and that language is needed to give meaning to social labor, that language restricted to the family and labor used to construct the Other's culture is death. In the final analysis, the idea of U.S. Hispanic linguistic rights is nothing more than the point of departure of a critically oriented U.S. Hispanic science of liberation (Habermas, 1972:301–17).

Language is not an instrument of power and money; it is not a tool that is to be mastered. Language is first and foremost what undergirds, defines, and sustains the cultural identity of the human being; it is what gives meaning to the totality of a life-trajectory. We have already suggested that today the critique of globalized neoliberal capitalism must take as its point of departure the critique of the idea of the "plurality of particulars" (i.e., the idea of "multiculturalism," of "identity politics"). We can now add that the critique of the idea of the "plurality of particulars" must take as its point of departure the struggle for the linguistic rights of minority and indigenous groups.

The UNESCO has for half a century now recognized linguistic rights to be an integral part of the international human rights agenda (UNESCO, 1953); and it has developed a framework to guide the struggle for those languages and cultures that are in danger of extinction (UNESCO, 2001). For instance, in a recent publication UNESCO declared that all minority and indigenous groups must be guaranteed the following four linguistic rights: the right to be educated in their maternal language; the right to the language of the majority group and the national educational system; the right to an intercultural education that promotes positive attitudes toward marginalized languages and cultures; and the right to be educated in at least one international language (2003:17). Indeed, in the final analysis the UNESCO understands the struggle for the linguistic rights of minority and indigenous groups to be a struggle against "subtractive bilingualism" — that is, when learning a second language interferes with the development of the first language — and a struggle in favor of "additive bilingualism" — that is, when learning a second language does not interfere with the perpetuation of the first language (Ibid.:18).

UNESCO's politics of language, however, must be understood together with the World Social Forum's struggle against global liberal-democratic capitalism. And this to the extent that the struggle for a plurilingual world implies a critique of the homogenizing logic of globalized liberal-democratic capitalism, and the struggle against global liberal-democratic capitalism implies a critique of the hegemonization of those cultures that control capital. From one side the World Social Forum proclaims: "Another world is possible" (Cassen,

2003). And from the other side, UNESCO proclaims: "A bilingual and plurilingual world is possible" (2003:30–34). The World Social Forum critiques capital as language and UNESCO critiques the language of capital. This insight is nothing more than the Marxian critique of political economy that has met the demands of the linguistic turn, and the linguistic turn that has come to terms with the Marxian critique of political economy. It is a practico-political formulation of the theoretico-philosophical perspective gained through a retrieval of the genealogy of the idea of psychoanalysis as a critically oriented science: namely, that the struggle against domination and for liberation must be conceptualized as the dialectic of the poietic transformation of the material-economic through labor and the praxeological transformation of the symbolic-cultural through language.

Today the U.S. Hispanic struggle for liberation must thus be concretized as a struggle against "subtractive bilingualism" and the "inevitability" of the Free Trade Area of the Americas. On the one hand, with UNESCO, U.S. Hispanics need to struggle to construct an educational system grounded in "additive bilingualism." On the other hand, with the World Social Forum, U.S. Hispanics need to struggle to construct a Hispanic America that is free from the logic of Anglo-American Capital.

U.S. Hispanic Religion

Mestizaje is the primordial category of U.S. Hispanic reality, and *popular religion* is the primordial category of U.S. Hispanic religion. Popular religion is subordinate to *mestizaje* to the extent that religion is grounded in reality. U.S. Hispanic popular religion is that primordial religious moment of U.S. Hispanic reality that is always already phenomenologically "there," prior to any institutionalized manifestation of religion. U.S. Hispanic popular religion is the set of beliefs and practices that attempt to grapple with the radical finitude of the *mestiza/o*. This finitude, we have suggested, manifests itself as being "thrown" into the dialectic of Anglo and Hispanic America, as losing the Spanish language. U.S. Hispanic popular religion posits the *mestiza/o*'s "ultimate concern" in light of this existential-ontological state of fragmentation (Tillich, 1967, vol. 1).

Popular religion is the metaphor of U.S. Hispanic desire, and it is the metonym of U.S. Hispanic lack of being. Indeed, a psychoanalytic approach to U.S. Hispanic religion analyzes the way U.S. Hispanic popular religious beliefs and practices function both *ideologically* to assimilate U.S. Hispanics into the Anglo-American mainstream, and *liberatively* as resistance and forward-looking hope in the face of fragmentation. In other words, a psychoanalytic approach to U.S. Hispanic religion analyzes the way U.S. Hispanic popular religious beliefs and practices generate both the desire to be recognized by the Other and the "courage to be" in the face of the anxiety that is generated by that primordial loss of *mestiza/o* language and *mestiza/o* labor.

Part Three

Rethinking
Theory, Power, and Identity
in Latina/o Religions

Chapter 9

Exhibiting Religious Erotics: Ethics of Machismo after Aztlán

Luis D. León

Eroticism is primarily a religious matter.... (Bataille, 1986:31)

The erotic is a resource within each of us that lies in a deeply female and spiritual plane.... (Lorde, 1984:53)

Sometimes the quickest way to your spirituality is through your sexuality. (El Vez: Boxing with God)[1]

What is machismo? The "macho" is a violent, menacing, misogynist, homophobic, racist, alcoholic beast who has no emotion but rage, and whose ritual activity is rife with deceit and cruelty aimed only at gratifying animalistic urges. For many, machismo is a Latin American invention. Yet, contrary to this popular mythology, Latinos did not invent vehement sexism. In spite of the macho's cultural power, Mexican men reject the tag and opt instead for models of *hombre*, or true men, which fly in the face of machista cultural practices. Men don't require the macho script in order to act with malice and evil, and yet it helps. For though the symbol of the macho bears many spiritual and cultural burdens, it has long existed as a counterpoint to the ideal European patriarch, who is imagined as kinder and gentler, or civilized (Paredes, 1966). And yet Latinos themselves have actively participated in the construction of the macho image, and each region of Latin America has distinct machista tropes.

---

1. El Vez, from the recording "Boxing with God: Songs from and Inspired by The Gospel Show" produced by El Vez, on Sympathy for the Record Industry.

Machismo's female counterpart is *marianismo,* the religious mandate for women to emulate Mary the mother of Jesus, cast as the long-suffering virgin mother. Throughout Mexico, she is known as Guadalupe (though she is conjured by numerous regional identities). Both machismo and marianismo are sacred symbols invested with authority by millions throughout the world. From them issue cultural scripts to whose significance we scholars of religion and theology must attend. And we must also attend for once to queer identities, which have been remarkably overlooked in Latino theology. While the mythology of Guadalupe and the rituals she models have been subjected to powerful scrutiny, for the most part, theology and religious studies have failed to critique the baleful image of the macho, especially in light of the homophobic drama it enacts. Yet, since the 1980s, Latina and Latino artists have deployed irony, parody, and literary critique to deconstruct the narrative and image of the macho (Castillo, 1996).

For Mexican Americans or Chicanas and Chicanos, deconstructing machista narratives has become a spiritual and religious practice that involves debunking sacred myths telling of a mythical Aztec homeland, the peregrination of the original mexica, or Aztecs, from their primal utopia, a place known as Aztlán. Mexica ruled Central Mexico at the time of Spanish arrival, and legitimized their tyrannical reign with a divine mandate to travel south, leaving their paradise of poetry, art, music, and "whiteness." Since that time Spanish explorers and Chicana/o political activists have theorized that Aztlán is actually the southwestern United States.[2] For Chicanos, Aztlán was ground zero for the reinvention of machismo.

In what follows I explore three sites in which visions of Aztlán and the machista drama it enacts are deconstructed and revised. Two are contemporary art exhibits, and the third is in the work of Chicano performance artist El Vez, whose gender-troubling rock-and-roll proposes fresh and uncannily ancient religious idioms. In between these sections, I offer a travel narrative, a road trip through Aztlán, demonstrating the centrality of the macho narrative to the construction of Latina/o and North American identities.

---

2. For a discussion of machismo in Mexico, see McKee Irwin, 2003; Murray, 1995.

Puro Macho: Born in Aztlán

Rejecting machismo's veracity does not deny the oppressive realities of patriarchy and violence against women which, tragically, exist
everywhere. Certainly the physical practices attributed to the macho
continue to plague Latin Americans and the world. In the Mexican
Americas, this machista narrative is activated by cultural expressions,
especially the performative pneumonic retrieval of a primal ancestral warrior who embodies aggressive hyper-masculinity, an original
macho archetype.[3] The Mexican American or Chicano civil rights
movement (1968–1980) in particular was perhaps symbolized best
by the classical Aztec silhouette gracing kitchen calendars throughout the borderlands: a sinewy warrior, glorified and triumphant with
a volcano in the background, a frame that is at once phallic aura
and full-body halo. But the image would not be complete without his
scantily clad princess reposed submissively on his lap.

The movement's philosophy was grounded in a spiritual and symbolic return to imagined Aztec values. Rejecting the presumed ways
of the colonizer was thought to be a socially redemptive strategy, for
it modeled an ethics and society once glorious and triumphant, prior
to the "brutal gringo invasion." But returning to this lost time and
place required a textual map, and this Chicanos found in the myth of
Aztlán — as many others had before them (see especially Anaya and
Lomeli, 1988; Anzaldúa, 1999).

Historical Aztlán is the mythical homeland of the Aztecs, as first
told by the ancient Mexica or Azteca whose bloody rule terrified
and controlled central Mexico immediately prior to the arrival and
conquest of the Spanish in 1521. The precious few surviving original storybooks of the Mexica depict the exodus from Aztlán and
the arrival in Central Mexico as a divine commission, ordained by
their principal deity, Huitzilopochtli (Duran, 1964:9–14). This story
is confirmed by Fray Diego Dúran, a Dominican priest who chron-
icled the conquest ethnographically. Aztlán is the lead peregrination
myth of the Aztecs, and only one of a complex system of mythology

---

3. For a discussion of the ways popular culture portrays and thus models male behavioral
codes, see Nixon, 1997.

conferring a holy blessing on their imperialism.[4] Their first homeland emerged as a paradisiacal utopia — a place of "whiteness," a
place of "herons," and of "seven caves" — where philosophy/poetry,
music, and all the arts flourished. The story became the Aztec master
narrative (Carrasco, 1982b:11–62).

In addition, this myth of beginnings wed Aztec origins with the
Maya of Tula. In the Aztec's reconstructed Aztlán, the great city
of Tenochtitlán, ancestral blood flows mixed and solidified in the
erection of the pyramids. Davíd Carrasco notes: "The historical reconstruction of a people struggling to fit into the developed world
of the lakes is a far cry from the glorious mythological story of divine guidance that appears in the sacred histories of Tenochtitlán"
(1982b:159–60). Similarly, Chicanos narrated stories of Aztlán as a
rallying cry for their divine and ancestral right to occupy the U.S.
Southwest.

The myth of Aztlán began to possess great allure for the pillaging
Spanish, who soon exhausted vast stores of Indian gold and turned
their focus north searching for this mythical glimmering city. The
Spanish believed they had actually found Aztlán in many places, especially in New Mexico. In fact, the "actual" or "historical" Aztlán
is thought to be somewhere near Albuquerque and Santa Fe (Chavez,
1984). Aztlán has functioned as a canvas and travel narrative on and
through which many have pictured and narrated their destinies and
identities, including the Aztecs, the Spanish conquistadores, the New
Mexican Chamber of Commerce, and Chicana/o revolutionaries. A
good myth is infinitely elastic.

For Chicanos, Aztlán was central to Chicano identity, and was first
spoken in their poetic manifesto:

THE SPIRITUAL PLAN OF AZTLÁN

In the spirit of a new people that is conscious not only of its
proud historical heritage but also of the brutal "gringo" invasion
of our territories, *we,* the Chicano inhabitants and civilizers of
the northern land of Aztlán from whence came our forefathers,

---

4. Two studies have traced the historical parameters of the Aztec myth of Aztlán: Pina,
1989; Boone, 1991.

reclaiming the land of their birth and consecrating the determination of our people of the sun, *declare* that the call of our blood is our power, our responsibility, and our inevitable destiny.

We are free and sovereign to determine those tasks which are justly called for by our house, our land, the sweat of our brows, and by our hearts. Aztlán belongs to those who plant the seeds, water the fields, and gather the crops and not to the foreign Europeans. We do not recognize capricious frontiers on the bronze continents.

Brotherhood unites us, and love for our brothers makes us a people whose time has come and who struggles against the foreigner "gabacho" who exploits our riches and destroys our culture. Before the world, before all of North America, before all our brothers in the bronze continent, we are a nation, we are a union of free pueblos, we are *Aztlán*.

To the chagrin of many, Chicano identity had become a mythical Aztec family romance structured by the twin mandates of machismo and an indigenous Marian fetishism, or marianismo (Laura Pérez, 1999).

The Macho/Marian Complex

Detractors of macho mythology in Mexico identify it as a foreign imposition, a cultural colonialism or "orientalism" that has emerged through social exchanges. For example, as late as 1995 an American, self-identified "homosexual sex researcher," declared with observed certainty and presumed impunity:

The Mexican mestizo culture places a high value on "manliness." A salient feature of the society is a sharp delimitation between the roles played by males and females. In general, men are expected to be dominant and independent and females to be submissive and dependent. The distinct boundary between male and female roles in Mexico appears to be due in part to a culturally defined hyper masculine ideal referred to as *machismo*. The ideal female role is generally believed to be the opposite of the ideal male role and may be referred to as marianismo. (Carrier, 1995:3–4)

"Marianismo" is a religious and cultural expectation that women imitate the patron saint of Mexico, La Virgen de Guadalupe, in her official role as "virgin mother," who is paralleled here with the fertility goddesses. Mesoamerican fertility goddesses were embodied in the myth of "Tonantzin," or "Our Mother" (Castillo, 1995). Inasmuch as identities require symbols and their attendant narratives, machismo derives from the symbol of the Indigenous warrior, an archetype further — and surprisingly — idealized as priest, philosopher, and poet (Alarcón, 1997). Both marianismo and machismo are sacred signifiers in the pantheon of Latin American holy ancestors. This fantastical and perfect gendered binary was reinscribed into Mexican consciousness by Octavio Paz during the 1950s, as a holy family romance. In this drama, *chingar,* meaning to violate or to make a preemptive strike, was the apotheosis of male virtue and carried with it the much coveted title *chingón.* Yet, Paz's analysis is brilliantly complicated by one now famous declaration: "It is likewise significant that male homosexuality is regarded with a certain indulgence insofar as the active agent is concerned. The passive agent is an abject, degraded being" (Paz, 1959:34). As he sees it, it is the division of the sex roles that determines who can enjoy macho status, not the act of homosexual sex itself; the receptive agent is considered a faggot, or *maricón*, while the delivering actor's macho status is enhanced, presumably, from the intimate violation of another male.

In the United States, sexual identity emerges from the gender of the erotic partner, not as a result of the sexual position. In contrast, Paz reports that in Mexico a man's sexual identity is determined by the sexual act — even if the partner is another man. Hence, the mythology of machismo is a complex mixture of erotic desire, delineated by the specific sexual activity, or ritual posturing, rather than by the gender of one's partner. Tomás Almaguer agrees with Paz and elaborates this theory in a San Francisco-based case study (Almaguer, 1993).

José Limón argues that the macho symbol is a necessary corrective to Mexican and Chicano society fraught with signifiers of male intimacy, bonding, and homo-eroticism existing at various levels of group consciousness and sexual play (1994:123–40). Similarly, Miguel De La Torre, a Cuban American, offers his former self as an example of machismo in Cuban culture. He writes: "It becomes the macho's responsibility, his burden, to educate those who fall below his perceived superior standards. Because of their gender, most men are complicit with sexist social structures. . . . Men prevail over women in the marketplace, in the church, in the community, and within *cubanidad* just because they are male" (2003:85).

Generally machismo is thought to be natural, existing outside of language, a reality of its own kind: it's as if the macho surrenders his body by force of ritual nature, abandoning his reason, while enacting an existential script that functions as an authoritative narrative of identification and raw, aggressive power.

I turn now to examine three cultural sites where machismo, masculinity, and Latina/o spiritual and religious values are actively questioned, re-worked, and re-symbolized.

The Road to Aztlán

Organized by curators Virginia M. Fields and Victor Zamudio-Taylor, the exhibition "The Road to Aztlán: Art from a Mythic Homeland," showed at the Los Angeles County Museum of Art, the Austin Museum of Fine Art, and the Albuquerque Museum of Art from May 2001 through April 2002. A collection of 250 pieces, the exhibition spanned two thousand years, divided into three periods: pre-Columbian (third century B.C.E.–1521), the colonial period (1521–1848), and modern times (1848–2000). In the words of the organizers: "Central to the conception of the exhibition is the notion of Aztlán as a metaphoric center place, reflecting a sacred geography and a social imaginary that incorporates economics, religion, history, and art" (Fields and Taylor, 2001:40).

Organizers of the show faced a difficult task: collecting and displaying centuries of art — from early Mesoamerica to contemporary Chicana/o and Mexicana/o arts. Rather than a show about Aztlán, it was a show of art from Atzlán — a broad rubric and defiant representation. The actual exhibit is a tactical deployment of the myth, insofar as its premise requires the pieces to work together to imagine and represent a community, from different times, in adjacent and overlapping places.

The objects in the first section originated in Mesoamerica and are mostly clay and stone sculpture with remarkably detailed colors, lines, and textures. This section also contains replicas of the Aztec codices, extended out in storybook fashion. Among the most popular in this space is the chronicle of the Aztec peregrination from Aztlán. The second grouping unfolds colonial aesthetics, disclosing the continuities between Native and Spanish-Moorish arts. Mestizo artists continued to develop their ideals in Christian forms, and those not so subtly disguised as Christian. The image of Guadalupe, as a *fait typique,* illustrates at least three main referents. The Christian influence is present in her general frame: Mary, the mother of God. But she is also Aztec inasmuch as she appears with dark skin, speaking Nahuatl. Her bright solar aura or full body halo suggests Aztec beliefs about celestial deities, as does her cape of stars. She stands on a crescent moon, emblematic of Islamic faith. Similar admixtures are visible in many of the oil paintings and sculptures that adorn this section of the exhibit (see Davalos, 2001).

Amalia Mesa-Bains's installation, "Reflections on a Transparent Migration" (2001, mixed media), marks a brilliant nodal point in the show's walking tour. It replicates the three fundamental levels of Aztec cosmology, while blending representations of public home spaces/domestic space/sacred space. The sculpture is made entirely of brilliant thin reflective mirrors, the lines sharp as glass. The scene is of a home altar doubling as a vanity table, seat, and mirror, surrounded by a maguey garden. The center of the piece is the apex of the vanity's mirror, which shoots directly into the sky as a pillar, connecting the scene with the heavens, the realm of the gods. Here, then, is the *axis mundi,* the sacred pole connecting the tripartite levels of life. The sculpture shines and reflects; it functions as source, receptacle, and transmitter.

The apex of Mesa-Bains's "Reflections" is narrow and pointed, resembling a church steeple. It delineates a phallic structure — but from an unlikely source, as it originates in the female domestic space. By redrawing the phallus as a trope in feminine domestic space and by demarcating that space as sacred center, Mesa-Bains has re-signified the master symbol of Western phallo-centric society, rendering it a tool within the feminine sacred, relocating it and thus its authority centrally within feminine space. Her shrine to the female sacral marked a glimmering pivot of the exhibit, whereupon two other signifiers hinged.

The first was the opening piece of the show entitled: "Rattlesnake Tail with Maize Ears."[5] The ancient giant basalt stone, sculptured by the Aztecs during their brief reign, was fashioned so that its posterior tip was capped and raised to resemble an erect phallus, complemented by the ears of corn to symbolize fertility. The exhibit's final room answered and cadenced the sculpture: an enormous installation by contemporary Mexican artist Teresa Serrano entitled "River."[6] A cloth tube made of rolled embroidered blankets flowed lazily from the apex of the wall and fell flat onto the ground; it hung from an iron three-ring holder, bound by men's trouser belts. The signifier here was flaccid.

In its framing and in many of its central pieces, "The Road to Aztlán" exhibition replicates phallic imagery, and thus glorifies the central symbol of macho virility, even while mocking, relocating, and troubling it. In Aztlán — recreated, reproduced — the phallic iconography and signification are inescapable.

American Ethos: The Detour on the Road to "The Road to Aztlán" Show, or Get Your Kitsch on Route 66

Travel itself has become a definitive trope of American identity, and two of the defining statements on American culture came as modern travel narratives, and moreover they came from French authors. Social theorists Alexis de Tocqueville and Jean Baudrillard seem unlikely bedfellows — one a modernist interested in U.S. democracy in the early nineteenth century, the other a postmodernist who documented the surrealistic character of North American road culture in the late

---

5. "Rattlesnake Tail with Maize Ears," Mexico, Aztec, 1325–1521, basalt, 39x21x49 in.
6. Teresa Serrano, "River," 1996, embroidered blankets, iron, leather belts, 177x21x31 in.

twentieth century. Still, both wrote in French about America, from an expressed French perspective. And both penned travel narratives. Tocqueville toured the nascent nation just before the "opening" of Aztlán to U.S. colonization, from the east; Baudrillard toured Aztlán. Both their conclusions stress the uncannily "phantasmagoric" quality of American life: Tocqueville called this "religious enthusiasm," more than he had previously witnessed in Europe. Baudrillard called this quality the "hyper-real," a utopian death state more real than reality itself, around which American identities took shape.

I also embarked upon a journey through and to Aztlán: traveling to the museum exhibits on Aztlán-produced narratives about Chicano homeland and machismo even before arriving at the museums. On my drive from Phoenix to Albuquerque to see the exhibit "The Road to Aztlán," I discovered another reprisal of the myth of primordial sacred homeland, on "historic" Route 66. Places the Indigenous mapped and the Spanish originally traveled seeking wealth and salvation are now coded in terms of their highway designations, particularly American historic Route Sixty-Six — which cuts through the heart of Aztlán. Each aspect of this area is visually stunning, continuously unveiling ever more spectacular natural beauty: red rock mountains to the north and forested plains to the south. Baudrillard deemed these Western places "utopia found," a place of "death." If human life is the search for utopia, then utopia discovered renders the loss of this life. Signs along the highway deem them "scenic."

The idea of a magical, enchanted past is central to American road culture, hence the popular belief that driving enables a return to a simpler time, an easier time, a less complicated time — what Renato Rosaldo calls "imperialist nostalgia" (Rosaldo, 1989). And yet, an escape from the presumed "corruption" of modern life is a plausible idea in the American imagination. Indeed, low-cost, minimum service roadside motels and restaurants are commonly named "Country Inn." The promise of the virtuous purity of the country is built into the road environment, as a commodity, ready to be consumed. The notion of escaping the contamination of the city for an authentic America is not exhausted by the literal pollution from the combustion engine, industry, and the population, but its meaning extends into the allegory of the immoral city and moral countryside that represents an older, more authentic, true America (Orsi, 1999). This America is symbolized by the American Indian, some in this area known as "Uto-Aztecan" tribes. Their myths also become commodities, capitalist artifacts, and can therefore open imaginary historical space for the teachings of Aztlán, machismo, and patriarchy to touch and influence individuals and societies.

One sign along "historic" Route 66 invites motorists to "experience the past." Another phrases it differently: "experience history," claiming the "best Indian *Ruins*" along the highway. The signage offers "Indian arts and crafts," reassuring the traveler that they are "made by real Indian artisans." One Indian "jewelry and gift store" boasts its wares as being "museum quality." The Indian today is a relic of Aztlán, one who is associated with a foregone past, innocent, a Shepherd of the present. This mythical past reveals itself in the cultural representation of today's Indians, rare, remote, removed from civilization. Seeing them, then, requires a long drive. For it seems that only a long drive can satisfy the tourist desire for reviving a human experience of pristine and "unspoiled" humanity now deemed remote from culture. "Take a picture with a real Indian," reads one sign. "Great family stop," reads another. Not only does this phantasmagoric road culture violate religious identities and life ways, but it has the uncanny ability to sanctify profane commercialization.

In the heart of the desert, dinosaur sculptures line the road, guarding the gas stations and still inhabiting highway museums while signifying a turn to a prehistoric time, a time of plausible fantasy, a time of myth. This is the American road to Aztlán, best seen from behind the automobile's looking glass. There, the visual and sensational world is highly *velocitized,* that is, one's body becomes de-sensitized to the effects of speed, or rate of movement through space. In this way, one loses perspective and the world is experienced through the opaque windshield veil, which frames images like a television screen, changing them rapidly, and cultivating human greed for consumer products. Like the television, the highway projects a desire-driven fantasy, hinging upon the image as framed for consumption, and as unmediated truth. American identity is simply a commodity in and product of a capitalist political economy, arrested and arranged from the movement, play, and signification of symbols — including especially those signs that tell of God, race, and gender.

Road semiotics create myths that are not nearly as much about the historic past as they are about the motorists who navigate them. Like the museum, the highways sell identity by providing historical fantasies in a space that is well-lighted, neatly organized, and pleasingly displayed. No one has captured the irony of identities normalized and naturalized by liquid crystal displays — be they car windshields, television and computer screens, or museum display cases — as has John Leanos in his brilliant installation entitled, "Remembering Castration: Discovery and Bloody Metaphors in Aztlán." I traveled from the West coast to the exhibit at New York's prestigious biennial exhibition, staged at the Whitney Museum.

Aztlán, Madison and 75th, Manhattan

During my flight from San Francisco to New York City to see the Leanos installation at the Whitney Museum of American Art, Delta Airlines screened free in-flight commercial videos that declared the Chicano rock band, Los Lobos, of East Los Angeles, "America's greatest band." The video clips were from the group's latest recording, "Good Morning, Aztlán." Band member David Hidalgo explained the album title: "With this recording Aztlán is now global; in Japan they will be speaking it."

Certainly they were speaking it in New York, thanks to the art of John Leanos, particularly his installation "Remembering Castration." His re-creation of ancestral homeland consciously distorts and thus disrupts the machismo embedded within sacred "ancestral" memory. Comprising over a dozen display cases that contained photographs, skeletal relics, maps, chronologies, and a blank note book, all pieces in the exhibit were entirely faux, an ironic challenge to notions of truth and the rarified places that produce it. Leanos articulates his premise of the exhibit as follows:

German archaeologist Helmut Mythusmacher [read: "mythmaker"] traveled to Mexico in 1840. Influenced by the codex borges, he departed Mexico city in 1846 to retrace the migratory route of the Aztec emissaries with the intention of relocating the ancient Mexico homeland, Aztlán. Mythusmacher wandered the north American desert for two years in search of signs of Aztec culture and in late 1847, he discovered several Aztec artifacts in a hoard along the Rio Grande marked by an Aztec cudgel. This discovery led to a major excavation of Aztlán on the salt lake river, Arizona in 1848.[7]

Mythusmacher's "discoveries" are collected and exhibited in Leanos's installation. It occupied a small room on the top floor at the Biennial, its walls painted a sanguine red. In the background Mexican boleros alternated with "American Indian" flute music. Each "artifact" was numbered, scientifically, telling an unordered story. In fact, on the first lighted story board, a timeline of Aztec events defied any clear chronology. "Artifacts" displayed behind glass museum cases mocked the authority of these same modern trappings as framers, and indeed revealers of truth.

Mythusmacher's findings revealed an Aztec ritual previously unknown: a ritual of warrior castration as a sign of submission to the moon goddess Coayalaxhui. One of Leanos's exhibit tags explained: "A BLOODY RITUAL REMINDS THE WARRIOR OF HIS FALLACIOUS STANCE, HIS IGNORANCE OF THE MOON, AND MEMORY'S DEPENDENCE ON FORGETTING."

The first case enclosed a small phallus, ossified, displaying a red slice through the base. The case was littered with red powder, and marked: "AZTLÁN/1451–2000: CASTRATED WARRIOR PHALLUS." The following display case held the diary of Mythusmacher, where stones, presumably ossified artifacts, were exhibited mostly without narrative description. The message became clear: the non-descript stones are meaningless, but when framed behind the crystal glass they are narrated as disclosers of human truth, evolutionary nodal points, reputed progressive cultural markers, and symbolic commodities available for identity construction. These are then made accessible to a high grade of consumer, the patron with the distinguished tastes

---

7. Many images from this exhibit, as well as many of the texts, can be found at John Leanos's website: *www.johnleanos.com*.

which the museum reflects. Still, the success of this capitalist venture depends on its ability to appeal to the television and highway logics of American identity construction: i.e., identity is the nominal historical location of the self, with self-reference to distinct cultural markers.

The next case in Leanos's exhibit crystallized this further. The imprint of an erect fist, clinched into the power symbol, raised questions, the caption asking: "FIST OR PHALLUS: IF WE CANNOT DECIPHER THIS RELIEF ITS MEANING IS IRRELEVANT." Reading the symbols gives them meaning. Hence, Leanos's work asks: What would happen if the stones were read in a different way? What if the story was re-narrated? What if the myth of Aztlán were told as that of male submission, rather than as the story of men as warriors and philosophers emergent in the classical Mexican pieta? The center light board brought it all together. Narratives captioning sepia photographs of empty landscapes proclaimed "AZTEC TEXTILES FOUND AT THIS SITE REVEAL" that Chicana/o culture is liquid, malleable, and evolving. The last case held an ossified lower half of a phallus that was narrated as follows: "AS THE SEVERED WARRIOR PHALLUS STANDS PETRIFIED AND UNCOVERED A CLEAN SLATE IS OFFERED TO THE IMAGINED NATION."

"Remembering Castration" explicitly asked its viewers to recognize not only the power of memory, but also the imperative to forget, and the awesome responsibility to make myth, and history. Leanos submits: "AZTLÁN TODAY AND TOMORROW REFUSES TO BE SEEN BUT NEVER CEASES TO BE IMAGINED." With this responsibility in mind, "The Road to Aztlán" show begs the question: where does the road lead? It is artists who are taking the responsibility for the spiritual deconstruction of machismo and for replacing it with myths and symbols that affirm and unite, for rejecting the machista register of value and in its place creating fresh models of Chicana/o and Latina/o identities. And they are doing so from the fragments of deconstructed oppressive myths that simplified sexuality and by appealing to the mind-set of the liquid crystal display generation.

Leanos's exhibit and the Road to Aztlán show agree that machismo and its ancient signifiers need to be rethought in ways that truly reflect the borderlands locality — at the crossroads of many different paths.

This new Latina/o identity is built upon the Christian ruined temples of Aztlán that were dedicated to the machista gods and goddesses. Artists are leading the way.

El Vez and the Religiously Erotic

Since the 1980s, performance artist El Vez, the self-proclaimed "Mexican Elvis," has broken new terrain by re-signifying/re-making borderlands religions and identities. He has produced nearly twenty-five recordings, both original work and also inscribing revolutionary and humorous lyrics over American and Mexican classics. Born Robert Lopez in East Los Angeles, he is best known for his ubiquitous live tours, accompanied by his back-up dancers known as the "El Vettes." In English, he explains, the phrase "el vez" means "the time." As he sees it, a new time has come — a time for a radically fresh way of conceptualizing all things, but especially Latino male identity.

Toward this end, his music and performances are charged with religious spirituality and symbolism — from Aztec deities, Christ and Christianity, to the manifold deities of Hinduism. One of El Vez's first recordings was entitled "Aztlán." In it he declares:

> I am looking for a land
> That belonged to Mexico
> But now holds no time or space
> In Aztlán, Aztlán

El Vez foregrounds Leanos's subsequent work. For both artists, recovery of an authentic Aztlán is neither possible nor desirable. Yet, El Vez, like Leanos, continues to search for an Aztlán in which, as El Vez puts it, "We all will be received" (El Vez, "Aztlán," 1994). Both renditions of Aztec mythological narratives come from the perspective of gay Chicanos and use camp and parody to re-navigate the familiar terrain of sacred ancestral cartography.

These efforts at re-mapping sacred Latina/o psychic and existential identities are revealed powerfully in El Vez's 2001 recording, *Boxing with God,* and the attendant staged performance, "The Gospel Show." I saw "Gospel Show" live in 2002, in Phoenix, Arizona. I understand the record and show as texts of ludic, erotic, sexualized, and indeed religious play emerging out of a Latino borderlands musical and visual aesthetic. In short, El Vez has brilliantly inscribed a musical text as spiritual path into a revolutionary and liberating religiosity, creating what I call a theology of religious erotics, especially the beginnings for an ethics of Latino masculinity. In the religiously erotic, sacrality joins profanity, destruction melds with creation, and sex finds spirit. According to El Vez, "Sometimes the quickest way to your sexuality is through your spirituality" (El Vez, 2001).

Since the beginning, El Vez's lyrics have been informed by the mythology of the ancient Aztecs, revisiting deities and the ancestral homeland, "Aztlán." His work mixes Mesoamerican, Christian, Hindu, and Buddhist doctrines and practices. In the first line of a song entitled "Quetzalcoatl," the third of eighteen tracks on the *Boxing* record, he begins telling the story by claiming, "when I was an Aztec before the empire fell." The last line of the same song is a recitation repeated at the album's conclusion; barely audible, a woman's voice speaking in Spanish claims: "I have resurrected the bones of the captives." It emerges as a chant and incantation. It is a conjuring ceremony that recalls the pre-Christian spirits.

Like Leanos, El Vez presents an alternative in a performative text, written, sung, and recorded. "The Gospel Show" opens and takes place as a traditional evangelical revival to the passionate beats of Gospel tunes with soulful rhythms. El Vez explodes onto the stage as an enthusiastic evangelist, flailing his arms as if in a state of ecstasy. The "El Vettes" and his male back-up vocalists incite the crowd by waving their hands in the air and performing as if they too were driven by the religious excess of spiritual and physical rapture. The crowd responds, immediately understanding and appreciating the (mock?) spiritual setting of the experience. The audience joins in and seeks salvation — as if all are erotically yoked together.

The first song on the album and the tour, a religious anthem, fuses border crossing and religious baptism, signifying Jesus as the primal border crosser: The initial sounds heard on the record are splashes, border crossers arising from the river separating rich from poor, first world from third, Protestants from Catholics, and more. The songwriter celebrates this crossing with the expression: "Orale," or "Right

On." The refrain is offered in choral call and response. "Oh orale, when Jesus walked into the U.S.A." Border crossing becomes a religious ritual, patterned by Christ himself, leading his followers into the U.S.A. "He crossed the land to stand and be part of the U.S.A. / To earn a wage." El Vez deftly weds comedy and tragedy. The list lines of the song proclaim: "a new beginning for family and friends / To share a better working way / Sail on silver girl oh happy day / Sail on by oh happy day / Your time has come to fly / You have no borders / See how they run across freeways / And peace just can't be found. / Like a bridge over troubled borders I will lay me down." And thus begins *Boxing with God*.

This piece is followed by a poetic exhortation, a sermon: "And the Preacher Said." "Brothers and sisters," the preacher exhorts, "now some people think AIDS is the wrath of God, now that's not my Jesus, that's not my Jesus, God invented condoms." Early on El Vez attacks the impulse to attribute AIDS to God's wrath — a hateful and evil diatribe arising from religious extremists and ideological terrorists to impugn millions of people across the world.

El Vez playfully, joyfully mocks received Christian teaching on sexuality that denies the realm of the spirit to the body and sexuality, whether sexuality be expressed in procreation or not, and proposes instead a Christianity infused with Mesoamerican teaching. In the piece entitled "Quetzalcoatl," the ancient Mesoamerican *hombre dios,* or Man-God, said to be at once human and divine, is again likened to Jesus Christ — an obvious categorical affinity that fueled theological debate during colonialism. In El Vez's rendition of the narrative, Quetzalcoatl does indeed return to "spread peace."

Following an encouraging, clever, and uplifting anthem entitled "Mexi-Can," he offers a puja of sorts to the Hindu mother deity: "Can You Kali?" In it he creates comedic and triumphant liberation theology, declaring in the final stanza: "Can you Kali? — she's so glad to meet cha / She was the mother of creation and destruction. / Sister brother of begin and termination. Like no other / oh Kali Kali we love you." Kali, at once the mother of destruction and life, symbolizes memory's utter dependence upon forgetting.

In the ballad entitled "Just Want to See His Face," the first of the three concluding tracks on the record, El Vez surreptitiously unfolds his theology of religious play: "Get up feel it Relax your mind / Stand up, shout it Relax your mind / My country god 'tis of thee. Does Jesus Christ believe in me?" The word Relax is capitalized, while the word God is not. "Country" and "god" are related concepts, from which Christ appears, and El Vez reverses the equation that belief in "god," here signifying the nation state, is conditioned upon a belief in Christ. Instead, he asks, "Does Christ believe in me?" Relaxing one's mind and asking Christ to believe in the self, or subject, reverses the agency of statecraft, the subject makes history, makes the nation, makes Christ, and makes God. Relax and forget the notions you have been taught. The final lyrics repeat the chorus: "Don't wanna walk and talk about Jesus Just wanna see his face / Just wanna see his face." What does the face of Jesus look like? That image is left to the artistic faculties of the believer.

This is followed by the bawdy "Lust for Christ," sung to the pounding background of Billy Idol's popular 1980s hit, "Lust for Life." Finally, the sultry "If He Ever Comes Now" officially concludes the recording, but after a few minutes of silence "Lust" is reprised. El Vez's remake deserves lengthy citation here:

> Hey man where'd you get that notion to fear God that's not devotion. You need something called love / yeah something called love. No Church, Cross or Santería Chickens / Jesus is just a modern guy with Christ you haven't got to fear no more! / I've got a Lust for Christ I've got a Lust for Christ / God's got a million surprises like the kiss army Zapatistas go, go, go! / Don't need a uniform or a government loan / To Hell with the devil, he despises... Jesus is just a modern guy with Christ you haven't got to fear no more! / I've got a Lust for Christ I've got a Lust for Christ.

The final song, the ribald "If He Ever Comes (Down) Now," suggests orgasmic relief and anticipation — a blissful union with God. El Vez's musical performance creates sex with God. It in fact involves Christ in all the details of life, including sex — an episteme central to one theologian's queer liberation: "Sexual ecstasy frequently accompanies spiritual ecstasy, and both may involve orgasmic release. For me, erotic prayer propelled me to a new intimacy with Jesus the

Christ, a new awareness of discipleship.... My theological goal has been to articulate a sexual theology that encompasses the integration of sexuality and spirituality, various configurations of relationships, the interconnection of love-making and justice-doing, and eros as revelation of God" (Goss, 2002:18).[8] This, too, appears to be a part of El Vez's theological performance, with a focus on deconstructing the profanity of machismo.

Deconstructing Machismo after the Fall: Toward a Theology of the Religiously Erotic

Early last century, African American scholar W. E. B. Du Bois proclaimed that the dilemma of the twentieth century is the problem of the color line, an opaque veil separating black society from white society. Not by contrast but rather by extension I believe the problem of the twenty-first century is the problem of the spiritual line, or spirituality, that is, the religious and theological line separating saved from damned, Christian from pagan, rich from poor, science from religion, and more — ironically creating the greatest cleavages in our (post)modern world. This predicament lies deep in the soul of the nation: at the level of the culturally sublime, a sacred place at once intimate and infinite, the nucleus of the individual and of the nation: a place of spirit and memory.

In this matrix, the religious field is intimately meshed with the political field. God's handiwork is today frequently cited as the source for historical calamities that cause the suffering of infinite multitudes. The so-called wall separating church and state has crumbled under the weight of aggregated fundamentalist, anti-modernist, anti-liberal values congealed at temples dedicated to the State, a God-sanctioned sociological construction of reality, what Nietzsche calls the "New Idol." Within it, "every people speaks its tongue of good and evil, which the neighbor does not understand. It has invented its own language of customs and rights" (Nietzsche, 1954:49). In the Mexican Americas, the language of Aztlán speaks an ethics of

---

8. I recognize the controversy surrounding Goss's work. While I believe that Goss's work would be stronger if it were documented more carefully, I also feel his theological work provides a starting point for a queer theology of liberation.

machismo and marianismo — a theology of oppression that emerges from the great Indigenous-Christian synthesis that characterizes Latin America, especially Mexico (León, 2004).

With this in mind, El Vez's *Boxing with God* denotes a conversation with the sacred, a dialogue that transforms an understanding of God, rather than dismissing God as a primitive fairytale. However, El Vez is by no means submissive, but struggling with a memory and reality, a battle with God (*mano a mano*). Central to this fresh theology is the release of the erotic from its fundamentalist religious constraints. Accepting Bataille's definition, we can say that eros is the will toward radical union unto death to the self so that fresh creation can emerge from union (1986:24). In this light, the erotics of El Vez reveals revolutionary potential inasmuch as he seeks to rejoin a spirituality that has been rent asunder from a Christian sexuality. El Vez, together with the exhibits "The Road to Aztlán," remind us, as articulated by John Leanos, that memory is reliant upon forgetting, and that a holistic expression of self and society must negotiate this dynamic: forgetting the myths that tear apart while remembering those erotic myths and rituals that bind people and communities, *religare,* throwing them together in ways that are whole and complete. Liberation and social progress require forgetting — as well as memory.

Toward this end, El Vez deploys what José Esteban Muñoz calls "disidentifications," a term "descriptive of the survival strategies the minority subject practices in order to negotiate a phobic and majoritarian public sphere that continuously elides or punishes the existence of subjects who do not conform to the phantasm of normative citizenship." In this regard, Muñoz cites a Cubana performance artist: "Marga [Gómez]'s disidentification with these damaged stereotypes recycled them as powerful and seductive sites of self-creation" (1999:4). Similarly, Cherríe Moraga performs a disidentification when re-deploying the myth of Aztlán. She writes:

> As we are forced to struggle for our right to love free of disease and discrimination, "Aztlán," as our imagined homeland begins to take on renewed importance. Without the dream of a free world, a free world will never be realized. Chicana lesbians

and gay men do not merely seek inclusion in the Chicano nation; we seek a nation strong enough to embrace a full range of racial diversities, human sexualities, and expressions of gender. We seek a culture that can allow for the natural expression of our femaleness and maleness and our love without prejudice or punishment. In a "queer" Aztlán, there would be no freaks, no "others" to point our fingers at. (Moraga, 1993:150)

A theology of the religiously erotic champions Moraga's "queer Aztlán" as the queendom of God, thoroughly infused with the passion for union and recreation along erotic lines. C. S. Lewis defines "Eros" as a kind of God: "Of all loves he is, at his height, most god-like; therefore most prone to demand our worship. Of himself he always tends to turn 'being in love' into a kind of religion" (1960:154). Religious erotics is the spiritual path to individual and social liberation.

Chapter 10

Nepantla Spirituality:
Negotiating Multiple Religious
Identities among U.S. Latinas

Lara Medina

I was born and live in that in-between space, *nepantla,* the
borderlands. (Anzaldúa, 1993:114)[1]

In 1987, Gloria Anzaldúa published *Borderlands/La Frontera: The
New Mestiza,* a foundational book for the further development of
Chicana feminist thought and praxis. At the time, I was completing a
masters' in theology at the Graduate Theological Union in Berkeley.
I considered the book to be a "new Chicana bible." Her articulation
of the pain yet creativity of living on physical, psychological, sexual,
and spiritual borders resonated profoundly with my own experiences
of growing up Chicana. Straddling borders or the spaces "wherever
two or more cultures edge each other" had become a way of life for
me and other brown women constantly learning how to survive in a
white-dominated society. All people of color in the United States share
this challenge, but Anzaldúa addressed this space of discomfort and
contradiction from a specific cultural and gendered perspective. Anzaldúa has gifted Chicanas with a theory with which to articulate our
personal and communal pain leading to a "new mestiza consciousness," one that moves toward "a more whole perspective, one that
includes rather than excludes" (1987:79). For Anzaldúa, a central

---

1. While I was completing this essay the great Chicana cultural theorist Gloria Anzaldúa
unexpectedly died on May 16, 2004, of complications related to diabetes. I most respectfully
dedicate this essay to her.

aspect of this new consciousness is the healing of the dark-skinned Indian woman within Chicanas/os who has been "silenced, gagged, caged, bound into servitude ... " (Ibid.:23). La India's voice, wisdom, and spirit could redeem the fragmentation of our spiritual, psychological, and physical selves that had conformed to the dualistic paradigm of Western thought and culture.

One year later, the publication of *Hispanic Women: Prophetic Voice in the Church* by Ada María Isasi-Díaz and Yolanda Tarango offered another foundational text for the articulation of Latina feminist thought and praxis. The authors wrote candidly of the alienation and hurt that Latinas have experienced in the Catholic Church and within Latino cultures due to sexism and internalized racism. Their starting point was the daily experiences of Latinas in a white dominant society and church. By intertwining cultural theology, feminist theology, and liberation theology they offered an accessible methodology to enable Latinas to articulate their "understandings of the divine" and to effect social change. Through sharing our stories, analyzing the systemic causes of our shared pain, liturgizing from a feminist perspective, and strategizing to bring forth change, Latinas could give birth "to new elements, to a new reality" (1988:xiii). Validating the fusion of Amerindian, African, and Christian beliefs and practices "as the most operative system of symbols used by Hispanic women ... [that] could well offer needed correctives to some of the religious understandings of official Christianity" (Ibid.: 67) sanctioned my own growing awareness of the critical need to recognize Indigenous epistemologies within a Chicana/o theology. My master's thesis would argue that the reinterpretation and reclamation of Indigenous epistemology is a vital task for a Chicano/a liberation theology as Indigenous ways of knowing are foundational to Chicano/a ways of being in the world. It is the deepest source for our valuing communal responsibility, interdependency, reciprocity, sacrifice, truth through artistic expression, intuitive knowledge, respect for elders, humility, sacredness within nature, and the interconnectedness of all living things. As Anzaldúa prophesied, the Indigenous mother was truly emerging from the darkness "to fight for her own skin and a piece of ground to stand on, a ground from which to view the world — a perspective, a home ground where she can plumb the rich ancestral roots into her own ample mestiza heart" (1987:23). The question for Anzaldúa and myself became, "How could I reconcile the two, the pagan and the Christian?" (Ibid.: 38).

Reconciling the pagan and the Christian for colonized and Christianized people can be an arduous process. The reconciling must take place in the depth of one's being rather than as a mere acceptance of a syncretic symbol system or a mestiza identity formed from the best of two or more cultures. The concept of *mestizaje,* although useful to emphasize the racial/ethnic mixture of Chicanos and other Latinos, and the blending of cultures that create a mestizo/a identity, can also easily diminish the significance of the Indigenous worldview within the *mestizaje* and the conditions under which it has struggled to survive. As Anzaldúa later stated, "Beware of *el romance del mestizaje.... Puede ser una ficción*" (1993:111).[2] True reconciliation between the Indigenous and the Christian requires the privileging of the mother culture, the Indigenous, until the Indigenous can be fully respected.

According to Webster's New World Dictionary, to reconcile means: (1) "to make friendly again or win over to a friendly attitude; (2) to settle (a quarrel or dispute) or compose (a difference); (3) to ... bring into harmony; and (4) to make content, submissive, or acquiescent (to) [to become reconciled to one's lot]." For mixed race peoples, existing in harmony is often an oxymoron and submitting or acquiescing is no longer a viable option. How then can "the pagan and the Christian" truly reconcile?

The ancestral experience of violent contact, colonization, miscegenation, and transculturation beginning in the sixteenth century between Indigenous, European, and African peoples that created the mestiza, the mulatto, and the Afro-mestizo, also created the potential for their descendants to hold diverse worldviews and religions in balance (Aguirre Beltrán, 1946; Bennett, 2003). But colonizing powers had a different agenda and the African and Indigenous epistemology would be supplanted or forced underground. Not being willing to give up their ancestral deities and being forced to accept a new way left many Indigenous people in between worlds, discerning how best

---

2. "Beware of romanticizing *mestizaje* ... it could be fictional."

to survive. The well-known phrase "idols behind altars" offered an attempt to understand one strategy of survival, but as David Carrasco so brilliantly elucidates, "There were idols behind altars but it is imperative to look at the entire scene, the idol and the altar as the relationship to be understood" (1995:74). Indigenous peoples did not merely resist the imposition of Christianity but they responded to the foreign tradition by crafting their religiosity, developing unsanctioned traditions, reinforcing their community networks, and ultimately asserting their religious autonomy.[3] They became Christian on their own terms and in the process Christianity was changed.

The first victims of colonization found themselves in *nepantla,* a Nahuatl term meaning in the middle, or the middle place.[4] According to Nahautl scholar Fermin Herrera, the word *nepantla* means a middle place and is usually attached to nouns.[5] For example, *tlalli* means land and *tlalnepantla* means middle of the earth. To be "in *nepantla*" could then imply to be at the center.

The use of *nepantla* was recorded by the Dominican friar Diego Durán, in the sixteenth century in *Historia de las Indias de Nueva España y Islas de Tierra Firme.* I quote the passage at length:

> Once I questioned an Indian regarding certain things, particularly why he had gone dragging himself about, gathering monies, with bad nights and worse days, and having gathered so much money through so much trouble he put on a wedding and invited the entire town and spent everything. Thus reprimanding him for the evil thing he had done, he answered me: Father, do not be frightened because we are still *nepantla,* and since I understood what he meant to say by that phrase and metaphor, which means to be in the middle, I insisted that he tell me in what middle it was in which they found themselves. He told me

---

3. Roberto R. Treviño named these aspects of religious agency in his study on turn-of-the-century Tejano Catholics. See "The Handbook of Texas Online," *www.tsha.utexas.edu/handbook/online/articles/print/MM/pqmcf.html.*

4. Nahuatl is the language of the Nahuas, the largest Indigenous ethnic/cultural group in the central valley of Mexico in the 1500s. Nahuatl is widely spoken today in this region of Mexico.

5. Fermin Herrera is a professor of Chicano/a studies at California State University, Northridge and author of *Nahuatl-English, English-Nahuatl,* Hippocrene Books Concise Dictionary, 2004.

that since they were still not well rooted in the faith, I should not be surprised that they were still neutral, that they neither answered to one faith or the other or, better said, that they believed in God and at the same time keep their ancient customs and demonic rites. And this is what he meant by his abominable excuse that they still remained in the middle and were neutral. (1867–80:268)

The friar's apparent lack of regard or understanding of Indigenous communal responsibility, communal obligations, and communal celebrations marking rites of passage clearly blurred his interaction with the native elder. Within indigenous epistemology, community participation symbolizes the strength of a community and is proof of one's belonging in a community.[6] Instead, the friar found this behavior to be an "evil thing" and condemned the actions. In addition to his lack of understanding of the traditions of the Nahuas, the possibility of their believing in the Christian God *and* maintaining their ancient customs repulsed the missionary.

According to the renowned scholar of Mesoamerican studies Miguel León-Portilla, this response of the "elder Indian" exemplified "the trauma of nepantlism." He elaborates:

The ancient institutions had been condemned and mortally wounded, while the ones the friars imposed were still strange and at times incomprehensible. Consequently, the Indians found themselves *nepantla,* "in between." The commitment to forcing change had wounded the very values and foundations of the indigenous world. (1990:10)

León-Portilla further adds:

The violent attacks against the indigenous religion and traditions, the death of the gods, and the difficulty in accepting the new teachings as true had already affected the people deeply

6. Examples of communal responsibility in helping to make celebrations a success can still be found in contemporary indigenous communities today. The communal participation is proof of one's belonging to the community. One example occurs in the video *Blossoms of Fire.*

and had brought about, as a consequence, the appearance of nepantlism. The concept of nepantlism, "to remain in the middle," one of *the greatest dangers* of culture contact ruled by the desire to impose change, retains its full significance, applicable to any meaningful understanding of similar situations. (Ibid.:11)

León-Portilla's often quoted interpretation of the exchange of words between the friar and the "wise old native" presumes indecisiveness on the elder's part. His use of the term *nepantla* is assumed to mean confusion and conflict, the result of imposed change. Clearly, the native peoples experienced psychological, physical, and spiritual violation, and subsequently found themselves caught or bound between worlds leading to inner and outer turmoil. But the elder himself stated that they were neutral, implying their unwillingness to take sides in the religious conquest. As a matter of survival, they would choose both religions. And as he told the friar, "Do not be frightened."

I would like to elaborate on the elder's response and suggest a different interpretation for his decision, an interpretation that broadens the concept of *nepantla* and illuminates the multifacetedness of "being in the middle." So I raise the following questions: Is it not possible that the elder was referring to his survival strategy of remaining in the middle, the neutral space, by describing how his people must and could incorporate Christianity into their native worldview, but also must and could hold on to their traditional beliefs and practices? Could the elder have been maneuvering the fissures, boundaries, and borders of his changed world by claiming the middle space, the center space, the space of meaning-making where his people's religious and cultural agency could construct new ways or simply provide space for both religions to coexist side by side? In other words, for the elder, the pagan and the Christian could coexist in harmony, in a middle space, a neutral space where one does not have power over the over. Perhaps what appeared to the friar and to León-Portilla to be a state of confusion and ambiguity was the manner in which the elder attempted to hold on to his dignity and to the ways of his ancestors. The elder wisely and consciously chose the middle space, the center, for his worldview was large enough to encompass multiple manifestations of the divine. From this perspective, *nepantla*, the middle place, presumes agency, not confusion.

My interpretation of *nepantla* in this manner suggests that there is duality within *nepantla*, a transparent side where there is clarity and self-determination, and a shadow side, where diversity confuses and creates disorientation. As such, I argue that *nepantla* is a multifaceted psychic and spiritual space composed of complementary opposites: obscurity and clarity.

Bipolar duality consisting of complementary opposites is a constant within Indigenous Mesoamerican understandings of the universe (Marcos, 1995) and illuminates the duality I propose within *nepantla*. As duality or complementary opposites exist in all things, neplanta itself is comprised of the shadow side or the bewildering state of uncertainty, and the transparent side or the state of clarity and meaning making.

According to Mexican anthropologist Sylvia Marcos, "the duality implicit in Mesoamerican cosmology was constantly in flux and never fixed or static...movement gave its impulse to everything...everything flowed between opposite poles" (1995:30). For border people, people who live in the physical and psychological terrain where diverse cultures clash, at times converge, and ultimately coexist (not without tension) there is constant movement, constant fluidity.

Whereas fluidity remains constant, the cosmos naturally reestablishes equilibrium as "the critical point of balance had to be found in continual movement" (Ibid.:30). Maintaining balance/equilibrium in all things, including oneself, is the moral responsibility of all individuals. Without balanced individuals, the community cannot exist in harmony. Balance was achieved not by "negating the opposite but rather by advancing toward it and embracing it, in an attempt to find the ever-shifting center of balance" (Ibid.:31). The confusion of *nepantla* must be embraced and worked through in order to reach the balanced state of clarity on the opposite pole within *nepantla*. The elder and his people had to move toward Christianity and embrace it as the opposite in order to survive and regain balance in their changing world. But the opposite, the native worldview, was/is held on to in order to sustain balance.

My use of *nepantla* differs from the concept of syncretism that refers to the blending of diverse beliefs and practices into new and distinct forms. The term "syncretism" is often used to describe Latin American religions resulting from the European imposition of Christianity upon native religions. Scholars are realizing the limitations of this term as it can easily silence complex historical contexts, power relations, and the "phenomenological distress" in which syncretic traditions evolved. According to David Carrasco, syncretism "can be useful when viewed as a 'tool for interpretation' rather than as a description of social patterns" (1995:71). As such, he suggests redesigning the tool to better understand the dynamics of Latino cultures and religions. Refining syncretism as shared culture, Carrasco illuminates what took place throughout colonial Latin America, in the "contact zone of incomplete and developing forms where the social and symbolic relations were permeated by conflict and loss, coercion and indigenous urging more than adherence" (Ibid.:78). Syncretism when understood as shared culture reveals the agency and ingenuity of the Indigenous to transform Christianity for their benefit. For example, a crucifix made of cornhusks conjoins the sacrifice of Christ with the sacredness of maize and "the cosmo-magical powers stemming from the earth" (Ibid.:76).

Syncretism as shared culture also exemplifies a middle space, and as such holds a place within *nepantla*, but as Klor de Alva points out, "*Nepantlaism* should never be confused with syncretism, which is, in both a historical and a psychological sense, the consequence of nepantlaism." *Nepantla* as a multifaceted psychological and spiritual space provides for pre-Christian Indigenous traditions and syncretic Christianity to coexist, side by side, in mutual harmony and respect. In *nepantla*, there is room for all. *Nepantla* provides a place where the Indigenous elders and their descendants can survive, rest, and prosper. In the transparency of *nepantla*, there are no power struggles regarding who holds "the truth." While *nepantla* as a harmonious space might seem to contradict the mystico-militarism that existed within the Mexica culture, it is important to remember that the poets and philosophers, the *tlamatinime*, advocated a peaceful coexistence with all of humanity. Mexica culture, like all cultures, was/is not homogeneous.

León-Portilla's interpretation of *nepantla* as a place of conflict and confusion has influenced the writing and artistic productions of many Chicana scholars and artists, but they too have broadened its meaning. Anzaldúa refers to "mental and emotional states of perplexity...psychic restlessness...mental nepantlism, an Aztec word meaning torn between ways" (1987:78). In later work, she refers to *nepantla* as the site of transformation. *Nepantla* is referred to as "the dark cave of creativity...one that brings a new state of understanding" (1993:113). Cultural theorist Laura Pérez (in chapter 11) refers to the "*susto* of *nepantla*" (the frightening of *nepantla*). But she also sees "that 'in between' space *al revés*, in reverse, not only as something powerful, but indeed as emblematic of the nature of being and meaning." Yreina Cervantez's lithograph triptych titled *Nepantla* images the severity of colonizing forces to obliterate and reconfigure the native, and the artist's response to move "beyond *nepantla*," into a place of power and self-determination. These insightful and groundbreaking works candidly describe the turmoil and self-doubt that exist within the shadow side of *nepantla* as well as calling the reader/viewer to transformation beyond the disorientation and obscurity of *nepantla*. *Nepantla* is the liminal space that can confuse its occupants but also has the ability to transform them.

Nepantla Spirituality in Pedagogy

In my teaching about Chicanos/as and religion, I encounter many students who are spiritually searching. They are searching for more knowledge about themselves and their God. Many express interest in learning about their Indigenous roots, knowledge that has been denied them in the Western educational system. Most have only studied religion in catechism classes and have never openly challenged Christian doctrine. The class intends to provide the opportunity to question religious "truths" constructed within historical and gendered contexts so they may think critically about their own traditions and their own cultures. It is through the process of critical thinking about religion that healing from the psychic wounds of spiritual colonization can occur. My emphasis on Indigenous epistemology challenges the majority to confront their internalized biases toward non-Christian and non-Western worldviews. For Chicanos/as who are products of cultural *mestizaje* within a legacy of colonization, reconciling the differences and discovering the similarities between Christian and Indigenous traditions offers healing. Healing in this context is about bringing forth self-knowledge and historical consciousness so that one may claim religious agency, or the ability to determine for oneself what is morally and ethically just, and what enables communication with spiritual sources. For the young women in the class, discussions about moral authority over one's body constitute a central part of the healing process. The personal nature of the student's interest in religion definitely influences the course design.

Many students reveal their parents' concern that in college they will leave their Christian upbringing behind and turn to Indigenous ways or forget about spirituality altogether. To help the students bridge their worlds, I introduce the concept of *nepantla* spirituality,[7] spirituality at the biological and cultural crossroads where diverse elements converge, at times in tension and at other times in cohesion. It is a spirituality that allows the Christian and the Indigenous to coexist in harmony. The use of the Nahuatl term to distinguish this spirituality privileges and reinforces the Indigenous epistemology active within *nepantla*.

As in any relationship coexistence is not always easy, but once the tensions of *nepantla* are understood and confronted, and the native-Self is recovered and continuously healed, *nepantla,* or the middle space, becomes a psychological, spiritual, and political space that Latinos/as transform as a site of meaning making and healing. Rather than being limited by confusion or ambiguity, Latinos/as act as subjects in deciding how diverse religious and cultural forces can or cannot work together. Like the native elder of the sixteenth century, they creatively maneuver the fissures, boundaries, and borders and consciously make choices about what aspects of diverse worldviews nurture the complexity of their spiritual and biological *mestizaje,* and what for them enables communication with spiritual forces. Within *nepantla,* Chicanas/os and other Latinos can have the wisdom of both the Indigenous and the Christian.

---

7. I define spirituality as the multiple ways in which persons maintain and nurture balanced relationships with themselves, others, the world, and their creator or creation.

A significant amount of class time is spent on understanding the Mexican Indigenous/Chicano tradition of honoring and communing with the dead through *Días de los muertos*. As in many Indigenous cultures around the world, with exceptions of course, the dead or the ancestors play a key part in cultural continuity. The ancestors guide the living, offer protection, and renew the living. Constructing sacred space in their honor, leaving them gifts of food and drink, spending time with their spirits, and sharing in oral tradition ensures family stability and most importantly reminds the living of their historical lineage. For marginalized peoples in the United States, the simple act of remembering their family history holds spiritual and political significance. Whether celebrating the dead takes place in public processions, cemeteries, gatherings in cultural centers, or in the privacy of a family altar, the tradition rejects mainstream attempts to ignore the histories and traditions of non-white and mixed race peoples. Through public ritual, marginalized "others" claim public space and reject any efforts to dismiss their presence in an increasingly segregated society. The tradition challenges a society that privileges youth and silences the dead. Teaching about this tradition underscores the distinctiveness of non-Western epistemologies where the living and the dead depend on each other.

Students are required to construct *ofrendas* (offerings) to a deceased member of their family or community. The *ofrenda* can be designed in a box that can be easily carried to class. They must design the container with symbols and photos that represent the life of the deceased. In their oral presentations they offer a brief biographical sketch followed by an explanation of the symbols they chose to represent the deceased. For many of the students, building the *ofrenda*, explaining it to the class, and writing a summary facilitates a healing process by enabling them to confront the pain of loss. Many students express how meaningful the assignment is not only for themselves, but also for their families. Oftentimes they will have to ask a parent to tell them more about a deceased family member and the exchange facilitates the sharing of family history previously untold.[8]

---

8. See Matovina and Riebe-Estrella, 2002, for a lengthy discussion of the Mexicano/ Chicano tradition of honoring the dead.

The symbols chosen by the students to represent family members oftentimes reflect *nepantla* spirituality as the *ofrendas* contain elements of Indigenous spirituality alongside elements found meaningful in Catholic Christianity. Catholic icons share physical space with Indigenous elements such as soil, water, fire, herbs, and images of Mesoamerican deities. The dual symbol system represents not confusion, but rather choice about what objects and natural resources reflect the fullness of their identity and spirituality.

To further the experience of *nepantla* spirituality, I respectfully offer those students seeking connection to their Indigenous ancestral ways the opportunity to participate in a *temazcal* or purification/sweat ceremony, an ancient ceremony indigenous to the Americas. Many Chicanas/os have learned the purification ceremony from Lakota people who have been willing to share their tradition, the *inipi*, as a way to bring balance to the world and strength to those in solidarity with native peoples.[9] Many Chicanas/os who are seeking their way home to the Indigenous mother have rediscovered the sweat ceremony. As Chief Lame Deer of the Lakota states, "it gives them their identity back" (1972:5). Some Chicanas/os also have learned the tradition from their Mexican Indigenous elders or peers who have maintained the purification ceremony. While the actual sweathouse will look different depending on the tradition being followed, the sweat ceremony is a sacred ceremony for many native peoples of the Americas and must not be taken lightly. It is centered on prayer, sacrifice, and both physical and spiritual renewal.

Native American (Abenaki) Joseph Bruchac, in his very useful book *The Native American Sweat Lodge: History and Legends*, describes some of the distinctive features of the Lakota *inipi* and the *temazcalli* of the Native peoples of Mexico.[10] The *inipi* is a semi-permanent dome structure made from willow branches:

---

9. I have been trained according to the Lakota *inipi* tradition, but I have also experienced the Mexican *temazcal*. The traditions differ in the structure of the sweat house, the use of herbs, the prayers and songs. I belong to a woman's spiritual circle that practices the *inipi* tradition.

10. There are many other kinds of sweathouses in the Americas depending on the region, traditions, and natural resources available. The Lakota *inipi* and the Mexican *temazcalli* are the most widely used today in North America.

[The] Vapor-bath sweat involves heating stones in a fire out-side the lodge. The stones are carried inside, the lodge is sealed [traditionally with animal skins but now with heavy blankets], and after cedar and sweet grass are placed on the stones, water is poured to create steam. When the sweat is concluded, the participants leave the sweat lodge. (1993:11)

In contrast, the *temazcalli:*

is a permanent structure ... made out of stone or adobe bricks. The fire for the *temescal* [*sic*] is built in an oven which is adjacent to the sweating chamber, sharing a wall with it and sometimes with a heating duct to conduct the fire's heat into the chamber. The fire heats the stones so thoroughly and intensely that the heat is conducted through them into the room where the sweat-ing takes place ... more often than not, water is poured onto the stones of that heated wall. Often, the water has special medicinal herbs mixed in with it. (Ibid.:11–13)

What Bruchac does not describe for both traditions is the lengthy process of building the sweathouse, gathering the lava rocks, build-ing the sacred fire, and the many prayers/songs and teachings that compose crucial parts of the ceremonies.

Temazcalli in Nahuatl means bathhouse or sweathouse. *Tema* is to bathe and *calli* is house. The custom of purifying and healing oneself through ritual sweating is an ancient tradition common to many northern and southern native peoples of this hemisphere. At the time of the European invasions of the Americas the sweat bath was an integral part of the daily practice of native peoples. The Span-ish missionaries wrote extensively on the tradition they encountered in Mexico. Diego Durán, the same missionary who encountered the elder previously discussed, described succinctly what he saw: "These bath houses can hold ten persons in a squatting position. The en-trance is very low and narrow. People enter one-by-one and on all fours" (Ibid.:17). And Friar Bernardino de Sahagún observed that ritual participants prayed and chanted as the *temazcalli* "restored their bodies, their nerves. Those who are as if faint with sickness are there calmed, strengthened" (Ibid.). According to Bruchac, "For the

Aztecs, the vapor bath was the favorite remedy for almost every ill" (Ibid.).[11]

Despite the presence of the sweat bath in parts of ancient Europe, for Spaniards and other Europeans from the fifteenth to the eighteenth century, bathing and sinfulness went hand in hand. The emphasis on bathing that the native people valued appeared appalling to the colonizers throughout the Americas. This helps to explain their efforts to eradicate ritual sweating, which was a form of cleansing and praying (Ibid.:17–18; see also Giedion, 1948).

The banning of the sweat bath for native peoples beginning in the sixteenth century proved devastating to their spiritual and physical well-being. Bruchac cites a poignant example based on an interview with a Mayan elder named Tata Julian from the pueblo Todos Santos:

> In the college we had to bathe in cold water. I went to the chief and said, "Señor, it is the custom in my pueblo for the *naturales* to take sweat baths. Here there is no sweat bath. Will you give me permission to heat a little water for a bath?" He would not give me permission. After I had been there a year and six months, we all became sick with much *chor* [dysentery]. All of us were sick, sick every day. They gave us just tea; no coffee. Many *naturales* died. We became so weak that we could not walk. More and more of the *naturales* died. Then my thoughts went back to *Todos Santos*. I knew that if I did not escape I would never see my pueblo again. Señorita, as weak as I was I escaped one night and I returned to my pueblo. (Ibid.:20)

Spanish missionaries denounced sweat baths, and by 1873 the U.S. government prohibited the tradition for Native Americans. Many native peoples in the United States lost the tradition over time. The Lakota, however, managed to withstand colonizing powers waged against the *inipi*. The Indigenous of the south also preserved this most important spiritual and cultural practice.

---

11. The practice of sweating also thrived in ancient Europe, specifically among the Greeks, Romans, Scythians (present-day Russia), Slavs, Scandinavians, and Celts, and also in the Arab world, ancient Japan, and parts of Africa. The Russian, Scandinavian, and African sweat traditions in particular, had physical and spiritual therapeutic properties as does the northern and southern Indigenous American sweat bath. See Bruchac, 1993:14–16; and also Aaland, 1978.

The *temazcal* has been referred to as "the mother of all medicines." As one Chicana says about her first experience in the purification ceremony:

> I felt like I was home. I felt like I went back five hundred years. I could feel the spiritual connection to those original ceremonies and to my ancestors, and I never felt like that before. I really felt a deep spiritual inner connection.[12]

When one enters the *temazcal* or the *inipi* on all fours and kisses mother earth to ask her permission to enter, one is beginning the return to the Indigenous mother. Entering the *temazcal* or the *inipi* is like (re)entering the womb of the creator mother. Being enveloped by her warmth and immersed in the darkness of her womb enables the participants to purge themselves of their burdens. Sitting in a circle in the darkness reminds us all of our inherent equality. It is a visceral returning to the unconditional love of the divine mother. Offering songs and prayers of thanksgiving to the four sacred cardinal directions of the universe, to the creator and to one's ancestors opens the communication between the living, the divine, and the dead. Prayers for one's personal needs and the needs of others are shared.

The lava rocks brought into the *inipi* embody the spirits of the ancestors. When the water is poured over them, they emit ancestral spirit and ancestral knowledge. The steam that is created offers the breath of the creator. Lakota Chief Lame Deer states, "The steam in essence is the Grandfather's breath combining together our prayers, the air, the water, the fire which is in the rocks, and our mother the earth" (1972:2).

The process of sweating in the ceremony requires physical and emotional sacrifice. It is a process of letting go of one's fears, of letting go of material and temporal concerns. It is a process that requires trust, trust in one's creator and trust in the ceremonial leader. Leading a *temazcal* requires specialized training, ceremonial knowledge, and intuitive skills. The water pourer or ceremonial leader ministers to the participants. He or she invites participation, shares teachings, leads in prayer and song, and paces the process of the ceremony. The

---

12. Interview conducted by author with Virginia Espino, March 1994.

inipi ritual is divided into four parts coinciding with the four cardinal directions and the four stages in life. The Lakota ceremony often includes the sharing of the sacred pipe during the four resting periods when the "door" of the sweathouse is opened.[13] The *temazcal* is often in two parts. Both ceremonies may be compared to the sacrament of the Eucharist in the Catholic tradition or *La Santa Cena* in the Pentecostal tradition in that the participants are led into communion with their creator and the participants are spiritually transformed.

When the ceremony is over, the participants crawl out of the sweathouse, the womb, feeling reborn, renewed, and purified. "We rinse off and the sweat from our bodies is an offering of ourselves back to Mother Earth, who gave us life" (Ibid.:4). Sacrifice, reciprocity, and renewal underscore the dynamics of the purification ceremony.

For students to reconcile with Christianity and the often-rigid paradigm they were taught, I draw from the theory of transformation proposed a decade ago by Chicano sociologist David Abalos. Essential to this theory is the awareness of one's true self or the sacred source within each individual that enables one to shape one's life based on justice, love, and solidarity with humankind. Fragmentation or alienation occurs when one has been conditioned to image the sacred source, or God, as solely outside of oneself, beyond one's personal and social reality. "A disconnection from one's sacred sources and from one's self leaves others to play god" (1986:5).

According to Abalos, it is the quality of the relationship between the person and the sacred that is important. He distinguishes between "three gods who correspond to three fundamentally different ways of living."

> Two of these gods are false gods or idols, and only the god of transformation allows us to fully participate. Thus the god of emanation is a divinity that embraces us and protects us. But we cannot struggle or talk back. We must be perpetual children to be protected by this mother-god-Church. Others link us to the god of incoherence that will help us triumph over others if we are good. This is a capitalistic god that urges us to ... seek power. It

---

13. The sacred pipe is shared only if a pipe carrier is present in the ceremony. The pipe is an extremely sacred object; the pipe and the tobacco are used to help send prayers to the Creator.

is only the transforming god who asks/needs our participation in completing the creation of divinity, community, world, and our own selfhood. (Ibid.:8)

The god of transformation requires humans to critique unhealthy relationships and systems of oppression, reconstruct new ones, and critique them again. This never-ending process will offer liberation, or the inherent right and ability to shape one's life and environment based on justice and solidarity. Liberation does not mean an irresponsible autonomy that allows one to do what is most advantageous for personal gain. Rather, liberation offers the freedom to create conditions that provide all persons with equal respect and opportunity.

All three gods can be found within Christianity, but individuals must choose which god they are to follow. Jesus' work offered hope to the marginalized as he challenged the oppressive religious and political structures of his time. His message required the "transformation of all reality — personal, social, and even cosmic" (Sobrino, 1978:356). Jesus did not believe in a God who was totally other, totally beyond the human situation. According to liberation theologian Jon Sobrino, "Jesus unmasked people's domination of others in the name of religion, people's manipulation of the mystery of God ... to avoid the obligations of justice" (Ibid.:366). Jesus challenged an access to God limited to worship, prayer, or academic knowledge. For Jesus access to God was in challenging injustice for the liberation of the oppressed. Jesus chose the god of transformation, yet the ecclesial institutions of power that came after in his name promoted the gods of emanation and incoherence.

Christian doctrine has presented Jesus primarily as the necessary sacrifice for individual salvation. He is considered to have paid the price for human redemption through his death, a once and for all act of penance demanded by an angry but forgiving God. Such a Christology does not concern itself with the social sin that brought Jesus to the cross or the manner in which the horror of the crucifixion affected Godself, the sacred source of life.

But when the death of Jesus is understood as the result of his bold criticism of unjust religious and political systems, then the god of transformation is revealed. This transforming love is revealed through the resurrection. When the followers of Jesus heard of his rising from the dead, they heard of a power that overcame the darkness of the cross, the darkness of the social sin that had killed him. They experienced a response from God that transformed the evil and they experienced hope against injustice. Understanding the resurrection requires hope in transformation. The resurrection then calls the hopeful to responsible action in the challenging and reconstruction of oppressive structures and relationships. Thus, resurrection occurs every time marginalized people attempt to challenge oppression. Christian faith cannot rest on the notion of personal salvation but ultimately must be a functional, just, and liberating way of acting in history.

Conclusion

Many Chicanos and Chicanas find empowering the possibility of being able to participate in both Indigenous and Christian spirituality. As one student states,

> I feel more at peace with myself now, there is nothing wrong with me trying to practice indigenismo.... I don't see myself as only Catholic.... I don't want to leave Catholicism, but I have always felt a strong connection to the earth, to herbs, and especially to the ocean. I now feel at peace being in the middle, being in *nepantla*.[14]

Or as another student wrote,

> *Nepantla* spirituality is a useful concept because many people feel that Catholicism alone will not satisfy their spiritual needs. *Nepantla* is the common ground, where both Indigenous and Christian religions can meet.

To be *en nepantla* is to exist on the border, on the boundaries of cultures and social structures, where life is in constant motion, in constant fluidity. To be *en nepantla* also means to be in the center of things, to exist in the middle places where all things come together.

---

14. Interview conducted by author with Celia Ramos, May 2004.

Nepantla, the center place, is a place of balance, a place of equilibrium, or, as discussed earlier, a place of chaos and confusion. Border people, *las mestizas y los mestizos,* constantly live *en nepantla.* We can never leave the middle space as that is where we were created, in "the contact zone" (Carrasco, 1995:78). As Anzaldúa stated, "As you make your way through life, *nepantla* itself becomes the place you live in most of the time — home" (2002:548). How we choose to occupy our home is crucial. *Nepantla* spirituality offers a choice, a choice to exclude or to include.

Chapter 11

Spirit Glyphs: Reimagining Art and Artist in the Work of Chicana Literature

Laura E. Pérez

Fruto del diálogo sostenido con su propio corazón, que ha ru-
miado, por así decir, el legado espiritual del mundo náhuatl, el
artista comenzará a transformarse en un yoltéotl, "corazón en-
diosado," o mejor, movilidad y dinamismo humano orientados
por un especie de inspiración divina.

(León-Portilla, 1988:168)[1]

But what, or who, can emerge intact from such traumatic crossings, in response to the passionate call of the originary language,
figured by the drum? Only the black trickster. (Gates, 1988:19)

The journey of this writing is as much a journey into the past
as it is into the future, a resurrection of the ancient in order
to construct the modern. It is a place where prophecy and past
meet and speak to each other. (Moraga, 1993:3)

A longer and slightly different version of this essay appeared in *Modern Fiction Studies* 40,
no. 1 (Spring 1998): 37–76. Due to space constraints, the present essay omits discussion of
the videos of Frances Salomé España, the lithograph prints of Yreina D. Cervántez, and the
prints of Ester Hernández. My thanks to *MFS* for permission to reprint this essay and to Duke
University Press, where a longer version of the essay will appear in my *Altarities: Chicana Art,
Politics, and Spirituality.*

1. "Fruit of the dialogue sustained with his own heart, that has ruminated, so to speak, the
spiritual legacy of the Nahuatl world, the artist will begin to transform himself into a yoltéotl,
"a deified heart," or better, human mobility and dynamism oriented by a kind of a divine
inspiration" (my translation).

Making Spirit Opposition

It seems that what individuals and groups perceive and represent as
the spiritual — that having to do with the s/Spirit(s) — is a socially
and politically significant field of differences and contention, as well
as of resonances, crossings, and hybridization.[2] Culturally specific
notions of the spiritual circulate unevenly, and with different political meaning, in the United States. Thus, though we might perhaps
be able to generalize about the notion of the spiritual sufficiently to
speak cross-culturally within and outside of the United States, doing
so within Euro-dominated discourse runs the risk of collapsing cultural differences of conception, experience, and representation. The
notion of the spiritual that I wish to discuss here, as it is invoked
and represented in contemporary Chicana writing and visual art,
derives its inspiration primarily, though not exclusively, from Mesoamerican, other American Indian, and African perceptions of belief,
concept, and experience: that there is an essential spiritual nature, and
thus an interconnectedness, of all beings, human and non-human.
Interestingly, this view is also present in less dominant versions of
Christianity (e.g., gnosticism) and Judaism (e.g., Kabala), even as it
is among the beliefs that are ascribed significant cultural difference
in dominant, Euroamerican thought, and projected onto people such
as U.S. Latina/os, African Americans, and Third World populations
more generally, as well as onto the rural or "uneducated."

Beliefs and practices that consciously make reference to the s/Spirit
as the common life force within and between all beings are largely
marginalized from serious intellectual discourse as superstition, folk
belief, or New Age delusion, when they are not relegated to the

---

2. For communications theorist H. L. Goodall Jr., "Spirit, it seems, is best read as a sign
that means to be taken as deeper clue." "To move toward the unifying awareness of Spirit in
our ordinary, everyday texts; social texts; and communal texts is to grant voice to the creative
powers of imagination and interpretation, from which emerges a fuller body for experiential
knowing capable of sustaining not only a rhetoric for the ordinary, the ritualized, and the
rational, but one ready to embrace a *poetics* of the extraordinary, the intuited, the felt, and
the lived. From this unifying awareness comes the possibility for genuine holistic dialogue, a
dialogue capable of learning from the body of experience without denying to Others what has
not been bodily experienced for oneself, a dialogue in which the full measure of truth is found
only in the quality of our lives" (1996:213).

socially controlled spaces of the orientalist study of "primitive animism," or of "respectable" religion within dominant culture. To speak about the s/Spirit and the spiritual in U.S. culture is risky business that raises anxieties of different sorts.[3] Yet, the very discomfort that attends talk of the spiritual outside of authorized and institutionalized spaces (i.e., churches, certain disciplines, old and new Eurocentric ideological and theory orthodoxies) alerts us to a tender zone constituted by the (dis)encounters of culturally different and politically significant beliefs and practices.

To speak of the spiritual with respect to the cultural practices of politically disempowered communities, particularly the work of women, is perhaps even more fraught with dangers. Given this loaded landscape, the invocation of the spiritual in the work of contemporary Chicana writers and visual artists, as a part of an oppositional politics, is especially provocative and ambitious. The linkages within imperialist and racist thinking between the spiritual, the female, and peoples of color are what make the conditions for talking about women, particularly women of color, and the spiritual, especially difficult. For, as Marianna Torgovnick writes in *Primitive Passions: Men, Women, and the Quest for Ecstasy,* "bit by bit, thread by thread, the West has woven a tapestry in which the primitive, the oceanic, and the feminine have been banished to the margins in order to protect — or so the logic went — the primacy of civilization, masculinity, and the autonomous self" (1997:212). Regardless of intention, then, it might seem that connections made between the spiritual and women of color finally reproduce dominant narratives about these as the inferior opposites to the rational, Christian, Western European, and male.

The stakes involved in the struggle over these narratives are not small. Nonetheless, the necessity of addressing the politics of spirituality from the perspective of the "Indian" other of Eurocentric cultures, and of claiming a belittled spiritual worldview, is crucial to

---

3. For, as Janice Hocker Rushing puts it: "Spirit was thus revealed by Nietzsche to have died, by Marx as a pretense to maintain political domination by the ruling classes, by Freud as an illusory and neurotic hedge against the finality of death, by feminists as an excuse for male domination, and by poststructuralists as the illusory transcendental signifier" (quoted in Goodall, 1996:212).

many, particularly if it is a personally and socially empowering one, and especially if it is so for women.[4] In the work of the Chicana artists under study, citations of the spiritual, whether Western, non-Western, or newer, hybrid forms, are brought into view as social discourse, for their manifest effects in the social and human bodies, and the natural environment. Spirituality in this work is inseparable from questions of social justice, with respect to class, gender, sexuality, culture, and "race."[5]

The "spirit work" of the Chicana visual, performing, and literary artists here suggests that the trivialization of the spiritual, particularly of beliefs and practices from non-Western traditions, as "folk religion," "superstitious," or "primitive," has the political effect of reinforcing Eurocentric cultural evolutionary arguments demeaning that which is culturally different as inferior. Such beliefs help to rationalize social and economic inequities as the "natural" outcome of "developed" and "underdeveloped" cultures and peoples. In none of the work of the women studied here is the "spiritual" an abstract or romantic notion, reproducing the idea of a binary split between

---

4. In Paula Gunn Allen's view: "We as feminists must be aware of our history on this continent. We need to recognize that the same forces that devastated the gynarchies of Britain and the Continent also devastated the ancient African civilizations, and we must know that those same materialistic, antispiritual forces are presently engaged in wiping out the same gynarchical values, along with the peoples who adhere to them, in Latin America. I am convinced that those wars were and continue to be about the imposition of patriarchal civilization over the holistic, pacifist, and spirit-based gynarchies they supplant. To that end the wars of imperial conquest have not been solely or even mostly waged over the land and its resources, but they have been fought within the bodies, minds, and hearts of the people of the earth for dominion over them. I think this is the reason traditionals say we must remember our origins, our cultures, our histories, our mothers and grandmothers, for without that memory, which implies continuance rather than nostalgia, we are doomed to engulfment by a paradigm that is fundamentally inimical to the vitality, autonomy, and self-empowerment essential for satisfying, high-quality life" (1986:214).

5. "Race, as a meaningful criterion within the biological sciences, has long been recognized to be a fiction. When we speak of 'the white race' or 'the black race,' 'the Jewish race' or 'the Aryan race,' we speak in biological misnomers and, more generally, in metaphors. Nevertheless, our conversations are replete with usages of race which have their sources in the dubious pseudoscience of the eighteenth and nineteenth centuries." "The sense of difference defined in popular usages of the term 'race' has both described and inscribed differences of language, belief system, artistic tradition, and gene pool, as well as all sorts of supposedly natural attributes such as rhythm, athletic ability, cerebration, usury, fidelity, and so forth. The relation between 'racial character' and these sorts of characteristics has been *inscribed* through tropes of race, lending the sanction of God, biology, or the natural order to even presumably unbiased descriptions of cultural tendencies and differences" (Gates, 1986:4–5).

a baser material, physical, and social reality and a nobler, separate realm of spirit, ideals, and intellect. Chicana artists whose work concerns itself with the intersections of the spiritual, the political, and art call attention both to what counts as respectable religion and to the more general ghostly status of egalitarian forms of spirituality in U.S. culture. Conjuring and reimagining traditions of spiritual belief, upon whose cultural differences discourses of civilization and modernization have justified subjugation and devaluation, are conscious acts of healing the cultural *susto,* that is, the "frightening" of spirit from one's body-mind in the colonial and neocolonial ordeals that result in the "in-between" state of *nepantla,* the post-conquest condition of cultural fragmentation and social indeterminacy.[6] Put in perhaps more familiar terms, such identification works toward the reintegration of the psyche fragmented by the internalization of loathing of the stigmatized native self, which Frantz Fanon described so vitally for a decolonizing practice in *Black Skin, White Masks* (1967). By braving differing degrees of cultural discontinuity with Amerindian traditions, and opposing a history of vilification and attempted destruction of the "pagan" Indian, African, and Asian philosophical and spiritual worldviews, many contemporary Chicana writers and artists seek to remember, reimagine, and redeploy ideas and practices culled from these as critique and alternative to male-dominated, Christian Eurocentric capitalist and imperialist cultures.

Many Chicana artists engage in what is in fact *curandera* (healer) work: reclaiming and reformulating spiritual worldviews that are empowering to them as women "of color," and reimagining what the social role of art and the artist might be.[7] In this spirit work, Chicana

---

6. "The words of a Náhuatl Indian from the middle of the sixteenth century refer to the risks, so closely related to cultural identity, that can present themselves in attempts at inducing acculturation. A Dominican friar, Diego Durán, had reprimanded a native for his behavior, pointing out that it was also in discord with the ancient indigenous customs and morals. The wise old native responded: 'Father, don't be afraid, for we are still *"nepantla"'* — in other words, 'in the middle,' or as he later added, 'we are neutral' " (León-Portilla, 1990:10).

7. "Perhaps the most prominent contemporary archetypal heroine in Chicana literature is the *curandera/partera* (healer/midwife) who is also the *bruja* (witch). As do most complex symbols, the *curandera/bruja* encodes both positive and negative attributes...." "The curandera possesses intuitive and cognitive skills, and her connection to and interrelation with the natural world is particularly relevant. She emerges as a powerful figure throughout Chicano writing" (Rebolledo, 1995:83). Also interesting to bear in mind with respect to *curanderismo*

writers and artists interrupt the reproduction of gendered, raced, and sexed politics of spirituality and of art. From a perspective of concern for social justice and environmental responsibility, and the belief in the political effects of art practices, this kind of art work rejects politically disempowering modern and postmodern Western narratives about the socially useless (i.e., economically unproductive), and thus marginal role of the writer/artist (Bürger, 1984); the commodification of art as signifier of cultural capital (Bourdieu, 1984a), that is, prestige; and art's value residing in its status as high-yielding economic investment.

In numerous ways that include the invocation and reworking of pre-Columbian Mesoamerican notions of art and artmaking represented in glyphs, codices, and the figures of the *tlacuilo* (glyphmaker) and the *tlamatini* (sage, decoder of the glyphs), these artists are "spirit tongues" of a metadiscourse of art whose social role is more broadly conceived and engaged than that of hegemonic Euroamerican and Eurodominated cultures.[8] The writers and artists mentioned structure their work like the painter-scribes of Mesoamerica, particularly those of the immediate aftermath of the Spanish invasion, in that the glyphs they trace, like those painted by the Nahua *tlacuilo*, are signs that always point beyond the sign system itself to that which cannot be captured by it. Chicana work inscribing culturally different and politically challenging views of art and spirituality points beyond Eurodominated languages and worldviews to the necessity of a more complex hermeneutics, one that is cross-cultural, interdisciplinary, and beyond sexist and heterosexist myopias.

What is particularly relevant and unique to the "spirit glyphs" of the Chicana artists citing or constructing culturally hybrid spiritualities in their work is their mapping of pathways beyond the alienation

---

are the conclusions of a classic study of Mexican American "folk" healing practices: "Indeed, the study of curanderismo questions specific techniques, philosophies, and goals of contemporary dynamic psychotherapy, which may have developed more for their compatibility with the ethos and value system of our own [*sic*] culture than for any well-founded scientific reason." "Finally, there is no evidence that dynamic psychotherapy is of more value than such forms of treatment as curanderismo" (Kiev, 1968:179, 183).

8. Grey, *The Mission of Art*, 1998; Haynes, *The Vocation of the Artist*, 1997; and Gablik, *The Reenchantment of Art*, 1991, are examples of contemporary Euroamerican artists and art writers arguing for the return of more socially meaningful and visionary art practices.

and disempowerment of the nepantlaism of today's cultural and geographical deterritorializations, indeed *back,* though not to some mythical Eden, sign of a hierarchical, jealous, punitive, and male God, but rather to some essential sense of personal wholeness, communal interdependence, purpose, and meaningfulness in the social, global, and cosmic web. The conscious identification with the culturally "different" spiritual beliefs and practices of socially marginalized and politically disempowered peoples enacted in some Chicana art is hardly nostalgic or reproductive of detrimental racialist essentialisms as progressives fear. It is part of a broader attempt to interrupt capitalist and imperialist visions of reality that benefit crucially from our exile from the field of spiritual discourse.

'Membering the Spirit

The politics of the spiritual for some Chicana/os is linked to a politics of memory, as has repeatedly been theorized by artists and thinkers of communities resisting the melting pot's selective dissolution of cultural difference. But lest this be understood as a politically paralyzing nostalgia, this is a tactic of remembering that has been understood in the work of the women in this study as a reimagining and, thus, as a reformulating of beliefs and practices. It is perhaps more precisely a politics of the will to remember: to maintain in one's consciousness, to recall, and to reintegrate a spiritual worldview about the interconnectedness of life, even if it is fragmented, circulating, as its pieces have, through colonial and neocolonial relations. Amalia Mesa-Bains, artist, art critic and scholar, perhaps best known for her altar installations, considers that:

It is through memory that we construct the bridge between the past and the present, the old and the new. The spiritual memory reflected in the works of contemporary Latino artists is a memory of absence constructed from losses endured in the destructive project of colonialism and its aftermath. This redemptive memory claims a broken reality that is made whole in the retelling. In this context, contemporary art is more than a mirror of history and

belief, it is a construction of ideology. Art becomes social imagination through which essential worldviews and identities are constructed, reproduced, and even redefined. Memory becomes the
instrument of redefinition in a politicizing spirituality. (1993:9)

The hybrid spiritualities claimed and practiced in the work of some
Chicana artists are, paradoxically, decolonizing cultural appropriations, in part, because the traditions or contemporary practices from
American Indian, U.S. Latina/o, Latin American, and African diaspora cultures from which they draw upon in their writing and art
are politically oppositional to (neo)colonizing cultural and religious
systems, but also because some of these traditions have not been altogether interrupted in the memory or practices of Chicana/o culture
itself.[9] Such cross-cultural borrowing and refashioning is the effect
of a kind of a "minority"/"Third World," post-national, cultural environment from which culturally kindred *forms* are recycled[10] from
(neo)colonization's "waste" to give expression to what is perceived
at heart to be a common worldview: the spiritual nature of all being,
and thus its interconnectedness — a view ultimately at odds with the
reigning transnational corporate culture of extreme exploitation of
the planet and an unskilled labor force that is disproportionately
female, and "of color."

For Gloria Anzaldúa, in her culturally acupunctural[11] *Border-
lands/La Frontera: The New Mestiza,* a "new mestiza" spirituality

---

9. "Like the ancients, I worship the rain god and the maize goddess, but unlike my father
I have recovered their names" (Anzaldúa, 1987:90).

10. With respect to the discursive power of what she calls third-degree kitsch in postmodern
art that incorporates religious imagery, Celeste Olalquiaga notes that "besides imploding the
boundaries of art and reality, the third degree carries out an active transformation of kitsch.
Taking religious imagery both for its kitsch value and its signifying and iconic strength, it absorbs the icon in full and recycles it into new meanings. These meanings are related to personal
spiritual experiences, recalling users' relationships to first-degree [kitsch] imagery, except that
the first-degree images are part of a given cultural heritage and as such they are readily available
and their usage is automatic. Third-degree kitsch, on the other hand, appropriates this tradition
from 'outside,' searching for an imagery that will be adequate to its expressive needs." "Instead
of appropriation annihilating what it absorbs, the absorbed invades the appropriating system
and begins to constitute and transform it." "Rather than speaking of active or passive cultures,
one can now speak of mutual appropriation" (1992:52–54).

11. From Richard feather Anderson's "Geomancy": "Until recent times every structure was
situated with regard for the patterns of biomagnetic energy within the earth's body. Geomancers

is inclusive and affirming of her multiple positionings as a feminist Chicana lesbian writer. The spiritual worldview, like the aesthetic of the book, "seems an assemblage, a montage, a beaded work with several leitmotifs and with a central core, now appearing, now disappearing in a crazy dance" (1987:66) of diverse American Indian, African, and African diaspora beliefs and practices, recoded patriarchal Christian and Aztec symbols (e.g., Virgen de Guadalupe and Coatlicue), and culturally relevant translations of archetypal psychology (expressed in her formulation of "the Coatlicue state"). Similarly, in the face of traditional, patriarchal Catholicism, Ana Castillo speaks of the right to craft spiritual practices from any traditions that make us "feel better, that is, stronger willed and self-confident" (Castillo, 1994:147), including elements from that same belief system. In his essay in *Ceremony of Memory: New Expressions in Spirituality among Contemporary Hispanic Artists,* Tomás Ybarra-Frausto observes:

> Creative reorganization of traditional religious systems from Indigenous and African religions continues in a dynamic process throughout the Spanish-speaking world. Within the United States, artists accentuating spiritual domains re-examine, reinterpret and redefine ancestral religious forms with multiple impulses; as counterparts to socio-political commentary, as symbolic and iconographic systems united to autobiographical exploration or as primal icons that illuminate and foreground social conditions. Contemporary artists reworking spiritual canons augment their power and beauty. New forms of spirituality reverberate with the presence and potency of an ancient living ethos expanded with modern signification. (1988:12)

Whether remembered through surviving traditional practices or reimagined and fused together from chosen traditions, in the work of many Chicana artists studied here invoking the spiritual is a politically significant, socially transformative, and psychically healing

---

were employed to maintain the most beneficial flow of ch'i within the veins of the earth's body, variously known as dragon paths or energy ley-lines. It was taboo in earth-centered cultures to sever these vital channels, for the same reason that it is suicidal to cut our own arteries. Where the flow of earth ch'i has stagnated, 'earth acupuncture' procedures can be used to stimulate the ch'i. Some earth mysteries researchers believe that the megalithic standing stones of Europe may have functioned as acupuncture needles for the planet" (1991:198).

practice. In such work, we are pushed even further beyond the in-creasingly familiar, if still relevant, observations about the survival, resistance, opposition, and transformative powers of the socially ab-ject other. For what also calls for reckoning in the work of these and other Chicana *tlamatinime*, as many of them are redefining this word, is the relevance of the spiritual, whether understood as the sacred and interconnected nature of self and world, and the empow-ering effects of that belief/knowledge, or conversely, as the beliefs and practices of politically oppressive religious institutions. In such work, the reality of a politically significant, socially and materially embod-ied s/Spirit is consciously re-membered, which we are called to witness and act upon, alongside other historically specific and related issues of "race," gender, sexuality, and class.

Spirit Tongues: Glyphs, Codices, and *Tlamatinime*

Chicana/o art practices in general are historically rooted in the 1960s reclamation of the spiritual within the Chicana/o movement, as evi-denced in the manifesto *El Plan Espiritual de Aztlán,* the poetry of Alurista, the spiritual *mitos* of Teatro Campesino, Rudolfo Anaya's novel *Bless Me, Ultima,* and countless pre-Columbian-themed murals and other visual art. The birth of Chicana/o consciousness through the reclamation and reimagining of the colonially despised Indian self and beliefs is well known in Chicana/o art and scholarship (Klor de Alva, 1986; Ybarra-Frausto, 1979; and Anaya, 1988). The work of Miguel León-Portilla has been particularly important in Chicana/o attempts to reintegrate the Indigenous. His studies of the philoso-phy and artistic traditions of the Nahua peoples, and his translations of pre- and post-conquest codices recording Nahua belief and prac-tices greatly influenced Chicana/os through books such as his *Aztec Thought and Culture* (1956, Spanish; 1963, English translation) and *Los antiguos mexicanos a través de sus crónicas y cantares* (1961).[12] Distinguishing between the new tradition of the imperialist Aztecs

---

12. See Klor de Alva, "California Chicano Literature and Pre-Columbian Motifs" in *Con-fluencia,* 1986. The scholar's translations in *Aztec Thought and Culture* were also quoted in an important anthology, *Aztlán: An Anthology of Mexican American Literature,* in the section "The Toltec (The Artist): He Makes Things Live" (Valdez and Steiner, 1972:347–53).

who burned codices of conquered peoples, rewrote histories, and appropriated cultures and the older Toltec tradition which they had displaced and to which they were related, León-Portilla writes:

Alejados de la visión místico-guerrera de Tlacaél, fueron estos tlamatinime nahuas quienes elaboraron una concepción hondamente poética acerca del mundo, del hombre y de la divinidad. ... Valiéndose de una metáfora, de las muchas que posee la rica lengua náhuatl, afirmaron en incontables ocasiones que tal vez la única manera posible de decir palabras verdaderas en la tierra era por el camino de la poesía y el arte que son "flor y canto." ... La poesía y el arte en general, "flores y cantos," son para los tlamatinime, expresión oculta y velada que con las alas del símbolo y la metáfora puede llevar al hombre a balbucir, proyectándolo más allá de sí mismo, lo que en forma misteriosa, lo acerca tal vez a su raíz. Parecen afirmar que la verdadera poesía implica un modo peculiar del conocimiento, fruto de auténtica experiencia interior, o si se prefiere, resultado de una intuición. (1988:124, 126)[13]

Chicana artists who use these concepts more often than not combine the functions of the glyph-makers, the *tlacuilo,* and their sagely readers, the *tlamatinime,* by perceiving them both as "Toltecs," people wise beyond technical mastery and in tune with a deep sense of the sacred purpose of their work, and therefore able to move those who behold the work along in the life-long process of "making face, making soul."[14] The Toltec or artist is in this way engaged in teaching

---

13. "Removed from the mystico-warrior vision of Tlacaél, it was these Nahua *tlamatinime* who elaborated a deeply poetic conception of the world, [hu]man, and divinity.... Relying upon one of the many metaphors that the rich Náhuatl language possesses, they affirmed on innumerable occasions that perhaps the only possible way to speak truthful words on earth was through the path of poetry and art, which are "flower and song." ... Poetry and art, in general, "flowers and songs," are for the *tlamatinime* occult and veiled expressions that with the wings of symbol and metaphor can lead a [hu]man to stutter, projecting him [her] beyond the self, which in mysterious form, brings him [her] closer perhaps to his [her] root. They appear to affirm that true poetry implies a peculiar mode of knowledge, fruit of an authentic interior experience, or, if one prefers, the result of an intuition." My translation.

14. See León-Portilla, 1988:146–54. This is a concept that Anzaldúa appropriates and redefines in the anthology she edits, *Making Faces, Making Soul: Creative and Critical Perspectives by Women of Color* (1990). " 'Making faces' is my metaphor for constructing one's identity. 'Usted es el moldeador [sic] de su carne tanto como el de su alma.' You are the shaper

and healing, in the sense of mediating the greater spiritual growth and well-being of the beholder.[15] León-Portilla's translations suggest that what was guiding the work of conscientious *tlacuilo* and *tlamatini* was concern for the ultimate meaning of their life's work. The worthy *tlacuilo,* the "good" glyph-maker, must therefore by necessity also be a spiritually guided sage. Conversely, the codices suggest that the *tlamatini* was also a *tlacuilo,* schooled in the painting of glyphs, like other select members of society.[16]

When writers and artists refer to themselves as *tlamatini* and to their work as glyphs or codices of our own times, as do Anzaldúa in *Borderlands,* the artists in the *Chicano Codices* show, and Moraga in "Codex Xeri," they are reimagining art and artist along broader social parameters, for in themselves glyphs, codices, and the words *"tlacuilo"* and *"tlamatini"* are signs that point beyond modern, Eurocentric cultural conceptions of art and artist. They point to different systems of reading visual signs, to different ways of knowing, and even more, to the insufficiency of one system of signs (visual, oral,

of your flesh as well as of your soul. According to the ancient *nahuas,* one was put on earth to create one's 'face' (body) and 'heart' (soul). To them, the soul was a speaker of words and the body a doer of deeds" (xvi). It is interesting to compare these understandings with that of Roger Lipsey in *An Art of Our Own: The Spiritual in Twentieth-Century Art:* "Oneself as one might be. The reminder of what one has forgotten is a call to action. The spiritual in art offers a transient experience of intensity, of a larger world and larger self. One begins to care again, reawakened to old longings, to remorse, perhaps to new thoughts and feelings, almost always to a clarified sense of direction. This blend of hope and remorse is a sign that one has encountered the spiritual in art. . . . The spiritual in art makes its contribution to the pilgrim's halting progress. It is a resource for those who look beyond, understand that there is work to do, and undertake it" (1988:16).

15. On the Toltec/artist see León-Portilla, 1980:208; on the *tlamatinime,* León-Portilla, 1988:62, 123–25; and León-Portilla, 1980:200.

16. Joyce Marcus points out, "The *calmecac* (literally, 'row of houses') was a set of priestly residences associated with the temples of Tenochtitlán. Children of nobles were brought here by their parents to receive an education in the priesthood. Chronicles differ on whether children entered the *calmecac* at age four (1992:22) or fifteen (ibid.:199–200). Apparently, some promising commoner children could be enrolled by parents who wanted them to enter the priesthood, but they appear to have been a very small minority. In the Florentine Codex, Sahagún makes clear the association of the *calmecac* with the education of well-born members of the society." "The *calmecac* curriculum apparently included astrology, star lore, divination and the calendars, hieroglyphic writing, and 'life's history' (*nemiliz tlacuilolli*); it is here that future scribes (not to mention priests and diviners) were started on their career trajectory. All nobles, including future rulers, received their education in one of the six or more *calmecac* located in Tenochtitlán. Following some years of education there, all those entering administration, law, or other important governmental positions would share a working knowledge of those subjects, including the use and role of the hieroglyphic writing" (Ibid.:50–51).

performative) to convey meaning and "truths" fully. Old and new glyphs call for broader cultural readings, like those constituted in the *tlamatini*'s performance of decipherment that take into account the space and occasion, as well as the knowledge specifically coded in the pictographs or ideograms.[17] Glyphs rooted in Mesoamerican worldviews are signs meant to point beyond themselves to that which is outside of verbal and visual language — meaning ultimately to the realm of the spiritual. Creative writing and visual art by artists such as Gloria Anzaldúa, Cherríe Moraga, Yreina D. Cervántez, and Delilah Montoya, for example, attempt to access the codices as signs of alternative spiritual and material knowledges and practices.

Beyond the *Susto* of *Nepantla*: Culture Cures

Much of the Chicana art that cites pre-Columbian pictographic conventions hybridizes the different cultural meanings and functions of preconquest "books," or *amoxtli* (as imagined and understood through scholars like León-Portilla), post-conquest codices, and contemporary books and artwork. As in the stylistically hybrid works of the first-generation post-conquest codices described by Serge Gruzinski, in such Chicana artwork we see the complex reworkings of the technologies and belief systems of the imposed dominating culture and the parallel inscription of alternative knowledges and practices.[18]

---

17. "The formal structure of a ceremony is as holistic as the universe it purports to reflect and respond to, for the ceremony contains other forms such as incantation, song (dance), and prayer, and it is itself the central mode of literary expression from which all allied songs and stories derive. The Lakota view all the ceremonies as related to one another in various explicit and implicit ways, as though each were one face of a multifaceted prism. This interlocking of the basic forms has led to much confusion among non-Indian collectors and commentators, and this complexity makes all simplistic treatments of American Indian literature more confusing than helpful. Indeed, the non-Indian tendency to separate things from one another — be they literary forms, species, or persons — causes a great deal of unnecessary difficulty with and misinterpretation of American Indian life and culture. It is reasonable, from an Indian point of view, that all literary forms should be interrelated, given the basic idea of unity and relatedness of all the phenomena of life. Separation of parts into this or that category is not agreeable to American Indians, and the attempt to separate essentially unified phenomena results in distortion" (P. G. Allen, 1986:62).

18. "[T]he effort to unite two cultures (often turning the conquerors' culture to the advantage of the conquered) is probably easiest to detect in the realm of images and pictographs. The creation of a twin system of expression — pictographic and alphabetical — was not merely a sign of compromise or collaboration. It also represented discovery of new formal strategies for

What follows are sightings of the different ways in which *la cultura cura* (culture cures) in contemporary "spirit glyphs" of Chicana writing and visual art practices.

In Anzaldúa's *Borderlands,* image and written or spoken word are inseparably linked, as image and spoken word are in the functioning of the Mesoamerican glyph (pictograph/ideogram). In a chapter titled *"Tlilli, Tlapalli/*The Path of the Red and Black Ink," she writes that "to write, to be a writer, I have to trust and believe in myself as a speaker, as a voice for the images," and that when writing "it feels like I'm creating my own face, my own heart — a Nahuatl concept. My soul makes itself through the creative act" (1987:73). "The stress of living with cultural ambiguity" also allows her, as a "mestiza writer," to be a *"nahual,* an agent of transformation, able to modify and shape primordial energy and therefore able to change herself and others into turkey, coyote, tree, or human" (Ibid.:74). From Anzaldúa's cultural perspective, writing is an image-making practice that as such can indeed shape and transform what we imagine, are able to perceive, and are able to give material embodiment. Understood, therefore, is the great responsibility and sacredness of the very real and consequential "transformative power" wielded by the image-makers, which literally "makes face, makes soul" in a reading process understood to be part of a larger performance. Following Robert Plant Armstrong's study of the cultural difference and "power of affecting presence" of African masks and statues, Anzaldúa speaks of her work as "invoked art," a being imbued with spiritual presence and power, unlike art that concerns itself primarily with aesthetic and technical virtuosity:

> My "stories" are acts encapsulated in time, "enacted" every time they are spoken aloud or read silently. I like to think of them as performances and not as inert and "dead" objects (as the aesthetics of Western culture think [*sic*] of art works). Instead, the work has an identity; it is a "who" or a "what" and contains the presences of persons, that is, incarnations of gods or ancestors

---

preserving two living traditions side by side. At the same time that they mastered Latin and massively adopted writing, painter-writers were preserving and enriching their pictographic heritage (Gruzinski, 1992:158–60).

or natural and cosmic powers. The work manifests the same needs as a person, it needs to be "fed," *la tengo que bañar y vestir.*

When invoked in rite, the object/event is "present"; that is, "enacted," it is both a physical thing and the power that infuses it. It is metaphysical in that it "spins its energies between gods and humans" and its task is to move the gods. This type of work dedicates itself to managing the universe and its energies.... Invoked art is communal and speaks of everyday life. It is dedicated to the validation of humans; that is, it makes people hopeful, happy, secure, and it can have negative effects as well, which propel one toward a search for validation. (Ibid.:67)

Anzaldúa understands the image-making process not only through the sacred and shamanic aspects of the *tlamatinime/tlacuilo*'s path of writing and wisdom that the red and black inks signify, but also through James Hillman's archetypal psychology in *Re-Visioning Psychology,* from which she selectively draws in conceptualizing identity as multiple and in reimagining the role of art and artist. In an interesting resonance with Mesoamerican thought, for example, Hillman writes: "Because our psychic stuff is images, image-making is a *via regia,* a royal road to soul-making. The making of soul-stuff calls for dreaming, fantasying, imagining.... To be in touch with soul means to live in sensuous connection with fantasy. To be in soul is to experience the fantasy in all realities and the basic reality of fantasy" (1975:23). Like Hillman's, Anzaldúa's interest in the image is both as sign of the language of the soul and as mediator of growth of the soul or soul-making.

Her truly important book may itself be thought of as a glyph pointing beyond the cultural and psychological location of *nepantla* by seeing that "in between" space *al revés,* in reverse, not only as something powerful, but indeed as emblematic of the nature of being and meaning. Her perception of the greater meaning of the resonances in different kinds of experiences of marginalization (e.g., geographical, cultural, psychological, spiritual, and sexual) is a politically significant reenvisioning of interrelated cultural discourses of history, location, and identity that produce hierarchical orderings of difference. As the

title of the book suggests, the borderlands are not invoked as yet
another valuable but peripheral resource in the center's production of
meaning. Rather, "borderlands" becomes a sign of the centrality of
the marginalized, the mutable, and the unarticulated in the construction of fuller and not merely partial and self-reflecting knowledges
and identities. Thus, through the glyph of the borderlands, Anzaldúa
points away from too literal an identification with the signs of individual and collective identities toward ways of knowing that allow for
the complexity of that which exceeds language and which, crucially,
allows us to re-envision other versions of self and reality. To this
end, she also returns to the center of our vision the importance of
marginalized ways of knowing through our spirits. *"La facultad,"* for
example, and other forms of "inner knowledge," affirm the "divine
within" (1987:50), as well as the "supernatural" (Ibid.:49) or "the
spirit world" (Ibid.:38), and represent alternative forms of perception
("seeing," Ibid.:39, 42, 45) and "other mode[s] of consciousness"
(Ibid.:37), and thus, other epistemologies and paths of knowledge
(Ibid.:37, 42) than the rational as it is understood and privileged in
Euroamerican and European dominant cultures.[19]

The widely circulating book *Woman Hollering Creek and Other
Stories* by Sandra Cisneros offers another interesting refiguration of
the glyph. The story "Little Miracles, Kept Promises" itself functions as an ex-voto, the visual and written sign left by the faithful
as material testimony of the miraculous, that is, of the presence and
intervention of spiritual power.[20] The story is thus made up of the

---

19. For early discussions of the spiritual concerns of *Borderlands* see Ramírez, 1989:185–
87; and Cáliz-Montoro, 1996. Since the original publication of this essay in its longer form,
Anzaldúa published *Interviews/Entrevistas* (2000) making her concerns for the spiritual even
more explicit.

20. Julio Ramos's observations on the ex-voto are useful here: "El género del exvoto
se inscribe en una economía de la reciprocidad, del intercambio de dones, y como tal
trabaja fundamentalmente la mediación, la articulación entre distintos niveles de órdenes
discontinuos.... Como si de algún modo la temática del viaje y de sus interrupciones con-
densara las condiciones mismas de producción del género y su insistente reflexión sobre el
límite — límite entre la vida y la muerte del sujeto accidentado — así como sobre la discon-
tinuidad y la mediación entre tiempos y espacios diferenciados. Se trata entonces, en varios
sentidos, de una forma que a lo largo de su historia (que por cierto antecede la colonización
de América) registra lúcidamente el devenir de distintas concepciones de la estabilidad y el
desequilibrio, de la causalidad y la contingencia, del accidente y la ley, del desastre y de la
intervención de las mismas prácticas pictórico-narrativas como modos de contener y reparar la

different testimonies of faith in the spiritual as represented by various saints, including the mestiza Virgen de Guadalupe, long since redefined by Chicanas through the Mesoamerican goddess Tonantzin, an aspect of Coatlicue.[21] One such testimony is crafted by Chayo, disaffected from Catholicism, and particularly from its oppression of women through the image and discourse of "Mary the mild." She writes a letter to the Virgin of Guadalupe, bearing witness to the huge *milagrito* (little miracle) of a newfound and empowering faith:

> I don't know how it all fell in place. How I finally understood who you are. . . . When I could see you in all your facets, all at once the Buddha, the Tao, the true Messiah, Yahweh, Allah, the Heart of the Sky, the Heart of the Earth, the Lord of the Near and Far, the Spirit, the Light, the Universe, I could love you, and, finally, learn to love me. (Cisneros, 1991:128)

Perhaps because the recuperation of a spirituality that is empowering to women is not one of the usually celebrated miracles in Latin American and U.S. Latina/o communities where *mestizo*-identity sways toward the Eurocentric and the patriarchal, Chayo cannot choose from the common stock of human-body-part and animal medallions referring to the afflicted and now healed self or property, but must create her own image or *milagrito* to accompany her letter of gratitude. Thus, in an eloquent and feminist glyph, Chayo offers her braid of hair, symbol of her body's gendering and racialization, in a sacrifice that understandably leaves her "heart buoyant" (Ibid.:125).

Cherríe Moraga's "Codex Xeri," published originally in the exhibition catalog *The Chicano Codices: Encountering Art of the Americas*

catástrofe" (1997:7–8). (The genre of the ex-voto is inscribed in an economy of reciprocity, of the exchange of gifts, and as such, fundamentally works mediation, the articulation between different levels of discontinuous orders. . . . As if in some way the theme of travel and its interruptions condensed the very conditions of the genre's production and its insistent reflection upon the limit — the limit between the life and death of the subject of the accident — as well as upon the discontinuity and mediation between differentiated times and spaces. We are dealing then, in various senses, with a form that throughout its history (which indeed predates the colonization of America) lucidly registers the development of different conceptions of stability and equilibrium, causality and contingency, accident and law, disaster and the intervention of the same pictorial-narrative practices as modes of containing and repairing the catastrophe [my translation].)

21. See, for example, "From Coatlicue to La Llorona: Literary Myths and Archetypes" (Rebolledo, 1995:49–81).

(1992), and then in *The Last Generation: Prose and Poetry* (1993), offers another important rearticulation of pre-Columbian notions of art and artmaking. Moraga specifically identifies herself and these two writings with the last generation of conquest-era *tlamatinime* that not only witnessed the subjugation of their world, but more positively, that succeeded in transmitting their worldviews through the codices they left, as her work exemplifies. In the introduction to *The Last Generation,* Moraga figures her writing as prayer, codex, prophecy, "a resurrection of the ancient in order to construct the modern," as picture book, as "queer mixture of glyphs," and as writing that responds to the political urgency of the times. For her, the prophetic, seeing with the mystical third eye (1993:137) is the politically resonant heart of writing and art making, particularly in the present times where selfishness, violence, and greed could make this the planet's last generation. Thus, she writes:

> As a Latina artist I can choose to contribute to the development of a docile generation of would-be Republican "Hispanics" loyal to the United States, or to the creation of a force of "disloyal" americanos who subscribe to a multicultural, multilingual, radical re-structuring of América. Revolution is not only won by numbers, but by visionaries, and if artists aren't visionaries, then we have no business doing what we do. (1993:56)

Like Anzaldúa, her invocation of the *tlamatinime,* glyphs, and codices is not a nostalgic inscription of cultural difference meant as a sign of resistance to cultural imperialism, but rather through these, Moraga attempts to "disenchant" and reempower artists through the recognition of the political power of their vision as it is externalized in their work. In "Codex Xeri," which closes both the exhibition catalog and her own book, she states:

> The Chicano scribe remembers, not out of nostalgia but out of hope. She remembers in order to envision. She looks backward in order to look forward to a world founded not on greed, but on respect for the sovereignty of nature....

As it was for the tlamatinime centuries ago, the scribe's task is to interpret the signs of the time, read the writing on barrio walls, decode the hieroglyphs of street violence, unravel the skewed message of brown-on-brown crime and sister-rape. The Chicano codex is *our* book of revelation. It is the philosopher's stone, serpentine and regenerative. It prescribes our fate and releases us from it. It understands the relationship between darkness and dawn. *"Mira que te has de morir. Mira que no sabes cuándo."* (Ibid.:190–91)[22]

"Codex Makers" are therefore also *tlamatinime* whose tasks are to remember, envision, and inscribe their readings of the meaning of the cultural signs of their day in illuminating and transformative ways.

---

22. "See that you shall die. See that you don't know when," quoted in Amalia Mesa-Bains's *Codex Amalia*, reproduced in *The Chicano Codices* (Sánchez-Tranquilino, 1992:15).

Chapter 12

Religion and Power
in the Study of Hispanic Religions

Miguel A. De La Torre

Even within marginalized groups, power structures exist. This fact can never be ignored, minimized, or forgotten, lest those oppressed today become tomorrow's oppressors. To recognize the existence of power structures does not imply that such structures are inherently good or evil; it simply acknowledges that such structures are present. Power, in and of itself, is amoral, and it is present in every social transaction, including transactions on the margins of society. The power that is found (regardless of its potence or impotence) within the Latina/o context creates religious expressions that define what will be "good" and what will be "evil." Those with sociopolitical power, even within disenfranchised communities, influence, if not determine, the foundational principles of religion and identity. Among Hispanic scholars of religion, those with the power to shape the discourse by determining the "classic" methodological approaches to be employed (e.g., autobiographical), the concepts to be accepted (e.g., *la raza cósmica, mestizo, mulatez, mujerista*) and the philosophical assumptions to be embraced (e.g., liberationist and postcolonial), have guided the Latino/a religious discourse over the past thirty years. This is not necessarily wrong — it just is.

Although power, in and of itself, is amoral, it still has the capacity to traverse and produce reality. Through power, knowledge and discourse are created. In this fashion, power can be positive, producing authenticity and creating the subject's opinion of what is "truth" (Foucault, 1984:60–61). Power will always be tolerated if it is able to mask a substantial part of itself (Foucault, 1978:86). As long as Latino/a scholars insist that their religious thoughts and paradigms originated among the oppressed, and thus their task is simply to articulate what the people are reportedly saying and doing, we mask the power of the articulator. Although it is true that most of what Hispanic scholars of religion proclaim is grounded within the marginalized faith community, a fine line exists between what comes from the faith community and what is produced by scholars who then either project their analysis onto that community, or claim to speak on its behalf. Again, this is neither good or bad — it just is. However, what if the scholars are unaware of how they produce critical religious analysis and thought that is then fused and confused with what occurs within marginalized faith communities? Hispanic scholars of religion may find themselves creating absolutes where the good is defined as whatever a particular Latino/a professes to be the good.

But the gravest danger that can arise by the refusal to seriously consider how power works *within* marginalized communities is the danger of emulating the oppressors. As Paulo Freire warned, during the initial stage of their struggle the oppressed almost always tend themselves to become oppressors (what he called "sub-oppressors") rather than strive for liberation (1994:27). The very thought process of Hispanics, like every other oppressed group, is shaped and constructed by the very oppressive context in which Latino/as find themselves. Liberation runs the risk of being defined along Euroamerican terms, usually as equality with the oppressor. In seeking equality, the disenfranchised emulate and model themselves along the existing power structures designed to privilege one group over against another. Liberation is reduced to surmounting present power structures rather than dismantling them so as to reconstruct a more just social system.

That the present power structures existing within society are designed to privilege the dominant Euroamerican culture is not in question. This reality is recognized by the writers of this anthology. Still, to solely attack the dominant culture for being complicit with the present power structures masks how existing intra-structures of oppression operate. We, as Latina/o scholars of religion, will achieve a new level of maturity when we move beyond what Edward Said terms "the rhetoric of blame," which is primarily to attack the dominant culture for being "white, privileged, insensitive, and complicit" (1994:14, 96, 228–30). Historically, it has always been easier to blame the dominant culture for the predicament of Latina/os; yet all Hispanic woes cannot be attributed solely to Euroamericans. Subscribing to Latino/a nativism accepts the consequences of U.S. racism and reinforces Hispanic subservience, even while attempting to reevaluate the Latino/a ethos. Regardless of any aggressive stance taken, Hispanics are in danger of becoming trapped within a defensive role. Recognizing our own structures of power, which can also oppress, does not minimize the repression imposed by the dominant culture, but rather, it places the focus upon the structures rather than a particular ethnic group — which in this day and time happens to be Euroamerican (De La Torre, 2004a:297).

Through power, as voiced in the religious discourse of Latino/a scholars, ministers, and lay leaders, a "truth" is created and normalized within their minds. This constructed "truth" at times creates an incongruity between religious justification for power that privileges some Hispanics (specifically those who are closer to the "white male" ideal) and a religious impulse for justice. To unmask how power operates within our own marginalized group, a rethinking is required — not just a rethinking of our religious concepts but, just as important, a rethinking of how we construct our very identity. Long-cherished notions of *Latinidad, mestizaje, mulatez, mujerista,* community, empowerment, and liberation must all be reexamined, questioned, and challenged as new concepts, theories, and research outside the traditional institutional religion (such as those examined in this anthology) are explored. Unfortunately, to seriously question or critique the power structure existing among marginalized Latina/os that originally formulated these cherished notions at times results in a junior scholar being ostracized for being a *vendepatria* (sellout) to the dominant culture — a fact proven simply by their use of the dominant culture's methodological tools. Those who question the established "truth" (read, those who do not agree with or quote "us") become a threat to "truth," and hence, they must be discredited, ignored, or silenced.

A dichotomy becomes established. The Latina/o scholar of religion either belongs to the community and unquestionably supports what those who chronologically came before him or her articulated as our religious expression. Or the said scholar is considered not truly part of the community, but rather seen as using it to climb over and get ahead of other Hispanics. Yet I insist that even those who rethink Latino/a religion and identity are still full-fledged members of the Hispanic community, for they challenge all forms of power structures that cause oppression, albeit also those structures that are being produced or maintained by their own ethnic group. For this reason, it becomes crucial for Latino/as to engage in defining and examining their identity — exploring what is usually hidden, legitimized, and normalized within the Latino/a religious experience in order to unmask Hispanic intra-structures of oppression. This process, in turn, affects how Hispanics construct their religious expressions.

Still, the intention is not to debunk the work of those Hispanic scholars who came before us but rather to foreground the dynamic work of a new emerging generation. We must never forget that this earlier generation of pioneering Latino/a scholars carved out a space within a hostile academy for the critical study of this hitherto ignored community. Yet neither must such respect constrain or silence our own work. Rather, our discourse must continue to stimulate social change through a critical dialectic that expands the vision of the Hispanic community, always cognizant that in the years to come, when we who are now considered "junior" scholars become senior scholars, a newer generation will be needed to refine, re-imagine, expand, and even challenge the work we have done, so that the work our community produces can always remain dynamic, cutting-edge, and relevant.

With our present task of rethinking Latino/a religion and identity, it is appropriate to examine three examples of how power works and manifests itself among Hispanic scholars of religion. Specifically, I wish to explore: (1) the way we structure ourselves in relationship to each other; (2) the power relation created between elder and junior scholars; and (3) the establishment of a so-called pan-Hispanic unity.

Rhizomes – Not Trees

Eurocentric thought is dominated by a structure of knowledge that poststructuralists Gilles Deleuze and Félix Guattari have called arborescent in their text *A Thousand Plateaus*. According to them, our way of knowing, of perceiving reality, is tree-like, that is, vertical. Such tree models, with a unifying central trunk from which branches of thought protrude, commonly appear within academic disciplines, e.g., chemistry (Porphyrian trees), biology (Linnaean taxonomies), psychoanalysis (Freudian interpretation of Schreiber's case), and linguistics (Chomskyan sentence trees). But by arranging knowledge genealogically along a tree model, a centralized hierarchy is imposed that artificially creates, limits, and regulates connections between components, as branches spread out from a single trunk — each thought stemming from an original oneness. These tree models are concerned with origins, ontologies, clear-cut beginnings and ends (Deleuze and Guattari, 1993:30–31).

Theological trees, specifically in the case of Latino/a trees of religious thought, also exist. One such tree model used among Hispanic scholars is how they arrange themselves in relationship to each other. An example can be found in Arturo J. Bañuelas's essay "U.S. Hispanic Theology: An Initial Assessment." At the outset of his essay he provides a list titled "First-Generation U.S. Hispanic Theologians." His list includes: Gilbert Romero, Harold Recinos, Sixto García, Juan José Huitrado-Hizo, Dolorita Martínez, Clemente Barron, Jaime Vidal, Arturo Pérez, Ana María Pineda, Gary Riebe-Estrella, Marina Herrera, Jeanette Rodríguez-Holguin, Fernando Segovia, Rosendo Urrabazo, and Dominga Zapata (1995:55–56). From the unifying trunk of Hispanic thoughts, these particular scholars represent a branch, and upon that branch, like twigs, another generation of scholars will sprout. This newer generation finds their connectiveness to the original trunk, that is, the unifying truth, through a particular senior scholar already listed as a branch.

This image comes into focus in the genealogical tree provided for us by Benjamín Valentín in his essay "Nuevos Odres para el Vino," which was published some three years after Bañuelas's. Valentín maps out a list of what he calls first and second tiers of Latino/a theological articulation. In his first tier he lists Virgilio Elizondo, Justo González, Orlando Costas, Marina Herrera, María Pilar Aquino, Ada María Isasi-Díaz, and Yolanda Tarango. His second tier includes Roberto Goizueta, Harold Recinos, Allan Figueroa Deck, Ana María Pineda, Jeanette Rodríguez-Holguin, Orlando Espín, Arturo Bañuelas, David Traverzo, and Eldin Villafane (1998:31). A comparison of Bañuelas's and Valentín's lists shows several inconsistencies between them as to who is defined as doing theological and/or religious scholarship. Obviously, agreement as to who should belong in which category can be a matter of debate, hence helping to explain why different sets of scholars exist. Some scholars may be listed in the group closer to the "trunk" of the tree, while others are listed in "second" place upon the branches. This unconformity attests to the fact that the lists are arbitrarily arranged by whoever develops such a list. Hence power is exerted by the list-maker. Who is chosen, what criteria are used to chose them, and who is excluded are all somewhat arbitrarily decided. And this decision legitimizes as the norm an intra-Hispanic paradigm that bestows privilege to some, less privilege to others, and rebuffs still others.

The comparison of Bañuelas's and Valentín's lists of theological thinkers is meant neither to disparage nor discredit the insightful work both men have done in their respective essays. Nor is it to argue which list is correct, nor to propose a different list. Why then call attention to such an inconsequential point? To illustrate how Hispanics (this author included) have been taught to "see" and categorize the reality that surrounds us. Arborescent models are employed by the marginalized because they reside within a social structure that has normalized and legitimized the use of arborescent models for the purpose of categorizing.

Now, whether Latina/o scholars are arranged by generations (as so often is the case) or tiers, a hierarchy is developed with those listed in the "first" generation or tier carrying greater prestige because they are closer to the trunk of "original truth," regardless of how this "truth" is defined or if these scholars make any claim to be closer to "truth." An arborescent hierarchy is established going from the privileged who are closer to the trunk, toward the less differentiated who dangle on the branches. For this reason, Deleuze and Guattari oppose vertical, tree-like structures of knowledge. They instead propose a rhizome model that has no beginning or end, but always a middle from whence it grows. This rhizome model provides for a radically horizontal structure that is antigenealogical, nonhierarchical, nonsignifying, and lacking any type of central automation, thus shattering the supposed linear unity of knowledge (1987:6, 21).

Their inspiration for a rhizome model came from the special relationship between philosophy and neurology, specifically the microbiology of the brain, which is organized more like grass than like a tree. Thinking doesn't begin with what is known about the brain, but rather by how new thought traces uncharted channels, making new connections and synapses. For them, tree-like structures are closed uncertain systems with quantum mechanisms, while rhizome models are open (Deleuze, 1995:149).

An example of a rhizome model, as a subterranean stem, is couchgrass. With couchgrass there is no one central root, but rather thousands. Unlike trees whose protruding branches connect separately to a main trunk, the offshoots of couchgrass interconnect randomly in an unregulated, acentric (not polycentric), constantly changing network of nodes. In short, not only can any line be connected to any other line, it in fact must be so. This is very different from a tree model that plots a point and fixes an order. Through the rhizome model, a move is made away from the binary subject/other structure prevalent in Euroamerican thought (Deleuze and Guattari, 1987:7, 9). As such, rhizomes are never complete. There is always an "and." Neat hierarchical lists are subverted as the "and" is added to the equation followed by yet another "and." Hence the model is never able to come to fruition. The opportunity for a matrix of voices, some of which have been kept silent due to the power held by those "closer to the trunk," now finally exists.

Respecting Elders

One casualty of moving from an arborescent model to a rhizome model is the assumption that those scholars who chronologically came first, and thus are closer to the tree trunk, are inherently closer to the "truth" of what is Latino/a religious thought. A rhizomatic model unmasks and dismisses this hierarchical power structure, thus providing space for all, even those whose thoughts are not necessarily connected to scholars who came before them. All the same, resistance can be expected for any attempt to move beyond an arborescent structure of knowledge toward a rhizomatic model.

For example, during a presentation given in the summer of 1998 to an audience predominantly composed of Latino/a religion graduate students, Ada María Isasi-Díaz gave a lecture titled "Doing Theology as Mission." A respected senior scholar who has made major contributions to the Latina/o religious discourse, Isasi-Díaz laid out the relationship that should exist between the junior scholars hearing her presentation and those who chronologically began their scholarship over a generation before. She was especially concerned when junior Latina/o scholars challenged, questioned, or criticized the assumptions or scholarship of senior Hispanic intellectuals who have been constructing a Latino/a-based religious expression for the past thirty years. According to Isasi-Díaz:

> Why then contribute to the minimizing and degrading of the Hispanic/Latino enterprise by criticizing or negating what others of us [senior scholars] have said? ... We need to build on each other instead of tearing each other down. We need to be a strong community to carry out the [struggle] instead of contributing to our own marginalization by arguing against each other, by excluding each other, by not listening to and taking into consideration what has happened historically in the academy with Latinas and Latinos. (1998:104)

How then are those junior Latino/a scholars who insist on critically analyzing the overall Latino/a religious discourse, specifically the work of senior scholars, to proceed? It becomes difficult, if not impossible, to be self-critical as a group when the junior scholar raising questions is portrayed as an ungrateful child. According to Isasi-Díaz:

> They are the [son or daughter] who thinks that they owe nothing to father or mother, grandmother or aunt.... They step on our heads by siding with the dominant group against our strategies;

they step on our heads by not taking our work seriously; they step on our heads by using the publications of the dominant group to attack our work; they step on our heads by allowing themselves to be used by organizations and movements that have dispensed with others of us because we have insisted on bringing along the perspectives and struggles of our communities. (Ibid.:102)

In effect, a community is created by senior scholars where their work, and only their work, is put out of reach of the rigorous scholastic inquiry of junior scholars within that community. This positioning was probably not the conscious intention of Isasi-Díaz's comments. Surely she would welcome criticism, but she prefers it be conducted "in house," among ourselves, lest we leave ourselves and the community we represent open for criticism and thus undermine our own long-term work and community. Still, her desire to protect the community causes indirect political consequences that reinforce the silencing, if not ostracizing, of certain junior scholars who challenge or disagree with their senior scholars. Of course this phenomenon is not unique to the Latina/o experience, and probably exists among other marginalized groups.

This power relationship is a kind of oppression, masking as *familia,* which when created erects a clear dichotomy between those junior scholars accepted into the community, demonstrated by their willingness to quote senior scholars in all of their works, and those who are outside the community for having the audacity to rethink how Hispanic identity and religion should be fashioned. Ironically, while the Latino/a religious community resists the dominant culture's oppressive social structures, it simultaneously creates its own forms of oppression, i.e., when senior members of the community take advantage of their positions, which hold considerable power and prestige. It is thus possible to create an oppressive structure within the domination of the overall Hispanic community by the dominant culture.

In the sociopolitical vacuum created by the overall repressive power structures designed to privilege Euroamericans, those

Latino/as recognized by the dominant culture as leaders within the Hispanic scholarly community become important and powerful figures, whether they want to or not. Within this disenfranchised space, structures take form along a hierarchy that is based on chronology, privileging those power holders whose positions are assured because of the overall system of Euroamerican supremacy. Although it is true that the Latina/o religious expressions these early scholars created contain the power to liberate, they also (and in most cases unconsciously) can suppress, mask, and delegitimize the complex realities of hitherto marginalized voices within the very community they seek to liberate. The senior scholar as powerbroker serves as mentor, legitimizer, and counselor to the junior scholars. Because of their longevity within academia, it is to them that the dominant culture usually turns to speak for the Hispanic community, evaluate the work of junior scholars facing tenure reviews, and serve on academic and editorial boards. From this position, they hold enormous power to assist or block a junior scholar from obtaining funding, having their works published, or obtaining employment. It is not unheard of for junior scholars who dare to question the dominant perspective within the Latina/o religious scholarly community to be denied dissertation funding by the senior scholars who sit on scholarship granting boards, or to receive negative reference letters hampering tenure during review. In short, these senior scholars, as gatekeepers, become the most important voices within the dominated group due to the socio-political vacuum created by the dominant Euroamerican culture's ethnic discrimination.

Concern of offending these senior scholars consciously or subconsciously impacts the work conducted by most junior scholars. It becomes a matter of academic survival to remain in the good graces of those senior scholars who can advance or retard the junior scholars' academic career. Some junior scholars may find themselves employing a strategy that determines whose scholarship is to be criticized, focusing on other junior scholars who lack the power to retaliate. Even though there are many senior Hispanic scholars who have flaws in their work similar to the junior scholars targeted, the junior scholars' work is severely criticized because they are "safer targets" in that they lack the power to initiate negative repercussions.

"Are We One?"

All too often, marginalized groups unite to create a clear and distinctive voice to address the oppressive structures they struggle against. A united front against oppression is strategically wise, but it contains its own pitfalls, specifically when the voices of those who are farthest from the "white ideal" become marginalized among the marginalized. Usually, the voices of women, nonwhite Latino/as, gays/lesbians, and the very poor are told to remain silent until the battle against the dominant culture is won. Once this is accomplished, their concerns will be dealt with. Historically, this seldom happens.

The creation of a so-called "cohesive" community of Latina/o scholars of religion is no easy feat. Ethnic and cultural diversity historically prevented unity. So, for the sake of unity, for the sake of creating a united front against the dominant culture, a conscious effort was made to minimize what kept the community separated by emphasizing commonalities. With time, the concept of a Latina/o pan-ethnic identity began to develop. Nonetheless, the desire of Latino/a scholars of religion to evoke a pan-ethnic unity masked the reality of intra-Hispanic structures that foster oppression within the Latino/a constructed social space, evident in the fact that most Hispanic scholars of religion, specifically theologians, are either white or have lighter skin pigmentation than Hispanics in general. They are also mostly male. And, interestingly enough, they are disproportionately of Cuban descent, probably because of an economic class that is closer to the dominant culture than other Latino/a groups.

While a "pan-Hispanic" construct may have been beneficial, if not necessary, over a quarter of a century ago as Latino/a religious thought was initially developing, we are now left to consider if such a construct remains necessary. If all religious thought is contextual, rooted within the social location of those who are formulating religious expressions, then the original assumptions that formed how Hispanic religiosity is presently understood primarily reveal the social forces that shaped today's Latino/a senior scholars' thoughts when they were completing their own religious studies.

But what happens when the social context changes? What occurs when a newer generation of Hispanic scholars of religion attempts to create a theological expression reflective of their social location and the societal forces that shape them — a social location vastly different than a generation ago? This present generation of Hispanic religion scholars needs to recontextualize its interpretative framework in light of its present circumstances. These scholars must explore and contextualize recent development in the study of Latino religions.

Rethinking

Some Euroamerican scholars of religion may hesitate to criticize the construction of Latina/o religiosity or theology, concerned their efforts would be misconstrued as being anti-Hispanic. Others, motivated by their own sense of superiority, would not hesitate to quote those Hispanic scholars engaged in critical thought about our academic community (like myself) to advance their own self-interest of securing their own power and privilege within the overall academy. Moreover, Latino/a scholars, as we have seen, also hesitate, concerned that their analysis would be misconstrued as betraying the community and that they would thus face ostracization. Consequently, an analysis that critically investigates the major theoretical and methodological approaches to the study of Latino/a religions over the past thirty years has yet to be fully developed. The underlying hope of a book like this is to take modest initial steps toward such an analysis by focusing on the theoretical and methodological approaches past Latina/o scholars of religion took to interpret their religiosity, manifested as Hispanic theology. In this final chapter I have tried to explore intra-Hispanic power structures to unmask and demonstrate areas where academic rhetoric among Hispanic scholars of religion is incongruent with the Latino/a reality. I did this specifically because of my commitment to *mi comunidad.*

Bibliography

Aaland, Mikkel. *Sweat: The Illustrated History and Description of the Finnish Sauna, Russian Bania, Islamic Hammam, Japanese Mushi-Buro, Mexican Temescal, and American Indian and Eskimo Sweat Lodge.* Santa Barbara: Capra Press, 1978.

Abalos, David T. *Latinos in the United States: The Sacred and the Political.* South Bend, IN: University of Notre Dame Press, 1986.

Abel, Theodore. *Protestant Home Missions to Catholic Immigrants.* New York: Institute of Social and Religious Research, 1933.

Acuña, Rodolfo. *Occupied America: A History of Chicanos.* London: Canefield Press, 1972.

Aguirre Beltrán, Gonzalo. *La población negra de México, 1519–1810.* Mexico City: Ediciones Fuente Cultural, 1946.

Alarcón, Daniel Cooper. *The Aztec Palimpsest: Mexico in the Modern Imagination.* Tucson: University of Arizona Press, 1997.

Alcoff, Linda Martín. "Is Latina/o Identity a Racial Identity?" In *Hispanics/Latinos in the United States: Ethnicity, Race, and Rights,* ed. Jorge J. E. Gracia and Pablo de Greiff. New York: Routledge, 2000.

Allen, Paula Gunn. *The Sacred Hoop: Recovering the Feminine in American Indian Traditions.* Boston: Beacon Press, 1986.

Allen, Prudence. *The Concept of Woman.* Vol. 1. *The Aristotelian Revolution, 750 BC–AD 1250.* Grand Rapids, MI: Wm. B. Eerdmans, 1997.

———. *The Concept of Woman.* Vol. 2. *The Early Humanist Reformation, 1250–1500.* Grand Rapids, MI: Wm. B. Eerdmans, 2002.

Almaguer, Tomás. "Chicano Men: A Cartography of Homosexual Identity and Behavior." In *The Lesbian and Gay Studies Reader,* ed. Henry Abelove et al. New York: Routledge, 1993.

Alreck, Pamela L., and Robert B. Settle. *The Survey Research Handbook: Guidelines and Strategies for Conducting a Survey.* Chicago: Irwin Professional Publishing, 1994.

Althaus-Reid, Marcella María. "Gustavo Gutiérrez Goes to Disneyland: Theme Park Theologies and the Diaspora of the Discourse of the Popular Theologian in Liberation Theology." In *Interpreting beyond Borders,* ed. Fernando F. Segovia. Sheffield, U.K.: Sheffield Academic Press, 2000.

Althusser, Louis. "Idéologie et appareils idéologique d'Etat." *La Pensée* 151 (1970):3–38.

Anaya, Rudolfo A. "Aztlán: A Homeland without Boundaries." In *Aztlán: Essays on the Chicano Homeland,* ed. Rudolfo A. Anaya and Francisco Lomelí. Albuquerque: Academia/El Norte, 1989.

———. *Bless Me, Ultima.* New York: Warner Books, reprint 1994.

Anaya, Rudolfo A., and Francisco Lomeli, eds. *Aztlán: Essays on the Chicano Homeland.* Albuquerque: University of New Mexico Press, 1988.

Anderson, Richard feather. "Geomancy." In *The Power of Place: Sacred Ground in Natural and Human Environments,* ed. James A. Swan. Wheaton, IL: Quest Books, 1991.

Anderson, Thomas. *Matanza.* Willimantic, CT: Curbstone Press, 1992.

Anzaldúa, Gloria. *Borderlands/La Frontera: The New Mestiza.* San Francisco: Aunt Lute Books, 1987.

———, ed. *Making Faces, Making Soul, Haciendo Caras: Creative and Critical Perspectives by Women of Color.* San Francisco: Aunt Lute Books, 1990.

———. "Border Arte: Nepantla, El Lugar de la Frontera." In *La Frontera/La Border; Art About the Mexico/U.S. Border Experience.* San Diego: Centro Cultural de La Raza and Museum of Contemporary Art San Diego, 1993.

———. *Borderlands/La Frontera: The New Mestiza.* 2nd ed. San Francisco: Spinsters Press, 1999.

———. *Interview/Entrevistas/Gloria Anzaldúa.* Ed. AnaLouise Keating. New York: Routledge, 2000.

———. "now let us shift...the path of conocimiento...inner work, public acts." In *This Bridge We Call Home,* ed. Gloria Anzaldúa and AnaLouise Keating. New York: Routledge, 2002.

Aponte, Edwin David. *¡Santo! Varieties of Latino Spirituality.* Maryknoll, NY: Orbis Books, 2006.

Appadurai, Arjun. *Modernity at Large: Cultural Dimensions of Globalization.* Minneapolis: University of Minnesota Press, 1996.

Aquino, María Pilar. "Perspectives on Latina's Feminist Liberation Theology." In *Frontiers of Hispanic Theology in the United States,* ed. Allan Figueroa Deck. Maryknoll, NY: Orbis Books, 1992.

———. "Directions and Foundations of Hispanic/Latino Theology: Toward a Mestiza Theology of Liberation." *Journal of Hispanic/Latino Theology* 1, no. 1 (1993): 5–21.

———. "Directions and Foundations of Hispanic/Latino Theology: Toward a Mestiza Theology of Liberation." In *Mestizo Christianity: Theology from the Latino Perspective,* ed. Arturo J. Bañuelas. Maryknoll, NY: Orbis Books, 1995.

———. "Latin American Feminist Theology." *Journal of Feminist Studies in Religion* 14 (Spring 1998): 94.

Aquino, María Pilar, Daisy L. Machado, and Jeanette Rodríguez. "Introduction." In *Religion and Justice: A Reader in Latina Feminist Theology.* Austin: University of Texas Press, 2002.

Arguedas, Alcides. *Raza de bronce.* La Paz: Gónzalez y Medina, 1919.

Atkins-Vásquez, Jane, ed. *Hispanic Presbyterians in Southern California: One Hundred Years of Ministry.* Los Angeles: Hispanic Commission, Synod of Southern California and Hawaii, 1988.

Atkinson, Ernest E. *A Selected Bibliography of Hispanic Baptist History.* Nashville: Historical Commission, Southern Baptist Convention, 1981.

Bakewell, Peter. *Silver and Entrepreneurship in Seventeenth-Century Potosí: The Life and Times of Antonio López de Quiroga.* Dallas: Southern Methodist University Press, 1988, 1995.

Balibar, Etienne, and Immanuel Wallerstein. *Race, Nation, Classe: Les identités ambiguës.* Paris: La Découverte, 1988.

Bañuelas, Arturo J. "U.S. Hispanic Theology: An Initial Assessment." In *Mestizo Christianity: Theology from the Latino Perspective,* ed. Arturo J. Bañuelas. Maryknoll, NY: Orbis Books, 1995.

Barrera, Mario, Carlos Muñoz, and Charles Ornelas. "The Barrio as an Internal Colony." In *La Causa Política: A Chicano Politics Reader,* ed. F. Chris García. Notre Dame: University of Notre Dame Press, 1972, 1974.

———. *Race and Class in the Southwest: A Theory of Racial Inequality.* Notre Dame, IN: University of Notre Dame Press, 1979.

Barthes, Roland. *Mythologies.* Trans. Annette Lavers. New York: Hill and Wang, 1972.

Barton, Paul, and David Maldonado Jr., eds. *Hispanic Christianity within Mainline Protestant Traditions: A Bibliography.* Decatur, GA: Asociación para la Educación Teológica Hispana, 1998.

Basch, Linda, Nina Glick Schiller, and Cristina Szanton Blanc. *Nations Unbound: Transnational Projects, Postcolonial Predicaments, and Deterritorialized Nation-States.* Amsterdam: Gordon and Breach Publishers, 1994.

Bataille, Georges. *Erotism: Death and Sensuality.* Trans. Mary Dalwood. San Francisco: City Lights Books, 1962, 1986.

Bazán, Nellie, with Elizabeth B. and Don Martínez Jr. *Enviados de Dios: Demetrio and Nellie Bazán.* Miami: Editorial Vida, 1987.

Belli, Humberto, and Ronald Nash. *Beyond Liberation Theology.* Grand Rapids, MI: Baker Book House, 1992.

Benhabib, Seyla. *Situating the Self: Gender, Community, and Postmodernism in Contemporary Ethics.* New York: Routledge, 1992.

Bennett, Hermann. *Africans in Colonial Mexico: Absolutism, Christianity and Afro-Creole Consciousness, 1570–1640.* Bloomington: Indiana University Press, 2003.

Beverley, John. *Subalternity and Representation: Arguments in Cultural Theory.* Durham: Duke University Press, 1999.

Bhabha, Homi. "Culture's In-Between." In *Questions of Cultural Identity,* ed. Stuart Hall and Paul du Gay. London: Sage, 1996.

Boff, Leonardo, and Clodovis Boff. *Introducing Liberation Theology.* Maryknoll, NY: Orbis Books, 1987.

Boone, Elizabeth Hill. "Migration as Ritual Performance." In *To Change Place: Aztec Ceremonial Landscapes,* ed. Davíd Carrasco. Boulder: University of Colorado Press, 1991.

Bourdieu, Pierre. *Distinction: A Social Critique of the Judgment of Taste.* Trans. R. Nice. Cambridge: Harvard University Press, 1984a.

———. *Homo academicus.* Paris: Éditions de Minuit, 1984b.

———. *Language and Symbolic Power.* Ed. John B. Thompson and trans. Gino Raymond and Matthew Adamson. Cambridge: Polity Press, 1991.

———. *Méditations pascaliennes.* Paris: Seuil, 1997.

Brackenridge, R. Douglas, and Francisco O. García-Treto. *Iglesia Presbiteriana: A History of Presbyterians and Mexican Americans in the Southwest.* San Antonio: Trinity University Press, 1974.

Brandon, George. *Santería from Africa to the New World: The Dead Sell Memories.* Bloomington: Indiana University Press, 1993.

Bresette, Linna E. *Mexicans in the United States: A Report of a Brief Survey.* Washington, DC: National Catholic Welfare Conference, 1929.

Brown, Diana DeG. *Umbanda: Religion and Politics in Urban Brazil.* New York: Columbia University Press, 1994.

Bruchac, Joseph. *The Native American Sweat Lodge: History and Legends.* Freedom, CA: Crossing Press, 1993.

Bürger, Peter. *Theory of the Avant-Garde.* Trans. Michael Shaw. Minneapolis: University of Minnesota Press, 1984.

Burke, John Francis. *Mestizo Democracy: The Politics of Crossing Borders.* College Station: Texas A & M University Press, 2002.

Burma, John. *Spanish-Speaking Groups in the United States.* Durham, NC: Duke University Press, 1954.

Busto, Rudiger V. "The Predicament of Nepantla: Chicana/o Religions in the 21st Century." *Perspectivas* 1 (Fall 1998): 7–21.

———. *King Tiger: The Religious Vision of Reies López Tijerina.* Albuquerque: University of New Mexico, 2005.

Butler, Judith. *Gender Trouble: Feminism and the Subversion of Identity.* New York: Routledge, 1990.

Cadena, Gilbert. "Religious Ethnic Identity: A Socio-Religious Portrait of Latinos and Latinas in the Catholic Church." In *Old Masks, New Faces: Religion and Latino Identities,* ed. Anthony M. Stevens-Arroyo and Gilbert R. Cadena. New York: Bildner Center for Western Hemisphere Studies, 1995.

Cáliz-Montoro, Carmen. "Poetry Is Not Made of Words: A Study of Aesthetics of the Borderlands in Gloria Anzaldúa and Marlene Nourbese Philip." Ph.D. diss., University of Toronto, 1996.

Campa, Arthur F. *Spanish Religious Folktheatre in the Southwest.* Albuquerque: Borgo Press, 1943.

Cantú, Benjamín, and José Ortega. *Historia de la Asamblea Apostólica de la Fe en Cristo Jesús, 1916–1966.* Mentone, CA: Sal's Printing, 1966.

Capps, Walter. *Religious Studies: The Making of a Discipline.* Minneapolis: Augsburg Fortress. New York: St. Martin's Press, 1995.

Cardoso, Fernando Henrique, and Enzo Faletto. *Dependencia y desarrollo en América Latina: Ensayo de interpretación sociológica.* México, D.F.: Siglo Veintiuno editores, 1969.

Cardoza-Orlandi, Carlos F. "Drum Beats of Resistance and Liberation: Afro-Caribbean Religions, the Struggle for Life, and the Christian Theologian." *Journal of Hispanic/Latino Theology* 3, no. 1 (1995).

Carpentier, Alejo. *El reino de este mundo.* Barcelona: Seix Barral, 1979.

Carrasco, David. "A Perspective for the Study of Religious Dimensions in Chicano Experience: *Bless Me, Ultima* as a Religious Text." *Aztlán: A Journal of Chicano Studies* 13, no. 1 and 2 (1982a): 195–221.

———. "The Sources: From Storybook to Encyclopedia." In *Quetzalcoatl and the Irony of Empire: Myths and Prophecies in the Aztec Tradition.* Chicago: University of Chicago Press, 1982b.

———. *Religions of Mesoamerica.* San Francisco: HarperSanFrancisco, 1990.

———. "Jaguar Christians in the Contact Zone." In *Enigmatic Powers: Syncretism with African and Indigenous Peoples' Religions among Latinos,* ed. Anthony M. Stevens-Arroyo and Andres I. Pérez y Mena. New York: Bildner Center for Western Hemisphere Studies, 1995.

———. "The Myth of the Chicano Borderlands: Shamanism and the Loco-Centric Imagination in the Work of Gloria Anzaldúa and Dr. Loco." In *Chicano Religions: Essays in the Mexican American Experience,* ed. Gastón Espinosa and Mario T. García. Durham, NC: Duke University Press, 2006a.

———. "Cuando Dios y Usted Quiere: Latino Studies between Religious Powers and Social Thought." In *Blackwell Reader on Latino Studies,* ed. Juan Flores and Renato Rosaldo. Oxford, UK: Blackwell Publishers, 2006b.

Carrier, Joseph. *De Los Otros: Intimacy and Homosexuality among Mexican Men.* New York: Columbia University Press, 1995.

Cassen, Bernard. *Tout a commencé à Porto Alegre.* Paris: Mille et Une Nuits, 2003.

Castañeda, Carlos. *The Teachings of Don Juan: A Yaqui Way of Knowledge.* Eagle's Trust: Washington Square Press, 1968, 1998.

Castañeda, Carlos E.. *Our Catholic Heritage in Texas, 1519–1950.* 7 vols. Austin, TX: Von Boekmann-Jones, 1936–58.

Castillo, Ana. *Massacre of the Dreamers: Essays on Xicanisma.* Albuquerque: University of New Mexico Press, 1994.

———. "Saintly Mother and Soldier's Whore: The Leftist/Catholic Paradigm." In *Massacre of the Dreamers: Essays on Xicanisma.* New York: Plume, 1995.

———, ed. *Goddess of the Americas: Writings on La Virgen de Guadalupe.* New York: Riverhead Books, 1996.

Castro, Fidel. *La historia me absolverá.* Buenos Aires: Grupo Editor de Buenos Aires, 1973.

Castro, Fidel, and Nelson Mandela. *How Far We Slaves Have Come! South Africa and Cuba in Today's World.* Atlanta: Pathfinder Press, 1991.

Chávez, Angélico. *The Old Faith and Old Glory: Story of the Church in New Mexico since the American Occupation, 1846–1946.* Santa Fe, NM: privately printed, 1946.

———. *Our Lady of the Conquest.* Albuquerque: History Society of New Mexico, 1948.

Chávez, César. "The Mexican American and the Church." *El Grito del Sol* 1, no. 4 (Summer 1968): 9–12.

———. "Mexican Americans and the Church." In *Voices: Readings from El Grito.* ed. Octavio I. Romano. Berkeley: Quinto Sol, 1973. As cited in Anthony M. Stevens-Arroyo, *Prophets Denied Honor: An Anthology on the Hispano Church of the United States.* Maryknoll, NY: Orbis Books, 1980.

Chavez, John. *The Lost Land: The Chicano Image of the Southwest.* Albuquerque: University of New Mexico Press, 1984.

Chestnut, R. Andrew. *Competitive Spirits: Latin America's New Religious Economy.* Oxford: Oxford University Press, 2003.

Chopp, Rebecca, and Sheila Greeve Davaney. *Horizons in Feminist Theology: Identity, Tradition, and Norms.* Minneapolis: Fortress Press, 1997.

Christian, Barbara. "The Race for Theory." In *The Black Feminist Reader,* ed. Joy James and T. Denean Sharpley-Whiting. New York: Blackwell, 2000.

Cisneros, Sandra. *Woman Hollering Creek and Other Stories.* New York: Random House, 1991.

Clifford, James, and George Marcus, eds. *Writing Culture: The Poetics and Politics of Ethnography.* Berkeley: University of California Press, 1986.

Cone, James. *Black Theology and Black Power.* New York: Seabury, 1969.

———. *A Black Theology of Liberation.* Philadelphia: J. B. Lippincott Company, 1970.

Coniff, Michael L., and Thomas J. Davis, eds. *Africans in the Americas: A History of the Black Diaspora.* New York: St. Martin's Press, 1994.

Copeland, M. Shawn. "Black, Hispanic, and Native American Theologies." In *The Modern Theologians: An Introduction to Christian Theology in the Twentieth Century,* ed. David F. Ford. 2nd ed. Cambridge: Blackwell, 1997.

Corbitt, Duvon Clough. *A Study of the Chinese in Cuba, 1847–1947.* Wilmore, KY: Asbury College, 1971.

Cornejo Polar, Antonio. "Mestizaje e hibridez: Los riesgos de las metáforas, Apuntes." *Revista Iberoamericana* 67, no. 200–201, (2002): 867–70.

Countryman, L. William. *Dirt, Greed, and Sex: Sexual Ethics in the New Testament and Their Implications for Today.* Philadelphia: Fortress Press, 1988.

Cros Sandoval, Mercedes. "Afro-Cuban Religion in Perspective." In *Enigmatic Powers: Syncretism with African and Indigenous Peoples' Religions among Latinos,* ed. Anthony M. Stevens-Arroyo and Andres I. Pérez y Mena. New York: PARAL/Bildner Center for Western Hemisphere Studies, 1995.

Culp, Alice Bessie. "A Case Study of the Living Conditions of Thirty-Five Mexican Families of Los Angeles with Special Reference to Mexican Culture." M.A. thesis, University of Southern California, 1921.

Cypress, Sarah. *La Malinche in Mexican Literature: From History to Myth.* Austin: University of Texas Press, 1991.

Dalton, Frederick John. *The Moral Vision of César Chávez.* Maryknoll, NY: Orbis Books, 2003.

Darío, Rubén. *Obras completas, V.* Madrid: A. Aguado, 1955.

Davalos, Karen Mary. *Exhibiting Mestizaje: Mexican (American) Museums in the Diaspora.* Albuquerque: University of New Mexico Press, 2001.

Dayan, Joan. *Haiti, History, and the Gods.* Berkeley: University of California Press, 1995.

de Beauvoir, Simone. *The Second Sex.* Trans. H. M. Parshley. New York: Vintage Books, 1989.

De Castro, Juan. *Mestizo Nations: Culture, Race, and Conformity in Latin American Literature.* Tucson: University of Arizona Press, 2002.

Deck, Allan Figueroa. *The Second Wave: Hispanic Ministry and the Evangelization of Culture.* New York: Paulist Press, 1989.

———. "Introduction." In *Frontiers of Hispanic Theology in the United States,* ed. Allan Figueroa Deck. Maryknoll, NY: Orbis Books, 1992.

de la Fuente, Alejandro. *A Nation for All: Race, Inequality, and Politics in Twentieth-Century Cuba.* Chapel Hill: University of North Carolina Press, 2001.

de la Fuente, Victor Hugo. "De Porto Alegre a Mumbay y Santiago." *Le Monde Diplomatique* 39, Edición Chilena (Marzo 2004): 3.

De la Garza, Rodolfo O., Louis DeSipio, Chris García, John García, and Angelo Falcón. *Latino Voices: Mexican, Puerto Rican, and Cuban Perspectives on American Politics.* Boulder, CO: Westview Press, 1992.

de las Casas, Bartolomé. *Breve relación de la destrucción de las Indias Occidentales presentada a Felipe II siendo principe de Asturias.* México, D.F.: Libros Luciérnaga, 1957.

De La Torre, Miguel A., "Confesiones de un macho cubano." *Perspectivas: Occasional Papers* no. 4 (Summer 2001): 65–87.

————. *The Quest for the Cuban Christ: A Historical Search.* Gainesville: University Press of Florida, 2002.

————. *La Lucha for Cuba: Religion and Politics on the Streets of Miami.* Berkeley: University of California Press, 2003.

————, ed. *Handbook on U.S. Theologies of Liberation.* St. Louis: Chalice Press, 2004a.

————. *Santería: The Beliefs and Rituals of a Growing Religion in America.* Grand Rapids, MI: Wm. B. Eerdmans, 2004b.

De La Torre, Miguel A., and Edwin David Aponte. *Introducing Latino/a Theologies.* Maryknoll, NY: Orbis Books, 2001.

De León, Victor. *The Silent Pentecostals.* Taylors, SC: Faith Printing Company, 1979.

Deleuze, Gilles. *Negotiations: 1972–1990.* Trans. Martin Joughin. New York: Columbia University Press, 1995.

Deleuze, Gilles, and Félix Guattari. *L'Anti-Oedipe: Capitalisme et schizophrénie.* Paris: Minuit, 1972.

————. *A Thousand Plateaus: Capitalism and Schizophrenia.* Trans. Brian Massumi. Minneapolis: University of Minnesota Press, 1987.

————. "Rhizome Versus Trees." In *The Deleuze Reader,* ed. Costantin V. Boundas. New York: Columbia University Press, 1993.

Delgado, Teresa. "Prophesy Freedom: Puerto Rican Women's Literature as a Source for Latina Feminist Theology." In *Religion and Justice: A Reader in Latina Feminist Theology,* ed. María Pilar Aquino, Daisy L. Machado, and Jeanette Rodríguez. Austin: University of Texas Press, 2002.

de Luna, Anita. *Faith Formation and Popular Religion: Lessons from the Tejano Experience.* Lanham, MD: Rowan & Littlefield, 2002.

DeStefano, Anthony M. *Latino Folk Medicine: Healing Herbal Remedies from Ancient Traditions.* New York: Ballantine Books, 2001.

Deutsch, Sarah. *No Separate Refuge: Culture, Class, and Gender on an Anglo-Hispanic Frontier in the American Southwest, 1880–1940.* New York: Oxford University Press, 1987.

Dewey, John. *Later Works.* Vol. 11: *Liberalism and Social Action.* Carbondale: Southern Illinois University Press, 1991.

Díaz, Miguel H. *On Being Human: U.S. Hispanic and Rahnerian Perspectives.* Maryknoll, NY: Orbis Books, 2001.

Díaz-Stevens, Ana María. "Latinas and the Church." In *Hispanic Catholic Culture in the U.S.: Issues and Concerns,* ed. Jay P. Dolan and Allan Figueroa Deck, S.J. Notre Dame: University of Notre Dame Press, 1994.

Dodson, Ruth. *Tone the Bell Easy.* Dallas: Southern Methodist University, 1932.

———. *The Healer of Los Olmos.* Austin: Texas Folklore Society, 1951.

Dolan, Jay P., and Allan Figueroa Deck, S.J. *Hispanic Catholic Culture in the U.S.: Issues and Concerns.* South Bend, IN: University of Notre Dame Press, 1994.

Dolan, Jay P., and Gilberto Hinojosa. *Mexican Americans in the Catholic Church, 1900–1965.* South Bend, IN: University of Notre Dame Press, 1994.

Dolan, Jay P., and Jaime R. Vidal. *Puerto Rican and Cuban Catholics in the U.S., 1900–1965.* South Bend, IN: University of Notre Dame Press, 1994.

Du Bois, W. E. B. *The Souls of Black Folk.* New York: Signet Classic, 1995.

Durán, Diego. *Historia de las Indias de Nueva España y Islas de Tierra Firme.* Vol. 2. Mexico City: N.p., 1867–80.

———. *The History of the Indies of New Spain.* Trans. Doris Heyden and Fernando Horcasitas. New York: Orion Press, 1964.

Dussel, Enrique. *Método para una filosofía de la liberación: Superación analéctica de la dialéctica hegeliana.* Salamanca: Ediciones Sígueme, 1974.

———. *A History of the Church in Latin America: Colonialism to Liberation (1492–1979).* Trans. Alan Neely. Grand Rapids, MI: Wm. B. Eerdmans, 1981.

———. *The Church in Latin America, 1492–1992.* Maryknoll, NY: Orbis Books, 1992.

Eagleton, Terry. *The Illusion of Postmodernism.* Cambridge: Blackwell, 1996.

Eliade, Mircea. *The Quest: History and Meaning in Religion.* Chicago: University of Chicago Press, 1984.

Elizondo, Virgilio. "Educación religiosa para el méxico-norteamericano." *Catequesis Latinoamericana* (1968).

———. *Anthropological and Psychological Characteristics of the Mexican American.* San Antonio: Mexican American Cultural Center, 1974.

———. *Christianity and Culture.* Huntington, IN: Our Sunday Visitor, 1975.

———. *Mestizaje: The Dialectic of Birth and Gospel.* San Antonio: Mexican American Cultural Center, 1978.

———. *La Morenita: Evangelizer of the Americas.* San Antonio: Mexican American Cultural Center, 1980.

———. *Galilean Journey: The Mexican-American Promise.* Maryknoll, NY: Orbis Books, 1983, 1994.

———. *The Future Is Mestizo: Life Where Cultures Meet.* Bloomington, IN: Meyer Stone Books, 1992.

———. "Mestizaje as a Locus of Theological Reflection." In *Mestizo Christianity: Theology from the Latino Perspective,* ed. Arturo Bañuelas. Maryknoll, NY: Orbis Books, 1995.

———. *Guadalupe: Mother of the New Creation.* Maryknoll, NY: Orbis Books, 1997.

———. *Beyond Borders: Writings of Virgilio Elizondo and Friends,* ed. Timothy Matovina. Maryknoll, NY: Orbis Books, 2000.

———. "Foreword to John Francis Burke." In *Mestizo Democracy: The Politics of Crossing Borders.* College Station: Texas A & M University Press, 2002.

Elizondo, Virgilio P., and Timothy M. Matovina. *Mestizo Worship: A Pastoral Approach to Litugical Ministry.* Collegeville, MN: Liturgical Press, 1998a.

———. *San Fernando Cathedral: Soul of the City.* Maryknoll, NY: Orbis Books, 1998b.

El Vez. "Aztlán." In *My Words to His Music y Más: A Selection of Lyrics by El Vez.* Los Angeles: Pepe Publishing, 1994.

———. *Boxing with God.* Los Angeles: Pepe Publishing, 2001.

Espín, Orlando. "Popular Religion as an Epistemology (of Suffering)." *Journal of Hispanic/Latino Theology* 2, no. 2 (November 1994): 66.

———. "Tradition and Popular Religion: An Understanding of the Sensus Fidelium." In *Mestizo Christianity: Theology from the Latino Perspective,* ed. Arturo J. Bañuelas. Maryknoll, NY: Orbis Books, 1995.

———. *The Faith of the People: Theological Reflections on Popular Catholicism.* Maryknoll, NY: Orbis Books, 1997.

———. "The State of U.S. Latino/a Theology: An Understanding." *Perspectivas: Occasional Papers,* no. 3 (Fall 2000): 15–55.

Espín, Orlando, and Miguel Díaz, eds. *From the Heart of Our People: Latino/a Explorations in Catholic Systematic Theology.* Maryknoll, NY: Orbis Books, 1999.

Espinosa, Aurelio M. "Spanish Folk-lore in New Mexico." *New Mexico Historical Review* 1 (1926): 135–55.

———. *España en Nuevo Méjico.* New York, 1937.

Espinosa, Gastón. "El Azteca: Francisco Olazábal and Latino Pentecostal Charisma, Power, and Faith Healing in the Borderlands." *Journal of the American Academy of Religion* 67, no. 3 (Fall 1999): 597–616.

———. " 'Your Daughters Shall Prophesy': A History of Women in Ministry in the Latino Pentecostal Movement in the United States." In *Women and Twentieth-Century Protestantism,* ed. Margaret Lamberts Bendroth and Virginia Lieson Brereton. Chicago: University of Illinois Press, 2002.

———. "Changements démographiques et religieux chez les hispaniques des Etats-Unis." *Social Compass: International Review of the Sociology of Religion* 51 (2004a): 303–20.

———. "The Pentecostalization of Latin American and U.S. Latino Christianity." *Pneuma: Journal of the Society for Pentecostal Studies* 26, no. 2 (Fall 2004b): 262–92.

———. "Latino Clergy and Churches in Faith-Based Political and Social Action in the United States." In *Latino Religions and Civic Activism in the United States,* ed. Gastón Espinosa, Virgilio Elizondo, and Jesse Miranda. New York: Oxford University Press, 2005.

Espinosa, Gastón, Virgilio Elizondo, and Jesse Miranda, eds. *Hispanic Churches in American Public Life: Summary of Findings.* South Bend, IN: Institute for Latino Studies, University of Notre Dame Press, 2003.

———. *Latino Religions and Civic Activism in the United States.* New York: Oxford University Press, 2005.

Espinosa, Manuel J. "The Virgin of the Reconquest of New Mexico." *Mid-America* 18 (1936): 79–87.

Fabian, Johannes. *Time and the Other: How Anthropology Makes Its Object.* New York: Columbia University Press, 1983.

Fanon, Frantz. *Black Skin, White Masks.* Trans. Charles Lam Markmann. New York: Grove Press, 1967.

Farley, Margaret. "Moral Imperatives for the Ordination of Women." In *Women and Catholic Priesthood,* ed. Anne Marie Gardiner. New York: Paulist Press, 1976.

Fernández, Abraham. "History of the Presbyterian Church, U.S.A. among the Spanish-Speaking People of the Southwest." B.D. thesis, San Francisco Theological Seminary, 1943.

Fernández, Eduardo. *La Cosecha: Harvesting Contemporary United States Hispanic Theology (1972–1998)*. Collegeville, MN: Liturgical Press, 2000.

Fernández, José Moreno. "The History and Prospects of Hispanic Methodism in the Southern California–Arizona Conference of the United Methodist Church." Ph.D. diss., Claremont School of Theology, 1973.

Fernandez-Calienes, Raul. "Bibliography of the Writings of Orlando E. Costas." *Missiology: An International Review* 17, no. 1 (1989): 87–105.

Fields, Virginia M., and Victor Zamudio Taylor. *The Road to Aztlán: Art From a Mythic Homeland*. Los Angeles: Los Angeles County Museum of Art, 2001.

Foucault, Michel. *The History of Sexuality*, vol. 1: *An Introduction*. Trans. Robert Hurley. New York: Vintage Books, 1978.

———. *Power/Knowledge: Selected Interviews and Other Writings, 1972–1977*. New York: Pantheon, 1980.

———. *The Foucault Reader*, ed. Paul Rabinow. New York: Pantheon Books, 1984.

———. *The Order of Things: An Archaeology of the Human Sciences*. New York: Vintage Books, 1994.

Fox, Geoffrey, "Honor, Shame, and Women's Liberation in Cuba." In *Female and Male in Latin America: Essays*, ed. Ann Pescatello. Pittsburgh: University of Pittsburgh Press, 1973.

Freire, Paulo. *Pedagogy of the Oppressed: New Revised 20th-Anniversary Edition*. Trans. Myra Bergman Ramos. New York: Continuum, 1972, 1994.

———. "Education, Liberation and the Church." *Religious Education* 79 (Fall 1984): 527–28.

Freud, Sigmund. *Civilization and Its Discontents*. New York: W. W. Norton, 1961.

Friedman, Milton. *Capitalism and Freedom*. Chicago: University of Chicago Press, 1962.

Fuentes, Carlos. "L'Amérique latine en mal d'Europe." *Le Monde diplomatique* (November 2003).

Fuss, Diana. *Essentially Speaking: Feminism, Nature, and Difference*. New York: Routledge, 1989.

Gablik, Suzi. *The Reenchantment of Art.* New York: Thames and Hudson, 1991.

Gallup, George, Jr., and D. Michael Lindsay. *Surveying the Religious Landscape: Trends in U.S. Beliefs.* Harrisburg, PA: Morehouse Group, 1999.

Galvan, Elias Gabriel. "A Study of the Spanish-Speaking Protestant Church and Her Mission to the Mexican American Minority." Ph.D. diss., Claremont School of Theology, 1969.

Gamio, Manuel. *Mexican Immigration to the United States: A Study of Human Migration and Adjustment.* Chicago: University of Chicago Press, 1930.

————. *The Mexican Immigrant: His Life-Story.* Chicago: University of Chicago Press, 1931.

García, Juan Castañon. "Healer Roles, Society and Healing Efficacy: An Anthropological Essay." *El Grito del Sol* 4, no. 1 (Winter 1979): 80–82.

García, Mario T. *Desert Immigrants: Mexicans and the Making of El Paso.* New Haven: Yale University Press, 1981.

————. *Mexican Americans: Leadership, Ideology, and Identity, 1930–1960.* New Haven: Yale University Press, 1989.

————. "Padres: Latino Community Priests and Social Action." In *Latino Religions and Civic Activism in the United States,* ed. Gastón Espinosa, Virgilio Elizondo, and Jesse Miranda. New York: Oxford University Press, 2005.

García Canclini, Néstor. *Hybrid Cultures: Strategies for Entering and Leaving Modernity.* Minneapolis: University of Minnesota Press, 1995.

García-Rivera, Alejandro. *The Community of the Beautiful: A Theological Aesthetics.* Collegeville, MN: Liturgical Press, 1999.

Garza, Isidro. "The Development of the Southern Baptist Spanish Speaking Work in California." M.A. thesis. Ph.D diss. Golden Gate Baptist Theological Seminary, 1954.

Gates, Henry Louis, Jr., ed. "Editor's Introduction: Writing 'Race' and the Difference It Makes." In *"Race," Writing, and Difference.* Chicago: University of Chicago Press, 1986.

————. *The Signifying Monkey: A Theory of African-American Literary Criticism.* New York: Oxford University Press, 1988.

Geertz, Clifford. *Interpretation of Culture.* New York: Basic Books, 1973.

Gerald, Geary J. *The Secularization of the California Missions.* Washington, DC: Catholic University of America, 1934.

Gibson, Delbert Lee. "Protestantism in Latin American Acculturation." Ph.D. diss., University of Texas, Austin, 1959.

Giedion, Siegfried. *Mechanization Takes Control*. New York: Oxford University Press, 1948.

Gilroy, Paul. *The Black Atlantic: Modernity and Double Consciousness*. Cambridge, MA: Harvard University Press, 1993.

Goizueta, Roberto S. *Caminemos con Jesús: Toward a Hispanic/Latino Theology of Accompaniment*. Maryknoll, NY: Orbis Books, 1995.

Gómez-Quiñones, Juan. "On Culture." *Revista Chicano-Riqueña* 5, no. 2 (1977): 29–39.

González, Justo. *Mañana: Christian Theology from a Hispanic Perspective*. Nashville: Abingdon Press, 1990.

———, ed. *Each in Our Own Tongue: A History of Hispanic United Methodism*. Nashville: Abingdon Press, 1991.

———. "Characteristics of Latino Protestant Theology," in *Hispanic Christianity within Mainline Protestant Traditions: A Bibliography*, ed. Paul Barton and David Maldonado, Jr. Decatur, GA: Asociación para la Educación Teológica Hispana, 1998.

González, Michelle A. *Sor Juana: Beauty and Justice in the Americas*. Maryknoll, NY: Orbis Books, 2003a.

———. "Unearthing the Latino(a) Imagination: Literature and Theology, Some Methodological Gestures." In *New Horizons in Hispanic/Latino(a) Theology*, ed. Benjamín Valentín. Cleveland: Pilgrim Press, 2003b.

González, Roberto O., and Michael La Velle. *Hispanic Catholics in the U.S.: A Socio-Cultural and Religious Profile*. New York: Northeast Hispanic Pastoral Center, 1985.

Goodall, H. L., Jr. *Divine Signs: Connecting Spirit to Community*. Carbondale: Southern Illinois University Press, 1996.

Goris, Anneris. "Rites for a Rising Nationalism: Religious Meaning and Dominican Community Identity in New York City." In *Old Masks, New Faces: Religion and Latino Identities*, ed. Anthony M. Stevens-Arroyo and Gilbert Cadena. New York: Bildner Center for Western Hemisphere Studies, 1995.

Goss, Robert. *Queering Christ: Beyond Jesus Acted Up*. Cleveland: Pilgrim Press, 2002.

Gould, Jeffrey. *Nicaraguan Indians and the Myth of Mestizaje, 1880–1965*. Durham, NC: Duke University Press, 1998.

Gouveia, Lourdes, and Rogelio Saenz. "Global Forces and Latino Population Growth in the Midwest: A Regional and Subregional Analysis."
Great Plains Research 10, no. 2 (2000): 305–28.

Gracia, Jorge. *Hispanic/Latino Identity: A Philosophical Perspective*. New
York: Routledge, 2000.

Gracia, Jorge J. E., and Pablo de Greiff, eds. *Hispanics/Latinos in the United
States: Ethnicity, Race, and Rights*. New York: Routledge, 2000.

Grandin, Greg. *The Blood of Guatemala: A History of Race and Nation*.
Durham, NC: Duke University Press, 2000.

Grebler, Leo, Joan W. Moore, and Ralph C. Guzman. *The Mexican American People: The Nation's Second Largest Minority*. New York: The Free
Press, 1970.

Greeley, Andrew. "Defections among Hispanics." *America* (July 30, 1988):
61–62.

———. "The Demography of American Catholics: 1965–1990." In *The
Sociology of Andrew W. Greeley*. Atlanta: Scholars Press, 1994.

———. "Defection among Hispanics." *America* 27 (September 1997): 12–
13.

Gregory, Stephen. *Santería in New York City: A Study in Cultural Resistance*. New York: Garland Publishing, 1999.

Grey, Alex. *The Mission of Art*. Boston: Shambhala, 1998.

Griffith, Beatrice. *American Me*. Boston: Houghton Mifflin Company, 1947.

Griffith, James S. *Folk Saints of the Borderlands: Victims, Bandits, and
Healers*. Tucson: Rio Nuevo Publishers, 2003.

Grijalva, Joshua, and Dorothy Grijalva. *Heirs of the Soil*. Atlanta: Home
Mission Board, Southern Baptist Convention, 1950.

———. *A History of Mexican Baptists in Texas 1881–1981*. Dallas: Office of Language Mission, Baptist General Convention of Texas in
Cooperation with the Mexican Baptist Convention of Texas, 1982.

———. "The Story of Hispanic Southern Baptists." *Baptist History and
Heritage* 18, no. 1 (1983): 40–47.

Groody, Daniel G. *Border of Death, Valley of Life: An Immigrant Journey
of Heart and Spirit*. Lanham, MD: Rowan & Littlefield, 2002.

Grotstein, James S. " 'Orphans of the Real': Some Modern and Postmodern
Perspectives on the Neurobiological and Psychosocial Dimensions of
Psychosis and Other Primitive Mental Disorders." In *Contemporary
Treatment of Psychosis: Healing Relationships in the "Decade of the
Brain,"* ed. Jon Allen and Dean Collins. Northvale, NJ: Jason Aronson,
1996.

Gruzinski, Serge. *Painting the Conquest: The Mexican Indians and the European Renaissance*. Trans. Deke Dusinbere. Paris: Flammarion, 1992.

Guerrero, Andrés. *A Chicano Theology*. Maryknoll, NY: Orbis Books, 1987.

Guillén, Miguel. *La Historia del Concilio Latino Americano de Iglesias Cristianas*. Brownsville, TX: Latin American Council of Christian Churches, 1982.

Gutiérrez, David G. *Walls and Mirrors: Mexican Americans, Mexican Immigrants, and the Politics of Ethnicity*. Berkeley: University of California Press, 1995.

Gutiérrez, Gustavo. *Teología de la Liberación*. Lima, Peru: CEP, 1971.

———. *A Theology of Liberation: History, Politics and Salvation*, ed. and trans. Sister Caridad Inda and John Eagleson. Maryknoll, NY: Orbis Books, 1973, 1988.

Gutiérrez, Ramón A. *When Jesus Came, the Corn Mothers Went Away: Marriage, Sexuality, and Power in New Mexico, 1500–1846*. Stanford, CA: Stanford University, 1991.

Guttman, Matthew. *The Meanings of Macho: Being a Man in Mexico City*. Berkeley: University of California Press, 1996.

Guzmán, Betsy. *Hispanic Population: Census 2000 Brief*. Washington, DC: U.S. Census Bureau, 2001.

Guzmán-Blocker, C. *Colonialism y revolución*. México, D.F.: Siglo XXI, 1975.

Habermas, Jürgen. *Knowledge and Human Interests*. London: Heinemann, 1972.

———. *Theory and Practice*. Boston: Beacon Press, 1973.

———. *Life-World and System: A Critique of Functionalist Reason*. Boston: Beacon Press, 1984.

Hackett, Charles W. *Revolt of the Pueblo Indians of New Mexico and Otermín's Attempted Reconquest, 1680–1682*. 2 vols. Albuquerque: University of New Mexico Press, 1942.

Hale, Charles. "Introduction." *Journal of Latin American Anthropology* 2, no. 1 (1996a): 2–3.

———. "Mestizaje, Hybridity and the Cultural Politics of Difference in Post-Revolutionary Central America." *Journal of Latin American Anthropology* 2, no. 1 (1996b): 34–61.

———. "Travel Warning: Elite Appropriations of Hybridity, Mestizaje, Antiracism, Equality, and Other Progressive-Sounding Discourses in

Highland Guatemala." *Journal of American Folklore* 112, no. 445 (1998): 297–315.

———. "Does Multiculturalism Menace? Governance, Cultural Rights, and the Politics of Identity in Guatemala." *Journal of Latin American Studies* 34 (2002): 485–524.

Hardt, Michael, and Antonio Negri. *Empire*. Cambridge, MA: Harvard University Press, 2000.

Harrison, David C. "A Survey of the Administrative and Educational Policies of the Baptist, Methodist, and Presbyterian Churches among Mexican-American People in Texas." M.A. thesis. University of Texas, Austin, 1952.

Harvey, David. *The Condition of Postmodernity: An Enquiry into the Origins of Cultural Change*. Cambridge, MA: Basil Blackwell, 1989.

Harwood, Thomas. *History of New Mexico Spanish and English Missions of the Methodist Episcopal Church from 1850 to 1910*. 2 vols. Albuquerque: El Abogado Press, 1908–10.

Haselden, Kyle. *Death of a Myth: New Locus for Spanish American Faith*. New York: Friendship Press Inc, 1964.

Haynes, Deborah J. *The Vocation of the Artist*. Cambridge: Cambridge University Press, 1997.

Heidegger, Martin. *Being and Time: A Translation of Sein and Zeit*. New York: Harper & Row, 1962.

Hernández, Edwin. "Relocating the Sacred among Latinos: Reflections on Methodology." In *Old Masks, New Faces: Religion and Latino Identities,* ed. Anthony M. Stevens-Arroyo and Gilbert Cadena. New York: Bildner Center for Western Hemisphere Studies, 1995.

———. "Social Science Literature on Hispanic Protestantism." In *Hispanic Christianity within Mainline Protestant Traditions: A Bibliography,* ed. Paul Barton and David Maldonado. Decatur, GA: Asociación para la Educación Teológica Hispana, 1998.

———. "Moving from the Cathedral to Storefront Churches: Understanding Religious Growth and Decline among Latino Protestants." In *Protestantes/Protestants: Hispanic Christianity within Mainline Traditions,* ed. David Maldonado Jr. Nashville: Abingdon Press, 1999.

Hernández, José. *Martín Fierro*. Barcelona: Labor, 1972.

Hernández-Avila, Inés. "La Mesa del Santo Niño de Atocha and the Conchero Dance Tradition of Mexico-Tenochtilín: Religious Healing in

Urban Mexico and the United States." In *Religion and Healing in America,* ed. Linda Barnes and Susan S. Sered. New York: Oxford University Press, 2005.

Hernández Cuevas, Marco Polo. *African Mexicans and the Discourse on Modern Nation.* Lanham, MD: University Press of America, 2004.

Hillman, James. *Re-Visioning Psychology.* New York: Harper Collins, 1975.

Hodges, B. A. *A History of Mexican Mission Work Conducted in the Synod of Texas.* Waxahachie, TX: n.p., 1931a.

———. *Our Mexican Missions in Texas.* Waxahachie, TX: n.p., 1931b.

Hoey, Brian A. "What Is Ethnography?" University of Michigan. Available online at *http://www-personal.umich.edu/~bhoey/General%20Site/general_defn-ethnography.htm,* 2004.

Holland, Clifton J. *The Religious Dimension in Hispanic Los Angeles: A Protestant Case Study.* South Pasadena, CA: William Carey Library, 1974.

Holloway, Joseph E., ed. *Africanisms in American Culture.* Bloomington: University of Indiana Press, 1990.

Hout, Michael, and Claude S. Fischer. "Why More Americans Have No Religious Preference: Politics and Generations." *American Sociological Review* 67 (2002): 165–90.

Hunt, Larry L. "The Spirit of Hispanic Protestantism in the United States: National Survey Comparisons of Catholics and Non-Catholics." *Social Science Quarterly* 79, no. 4 (1998): 828–45.

———. "Hispanic Protestantism in the United States: Trends by Decade and Generation." *Social Forces* 77, no. 4 (1999): 1601–24.

———. "Religion and Secular Status among Hispanics in the United States: The Varieties of Hispanic Protestantism." *Social Science Quarterly* March 2000: 344–62.

Hunt, Mary Elizabeth. "Feminist Liberation Theology: The Development of Method in Construction." Ph.D. diss., Graduate Theological Union, Berkeley, 1980.

Huntington, Samuel. "The Hispanic Challenge." *Foreign Policy.* Electronic edition. March–April 2004.

Hurtado, Juan. *An Attitudinal Study of Social Distance between the Mexican American and the Church.* San Antonio: Mexican American Cultural Center, 1975.

Hymer, Evangeline. "A Study of Social Attitudes of Adult Mexican Immigrants in Los Angeles and Vicinity." M.A. thesis, University of Southern California, 1923.

Isasi-Díaz, Ada María. "Mujeristas: A Name of Our Own." In *The Future of Liberation Theology: Essays in Honor of Gustavo Gutiérrez,* ed. Marc C. Ellis and Otto Maduro. Maryknoll, NY: Orbis Books, 1989.

———. *En la Lucha, In the Struggle: A Hispanic Woman's Liberation Theology.* Minneapolis: Fortress Press, 1993, 2004.

———. *Mujerista Theology.* Maryknoll, NY: Orbis Books, 1996.

———. "Doing Theology as Mission." *Apuntes* 18, no. 4 (Winter 1998): 99–111.

———. "Response." In *The Ties That Bind: African American and Hispanic/Latino/a Theologies in Dialogue,* ed. Anthony Pinn and Benjamín Valentín. New York: Continuum, 2001a.

———. "A New Mestizaje/Mulatez: Reconceptualizing Difference." In *A Dream Unfinished: Theological Reflections on America from the Margins,* ed. Eleazar Fernandez and Fernando Segovia. Maryknoll, NY: Orbis Books, 2001b.

———. *La Lucha Continues: Mujerista Theology.* Maryknoll, NY: Orbis Books, 2004.

Isasi-Díaz, Ada María, Milagros Peña, and Yolanda Tarango. *Latina Women's Religion, Sexuality, and Corporeality Study.* Madison, NJ: Drew University, 1996.

Isasi-Díaz, Ada María, and Yolanda Tarango. *Hispanic Women: Prophetic Voice in the Church.* San Francisco: Harper and Row, 1988.

Jacobson, Matthew Frye. *Whiteness of a Different Color: European Immigrants and the Alchemy of Race.* Cambridge, MA: Harvard University Press, 1998.

James, William. *Pragmatism and Other Writings.* Cambridge, MA: Harvard University Press, 1975.

Jameson, Fredric. *Postmodernism, or, the Cultural Logic of Late Capitalism.* London: Verso, 1991.

Johnson, J. B. "The Allelujahs: A Religious Cult in Northern New Mexico." *Southwest Review of the World* (July 1923): 131–39.

Jones, Robert C., *The Religious Life of the Mexican in Chicago.* Report, n.p., 1929.

Jones, Robert C., and Louis R. Wilson. *The Mexican in Chicago.* Chicago: Comity Commission of the Chicago Church Federation, 1931.

Jones, Serene. *Feminist Theory and Christian Theology: Cartographies of Grace.* Minneapolis: Fortress Press, 2000.

Jones Walker, Randi. *Protestantism in the Sangre de Cristos, 1850–1920.* Albuquerque: University of New Mexico Press, 1991.

Jordan, Winthrop D. "American Chiaroscuro: The Status and Definition of Mulattoes in the British Colonies." *William and Mary Quarterly* 3d ser. (April 1962): 183–200.

Kibbe, Pauline R. *Latin Americans in Texas.* Albuquerque: University of New Mexico Press, 1946.

Kienle, John E. "Housing Conditions among the Mexican Population of Los Angeles." M.A. thesis, University of Southern California, 1912.

Kiev, Ari. *Curanderismo: Mexican-American Folk Psychiatry.* New York: Free Press, 1968.

Klor de Alva, Jorge. "California Chicano Literature and Pre-Columbian Motifs: Foil and Fetish." *Confluencia: Revista Hispánica de Cultura y Literatura* 1 (1986): 18–26.

———. "Postcolonialization of the (Latin) American Experience: A Reconsideration of 'Colonialism,' 'Postcolonialism,' and 'Mestizaje.' " In *After Colonialism*, ed. Gyan Prakash. Princeton: Princeton University Press, 1995.

Köhler, Angelika. "The New World Man: Magical Realism in Rudolfo Anaya's *Bless Me, Ultima.*" In *U.S. Latino Literatures and Cultures: Transnational Perspectives,* ed. Francisco A. Lomelí and Karin Ikas. Heidelberg, Germany: Universitatsverlag C. Winter, 2000.

Kosmin, Barry, and Seymour Lachman. *One Nation Under God: Religion in Contemporary American Society.* New York: Harmony Books, 1993.

Kosmin, Barry, Egon Mayer, and, Ariela Keysar. *American Religious Identification Survey 2001.* New York: Graduate Center of the City University of New York, 2001.

Lacan, Jacques. *Écrits.* Paris: Editions du Seuil, 1966.

———. *Les quatre concepts fondamentaux de la psychanalyse.* Paris: Éditions du Seuil, 1973.

Lambert, Frank. *The Founding Fathers and the Place of Religion in America.* Princeton: Princeton University Press, 2003.

Lame Deer, John, and Richard Erdoes. *Lame Deer, Seeker of Visions.* Englewood Cliffs, NJ: Simon & Schuster, 1972.

Lara-Braud, Jorge. "Our Spanish-American Neighbors." *Christian Century* 85, no. 2 (1968): 43–45.

Lawrence, Una Roberts. *Winning the Border: Baptist Missions among the Spanish-Speaking Peoples of the Border.* Atlanta: Home Mission Board, Southern Baptist Convention, 1935.

León, Luis D. "Foreword." In *Curanderismo: Mexican American Folk Healing*, by Robert T. Trotter II and Juan Antonio Chavira. 2nd ed. Athens, GA: University of Georgia Press, 1997.

———. " 'Soy una Curandera y Soy una Católica": Poetics of a Mexican Healing Tradition." In *Horizons of the Sacred: Mexican Traditions in U.S. Catholicism*, ed. Timothy Matovina and Gary Riebe-Stressa, SVD. Ithaca, NY: Cornell University Press, 2002.

———. *La Llorona's Children: Religion, Life and Death in the U.S.-Mexican Borderlands*. Berkeley: University of California Press, 2004.

———. "César Chávez and Mexican American Civil Religion." In *Latino Religions and Civic Activism in the United States*, ed. Gastón Espinosa, Virgilio Elizondo, and Jesse Miranda. New York: Oxford University Press, 2005.

León-Portilla, Miguel. *Los antiguos mexicanos a través de sus crónicas y cantares*. Mexico: Fondo de Cultura Económica, 1961, 1988.

———. *Aztec Thought and Culture: A Study of the Ancient Náhuatl Mind*. Trans. Jack Emory Davis. Norman: University of Oklahoma Press, 1963.

———, ed. *Native Mesoamerican Spirituality: Ancient Myths, Discourses, Stories, Doctrines, Hymns, Poems From the Aztec, Yucatec, Quiché-Maya and Other Sacred Traditions*. Trans. Miguel León-Portilla, J. O. Arthur Anderson, Charles E. Dibble, and Munro S. Edmonson. Ramsey, NJ: Paulist Press, 1980.

———. *Endangered Cultures*. Dallas: Southern Methodist University Press, 1990.

Levitt, Peggy, Josh DeWind, and Steven Vertovec. "Transnational Migration: International Perspectives." Special Issue. *International Migration Review* 37, no. 3 (2003).

Lewis, C. S. *The Four Loves*. New York: Harcourt, 1960.

Limón, José. *Dancing with the Devil: Society and Cultural Poetics in Mexican-American South Texas*. Madison: University of Wisconsin Press, 1994.

Lipsey, Roger. *An Art of Our Own: The Spiritual in Twentieth-Century Art*. Boston: Shambhala Publications, 1988.

Lipsitz, George. *The Possessive Investment in Whiteness: How White People Profit from Identity Politics*. Philadelphia: Temple University Press, 1998.

Lloyd-Moffett, Stephen R. "The Mysticism and Social Action of César Chávez." In *Latino Religions and Civic Activism in the United States*, ed. Gastón Espinosa, Virgilio Elizondo, and Jesse Miranda. New York: Oxford University Press, 2005.

Lomelí, Francisco, and Karin Ikas, eds. *U.S. Latino Literatures and Cultures.* Heidelberg: Universitätsverlag, 2000.

López Pulido, Alberto. *The Sacred World of the Penitentes.* Washington, DC: Smithsonian Institution Press, 2000.

Lorde, Audrey. "Uses of the Erotic: The Erotic as Power." In *Sister Outsider.* Trumansburg, NY: Crossing Press, 1984.

Los Lobos. "Good Morning Azltán," musical recording, and "The Making of 'Good Morning Aztlán' Documentary." New York: Mammoth Records, 2002.

Lucero-White, Aurora. "Los Pastores de Las Vegas." M.A. thesis, New Mexico Normal University, Las Vegas, 1932.

———. *The Folklore of New Mexico.* Santa Fe, NM: n.p., 1941.

Lugones, María. "Structure/Antistructure and Agency under Oppression." *Journal of Philosophy* 81 (1990): 504–5.

———. "On the Logic of Pluralist Feminism." In *Feminist Ethics,* ed. Claudia Card. Lawrence, KS: University Press of Kansas, 1991.

Machado, Daisy L. "The Writing of Religious History in the United States: A Critical Assessment." In *Hispanic Christianity within Mainline Protestant Traditions: A Bibliography,* ed. Paul Barton and David Maldonado Jr. Decatur, GA: Asociación para la Educación Teológica Hispana, 1998.

———. *Of Borders and Margins: Hispanic Disciples in Texas, 1888–1945.* New York: Oxford University Press, 2003.

Macklin, June. "Curanderismo and Espiritismo: Complementary Approaches to Traditional Health Services." In *The Chicano Experience,* ed. Stanley A. West and June Macklin. Boulder, CO: Westview Press, 1979.

Madsen, Claudia. *A Study of Change in Mexican Folk Medicine.* New Orleans: Tulane University Middle American Research Institute, 1965.

Madsen, William, and Claudia Madsen. *A Guide to Mexican Witchcraft.* Claremont, CA: Ocelot Press, 1977.

Maduro, Otto. "Some Theoretical Implications of Latin American Liberation Theology for the Sociology of Religion." In *Religion and Social Order,* ed. David G. Bromley. Greenwich, CT: JAI Press, 1991.

———. "Directions for a Reassessment of Latina/o Religion." In *Enigmatic Powers: Syncretism with African and Indigenous Peoples' Religions among Latinos,* ed. Anthony M. Stevens-Arroyo and Andres I. Pérez y Mena. New York: Bildner Center for Western Hemisphere Studies, 1995.

Maldonado, David, Jr., ed. *Protestantes/Protestants: Hispanic Christianity within Mainline Traditions*. Nashville: Abingdon Press, 1999.

Mallon, Florencia. "Constructing Mestizaje in Latin America: Authenticity, Marginality and Gender in the Claiming of Ethnic Identities." *Journal of Latin American Anthropology* 2, no. 1 (1996): 170–81.

Mannheim, Karl. *Ideology and Utopia: An Introduction to the Sociology of Knowledge*. New York: Harcourt Brace Jovanovich, 1936.

Marcos, Sylvia. "The Sacred Earth." *Concilium,* ed. Leonardo Boff and Virgilio Elizondo. Vol. 5, no. 261 (1995): 27–37.

Marcus, Joyce. *Mesoamerican Writing Systems: Propaganda, Myth, and History in Four Ancient Civilizations*. Princeton, NJ: Princeton University Press, 1992.

Marcuse, Herbert. *Eros and Civilization: A Philosophical Inquiry into Freud*. Boston: Beacon Press, 1966.

Martell-Otero, Loida. "Women Doing Theology: Una Perspectiva Evangélica." *Apuntes* 14 (1994): 67–85.

———. "Of Santos and Saints: Salvation from the Periphery." In *Perspectivas: Occasional Papers* 4 (Summer 2001): 7–38

Martí, José. " 'Carta a Manuel A. Mercado,' Campamento de Dos Ríos, 18 de mayo de 1895." In *Obras Completas* 20. La Habana: Editorial Nacional de Cuba, 1963–66.

———. *Nuestra América*. Caracas: Biblioteca Ayacucho, 1977.

Matovina, Timothy. *Tejano Religion and Ethnicity: San Antonio, 1821– 1860*. Austin: University of Texas Press, 1995.

Matovina, Timothy, and Gerald E. Poyo, eds. *¡Presente! U.S. Latino Catholics from Colonial Origins to the Present*. Maryknoll, NY: Orbis Books, 2000.

Matovina, Timothy, and Gary Riebe-Estrella. "Días de los Muertos." In *Horizons of the Sacred: Mexican Catholic Traditions in U.S. Catholicism,* ed. Timothy Matovina and Gary Riebe-Estrella. Ithaca: Cornell University Press, 2002.

McClintock Fulkerson, Mary. *Changing the Subject: Women's Discourse and Feminist Theology*. Minneapolis: Fortress Press, 1994.

McCombs, Vernon M. *From over the Border: A Study of the Mexican in the United States*. New York: Council for Women for Home Missions and Missionary Education Movement, 1925.

McEuen, William. "A Survey of the Mexicans in Los Angeles." M.A. thesis, University of Southern California, 1914.

McGarrity, Gayle, and Osvaldo Cárdenas. "Cuba." In *No Longer Invisible: Afro-Latin Americans Today,* ed. Minority Rights Group. London: Minority Rights Publications, 1995.

McGuire, Meredith. "Linking Theory and Method for the Study of Latino Religiosity in the United States Context." In *Old Masks, New Faces: Religion and Latino Identities,* ed. Anthony M. Stevens-Arroyo and Gilbert R. Cadena. New York: Bildner Center for Western Hemisphere Studies, 1995.

McKee Irwin, Robert. *Mexican Masculinities.* Minneapolis: University of Minnesota Press, 2003.

McLean, Robert N. "Getting God Counted among the Mexicans." *Missionary Review of the World* (May 1923): 363.

———. *The Northern Mexican.* New York: Home Mission Council, 1930.

McNamara, Patrick. "Dynamics of the Catholic Church from Pastoral to Social Concerns." In *The Mexican American People,* ed. Leo Grebler, Joan Moore, and Ralph Guzman. New York: Macmillan Free Press, 1970.

———. "Catholicism, Assimilation and the Chicano Movement: Los Angeles as a Case Study." In *Chicanos and Native Americans,* ed. Rodolfo O. de la Garza, Z. Anthony Kruszewski, and Tomás A. Arciniega. Englewood Cliffs, NJ: Prentice Hall, 1973.

———. "Assumptions, Theories, and Methods in the Study of Latino Religion after 25 Years." In *Old Masks, New Faces: Religion and Latino Identities,* ed. Anthony M. Stevens-Arroyo and Gilbert R. Cadena. New York: Bildner Center for Western Hemisphere Studies, 1995.

McNeil, Norman. *Curanderos of South Texas and Horns on the Toads.* Dallas: Southern Methodist University, 1959.

Medina, Lara. "Broadening the Discourse at the Theological Table: An Overview of Latino Theology 1968–1993." *Latino Studies Journal 5,* no. 3 (September 1993): 10–36.

———. "Communicating with the Dead: Spiritual and Cultural Healing in Chicano/a Communities." In *Religion and Healing in America,* ed. Linda Barnes and Susan S. Sered. New York: Oxford University Press, 2005.

Medina, Lara, and Gilbert R. Cadena. "Días de los Muertos: Public Ritual, Community Renewal, and Popular Religion in Los Angeles." In *Horizons of the Sacred: Mexican Catholic Traditions in U.S. Catholicism,* ed.

Timothy Matovina and Gary Riebe-Estrella. Ithaca: Cornell University Press, 2002.

Mejido, Manuel. "A Critique of the 'Aesthetic Turn' in U.S. Hispanic Theology: A Dialogue with Roberto Goizueta and the Positing of a New Paradigm." *Journal of Hispanic/Latino Theology* 8, no. 3 (2001): 18–48.

———. "Propaedeutic to the Critique of the Study of U.S. Hispanic Religion: A Polemic against Intellectual Assimilation." *Journal of Hispanic/Latino Theology* 10, no. 2 (2002): 31–63.

Mencke, John G. *Mulattoes and Race Mixture, American Attitudes and Images: 1865–1918.* Ann Arbor: University of Michigan Research Papers, 1979.

Mesa-Bains, Amalia. "Curatorial Statement." In *Ceremony of Spirit: Nature and Memory in Contemporary Latino Art.* San Francisco: Mexican Museum, 1993.

Mills, C. Wright, Clarence Senior, and Rose Kohn Goldsen. *The Puerto Rican Journey.* New York: Harper & Row, 1950.

Montejo, Esteban. *The Autobiography of a Runaway Slave.* Ed. Miguel Barnet. Trans. Jocasta Innes. New York: Pantheon Books, 1968.

Moore, Carlos. *Castro, the Blacks, and Africa.* Los Angeles: Center for Afro-American Studies, University of California, 1988.

Moore, Joan. "Protestants and Mexicans." In *The Mexican American People,* ed. Leo Grebler, Joan Moore, and Ralph Guzman. New York: Macmillan Free Press, 1970.

Moore-Gilbert, Bart. *Postcolonial Theory: Contexts, Practices, Politics.* London: Verso, 1997.

Moraga, Cherríe. *The Last Generation: Prose and Poetry.* Boston: South End, 1993.

Morales, Adam. *American Baptists with a Spanish Accent.* Los Angeles: Judson Press, 1964.

Morales, Ed. *Living in Spanglish: The Search for Latino Identity in America.* New York: LA Weekly Books/St. Martin's Press, 2002.

Muñoz, José Esteban. *Disidentifications: Queers of Color and the Performance of Politics.* Minneapolis: University of Minnesota Press, 1999.

Muoss, Meryl. *Midcentury Pioneers and Protestants.* New York: Protestant Council of the City of New York, 1954.

Murphy, Joseph M. *Santería: African Spirits in America.* Boston: Beacon Press, 1993.

————. *Working the Spirit: Ceremonies of the African Diaspora.* Boston: Beacon Press, 1994.

Murray, Stephen O. *Latin American Male Homosexualities.* Albuquerque: University of New Mexico Press, 1995.

Nañez, Alfredo. *History of the Rio Grande Conference of the United Methodist Church.* Dallas: Bridwell Library, Southern Methodist University, 1980.

Nañez, Clotilde. "Hispanic Clergy Wives: Their Contribution to United Methodism in the Southwest, Later Nineteenth Century to the Present." In *Women in New Worlds: Historical Perspectives on the Wesleyan Tradition,* ed. Hilah F. Thomas and Rosemary Kinner Keller. Nashville: Abingdon Press, 1981.

National Catholic Welfare Conference. *The Spanish-Speaking of the Southwest and West.* Washington, DC: National Catholic Welfare Conference, 1943.

National Opinion Research Center (NORC). *General Social Surveys, 1972–2000: Cumulative Codebook.* Chicago: University of Chicago Press, 2001.

Nederveen Pieterse, Jan. *Globalization and Culture: Global Melange.* Lanham, MD: Rowman and Littlefield, 2004.

Neuman, Lawrence. *Social Research Methods: Qualitative and Quantitative.* Vols. 1 and 2. Boston: Allyn and Bacon, 1991.

Nicholson, Linda, ed. *Feminism and Postmodernism.* New York: Routledge, 1990.

Nieto, Leo D. "The Chicano Movement and the Churches in the United States." *Perkins Journal* 29, no. 1 (1975): 32–41.

Nietzsche, Friedrich. *Thus Spoke Zarathustra: A Book for None and All.* Trans. Walter Kaufmann. New York: Penguin Publishing, 1954.

Nixon, Sean. "Exhibiting Masculinity." In *Representation: Cultural Representations and Signifying Practices,* ed. Stuart Hall. London: SAGE Publications, 1997.

Olalquiaga, Celeste. *Megalopolis: Contemporary Cultural Sensibilities.* Minneapolis: University of Minneapolis Press, 1992.

Omi, Michael, and Howard Winant. *Racial Formation in the United States: From the 1960s to the 1990s.* New York: Routledge, 1994.

Orozco, E. C. *Republican Protestantism in Aztlán.* Glendale, CA: Petereins Press, 1981.

Orsi, Robert O., ed. *Gods of the City: Religion and the American Urban Landscape.* Bloomington: Indiana University Press, 1999.

————. "Religious Thought and Practice among Mexican Baptists of the United States, 1900–1947." Ph.D. diss., University of Southern California, 1950.

Ortegón, Samuel M. "Mexican Religious Population of Los Angeles." M.A. thesis, University of Southern California, 1932.

————. "The Religious Thought and Practice among Mexican Baptists of the United States, 1900–1947." Ph.D. diss., University of Southern California, 1950.

Ortiz, Fernando. *El engaño de las razas.* La Habana: Editorial de Ciencias Sociales, 1975.

Oxnam, Bromley G. "Mexican Americans from the Standpoint of Religious Forces of the City." *Annals of the American Academy* 93 (1921): 130–33.

Paden, William E. "A New Comparativism: Reply to Panelists." *Method and Theory in the Study of Religion* B-1 (1996): 37–49.

Paredes, Americo. "Estados Unidos, Mexico, y el machismo." *Journal of Inter-American Studies* 9, no. 1 (1966): 65–84.

Park, Yong Hak. "A Study of the Methodist Mexican Mission in Dallas." M.A. thesis, Southern Methodist University, 1936.

Parker, Everett C. "New York's Spanish-Speaking Churches." *The Christian Century* 12 (April 1961): 162–64.

Paz, Octavio. *El laberinto de la soledad.* Mexico, D.F.: Fondo de Cultural Económica, 1959.

Peirce, Charles Sanders. *Collected Papers. Vol. 5, Pragmatism and Pragmaticism.* Cambridge, MA: Harvard University Press, 1934.

Peña, Milagros. "Devising a Study on Religion and the Latina Experience." *Social Compass: International Review of the Sociology of Religion* 49, no. 2 (2002): 281–94.

Peña, Milagros, and Lisa Frehill. "Latina Religious Practice: Analyzing Cultural Dimensions in Measures of Religiosity." *Journal for the Social Scientific Study of Religion* 37, no. 4 (1998): 620–35.

Pérez, Laura. "Spirit Glyphs: Reimagining Art and Artist in the Work of Chicana Tlamatinime." *Modern Fiction Studies* 40, no. 1 (Spring 1998): 37–76.

————. "El Desorden, Nationalism, and Chicana/o Aesthetics." In *Between Woman and Nation: Nationalisms, Transnational Feminisms, and the State,* ed. Caren Kaplan, Norma Alarcón, and Minoo Moallem. Durham, NC: Duke University Press, 1999.

————. "Hybrid Spiritualities and Chicana Altar-Based Art: The Work of Amalia Mesa-Bains." In *Mexican American Religions,* ed. Gastón Espinosa and Mario T. García (Durham, NC: Duke University Press, 2007).

Pérez, Louis A., Jr. *On Becoming Cuban: Identity, Nationality, and Culture.* Chapel Hill: University of North Carolina Press, 1999.

Perrone, Bobette, H. Henrietta Stockel, and Victoria Krueger. *Medicine Women, Curanderas, and Women Doctors.* Norman: University of Oklahoma Press, 1989.

Pina, Michael. "The Archaic, Historical, and Mythicized Dimensions of Aztlán." In *Aztlán: Essays on the Chicano Homeland,* ed. Rudolfo A. Anaya and Francisco Lomeli. Albuquerque: University of New Mexico Press, 1989.

Polk, Patrick A., Michael Owen Jones, Claudia J. Hernández, and Reyna C. Ronelli. "Miraculous Migrants to the City of Angels: Perceptions of El Santo Niño de Atocha and San Simón as Sources of Health and Healing." In *Religion and Healing in America,* ed. Linda Barnes and Susan S. Sered. New York: Oxford University Press, 2005.

Portes, Alejandro, and Alex Stepick. *City of the Edge.* Berkeley: University of California Press, 1994.

Pulido, Alberto L. *The Sacred World of the Penitentes.* Washington, DC: Smithsonian Institution Press, 2000.

Ramírez, Arthur. "Review of 'Borderlands/La Frontera: The New Mestiza' by Gloria Anzaldúa." *Americas Review* (Fall–Winter 1989): 185–87.

Ramos, Julio. "Memorial de un accidente: Contingencia y tecnología en los exvotos de la Virgen de Quiche." Keynote address. New York University and Columbia University Graduate Student Conference. New York, February 1, 1997.

Rankin, Melinda. *Twenty Years among the Mexicans: A Narrative of Missionary Labor.* Cincinnati: Chase and Hall Publishers, 1875.

Rebolledo, Tey Diana. *Women Singing in the Snow: A Cultural Analysis of Chicana Literature.* Tucson: University of Arizona Press, 1995.

Recinos, Harold J. "Popular Religion, Political Identity, and Life-Story Testimony in an Hispanic Community." In *The Ties That Bind: African American and Hispanic American/Latino/a Theologies in Dialogue,* ed. Anthony B. Pinn and Benjamín Valentín. New York: Continuum, 2001.

Reyes, Ruben. "Prolegomena to Chicano Theology." D.Min Project, Claremont School of Theology, 1974.

Ríos, Elizabeth D. "The Ladies Are Warriors": Latina Pentecostalism and Faith-Based Activism in New York City." In *Latino Religions and Civic Activism in the United States,* ed. Gastón Espinosa, Virgilio Elizondo, and Jesse Miranda (New York: Oxford University Press, 2005), 197–217.

Rodó, José Enrique. *Ariel.* Barcelona: Editorial Cervantes, 1930.

Rodríguez, Jeanette. *Our Lady of Guadalupe: Faith and Empowerment among Mexican American Women.* Austin: University of Texas Press, 1994.

———. *Stories We Live: Cuentos que vivimos.* New York: Paulist Press, 1996.

Rodríguez, José David, and Loida I. Martell-Otero, eds. *Teología en Conjunto: A Collaborative Hispanic Protestant Theology.* Louisville: Westminster/John Knox Press, 1997.

Rodríguez-Díaz, Daniel R. and David Cortés-Fuentes. *Hidden Stories: Unveiling the History of the Latino Church.* Decatur, GA: AETH, 1994.

Roeder, Beatrice A. *Chicano Folk Medicine from Los Angeles, California.* Berkeley: University of California Press, 1988.

Romano, Octavio I. *Voices: Readings from El Grito.* Berkeley, CA: Quinto Sol, 1973.

Romero, C. Gilbert. *Hispanic Devotional Piety: Tracing the Biblical Roots.* Maryknoll, NY: Orbis Books, 1991.

Romero, Juan, and Moises Sandoval. *Reluctant Dawn: Historia del Padre A. J. Martínez, Cura de Taos.* San Antonio: Mexican-American Cultural Center Press, 1975.

Romo, Ricardo. *East Los Angeles: History of a Barrio.* Austin: University of Texas Press, 1983.

Roof, Wade Clark. *Spiritual Marketplace: Baby Boomers and the Remaking of American Religion.* Princeton: Princeton University Press, 1999.

Rorty, Richard. *Consequences of Pragmatism: Essays, 1972–1980.* Minneapolis: University of Minnesota Press, 1982.

Rosaldo, Renato. *Culture and Truth: The Remaking of Social Analysis.* Boston: Beacon Press, 1989.

Rosales, F. Arturo. *Chicano! The History of the Mexican American Civil Rights Movement.* Houston: Arte Público, 1997.

Rostow, W. W. *The Stages of Economic Growth: A Non-Communist Manifesto.* Cambridge: Cambridge University Press, 1962.

Roundy, Robert W. "The Mexican in Our Midst." *Missionary Review of the World* (May 1921).

Rout, Leslie B., Jr. *The African Experience in Spanish America: 1502 to the Present Day.* Cambridge: Cambridge University Press, 1976.

Rueter, Edward Byron. *Race Mixture: Studies in Intermarriage and Miscegenation.* New York: Johnson Reprint Corporation, 1970.

Ruether, Rosemary Radford. "A Feminist Perspective." In *Doing Theology in a Divided World,* ed. Virginia Febella and Sergio Torres. Maryknoll, NY: Orbis Books, 1985.

Ruíz, Vicki. *Cannery Women, Cannery Lives: Mexican Women, Unionization, and the California Food Processing Industry 1930–1950.* Albuquerque: University of New Mexico Press, 1987.

——. *From Out of the Shadows: Mexican Women in Twentieth-Century America.* New York: Oxford University Press, 1998.

Ruiz Baia, Larissa. "Rethinking Transnationalism: Reconstructing National Identities among Peruvian Catholics in New Jersey." *Journal of Interamerican Studies and World Affairs* 41, no. 4 (1999): 93–109.

——. "Rethinking Transnationalism: National Identities among Peruvian Catholics in New Jersey." In *Christianity, Social Change, and Globalization in the Americas,* ed. Anna Peterson, Manuel Vásquez, and Philip Williams. New Brunswick, NJ: Rutgers University Press, 2001.

Russell, Letty. *Human Liberation in a Feminist Perspective — A Theology.* Philadelphia: Westminster Press, 1974.

Saenz, Rogelio, and Cruz Torres. "Latinos in Rural America." In *Challenges to Rural America in the Twenty-First Century,* ed. David L. Brown and Louis E. Swanson. University Park: Pennsylvania State University Press, 2003.

Said, Edward W. *Culture and Imperialism.* New York: Vintage Books, 1994.

Salpointe, Jean Baptiste. *Soldiers of the Cross: Notes on the Ecclesiastical History of New Mexico, Arizona, and Colorado.* Banning, CA: St. Boniface's Industrial School, 1898.

Sánchez, George. *Becoming Mexican American: Ethnicity, Culture and Identity in Chicano Los Angeles, 1900–1945.* New York: Oxford University Press, 1993.

Sánchez-Tranquilino, Marcos, curator. *The Chicano Codices: Encountering Art of the Americas.* San Francisco: Mexican Museum, 1992.

Sánchez-Walsh, Arlene M. *Latino Pentecostal Identity: Evangelical Faith, Self, and Society.* New York: Columbia University Press, 2003.

Sandoval, Moises, ed. *Fronteras: A History of the Latin American Church in the U.S.A. since 1513.* San Antonio: Mexican American Cultural Center, 1983.

————. *On the Move: A History of the Hispanic Church in the United States.* Maryknoll, NY: Orbis Books, 1990.

Sanjinés, Javier. *Mestizaje Upside-Down: Aesthetic Politics in Modern Bolivia.* Pittsburgh: University of Pittsburgh Press, 2004.

Saragoza, Alex M. "Recent Chicano Historiography: An Interpretive Essay." *Aztlán: A Journal of Chicano Studies* 19, no. 1 (1999): 1–77.

Sarmiento, Domingo Faustino. *Facundo: Civilización y barbarie.* Madrid: Cátedra, 1990.

Sathler, Josué A., and Amós Nascimento. "Black Masks on White Faces: Liberation Theology and the Quest for Syncretism in the Brazilian Context." In *Liberation Theologies, Postmodernity, and the Americas,* ed. David Batstone, Eduardo Mendieta, Lois Ann Lorentzen, and Dwight N. Hopkins. London: Routledge, 1997.

Saussure, Ferdinand. *Course in General Linguistics.* Ed. Charles Bally and Albert Sechehaye. Trans. Wade Baskin. New York: Philosophical Library, 1959.

Scholes, France V. "Documents for the History of New Mexican Missions in the Seventeenth Century." *New Mexico Historical Review* 4 (1929): 195–99.

————. "The First Decade of the Inquisition in New Mexico." *New Mexico Historical Review* 10 (1935): 195–241.

————. "Church and State in New Mexico, 1610–1650." *New Mexico Historical Review* 11 (1936): 9–76 and 15 (1940): 78–106.

————. *Troublous Times in New Mexico, 1659–1670.* Albuquerque: University of New Mexico Press, 1942.

Schüssler Fiorenza, Elisabeth. *Rhetoric and Ethic: The Politics of Biblical Studies.* Minneapolis: Fortress Press, 1999.

Schutte, Ofelia. "Negotiating Latina Identities." In *Hispanics/Latinos in the United States: Ethnicity, Race, and Rights,* ed. Jorge J. E. Gracia and Pablo de Greiff. New York: Routledge, 2000.

Segovia, Fernando F. "Two Places and No Place on Which to Stand: Mixture and Otherness in Hispanic American Theology." *Journal of Religion and Culture* 27, no. 1 (Winter 1992): 26–40.

————. "Two Places and No Place on Which to Stand: Mixture and Otherness in Hispanic American Theology." In *Mestizo Christianity: Theology from the Latino Perspective,* ed. Arturo J. Bañuelas. Maryknoll, NY: Orbis Books, 1995.

————. "Introduction: Minority Studies and Christian Studies." In *A Dream Unfinished: Theological Reflections on America from the Margins,* ed.

Eleazar Fernandez and Fernando Segovia. Maryknoll, NY: Orbis Books, 2001.

Sharpe, Eric J. *Comparative Religion: A History.* London: Duckworth, 1987.

Sherkat, Darren E. "Tracking the Restructuring of American Religion: Religious Affiliation and Patterns of Religious Mobility, 1973–1998." *Social Forces* 79, no. 4 (2001): 1459–93.

Simmons, Marc. *Witchcraft in the Southwest: Spanish and Indian Supernaturalism on the Rio Grande.* Lincoln: University of Nebraska Press, 1980.

Smart, Ninian. *The Phenomenon of Religion.* London: Macmillan, 1973.

Smith, Andrea. "Anthropology." In *Handbook on U.S. Theologies of Liberation,* ed. Miguel A. De La Torre. St. Louis: Chalice Press, 2004.

Smith, Clara Gertrude. "The Development of the Mexican People in the Community of Watts." M.A. thesis, University of Southern California, 1933.

Smith, H. W. *Strategies of Social Research: The Methodological Imagination.* Englewood Cliffs, NJ: Prentice Hall, 1975.

Smith, Jonathan Z. *Imagining Religion: From Babylon to Jonestown.* Chicago: University of Chicago Press, 1988.

Smith, R. Drew. *African American Churches and Civic Culture in Post–Civil Rights America.* Durham, NC: Duke University Press, 2003.

Smith, Rosemary E. "The Work of Bishops' Committee for the Spanish-Speaking on Behalf of the Migrant Worker." M.A. thesis, The Catholic University of America, 1958.

Sobrino, Jon. *Christology at the Crossroads.* New York: Orbis Books, 1978.

Soto, Antonio. *The Chicano and the Church: Study of a Minority within a Religious Institution.* Denver: Marfel Associates, 1975.

Spelman, Elizabeth V. *Inessential Woman: Problems of Exclusion in Feminist Thought.* Boston: Beacon Press, 1988.

Spivak, Gayatri. "Can the Subaltern Speak?" In *Marxism and the Interpretation of Culture,* ed. Carry Nelson and Lawrence Grossberg. Urbana: University of Illinois Press, 1988.

Stapleton, Ernest. "The History of the Baptist Missions in New Mexico, 1849–1866." M.A. thesis, University of New Mexico, 1954.

Stavans, Ilan. *Spanglish: The Making of a New American Language.* New York: HarperCollins, 2003.

Steensland, Brian, Jerry Z. Park, Mark D. Regnerus, Lynn D. Robinson, W. Bradford Wilcox, and Robert D. Woodberry. "The Measure of

American Religion: Toward Improving the State of the Art." *Social Forces* 79, no. 1 (September 2000): 291–318.

Stevens-Arroyo, Anthony M. *Prophets Denied Honor: An Anthology on the Hispano Church of the United States.* Maryknoll, NY: Orbis Books, 1980.

Stevens-Arroyo, Anthony M., and Gilbert Cadena, eds. *Old Masks, New Faces: Religion and Latino Identities.* New York Bildner Center for Western Hemisphere Studies, 1995.

Stevens-Arroyo, Anthony M., and Ana María Díaz-Stevens, eds. *An Enduring Flame: Studies on Latino Popular Religiosity.* New York: Bildner Center for Western Hemisphere Studies, 1994.

———. *Recognizing the Latino Resurgence in U.S. Religion: The Emmaus Paradigm.* Boulder, CO: Westview Press, 1998.

Stevens-Arroyo, Anthony M., and Segundo Pantoja, eds. *Discovering Latino Religion: A Comprehensive Social Science Bibliography.* New York: Bildner Center for Western Hemisphere Studies, 1995.

Stevens-Arroyo, Anthony M., and Andres I. Pérez y Mena, eds. *Enigmatic Powers: Syncretism with African and Indigenous Peoples' Religions among Latinos.* New York: Bildner Center for Western Hemisphere Studies, 1994.

Stowell, Jay S. *A Study of Mexicans and Spanish Americans in the United States.* New York: Home Missions Council and the Council of Women for Home Missions, 1920.

———. *The Near-Side of the Mexican Question.* New York: Home Missions Council, 1921.

Stratton, David H. "A History of Northern and Southern Baptists of New Mexico 1849–1950." M.A. thesis, University of Colorado, 1953.

Suárez-Orozco, Marcelo, and Mariela and Páez, eds. *Latinos: Remaking America.* Berkeley: University of California Press, 2002.

Subcomandante Marcos. *Detrás de nosotros estamos ustedes.* México, D.F.: Plaza y Janés, 2000.

Suro, Roberto. *The 2004 National Survey of Latinos: Politics and Civic Participation, Summary and Chartpack.* Washington, DC: Pew Hispanic Center/Kaiser Family Foundation, 2004.

Sylvest, Edwin E. "The Hispanic American Church: Contextual Considerations." *Perkins Journal* 29, no. 1 (1975): 22–31.

———. "Hispanic American Protestantism in the United States." In *Fronteras: A History of the Latin American Church in the U.S.A. since 1513,* ed. Moises Sandoval. San Antonio: Mexican American Cultural Center, 1983.

Tatum, Inez. "Mexican Missions in Texas." M.A. thesis, Baylor University, 1939.

Tillich, Paul. *Systematic Theology.* New York and Evanston: University of Chicago Press/Harper & Row, 1967.

Torgovnick, Marianna. *Primitive Passions: Men, Women, and the Quest for Ecstasy.* New York: Knopf, 1997.

Tortora, Robert D. "Response Trends in a National Random Digit Dial Survey." *Metodoloski zvezki* 1, no. 1 (2004): 21–32.

Traverzo Galarza, David. "A New Dimension in Religious Education for the Hispanic Evangelical Church in New York." M.A. thesis, New Brunswick Theological Seminary, New Brunswick, NJ, 1979.

———. "Evangélicos/as." *Handbook of Latina/o Theologies,* ed. Edwin David Aponte and Miguel A. De La Torre. St. Louis: Chalice Press, 2006.

Trotter, Robert, II, and Juan Antonio Chavira. *Curanderismo: Mexican American Folk Healing.* Athens: University of Georgia Press, 1981.

UNESCO. *Empleo de las lenguas vernáculas en la enseñanza.* Paris: UNESCO, 1953.

———. *Atlas of the World's Languages in Danger of Disappearing.* Paris: UNESCO, 2001.

———. *La educación en un mundo plurlingüe.* Paris: UNESCO, 2003.

Valdez, Luis, and Stan Steiner. *Aztlán: An Anthology of Mexican American Literature.* New York: Vintage Books, 1972.

Valentín, Benjamín. "Nuevos Odres para el Vino: A Critical Contribution to Latino/a Theological Construction." *Journal of Hispanic/Latino Theology* 5, no. 4 (May 1998): 30–47.

———. *Mapping Public Theology: Beyond Culture, Identity, and Difference.* Harrisburg, PA: Trinity Press International, 2002.

Vasconcelos, José. *La raza cósmica.* México: Espasa-Calpe Mexicana, 1948.

———. *The Cosmic Race: A Bilingual Edition.* Trans. Didier T. Jaen. Baltimore: Johns Hopkins University Press, 1997.

Vásquez, Manuel, and Marie Marquardt. *Globalizing the Sacred: Religion across the Americas.* New Brunswick, NJ: Rutgers University Press, 2003.

Wakefield, Dan. *Island in the City: Puerto Ricans in New York.* New York: Citadel Press, 1960.

Walsh, Albeus. "The Work of Catholic Bishops' Committee for the Spanish-Speaking in the United States." M.A. thesis, University of Texas, Austin, 1958.

Warren, Kay. *Indigenous Movements and Their Critics: Pan-Mayan Activism in Guatemala.* Princeton, NJ: Princeton University Press, 1998.

Weatherby, Lela. "A Study of the Early Years of the Presbyterian Work with the Spanish-Speaking People of New Mexico and Colorado and Its Development from 1850–1920." M.A. thesis, Presbyterian College of Christian Education, 1942.

West, Cornel. *The American Evasion of Philosophy: A Genealogy of Pragmatism.* Madison: University of Wisconsin Press, 1989.

Wiebe, Donald. *The Politics of Religious Studies: The Continuing Conflict with Theology in the Academy.* New York: St. Martin's Press, 1999.

Wiegman, Robyn. "Whiteness Studies and the Paradox of Particularity." *Boundary 2* 26, no. 3 (1999):115–50.

Williamson, Joel. *New People: Miscegenation and Mulattoes in the United States.* New York: Free Press, 1980.

Winant, Howard. *Racial Conditions: Politics, Theory, Comparisons.* Minneapolis: University of Minnesota Press, 1994.

———. "Behind Blue Eyes: Whiteness and Contemporary U.S. Racial Politics," in *Off White: Readings on Race, Power, and Society,* ed. Michelle Fine, Lois Weis, Linda C. Powell, and L. Mun Wong (New York: Routledge, 1997).

Ybarra-Frausto, Tomás. "Alurista's Poetics: The Oral, the Bilingual, the Pre-Columbian." In *Modern Chicano Writers. A Collection of Critical Essays,* ed. Joseph Sommers and Tomás Ybarra-Frausto. Englewood Cliffs, NJ: Prentice Hall, 1979.

———. "Cultural Context." In *Ceremony of Memory: New Expressions in Spirituality among Contemporary Hispanic Artists.* Santa Fe, NM: Center for Contemporary Arts, 1988.

Young, Iris Marion. "Gender as Seriality: Thinking about Women as a Social Collective." In *Intersecting Voices: Dilemmas of Gender, Political Philosophy, and Policy.* Princeton, NJ: Princeton University Press, 1997.

Žižek, Slavoj. *The Sublime Object of Ideology.* London: Verso, 1989.

———. "The Spectre of Ideology." In *Mapping Ideology,* ed. Slavoj Žižek. London: Verso, 1994.

———. *The Ticklish Subject: The Absent Centre of Political Ontology.* London: Verso, 1999.

———. "Class Struggle or Postmodernism? Yes, Please!" In *Contingency, Hegemony, Universality,* ed. Judith Butler, Ernesto Laclau, and Slavoj Žižek. London: Verso, 2000.

———. *Did Somebody Say Totalitarianism?* New York: Verso, 2001.

Zuñiga, Victor. " 'Making Carpet by the Mile': The Emergence of a Mexican Immigrant Community in an Industrial Region of the U.S. Historic South." *Social Science Quarterly* 81, no. 1 (2000): 49–66.

Zuñiga, Víctor, and Hernández-León, Rubén. *New Destinations: Mexican Immigration in the United States.* New York: Russell Sage, 2005.

Contributors

Edwin David Aponte is Vice President of Academic Affairs and Dean and Professor of Religion and Culture at Lancaster Theological Seminary in Lancaster, Pennsylvania. His books include *Introducing Latino/a Theologies* (2001), co-authored with Miguel A. De La Torre, and *Handbook of Latino/a Theologies*, co-edited with De La Torre (2006). He has also published several articles and chapters in books. Currently he is writing two books, one on the varieties of Latino/a spirituality, the other on exploring contextual Christianity.

Jorge A. Aquino is Assistant Professor of Theology and Religious Studies, and Latin American and Latino Studies, at the University of San Francisco. A former lecturer in the Ethnic Studies department at the University of California, Berkeley, Aquino is completing his dissertation at the Graduate Theological Union. His research studies Cuban and Caribbean racial history as a means of situating discourses of ethno-racial identity within U.S. Latino theology. A longtime journalist, Aquino worked or freelanced for a variety of print news organizations, including the *Oakland Tribune, American Lawyer Media, New Times,* and Religion News Service.

Miguel A. De La Torre is Associate Professor of Social Ethics at Iliff School of Theology and Director of Iliff's Justice and Peace Institute in Denver, Colorado. His books include *The Quest for the Cuban Christ: A Historical Search* (2002); *Reading the Bible from the Margins* (2002); *La Lucha for Cuba: Religion and Politics on the Streets of Miami* (2003); *Doing Christian Ethics from the Margins* (2004); and *Santería: The Beliefs and Rituals of a Growing Religion in America* (2003). He co-authored *Introducing Latino/a Theologies* with Edwin D. Aponte (2001). He also edited *Handbook on U.S. Theologies of Liberation* (2004) and the *AAR Career Guide for Racial* *and Ethnic Minorities* (2005); and co-edited *Handbook on Latino/a Theologies* (2006) with Edwin Aponte. He has also published several articles, chapters in books, and encyclopedia and dictionary entries. Presently he is writing three books. The first deals with re-imagining Christian sexuality, the second examines the formation of a biblical ethics of reconciliation, and the final project explores liberation theology within world religions.

Gastón Espinosa is Assistant Professor of Religious Studies at Claremont McKenna College. He is co-editor of *Latino Religions and Civic Activism in the United States* (2005) and *Mexican American Religions* (2007). His work has appeared in the *Journal of the American Academy of Religion, Social Compass: The International Review of the Sociology of Religion,* and *Church History.* He served as project manager of the $1.3 million Pew Charitable Trusts-funded Hispanic Churches in American Public Life research project and national survey. In 2002, he spoke at the first Hispanic Presidential Prayer Breakfast in Washington, D.C., along with President George W. Bush and Senator Joseph Lieberman. The Generations Center of Princeton named Espinosa one of the Nation's Top 100 Positive Men of Color.

Michelle A. González is Assistant Professor of Religious Studies at the University of Miami. She is the author of *Sor Juana: Beauty and Justice in the Americas* (2003) and *Afro-Cuban Theology: Religion, Race, Identity, and Culture* (2006). She has also published several articles, chapters in books, and encyclopedia and dictionary entries. She recently completed an introduction to theological anthropology from a feminist hermeneutic.

Luis D. León is Assistant Professor of Religious Studies at Denver University. He is the author of *La Llorona's Children: Religion, Life, and Death in the United States-Mexican Borderlands* (2004), and co-editor of *Religion and American Culture: Multicultural Traditions and Popular Religious Expressions* (2003). He is completing a book on the intersections of religiosity, politics, and erotics in the life and work of César Chávez.

Lara Medina is Associate Professor of Chicana/o Studies at California State University, Northridge. She is the author of *Las Hermanas:*

Chicana/Latina Religious Political Activism (2004). She has also authored several articles, book chapters, and encyclopedia entries, including "Communing with the Dead: Spiritual and Cultural Healing among Chicana/o Communities" in *Religion and Healing in America* (2005); "Women: The U.S. Latina Religious Experience" in *Introduction to the U.S. Latina and Latino Religious Experience* (2004); and several entries in the forthcoming *Latinas in the United States: An Historical Encyclopedia*.

Manuel Mejido C. is Visiting Professor at the Department of Sociology and visiting researcher at the Laboratory for Social Research and Political Analysis (RESOP) of the University of Geneva.

Laura E. Pérez is Associate Professor in the Department of Ethnic Studies and an affiliated member of the Departments of Women's Studies and Dance, Theater, and Performance at the University of California, Berkeley. She writes on contemporary U.S. Latina/o and Latin American feminist and queer literary, visual, and performance arts, spirituality, and decolonizing politics. She is the author of *Altarities: Chicana Art, Politics, and Spirituality* (2006).

Manuel A. Vásquez is Associate Professor of Religion and Latin American Studies at the University of Florida, Gainesville. He is the author of *The Brazilian Popular Church and the Crisis of Modernity* (1998), co-author of *Globalizing the Sacred: Religion across the Americas* (2003), and co-editor of *Christianity, Social Change, and Globalization in the Americas* (2001), and of *Immigrant Faiths: Transforming Religious Life in America* (2005). Currently he is co-directing an interdisciplinary, multiyear research project entitled *Latino Immigrants in Florida: Lived Religion, Space, and Power*, which is supported by a grant from the Ford Foundation. He is also a member of the planning committee for a comparative project on transnational migration and religion based at the Social Science Research Council (SSRC). The project studies the interplay of religion and migration in sites such as London, Durban, Kuala Lumpur, and Atlanta.

Index

Printed in the United States
64157LVS00003B/85-264